DICKENS STUDIES ANNUAL
Essays on Victorian Fiction

EDITORS

Michael Timko
Fred Kaplan
Edward Guiliano

DICKENS STUDIES ANNUAL

Essays on Victorian Fiction

VOLUME
20

Edited by
Michael Timko, Fred Kaplan,
and Edward Guiliano

AMS PRESS

NEW YORK

DICKENS STUDIES ANNUAL
ISSN 0084-9812

International Standard Book Number
Series: 0-404-18520-7
Vol. 20: 0-404-18540-1

Dickens Studies Annual: Essays on Victorian Fiction welcomes essay and monograph-length contributions on Dickens as well as on other Victorian novelists and on the history of aesthetics of Victorian fiction. All manuscripts should be double-spaced, including footnotes, which should be grouped at the end of the submission, and should be prepared according to the forma: used in this journal. An editorial decision can usually be reached more quickly if two copies are submitted. The preferred editions for citations from Dickens' works are the Clarendon and the Norton Critical when available, otherwise the Oxford Illustrated or the Penguin.

Please send submissions to the Editors, *Dickens Studies Annual*, Room 1522, Graduate School and University Center, City University of New York, 33 West 42nd Street, New York, N.Y. 10036: please send subscription inquiries to AMS Press, Inc., 56 East 13th Street, New York, N.Y. 10003.

Manufactured in the United States of America

Contents

Preface

The editors continue to be grateful for the services of the members of the editorial and advisory boards. Special thanks go to those who wrote the comprehensive review essays. We also thank the participants in the annual Santa Cruz Dickens Conference, especially John Jordan. Alicia Carroll, the editorial assistant from CUNY, and Jack Hopper, AMS Press, deserve special commendation.

We note and express our gratitude to those in administrative posts in different institutions who continue to provide supports of various kinds: Chancellor Anne Reynolds, CUNY; former President Harold Proshansky; Acting President and Provost Stephen Cahn; Executive Officer, Ph.D. Program in English, Joseph Wittrich, The Graduate School and University Center, CUNY; Dean of Humanities Michael Spitzer, The New York Institute of Technology; President Shirley Strum Kenny, Dean John Reilly, and Chair, English Department, Charles Molesworth, Queens College, CUNY; and Gabriel Hornstein, President, AMS Press, whose encouragement has always been a constant source of strength.

—THE EDITORS

Notes on Contributors

JAMES ELI ADAMS is Assistant Professor of English and Victorian Studies at Indiana University. His essays have recently appeared in *ELH, Victorian Studies,* and *SEL.* He is currently at work on a book-length study of Victorian masculinities.

ROSEMARIE BODENHEIMER is Professor of English at Boston College, and the author of *The Politics of Story in Victorian Social Fiction.* She is currently writing a book on George Eliot's letters and novels.

BRIAN CHEADLE is Professor of English at the University of Witwatersrand, Johannesburg.

MARILYN GEORGAS received her Ph.D. from the University of Texas at Austin and is Professor of English at Lamar University in Beaumont, Texas. She has published articles on Sir Philip Sidney, on James Hogg, on *Blackwood's Edinburgh Magazine* and on Dickens' *Hard Times* and *Bleak House.*

LEWIS HORNE is Professor of English at the University of Saskatchewan, Saskatoon.

DAVID KELLOGG is currently completing his Ph.D. in English at the University of North Carolina at Chapel Hill.

CHRISTOPHER KENT is Professor of History at the University of Saskatchewan, Saskatoon. He is the author of *Brains and Numbers: Elitism, Comtism and Democracy in Mid-Victorian England,* and several articles on literature and history, and Victorian bohemia. He is currently writing a book: "Michel Foucault: Undisciplined Historian."

JOHN KUCICH is Professor of English at the University of Michigan, Ann Arbor. He is the author of *Excess and Restraint in the Novels of Charles Dickens* and *Repression in Victorian Fiction,* as well as numerous essays on Victorian fiction, contemporary fiction, and literary theory. His book-in-progress is tentatively titled "The Power of Lies: Transgression, Gender, and Class in Victorian Fiction."

SYLVIA MANNING is Professor of English and Executive Vice Provost at the University of Southern California. She is the author of *Dickens as a Satirist* (1970) and *Hard Times: An Annotated Bibliography* (1984), as well as numerous essays on Dickens, Thackeray, and Tennyson. An earlier version of this essay was delivered as a lecture for the Dickens Universe, a project of the University of California at Santa Cruz.

PATRICK J. MCCARTHY is Professor of English at the University of California at Santa Barbara and has written on the Victorians, particularly Matthew Arnold and Charles Dickens. He is at present completing a book-length study of Dickens and language.

CATHERINE PETERS is the author of *Thackeray's Universe* and *The King of Inventors*. She teaches English Literature at Somerville College, Oxford.

PAUL SCHLICKE teaches in the Department of English at the University of Aberdeen, Scotland.

MARJORIE STONE is Associate Professor of English at Dalhousie University, Halifax, Canada. She has published in *Victorian Poetry* and *Atlantis* on Dickens, the female breast in Victorian poetry, and New England women writers. She is currently completing a book on Elizabeth Barrett Browning for the Macmillan Women Writers series.

JOHN SUTHERLAND is a Professor of English at the California Institute of Technology in Pasadena.

DOUGLAS THORPE teaches Victorian Literature at the University of Saskatchewan. He has published on Stevenson, Wilde, Arnold, and George MacDonald.

MALCOLM J. WOODFIELD teaches at the University of Pennsylvania. He is the author of *R. H. Hutton: Critic and Theologian, A Victorian Spectator*, and *Defending Romanticism*, as well as essays on Victorian literature and culture, on narrative theory, and the history of literature and genre theory.

The Showman of *The Pickwick Papers*

Paul Schlicke

One of the most fascinating and challenging aspects of Dickens' creativity is his ability to draw vital sustenance from popular forms of ephemeral entertainment, even as he aspired to emulate the greatest literary artists who preceded him. In his hands the stereotypes of popular fiction, theater, and song are transformed into fresh and original art, which simultaneously manifests the influence of Shakespeare, Fielding, and Scott. The interfusion of high and low is a defining characteristic of his art, and although readers of more refined taste have repeatedly denounced Dickens for what they see as his vulgarity, others have happily enjoyed the variety of riches which he provides. Over the past generation, while his reputation as one of the giants of English literature has grown ever more firmly established, the need to assess the function of popular conventions in his art has become increasingly pressing, and several modern scholars have offered illuminating insights into these issues.[1]

Nowhere is this mixture more evident than in the first novel he wrote, *The Pickwick Papers*. Having been approached in the first instance to supply letterpress for a series of engravings of Cockney sporting life, which were intended to be the publication's chief attraction, Dickens promptly took charge, rejecting some of Seymour's illustrations and redefining the nature of the project. This behaviour was an early instance of Dickens' customary disposition to dominate any activity in which he took part, but it was also an attempt by him to raise the stature of *Pickwick* from the level of hack work to serious comic art. Dickens was never fully clear in his own mind just how seriously he took *Pickwick*, as his later preferences reveal (see Butt and Tillotson, 65–66), but one thing is patent: *The Pickwick Papers* is both a highly conventional and a highly original work. Depending on the formulas

1

of ephemeral entertainment, it is an enduring masterpiece of unique achievement.

In the present essay I would like to offer an approach to these issues by stepping back from the novel to examine two closely related traditions which demonstrably fed Dickens' imagination, namely the theater of the English fairgrounds, in particular the booth theater of the foremost showman of the early nineteenth century, John Richardson, and the production of Shakespearean drama, in adaptations devised to increase the breadth and immediacy of appeal of the plays for eighteenth- and nineteenth-century audiences. Both of these types of theater combined artistic seriousness with broad-based popularity, and as I will proceed to show, Dickens was consciously responding to both of these traditions during the months in which he was writing *Pickwick*. The fact that he could comfortably accommodate his high esteem for Shakespeare with his unashamed delight in rollicking fairground theater is deeply revealing of his own conception of popular art. The combination of unpretentious seriousness with carefree fun touched resonant chords in his imagination, and an understanding of these forms can, I believe, suggest much not only about the nature of *Pickwick* but about Dickens' fiction generally.

In the early decades of the nineteenth century, before and during Dickens' childhood, the centerpiece of English fairgrounds was the large theater booth of "Muster" John Richardson. Outside the booth his actors paraded in full costume to attract patrons, and on the stage the emphasis was firmly upon spectacle and action: a play at Richardson's consisted of a rapid sequence of ghosts, sword fights, mad scenes, and deaths. In *Sketches by Boz* Dickens describes one production of Richardson's in detail and observes that, although a new play was put on each day, the story was "always pretty much the same" (116). This assessment of the formulaic nature of Richardson's shows is corroborated in a retrospective essay written by John Oxenford in 1869, who recalled that plays in the booth theater, "if not identical in plot, resembled each other as closely as possible in the principle of construction and in the arrangement of the effects" (83). Performance was complete in less than an hour and was repeated a dozen times or more in a single day. For nearly half a century Richardson's theater was a byword for the fun of the fair, and the showman himself, although born like Oliver Twist in a workhouse, amassed a fortune by the time of his death.

Dickens' enthusiasm for Richardson is easily documented. In his April 1835 sketch "Greenwich Fair" he described Richardson's show as "the very centre and heart of the fair" (115). In January 1837, acting in his capacity as editor of *Bentley's Miscellany*, he revised an obituary article on Richardson by William Jerdan which praised the showman as manager of what could be designated the "national theater" (Jerdan, 184). On 22 June 1837, finishing work on the fifteenth serial part of *Pickwick*, he arranged an outing with his friend and fellow-novelist Harrison Ainsworth to see a performance by Richardson's leading tragic actor, John Cartlitch, and promised "to lend my mite of applause to Mr. Cartlitch and the other wild beasts" (*Letters* Pilgrim I: 276). The introductory chapter of *Memoirs of Grimaldi*, dated January 1838, records Dickens' childhood delight in the pantomime which Richardson's waggons brought at fair time to the "dull little town" where he grew up (xii). And years later, the collection of dummy books which he had installed in his study at Tavistock House and which were later removed to Gad's Hill Place included a twelve-volume set entitled *"Richardson's Show of Dramatic Literature"* (*Letters* Nonesuch II: 353-54; Johnson 2: 963). From the outset of his career as a writer, in short, Dickens had thorough familiarity with Richardson's theater, and he had not forgotten it long after the show had closed forever.

Of Dickens' several allusions to Richardson, by far the most interesting in its implications for his own art is to be found in the announcement appended to Part 10 of *The Pickwick Papers*, in which he declared his intention of "confining his work to twenty numbers." Dated "December 1836," a month after the great showman's death, the notice has the topicality of an obituary tribute, and placed as it is at the conclusion of Dickens' statement of intention regarding the "plan" of his work in progress, the invocation of Richardson serves as a revealing indication of the young author's conception of that work halfway through its composition. Referring to himself as "Mr. Pickwick's Stage-Manager," Dickens explicitly compares his role as author to that of "the late eminent Mr. John Richardson." He then quotes, as being appropriate to his own purposes, the address with which the showman closed each performance:

> "Ladies and gentlemen, for these marks of your favour, we beg to return you our sincere thanks; and allow us to inform you, that we shall keep perpetually going on beginning again, regularly, until the end of the fair" *Pickwick* 882).

Overtly, this address is an expression of gratitude to his readers for purchasing his work and a pledge to continue bringing out monthly numbers for a further ten months, at which time the serial will have reached its conclusion. More fundamentally, the comparison with Richardson suggests that Dickens conceived the provision of entertainment to be his proper duty as a creative artist and that he intended the appeal of his work to be broad-based and popular, like the amusements at a fair. By the time he finished *Pickwick,* Dickens was taking his work more elegantly, when he turned to the precedent of "some of the greatest novelists in the English language" to defend its variety of incidents, but even then he continued to claim entertainment as his guiding purpose. In the preface to the original edition he declared,

> The author's object in this work, was to place before the reader a constant succession of characters and incidents; to paint them in as vivid colours as he could command; and to render them, at the same time, life-like and amusing
> (xcix).

From beginning to end *The Pickwick Papers* is the performance by a popular showman, and John Richardson was the model Dickens consciously emulated.

On the face of it, the proposition that *Pickwick* is like fairground entertainment appears to relegate Dickens' first extended work of fiction to the lowly status of ephemera. In certain respects such a judgment is correct. The initial conception of the work as comic scenes of Cockney sporting life was a stock formula of tested popularity; the project was initiated not by Dickens but by the illustrator Robert Seymour and his publishers Chapman and Hall; it was the only one of Dickens' novels begun with no initial period of gestation; and during the months of composition Dickens freely entered into several contracts for additional creative writing. For these reasons, as John Butt and Kathleen Tillotson have shown, *The Pickwick Papers* is by far the most improvisatory of Dickens's works, produced as journalistic entertainment rather than as a "real" novel (Butt and Tillotson 62–75). In its lasting appeal, however, *Pickwick* is emphatically more than ephemeral hack-work, and awareness in the traditions of popular entertainment to which Dickens himself referred in his address following Part 10 of the novel can help to show why it is something more.[2] The entertainment of fairground booth theaters and of other venues of theatricality devoid of literary merit existed in a curiously complex relationship with the most serious dramatic art of the day. A clarifying factor to the nature of such entertainment is the presence of Shakespearean adaptations within its repertoire—and, after *Pickwick* had achieved popularity, the presence of Dickensian adaptations in these theaters, occasionally on the same program alongside plays by Shakespeare.[3] By considering the traditions of booth theater production and of Shakespearean adaptation we can understand more fully what kind of work Dickens thought he was creating when he compared himself to "Muster" Richardson the showman.

A play at Richardson's was brief, vigorous, spectacular melodrama, repeated more or less hourly throughout each afternoon and evening during
fairtime. Between performances, in order to attract new customers, the actors
paraded on the elevated platform in front of the booth, the clown told jokes,
and the barker harangued the crowd. Since the booth, large enough to hold
an audience of "nearly a thousand," had to be cleared of patrons and then
refilled before the next performance could begin, speed and concentration
were, as Sybil Rosenfeld has observed, "essential."[4] As Dickens describes it,
one of Richardson's plays consisted of starkly contrasted moral polarities—a
rightful heir and a wrongful heir, a good assassin and a bad assassin—and
vigorous action leading to mortal combat, with the plot resolved by the
appearance of a ghost. His summary is corroborated by other observers:
although the main attraction was changed daily, whatever the nominal interest
of the particular play, its substance was invariably the same. Lurid action,
fights and death scenes, last minute escape—and a ghost—were the staples.
In *The Wandering Outlaw*, witnessed by William Hone, the action moved
between forest, castle, old church, market place and cliff, with a murder, an
"unexecuted execution," and the hero saved by the ghost (Hone I: 596).
Richardson's *Virginius*, as described by John Oxenford, was substantially
modified from the wooden tragedy of Sheridan Knowles; in the fair booth the
heroine, crossed in love, is wrongly imprisoned until a spectre appears, reveals a horrid murder, and drives the villain to wordy remorse and lingering
suicide (Oxenford 83). Another Richardson favorite, *The Warlock of the
Glen*, centers on the perils and rescue of a beleaguered heroine; in this play
the mysterious deus ex machina is not an actual ghost but only the returned
hero, long assumed dead—a diminution of customary spectral interest which
may be explained by the fact that the most circumstantial summary, hilari-
ously recounted by Thackeray, is based not on a booth performance but on a
provincial theater production he saw in Brighton (Thackeray 328–30).

Although Dickens has left abundant testimony as to the delight he took
in theatricality of this sort,[5] the affinities with *Pickwick* would be slight indeed
if improbable plotting and supernatural wonders were the only ingredients of
fairground melodrama. *Pickwick* achieves variety through contrasting scenes,
but melodramatic polarities are far less prominent as organizational method
than they were to be in Dickens' next novel, *Oliver Twist*, in which the
"streaky bacon" principle of structure is articulated (105). Ghosts, madness,
and horrible deaths are confined in *Pickwick* to the interpolated tales, and the
novel's sheer abundance of character and incident—to say nothing of its

central focus on the developing relationship between Mr. Pickwick and Sam—precludes the rapid plotting of a brief stage play.

What is of deeper significance is the spirit with which the entertainment was offered in Richardson's theater. The showman had no pretensions to lofty aesthetic achievement, but it is abundantly clear from contemporary accounts that he took considerable pride in his productions. Admission charges for his brief show, at 2s for boxes, 1s for pit, and 6d for gallery, were high in comparison to provincial theaters, where charges were normally 3s, 2s, and 1s for an entire evening's entertainment, and to most other attractions at the fairgrounds, where only menageries charged as much as 6d and the price to see lesser novelties ranged from 3d down to 1/2d (Daniel 2: 192–93; Rosenfeld *Popular Theater* 112). In return for what he charged, Richardson offered elaborate scenery and costumes. He hired scene painters from Drury Lane and was able to effect scene changes as often as seven times in a single brief play (Rosenfeld *Popular Theater* 117). Pierce Egan reported that the front of Richardson's theater alone cost £600 and estimated that the worth of his wardrobe was thousands of pounds (Egan *Life* 70). The costumes, reputedly superior to those at Covent Garden and Drury Lane, had to be of high quality since they were seen not only by the flicker of lamps at night but in the full glare of daylight. Jerdan reported that when Richardson died 334 lots of show property were auctioned off at a fraction of their real worth (185).

But it was not only in physical trappings that Richardson's theater excelled. In contrast to most other travelling companies, in which actors were told a plot, given a character, and left to extemporize lines as best they could, Richardson's company were required to learn their lines. "Gagging," or making up words as one went along, not infrequently collapsed into miserable results, but Richardson's actors, having studied their parts and recited them repeatedly, were able to perform with seemingly effortless spontaneity (Egan *Pilgrim* 85; Mayhew 3: 139; Paterson, 49). His actors moved back and forth between his booth and the circus, and several of them, most notably Edmund Kean, graduated from the fairground to success in the patent theaters. Kean, in his prime one of the most celebrated actors of all time, got his start as a child prodigy under Richardson, and is said to have visited his old manager on several occasions after achieving fame and once to have contacted Richardson to request a loan of costumes (Egan *Pilgrim* 92, 899; Rosenfeld *Popular Theater* 115–16). Richardson himself claimed to have seen "more real talent exhibited at *Feers* than I ever saw at any of the licensed theatres," and always welcomed as "one of us" any "hactor" from Covent Garden or Drury Lane who came to see the show (Egan *Pilgrim* 112).

Pierce Egan, by far the most fully informed and circumstantial of contemporary witnesses to write about Richardson, was at pains to stress the genuine merit of the showman's theater. In *The Life of an Actor* the hero, Proteus, has initial misgivings when offered a position with Richardson, but he is quickly impressed by the high standards and hard work he finds in the booth (68–70). In *The Pilgrims of the Thames in Search of the National*, Peter Makemoney and his companions are impressed to perceive "talents, abilities, and an anxiety to please; and if we may judge as a criterion from the applause which were bestowed on their exertions, I should say the audience were gratified. I hate anything in the shape of *hypercriticism*" (Egan 86). Egan, best known as the creator of Tom and Jerry in his urban picaresque novel *Life in London*, was the foremost spokesman on Regency "flash" culture, and his words carry authority, but his standards of quality are, perhaps, open to question. Certainly Dickens was eager to dissociate his name from Egan's when he asked Frederick Yates "not to compare Nicholas to Tom and Jerry" in advertisements for a stage adaptation of *Nicholas Nickleby* (*Letters* Pilgrim 1: 463). Nevertheless, Dickens appears to have shared Egan's admiration for Richardson, and Sybil Rosenfeld, the eminent modern historian of fairground theaters, judges that Richardson's methods were able to "infuse new life into the fair in the nineteenth century" (*London Fair* 70).

Furthermore, Richardson personally was a man of a sort immediately attractive to Dickens. The showman was empathically a "character," with eccentric mannerisms, attitudes, and speech habits. His colorful personality as an individual was a chief quality singled out by Jerdan in the obituary notice of Richardson that Dickens revised for publication in *Bentley's Miscellany*. Richardson's life was simple and unaffected; he never married, preferred living in his caravan to staying in a house, and when he died was buried at his own request in a grave beside that of his beloved "spotted boy," George Alexander, whom he had exhibited at the fairs in 1810. In addition, Richardson's charitable generosity was legendary: ever ready with financial assistance for showmen in distress, magnanimous to his actors, on one occasion he donated £100 to a subscription for victims of a fire in St. Albans (Anon. 326–27). In all of Dickens' thinking about amusement and imagination, it was axiomatic that expansiveness, fellow-feeling, and selflessness were essential concomitants. The value of entertainment, in Dickens' view, lay precisely in its capacity to nurture human accord. The combination of human warmth and of a disposition to seek enjoyment is central to Mr. Pickwick's character, and its worth is the lesson which Jingle learns from Mr. Pickwick in the Fleet because John Richardson spent his lifetime providing entertainment for the enjoyment of others in a spirit of good humor and good will, he embodied to the core a disposition singularly appropriate for Dickens to invoke for his own work. His show was living proof that entertainment avowedly popular in its appeal could be artistically devised with thought and care; for Richardson popularity was the very reverse of slapdash.

Reciprocally, in the tradition of Shakespearean adaptation in theaters such as Richardson's, Dickens had at hand an example of great art that was vigorously popularized. For it is a striking fact that the greatest of all English dramatists has never been the exclusive property of an elitist culture, despite legal regulations in force throughout the eighteenth century and nearly half of the nineteenth, framed specifically to restrict production of his plays to patent theaters alone. Shakespeare's works regularly percolated down to the lowliest stages in the land, and Shakespearean adaptation was a burgeoning phenomenon in the decade during which *Pickwick* first saw light of day. It is also a well-established and noteworthy fact that Shakespeare's works mattered intensely to Dickens from his youthful days when literary creation was the merest gleam in his eye. Among the books he is known to have consulted in the British Museum, to which he gained admission the day after his eighteenth birthday, the earliest age permissible, was a set of Shakespeare's works (*Letters* Pilgrim 1: 10n.). In 1833, at the age of twenty-one, he wrote and produced a travesty of Shakespeare entitled *O'Thello* (Haywood 67–88). During William Charles Macready's management of Covent Garden from 1837 to 1839, Dickens enthusiastically supported the efforts of the Eminent Tragedian to upgrade the quality of Shakespearean production; he was a close friend of Macready and a trusted adviser (Downer 170, 175, 180, 184). In 1838 he visited Shakespeare's birthplace in Stratford-upon-Avon and left his autograph there (*Letters* Pilgrim 1: 447, 634). Between 1838 and 1839 he was an active member of the Shakespeare Club, which had been formed to foster "intellectual with social enjoyment" through discussions, readings, and papers (*Letters* Pilgrim 1: 392n; Dexter 40–41). A number of his letters from these years contain verbal allusions to lines from Shakespeare, as does *Pickwick* (*Letters* Pilgrim 1: 5, 14, 29, 79, 207, 408, 489, 542, 610). It was thus wholly appropriate that his publishers Chapman and Hall, presenting him with a token of their esteem on the anniversay of the publication of the first serial part of *Pickwick,* should select as their gift a set of Shakespeare's works (*Letters* Pilgrim 1: 244n). It is abundantly clear, in short, that Dickens from an early age was actively forging an intimacy with Shakespearean drama, just as he was frequenting the fairground, circus, and popular theater.

At Richardson's booth itself he would have been unlikely to have come across Shakespeare in any form. One historian has claimed that Kean, when he was with Richardson, gave a recital of Shakespearean speeches at Windsor Castle before George III, but Richardson himself, who told Egan about the command performance, mentioned only "passages from different plays," without naming Shakespeare, and Kean had been performing *Tom Thumb* at the time he attracted the king's notice (McKechnie 52; Egan *Pilgrim* 92). Again, the barker outside Richardson's who appears in *The Pilgrims of the Thames* invokes the legacy of Shakespeare and itemizes *Othello* among plays to be seen inside the booth, but there is no other evidence that I have seen to suggest that Shakespearean tragedy ever was actually performed at Richardson's (Egan *Pilgrim* 82). Indeed, apart from quoting the occasional line from the bard, Richardson did not, according to Egan, "boast of any great knowledge with the plays of Shakespeare" (*Pilgrim* 100).

Nevertheless, there was a long history linking Shakespeare with the fairground theaters. As Sybil Rosenfeld has documented, principal actors and actresses from Covent Garden and Drury Lane realized by the late seventeenth century that a quick way to cash in on their fame and make money during the offseason was to perform in the fairground booths. Thus William Penkethman of Drury Lane appeared in *Jephtha's Rash Vow* at Bartholomew Fair in 1698, and Mrs. Elmy, who was later to play Shakespearean heroines opposite Garrick, made several appearances at Bartholomew Fair in the 1730s. After the duration of Bartholomew Fair was reduced in 1735 from a fortnight to three days, the actors found it more profitable to turn to the provinces when the London theaters were closed, but even after the players from the patent houses had deserted the fair, the plays remained: Sybil Rosenfeld records versions of *The Merchant of Venice, Henry IV, The Tempest,* and *A Comedy of Errors* at Southwark Fair, Bartholomew Fair, and Tottenham Court Fair between 1719 and 1749. Emphatically, these were not full versions of Shakespearean drama, but adaptations carved out of Shakespeare to make his works suitable for the fair booths. They were shortened to reduce complexity and to heighten comedy, spectacle, and action. New titles indicated the elements of appeal, as in a 1733 adaptation, *The Comical Humours of Sir John Falstaff, Justice Shallow, Ancient Pistol, and Others* (Rosenfeld *London Fairs* 9, 42, 147).

But if the booth theaters were not faithful to the Shakespearean text, neither were the most prestigious playhouses in the land. It was an age of wholescale tampering with Shakespeare, as Nahum Tate, Colley Cibber, and their ilk rewrote plays to suit the taste of their time. And a long time it was: not until

1838 did a production of *King Lear* based on Shakespeare's text appear on an English stage in place of Tate's version with its love interest between Cordelia and Edgar and its happy-ever-after ending.[6] There remained a great distance, of course, between a full-length production in an elegant playhouse and a booth theater performance competing for patrons with freak shows, rope dances, gingerbread stalls, and puppet plays. But the point stands that the legacy of eighteenth-century Shakespeare production at all levels was one of adaptation. In this context one can appreciate why Dickens, with his passionate devotion to the theater, so highly valued Macready's endeavors to mount productions which took Shakespeare's dramatic and literary quality seriously. But one can also see that Dickens would find nothing extraordinary in the notion that excellence and popularity could be bedfellows. In the theatrical tradition which he inherited the difference was one of degree rather than of rigid compartmentalization.

Compartmentalization, however, was precisely what the licensing law was designed to enforce. Enacted in 1737 and not revoked until 1843, the law decreed that spoken drama could be performed only in the two patent theaters. The act met with ineffective resistance in the eighteenth century, but by the early nineteenth century, as theaters proliferated in response to the rapid increase in urban population, the monopoly restrictions began to be circumvented. As Michael Booth has suggested, the law forced unpatented theaters to become innovative to create attractive entertainment without breaking the law (Booth 44). Since straight drama could not legally be presented outside the patent theaters, two courses were open to managements wishing to produce Shakespeare: illegal production, or adaptation away from spoken text into mime, music, and spectacle. In either case, Shakespearean drama was what it had been in the eighteenth-century fairground: a vigorously popularized form.

In the unlicensed penny gaffs, which flourished throughout the nineteenth century and were by many accounts the nadir of theatrical activity, Shakespeare's plays took their place alongside the most scabrous melodrama. As in the fair booths, an entire program, including two or three separate items, took less than an hour to perform and was repeated several times each night. Heavy emphasis on murder, madness, ghosts, fights, and deaths make it easy to imagine—even without the help of Tom Stoppard's one-minute version of Shakespeare in *Dogg's Hamlet*—how *Hamlet* and *Macbeth* could fit so easily into the repertoire of the gaffs (Sheridan 3, 6, 13, 23, 54, 57).

More respectably, in the minor theaters, which saw much of the creative innovation in nineteenth-century production, Shakespeare was squeezed to fit within the letter of the patent laws. In 1809 R. W. Elliston produced at the Surrey Theater a "ballet of music and action" entitled *The History, Murders, Life, and Death of Macbeth,* which skirted the law by virtually eliminating dialogue and concentrating on action and spectacle, heightened by music. Twenty years later, with the monopoly eroding rapidly, Ellison acted the roles of Hamlet, Othello, Mercutio, and Falstaff, in shortened musical versions of Shakespearean drama (Murray 22–25; Sprague "Shakespeare" 2–3, "Macbeth" 80–101).

In 1834 and 1835 Astley's Circus presented plays based on Shakespeare under the titles *The Life and Death of King Richard II; or, Wat Tyler and Jack Straw* and *The White and Red Rose; or, The Battle of Bosworth Field.* At Astley's drama was enacted on horseback according to the dictum of the manager and star of the arena, Andrew Ducrow, "Cut out the dialect and come to the 'osses," and in the 1835 production John Cartlitch, the tragedian from Richardson's, took the role of Richmond (Saxon 179, 286).

Meanwhile an increasing number of burlesques of Shakespeare began to appear. The weakening of the patent regulations meant that theaters could place greater reliance on spoken dialogue without facing prosecution, and as we have seen, Dickens contributed his mite to the vogue with a travesty of his own, *O'Thello.* Stanley Wells, who has selected a sufficient quantity of nineteenth-century Shakespearean burlesques to fill five volumes, observes that the emergence of Shakespearean burlesque coincided with the rise of a new seriousness about textual matters and about historical accuracy in major productions (Wells 1: xiii and 2: x). Popularization and attention to excellence once again converge.

Dickens clearly recognized in Shakespeare one of the great creative writers and dramatists in the language. He was alert to the gulf between ambitious, faithful dramatization and vulgar trivializing; as he said in a letter to Macready in 1839 (glancing at the packed houses the lion-tamer Isaac Van Amburgh attracted to Drury Lane that winter), "I hold any society to be valuable which recognizes something of slight interest in the Drama shorn of Lions and Tigers" (*Letters* Pilgrim 1: 497). At the same time, Dickens was far from Solemn in his veneration for The Bard; the early *O'Thello* and the late portrayal of Wopsle as Hamlet are evidence in point. What I wish to suggest is not that Dickens was incapable of distinguishing between the great tragedies of Shakespeare on the one hand and on the other the brisk melodramas of Richardson, the wretched depravity in the penny gaffs, or the derisory incompetence in private theaters. Without question, he knew the difference.

Rather, Dickens saw that Shakespeare was freely appropriated by the most unpretentious theaters, catering to poorly educated audiences for whom, according to one of Mayhew's informants, a faithful production of Shakespeare was incomprehensible. In this coster's opinion, *Hamlet* was better when confined to the ghost scenes, the funeral, and the final killings, and *Macbeth* to the witches and the fighting (Mayhew 1: 15). Dickens knew from close and extensive observation how the lower classes chose to amuse themselves, and he expressed confidence in his anti-Sabbatarian pamphlet *Sunday Under Three Heads,* written when *Pickwick* was just underway, that most people prefer good entertainment to bad. He was later, in his important *Household Words* essay "The Amusements of the People," to articulate his conviction that people were susceptible of improvement through entertainment, because love of dramatic representation was "inherent in human nature" (Dickens "Amusements" 58). This is not the crude condescension of a "moral uplift" theory of art, but a belief that, properly presented, artistic excellence would appeal to a broad audience. From this perspective, one facet of Shakespeare's genius was to have a core of artistry which appealed to the sophisticated and the unsophisticated alike. The presence of Shakespearean adaptations outside the patent theaters offered Dickens a supreme example that popularity need not mean hackneyed frivolousness, and that achievement of lasting worth could exist within popular forms.

The Pickwick Papers is an essentially popular work of art. It taps stock formulas, character types, farcical misadventures, variety, exuberance, and repetitiveness. Some of its popular ingredients are specifically theatrical, and not only as seen in the figure of the strolling player Jingle. The bold posturing of the characters, the set-piece situations, and the finales in tableaux, memorably recorded by Phiz, all evince a robust theatricality. *Pickwick* shares these qualities with types of ephemeral entertainment long forgotten save by dry-as-dust scholars. At the same time, *Pickwick* is not itself ephemeral but stands as one of the sublime comic achievements in English literature. It reveals a breadth of humanity and generosity of spirit of which only great art is capable, and especially in the dynamic, complex, magical yet believable relationship between the innocent old gentleman and his worldly-wise manservant, Dickens has given us a triumph of comic invention.

It has not been my purpose to trace specific Shakespearean echoes in *Pickwick,* nor to look for mechanical resemblances between Richardson's theater and Dickens' novel. Instead, I have tried to suggest that the adaptibility of Shakespeare to unsophisticated theatrical production offered to Dickens an example of artistic legitimacy found within one form of popular entertainment. Shakespearean drama was living proof to Dickens that to work within the tradition represented by John Richardson need involve no clash between an art which had value in addition to—not in opposition to—its popularity. What Nicholas Nickleby was to say of Shakespeare in Dickens' next novel but one could equally well be applied to the showman of *The Pickwick Papers*: "He brought within the magic circle of his genius, traditions peculiarly adapted for his purpose, and turned familiar things into constellations which should enlighten the world for ages" (*Nicholas Nickleby* 633).

WORKS CITED

Anon. "Obituary—Mr. John Richardson." *Gentleman's Magazine* (March 1837): 326–27.

Axton, William F. *Circle of Fire: Dickens' Vision and Style and the Popular Victorian Theater*. Lexington: Kentucky UP, 1966.

Booth, Michael. *"The Social and Literary Context." The Revels History of Drama in English*. Eds. Clifford Leech and T. W. Craik. London: Methuen, 1975, 6: 1–57.

Butt, John, and Kathleen Tillotson. *Dickens at Work*. London: Methuen, 1957.

Daniel, George. *Merrie England in the Olden Time*. 2 vols. London: Bentley, 1842.

D[exter], W[alter]. "The Shakespeare Club." *Dickensian*. 41 (1945): 40–41.

Dickens, Charles. "The Amusements of the People." *Household Words* 1 (1850): 13–15 and 57–60.

———. "Greenwich Fair." *Sketches by Boz*. London: Oxford UP, 1957, 111–18.

———. *The Letters of Charles Dickens*. The Pilgrim edition. Eds. Madeline House. Graham Storey, et al. 6 vols. Oxford: Clarendon, 1965—.

———. *The Letters of Charles Dickens*. The Nonesuch Edition. Ed. Walter Dexter. 3 vols. London: Nonesuch, 1938.

——— [as "Boz"], ed. *Memoirs of Joseph Grimaldi*. 2 vols. London: Bentley, 1838.

———. *Nicholas Nickleby*. Ed. Paul Schlicke. Oxford: Oxford UP, 1990.

———. *Oliver Twist*. Ed. Kathleen Tillotson. Oxford: Clarendon, 1966.

———. *The Pickwick Papers*. Ed. James Kinsley. Oxford: Clarendon, 1986.

Downer, Alan S. *The Eminent Tragedian, William Charles Macready*. London: Oxford UP 1966.

Egan, Pierce. *The Life of an Actor*. London: Arnold, 1825.

————. *The Pilgrims of the Thames in Search of the National*. London: Strange, 1838.

Eigner, Edwin M. *The Dickens Pantomime*. Berkeley/Los Angeles: California UP, 1989.

Haywood, Charles. "Charles Dickens and Shakespeare; or, The Irish Moor of Venice, O'Thello, with Music." *Dickensian* 73 (1977): 67–88.

Hone, William. *Every Day Book*. 2 vols. London: Tegg, 1826–27. [Jerdan, William.] "Biographical Sketch of Richardson, the Showman. With a Peep at Bartholomew Fair." *Bentley's Miscellany* 1 (1837): 178–86.

Johnson, Edgar. *Charles Dickens: His Tragedy and Triumph*. 2 vols. Boston, MA: Little, Brown, 1952.

McKechnie, Samuel. *Popular Entertainments through the Ages*. London: S. Low, Marston, 1931. Rpt. B. Blom.

Mayhew, Henry. *London Labour and the London Poor*. 4 vols. London: Griffin, Bohn, 1861–62.

Murray, Christopher. *Robert William Elliston Manager*. London: Society for Theater Research, 1975.

Oxenford, John. "Richardson's Show." *The Era Almanack* (1869), 82–83.

"Paterson, Peter" [pseud. James Glass Betram]. *Glimpses of Real Life*. Edinburgh: Nimmo, 1864.

Rosenfeld, Sybil. "Muster Richardson—'The Great Showman.' " *Western Popular Theatre*. Eds. David Mayer and Kenneth Richards. London: Methuen, 1977.

————. *The Theater of the London Fairs in the 18th Century*. Cambridge: Cambridge UP, 1960.

Saxon, A. H. *The Life and Art of Andrew Ducrow and the Romantic Age of the English Circus*. Hamden, CT: Archon, 1978.

Schlicke, Paul. *Dickens and Popular Entertainment*. London: Allen and Unwin, 1985. With revisions Unwin Hyman, 1988.

————. " 'A Discipline of Feeling': Macready's *Lear* and *The Old Curiosity Shop*." *Dickensian* 76 (1980): 78–90.

Sheridan, Paul. *Penny Theatres of Victorian London*. London: Dobson, 1981.

Smith, Grahame. "Dickens: the Early Novels." *The Novel and Society: Defoe to George Eliot*. London: Batsford, 1984, 174–92.

Sprague, Arthur Colby. "Shakespeare and Melodrama." *Essays and Studies* n.s. 18 (1965): 1–12.

————. "A Macbeth of Few Words." *All These to Teach: Essays in Honor of C. A. Robertson*. Eds. Robert Bryan, et al. Gainsville, FL: Florida UP, 1965, 80–101.

Thackeray, William Makepeace. *"A Brighton Night Entertainment." Contributions to Punch*. London: Caxton, n.d., 328–30.

Wells, Stanley, ed. *Nineteenth-Century Shakespeare Burlesques*. 5 vols. London: Diploma, 1977.

NOTES

1. See in particular Axton, Smith, and Eigner.
2. For a more wide-ranging examination of the traditions of amusements which helped to shape Dickens' art, see my *Dickens and Popular Entertainment*.
3. To cite three instances, W. T. Moncrieff's *Sam Weller; or, The Pickwickians* appeared on a bill for the Theater, Sheffield, on 21 October 1837, with *Romeo and Juliet* as the afterpiece; W. T. Murray's *Scraps from Pickwick* appeared alongside *As You Like It* on several occasions at the Theatre Royal, Edinburgh, between 27 November and 21 December 1837; in London at the Strand Theatre Moncrieff's *Pickwick* adaptation ran for upwards of 120 nights during the 1837–38 season, with *Hamlet Travestie* among the plays produced in tandem with it. I am indebted to Philip Bolton for these examples.
4. Jerdan gives the estimate of the booth's audience capacity (Jerdan, 181). Rosenfeld assesses the shows and counts 44 plays, 20 pantomimes, and 9 panoramas advertised by Richardson in surviving playbills (Rosenfeld, 1977, 113).
5. *Sketches by Boz* alone contains several depictions of inferior theatrical events, each served with relish by the fascinated Boz.
6. For a discussion of the importance of Macready's 1838 restoration of *King Lear* to Dickens' art, see my article " 'A Discipline of Feeling.' "

The Curious Road to Death's Nell

Patrick J. McCarthy

Not the least of the puzzles about *The Old Curiosity Shop* is that on the one hand it can be dubbed ''Dickens' least successful novel'' and that on the other it has received considerable attention in its own day and almost endless scrutiny in ours. In their fine bibliographical study Priscilla and Paul Schlicke deal with 152 reviews and critical pieces from the nineteenth century and some 650 from the twentieth. Readers may raise objections to the novel, but they read it, usually to the end. Two of its famous attackers, Oscar Wilde and Aldous Huxley, were interested readers: their reactions may be thought a measure of its power. Stephen Marcus, the critic who called it Dickens' least successful work, went on to write a stunning forty-page essay about it.

What has kept readers reading *The Old Curiosity Shop* is a question that still needs to be asked, and I wish to ask it not of the richly comic or comic-horrific sections, of Swiveller, Brass, and Quilp, but of its central action, its astonishing, prolonged, implausible progress telling and tolling the way to dusty death. Modern readers, unlike those famed hangabouts on the American docks clamoring to know Nell's fate, are likely to know before they begin the novel that Nell will die in its pages. But whether in on the secret or not, they discover multiple inducements to continue reading. The inducements may be classified as in part local—the way page after page draws us in and on—in part what I may call infused—that is the continual but not ultimate or final lures—and in part overarching, that sense that the book has a particular destiny toward which it is driving.

After creating a dynamically rich and contrasting world, Dickens leaves half of it behind—including the linguistically fascinating characters Swiveller, Quilp, and Sampson Brass—in order to accompany two physically weak characters on a kind of walking tour. We follow along. Not all of our reasons for doing so can be explored here: our simple love of story and local suspense, say, or our interest in the journey motif, or the handling of the double plot.[1] I shall rather wish to look at how the novel sets itself up and establishes linguistic energies and counters for all that follows. These include the contexts for various sorts of curiosity, a sense of shifting paradox and bi-play, and, for the dock habitué in us all, a steady concentration on death. In short, the book draws us into its extraordinary story by methods to match its strangeness: a language shaped to unusualness, an insistence on curiosities, and a well-nigh manic fixation on mortality.

Though the road to Nell's death leads by a series of indirections and misdirections to an end that Dickens may not have seen clearly when he started, but felt coming, it begins with Master Humphrey's account of his nocturnal meanderings.[2] In the half-light of street lamps he fashions stories about those he comes upon, the glimpsed faces amid passing crowds, and, like Baudelaire ("Swarming city, city full of dreams, / Where the specter in broad daylight accosts the passer by") and Eliot on London Bridge ("So many, / I had not thought death had undone so many"), Master Humphrey thinks of death. Like the speaker in Tennyson's *Maud*, he thinks particularly of a dead man, lying "dead but conscious," with "the hum and noise being always present to his senses, and of the stream of life that will not stop, pouring on, through all his restless dreams" (43). He thinks of would-be suicides on the London bridges, and he thinks of imprisonment in life, of captive birds in Covent Garden Market at dawn as it bursts into bright and fragrant life. Though some shrink "from the hot hands of drunken purchasers," others, freshened and watered, will make "old clerks . . . wonder what has filled their breasts with visions of the country." Like his creator, Master Humphrey is fascinated by stories, by vitality, by energies made captive, by death in life, and by life in death.

The self-described man of curiosity is addressed by a child. "Sweet," "soft," "pretty," "slight," and "small" are the adjectives he early applies to her, but it is the word "little," used a half-dozen times in the first two pages, that serves to encapsulate her. (Robert Graves described "little" as "the tender catch in the voice of every friendly Dickens character" (8). Master Humphrey's curiosity is met first by a curious look from the child herself, and he notes that his "curiosity and interest [are] at least equal to the child's" (45). Soon we are with them in the curiosity shop proper where the objects of attention are labeled as "old," "odd," "musty," "rusty," "fantastic," "distorted," and of course "curious." Since they may be spoils from "old churches and tombs and deserted houses," they lurk about and hide "in jealousy and distrust." In their midst is an appropriate old man: we are told that "there was nothing in the whole collection but was in keeping with himself; nothing looked older or more worn than he" (47).

But the old man is "little," and Humphrey immediately tells his "little" story, and we see a "little" bed in a "little" room and we are more than a little at sea. Master Humphrey charges the old man to take better care of the child. The old man, her grandfather, does not shed remorseful tears. Instead, he is indignant: he insists that no one could love a child so much as he. We wonder what he can mean. Complications sharpen our curiosity: the child refuses to say what she has been doing out alone at night. There is a secret, and she herself does not know what it is. There is talk of great expectations, and a comic lad stands sideways to talk, laughs in a way perilously close to weeping, and sets the child to laughing though she, too, is on the verge of tears. Gradually, the little old man shifts the burden of maturity to the child. "In many respects," he says, "I am the child, and she is the grown person" (52). To our further surprise, he goes out after midnight, and Master Humphrey fears for the child at home the normal perils of midnight London—robberies, fires, and even murders—but he is on the wrong track. As a fairy princess willingly imprisoned in a lumber-room of oddities, she must face other than usual perils.

Dickens' language heightens surprise. It will not permit us to develop any appropriate sense that the scene we are witnessing is unremarkable. What words can do they do, stretching themselves into ultimates of their kind. Nell, seeking to account to Master Humphrey for her grandfather's nightly absences, uses words suggesting singularity, reach, and exclusiveness ("always," "every," "all," "ever," "great," "long," "one," "only") and finds they do not nearly suffice (54). The language describing the comic lad, Kit, pushes toward the same intemperate extravagance. He "bawls," "roars," laughs "violently" and "like a stentor," eats "with great voracity," taking "a most prodigious sandwich at one bite" (50–52). There is more than a touch of forcedness, too, as Nell bids her grandfather goodnight. She "cheerfully" helps him dress, she runs to kiss him, she promises "fervently" to say her prayers, she says a "clear" and "tender" farewell and "gently" closes the door (53–54). The mystery and sense of forward movement endorse such verbal pressing.

Humphrey returns to "a cheerful fire . . . [a] lamp burn[ing] brightly," everything "warm and cheering," but the images surrounding Nell have taken "possession of [his] brain." At this moment, as he first finishes Chapter

One, the burden of evidence suggests that he and his creator with him do not quite know where they are heading. We know from letters that Dickens thought "the little child-story" would serve as contrast to Master Humphrey's "quiet way," not to mention his drab friends, and next day considered naming "that little tale" *The Old Curiosity Shop and the Child* (*Letters* II: 49). As Nell takes possession of Dickens' imagination, the contrast deepens and widens not just to Master Humphrey but to all about her.

He tells us so, explicitly, and his language makes clear the manner, the extent, and the directions in which his conception of her besieged his attention (italics mine): "I had her image," says Master Humphrey, "without *any* effort of imagination, *surrounded* and *beset* by *everything* that was foreign to its nature, and *furthest* removed from the sympathies of her age and sex" (56).

This sentence did not appear in the text before the novel's first publication as a separate volume in 1841, and it now occurs in the middle of four paragraphs which Dickens inserted just before the last paragraph of Chapter One. What induced him to make the additions was a review by Thomas Hood of the first volume of *Master Humphrey's Clock* in October of 1840. With about half of *The Old Curiosity Shop* before him, Hood drew attention to "the Artist's picture of the Child, asleep in her little bed, surrounded, or rather mobbed, by ancient armour and arms, antique furniture, and relics sacred or profane, hideous or grotesque: —it is like an Allegory of the peace and innocence of Childhood in the midst of Violence, Superstition, and all the hateful or hurtful Passions of the world" (96). Dickens admired Hood's review and in his four-paragraph addendum picks up from it certain key words. Having seen Nell amid "the heaps of fantastic things," he writes,

> . . . she seemed to exist as a kind of allegory; and having these shapes about her, claimed my interest so strongly, that . . . I could not dismiss her from my recollection, do what I would.
> "It would be a curious speculation," said I, after some restless turns across and across the room, "to imagine her in her future life, holding her solitary way among a crowd of wild grotesque companions; the only pure, fresh, youthful object in the throng. It would be curious to find—"
> I checked myself here, for the theme was carrying me along with it at a great pace, and I already saw before me a region on which I was little disposed to enter.   (56)

With Hood's help Dickens now has seen clearly what he has been about. "Sweet," "soft," "pretty," "little" Nell, the intended contrast to Master Humphrey, placed amid the old, deformed, and the grotesque has set that world by the ears. Her dissimilarity to all about her has been so stunning as to make her a curiosity of a reverse sort. But reverse or not, she is defined by the curiosities and may not depart their company.

What is more, Nell, "childish" Nell, is surrounded by sweepings of time and age that persist into a kind of life. What is their challenge to her? They survive, decaying slowly and meaninglessly. And she? What can be her meaning? Not in surviving as they have done but as moving alone toward the region on which her creator "was little disposed to enter." She must die.

Conceived from the outset, then, as contrastive, destined to live among the contrasting elements so as to enact a meaning, Nell fulfills her destiny best as an allegorical figure. Her pure, self-abnegating innocence, for example, sweetens her essential self, the mortal child. She is denied the kind of full, rounded existence that can embody self-generated contradictions and surprises. Her strength is narrow and defined; her weakness, an absence of generous, unordered particularity.[3] She is pared down to essentials and made solitary: her grandfather, too, exists primarily as aspects of herself and her condition (fear, helplessness, hope) and in part what she is fleeing from (greed, violation, and imprisonment).

Dickens, the practiced story-teller, now had two major inducements to keep himself and his readers interested. The first, the curiosities, would be a continual one, and give him more delight than trouble. For them, particularly living curiosities, he had a lively interest all his life.[4] It was as though oddities, freaks, and extravagances of form and behavior held secrets for him, that they were ways to understand the nature of man. It was not that the quotidian and the ordinary were inscrutable—he read them with a wizard's eye—but that scrutiny of the odd and distorted unleashed his fascinated imagination.

The second inducement is death itself which—to adapt Mark Twain's famous dictum—tends to concentrate the mind. In its most distressing form, the death of the young and innocent, we are appalled but we want to understand and if possible to get a measure of control over it, even the control of having experienced it vicariously through the death of a fictional child.

Certain modern theory goes further on the point. We have moved quite away from the cocktail-party commonplace that the modern liberal intelligence does not wish to think of death, that for us it is as forbidden a subject as sex among the Victorians. In his challenging study of Victorian fiction, John Kucich has boldly argued that "understand[ing] self-negation or destabilization as the end of human desire" is "explicitly at the heart of most postmodernist ideas about pleasure," and that "human life becomes a kind of impossible flirtation with death, an attempt to represent or experience its finality without actually suffering it."[11] (*Repression* 20–21). According to this view, we want to experience death while still living, and specifically to do so we have created certain ordered, symbolic forms which make it possible. The appeal of Dickens' novels, then, resides in their centering on death and thereby providing us a vicarious but liberating experience. Thus Dickens "authenticates the lives of those who can internalize [death's] negative power" (Kucich "Forum" 87).

Whether or not we wish to go so far as this, the novels, and *Old Curiosity Shop* most assuredly, draw upon the usually secret, unacknowledged energy of death. Through Nell Dickens reaches toward a meaning outside the individual child. True, he had killed off at least fifteen characters in his first three novels with varying degrees of luridness. As for the young and the good, he had explored with the near-fatal illness of Rose Maylie in *Oliver Twist* what an onlooker would feel, and Smike's mistreatment and death in *Nicholas Nickleby* are central to that novel's groundwork of feeling but not its major theme. Nell is of quite another order. She is his central figure, her story the spine of the work.

In responding to this major Dickensian concern, we need not think ourselves markedly different from the Victorians, though we may respond differently from them. Like them we fear death and find it fascinating; we abhor it and seek it out. Our doubleness of attitude may seem to us less patent than Dickens', but his doubleness as it appears in the novels is in fact part of his own engagement with death. Undeniably, in any case, his energy and the energy of his subject beckon us along the curious road to the death of Nell.

Beginning with the second chapter, then, new orders of curiosity must be found, and Dickens will be at no loss for them. But as his next figures are introduced, Dickens seems first to have thought of lesser contrasts: Quilp as "elderly" and sly and grasping; Frederick as brash, drunken, and profligate; Dick Swiveller as dirty, careless, and whimsical, an idle hanger-on and frequenter of music halls and drinking societies. Swiveller is a figure of whom Dickens later wrote that he "*mean*[t] to make much," but the character will be passive for yet a while, as Dickens said, "the sport of destiny" (*Letters* II: 70,75). Frederick, Nell's older brother, clearly will not do, not being extravagant enough or sufficiently unique, and so he is whirled out of the novel and onto a slab in the Paris morgue. Even Quilp is a trifle slow to take on his terrifying, aggressive, preternaturally knowing self. Nell, who has met him before, shows no signs of fright as she enters with him. Nor does Quilp yet know Trent's secret: he has lent money to him without knowing how it is being spent.

At this point, three passages, chosen as the three lead characters emerge into full selfhood, will illustrate and compare the verbal coordinates within which they move. Nell, first introduced as contrast to Master Humphrey, now generates Quilp as full opposite to herself. Quilp becomes ineluctably Quilpish as he first talks to Swiveller, then as we follow him to his wharf, to his dwelling on Tower Hill, and back to his wharf. A long paragraph describes his passage across the river:

> A fleet of barges were coming lazily on, some sideways, some head first, some stern first; all in a wrong-headed, dogged, obstinate way, bumping up against the larger craft, running under the bows of steamboats, getting into every kind of nook and corner where they had no business, and being crunched on all sides like so many walnut-shells; while each with its pair of long sweeps struggling and splashing in the water looked like some lumbering fish in pain. In some of the vessels at anchor all hands were busily engaged in coiling ropes, spreading out sails to dry, taking in or discharging their cargoes; in others no life was visible but two or three tarry boys, and perhaps a barking dog running to and fro upon the deck or scrambling up to look over the side and bark the louder for the view. Coming slowly through the forest of masts was a great steam ship, beating the water in short impatient strokes with her heavy paddles as though she wanted room to breathe, and advancing in her huge bulk like a sea monster among the minnows of the Thames. On either hand were long black tiers of colliers; between them vessels slowly working out of harbour with sails glistening in the sun, and creaking noise on board, re-echoed from a hundred quarters. The water and all upon it was in active motion, dancing and buoyant and bubbling up; while the old grey Tower and piles of building on shore, with many a church-spire shooting up between, looked coldly on, and seemed to disdain their chafing, restless neighbour.   (86–87)

This is typical Dickensian jumblement at its richest and best, reminiscent of a similar scene in *Martin Chuzzlewit* and comparable scenes in *Dombey and Son* and *Bleak House*. Crackling with multi-directional energy, it mirrors Dickens' elementary conviction that all things seek to affirm themselves amid a welter of contending forces and that the resulting anarchy is dangerous. Quilp's connection with the scene is purely metonymic, needing nothing else; it is the kind of world which suits him and in which he flourishes.

Dick Swiveller, my second example, undergoes his transformation from Frederick Trent's loutish friend to comic immortal before he must seriously deal with Quilp and the Brasses. His delicious dalliance with Sophy Wackles achieves for his characterization what the scenes of domestic sportfulness do for Quilp. His surroundings are no less disorderly than Quilp's, but his imaginative mastery of them evokes a vocal pitch from the narrator that suggests that Swiveller's style has taken him over as well. The tone is that of a charmed but dotty tour guide:

> It may not be uninteresting or improper to remark that even [his saying, "Pass the rosy wine"] partook in a double sense of the figurative and poetical character of Mr. Swiveller's mind, as the rosy wine was in fact represented by one glass of cold gin-and-water which was replenished as occasion required from a bottle and jug upon the table, and was passed from one to another in a scarcity of tumblers which, as Mr. Swiveller's was a bachelor's establishment, may be acknowledged without a blush.   (101)

The languagae and style of Nell eschews such playfulness; her plight finds a thrumming plangency of expression. Here she determines to flee with her grandfather: "If you are sorrowful," she says to him, "let me know why and be sorrowful too; if you waste away and are paler and weaker every day, let me be your nurse and try to comfort you. If you are poor, let us be poor together . . ." and so on for two paragraphs (122). Within a narrow range of reference, the anaphoras roll out predictably: "Let us be beggars. . . . Let us walk. . . . Let us never set foot in dark rooms" (122). She bids farewell to her room, a fairy-tale leave-taking. The narrator lingers on repetitions of words including "little," ignores her restless nights there, and regrets the trifles she leaves behind without, we note, specifying them.

> Her own little room too, where she had so often knelt down and prayed at night—prayed for the time which she hoped was dawning now—the little room where she had slept so peacefully, and dreamed such pleasant dreams—it was hard not to be able to glance round it once more, and to be forced to leave it without one kind look or grateful tear. There were some trifles there—poor useless things—that she would have liked to take away; but that was impossible.
> (149)

It would appear that Swiveller that "creature compact of great phrases," (Priestley 196), and Quilp, begetter and scion of everything that "goes bump in the night," are poised to take over the verbal energies of the book. Nothing so extreme happens. Soon after starting out, Nell and her grandfather move through a landscape of deprivation and decay, but the language is contrastingly profuse and exuberant. Its energetic participles almost burst the tattered seams of the subject. Nell and her grandfather, vulnerable and weak, exist amid a verbal liveliness comparable to what other characters generate.

> Children, scantily fed and clothed, spread over every street, and sprawling in the dust—scolding mothers, stamping their slipshod feet with noisy threats upon

the pavement—shabby fathers, hurrying with dispirited looks to the occupation which brought them ''daily bread'' and little more—mangling-women, washer-women, cobblers, tailors, chandlers, driving their trades in parlours and kitchens and back rooms and garrets, and sometimes all of them under the same roof—brick-fields, skirting gardens paled with staves of old casks, or timber pillaged from houses burnt down and blackened and blistered by the flames—mounds of dock-weed, nettles, coarse grass and oyster shells, heaped in rank confusion—small dissenting chapels to teach, with no lack of illustration the miseries of Earth, and plenty of new churches, erected with superfluous wealth, to show the way to Heaven.   (172/73)

Comparing two further scenes, one under the domination of Quilp, the other of Nell, also makes the point further. When the ''strong men in carpet caps'' are emptying the curiosity shop of furnishings, Quilp performs prodigies of strength and energy, bumping, knocking, and hustling about ''like an evil spirit.'' Readers remember the exactly rendered scene and Quilp's caperings. Just as specifically executed is the road-side cottage at which Nell purchases milk on the pilgrims' first day out of London. Nell has her ''little'' basket, of course, and she sits quietly, but the description points precisely to ''a stock of crockery and delf'' and ''a gaudy tea-tray, representing a lady in bright red, walking out with a very blue parasol'' (178).

Nell, never far from curiosities, gets contextual support from them, her scenes with them rich in paradoxes of life and death, freedom and imprisonment, vulnerability and power. Much has been made, and deservedly, of the splendid double-directness of the moment in the churchyard when Nell and the grandfather come upon the Punch exhibitors Codlin and Short. They exchange looks of curiosity, this curious foursome; the old man expresses ''delight'' with what Codlin calls ''delusion,'' Nell mends the clothes of the battered Judy; lifeless Punch, atop a tombstone, points at and chuckles at a ''most flourishing epitaph''; and Codlin, the master, soon bends under the weight of Punch and his Punch's temple as he carries them off. They repair to the ''glorious fire,'' the ''cheerful sound[s],'' and the ''delicious'' odors of the Jolly Sandboys, but its sensuous joys dissipate quickly as Short plans to ''take measures for detaining'' Nell and her grandfather (199). Alert to treachery, she is put ''in a state of extreme surprise'' by Codlin's protestations of friendship, and when they get to the town where the races are to take place, a ''delirious scene'' of noisy drunkenness and rioting determines her to flee.

We tend not to ask what precisely Nell and her grandfather are fleeing. But if we do, the reasons we come up with, and even less the ones concocted by Nell for her grandfather, do not meet the case. The motifs of imprisonment and freedom are constants of Dickens' imaginative world: forces within it, almost all of them, will bind to their wills at any chance the weak and forceless. Nell and her grandfather, the imagery tells us, have left behind a London where birds in cages, beasts in dens, and men in dungeons (171) are restrained "close and dark." Now Nell wants to "escape" again, to "steal away," an unspecified, general "they" threatens to lock up Trent "in a stone room, dark and cold, and chain [him] to the wall," and as the chapter ends the couple makes "for the open fields" (214).

Nell's fears and hopes are as unspecified and as real-unreal as those of fairy tale. Language, too, and the fictions it generates, are also subject to pressures of fable and meaning. Before leaving the company of the Punch players, Nell visits a churchyard where she takes "a curious kind of pleasure in lingering among these houses of the dead, and read the inscriptions on the tombs of the good people . . . , and passing on from one to another with increasing interest." Here birds skim to and fro, their clamor noisily "satiriz[ing] the old restlessness of those who [lie] so still beneath the moss . . . , and the useless strife in which they had worn away their lives." She "loiter[s] from grave to grave," and peeps into a church where "the very bell-rope [is] frayed into a fringe, and hoary with old age (187)." An old woman, long survivor of a young husband, tells her that "death doesn't change us more than life" (188).

The free birds, that is to say, implausibly deride the once lively energy of men now imprisoned forever. The old woman, altered and bent by time, suggests no doubt a real ambiguity in time's effects but can do so only by ignoring the moldering of her husband's "manly beauty." The scene puzzles us. Nell takes pleasure in the tombs? She is developing the sensibility of a graveyard poet, meditating in the style of Blair, Gray, and Collins? We cannot deny the implausibility, and the inconsistency of language is clear. Images which represent life as restlessness and undesirable change, death as freedom and permanence, deny and overturn their former meanings.

Shortly after, with Codlin and Short safely behind, Nell conspires in her own fiction that a bird is leading them to freedom. It leads them not to freedom but "downward in a steep descent" to a hamlet where death had just marked a young victim (247–48). It takes the schoolmaster's dull but normal boys to put language to rights again. They "long[ ] to be outside" (256) and once "free" emit "a joyous whoop" (258).

Coming next upon Mrs. Jarley's caravan moves us into another curious cycle of heightened and then declining life.

It was not a shabby, dingy, dusty cart, but a small house upon wheels, with white dimity curtains festooning the windows. . . . Neither was it a poor caravan drawn by a single donkey or emaciated horse. . . . Neither was it a gypsy caravan, for at the open door (graced with a bright brass knocker) sat a Christian lady. . . . And that it was not an unprovided or destitute caravan was clear from this lady's occupation.   (263)

The anaphora is neither tired nor misplaced since it is full of gentle surprises; the woman's "occupation" is pleasurable eating, she invites the travelers to partake, and we know—as in all Dickensian scenes of happy ingestion—that we are in benevolent surroundings. But the deadly undertow soon exerts itself on Nell. Quilp makes brief monitory appearances under the town arch, in Nell's uneasy dreams, and in her dread imaginings brought on by the wax figures (289). Nell is also stripped of all close human company by the return of her grandfather's gambling compulsion. She slips into depression and illness. The text casts about to find consolations for her. Again they are contrary ones. She is said to find "deep delight," "softened pleasure," "pleasure or relief from care," as she observes "from a humble distance" the joys of the united Edwards sisters (316). Of them, too, she is soon deprived, and "past, present, and what was yet before her" are elided into a symbol of eternity.

She raised her eyes to the bright stars, looking down so mildly from the wide worlds of air, and, gazing on them, found new stars burst upon her view, and more beyond, and more beyond again, until the whole great expanse sparkled with shining spheres, rising higher and higher in immeasurable space, eternal in their numbers as in their changeless and incorruptible existence. She bent over the calm river, and saw them shining in the same majestic order as when the dove beheld them gleaming through the swollen waters, upon the mountain top down far below, and dead mankind, a million fathoms deep.   (396–97)

Allow the familiar symbols of order and permanence and incorruptibility, and concede that the gothic image of the dove looking down on the deeply drowned dead is striking.[5] Dickens was proud of it and considered the last part "the best thing" in the sentence, explaining that it was "the fruit . . . of a solitary walk" (*Letters* II: 131). The ideas and particularly the deft Biblical allusion, however, are not (as represented) those of a fourteen-year-old child. The narrator has supplied her with thoughts and language. He directs her along her descending path and watches her descend while still bent on finding sources of comfort.

In the tumultuous industrial town to which the travelers then flee, Dickens' verbal power is unleashed in onomatopoeic clatterings, hammering repetitions, and a stunning multitudinousness of referent and analogy. The Ancient

Mariner, Pandemonium, the Hall of the Mountain King, Vulcan's forge—critics have found all and more here.[6] Not the least impressive feature of the writing is the rendering of scene into oppressive dream, keeping Nell at its focus so that Dickens draws on contemporary fears of anarchy and yet locates them in her sensibility.[7] The cost to Nell is the wasting cost of contrast, as, in the words of Garrett Stewart, "the objective pass[es] over into the subjective" (108). After the wasteland scenes she is now the "wasted" child (434). The battle of life in such conditions has been too fierce for her. The schoolmaster rescues her but for appropriate death rather than life. He finds for her a gently moving "stage-waggon," and her two-day ride in it simulates a journey by funeral cortege and predicts apotheosis. Nell goes to sleep to the waggon's lulling movement "until it stopped abruptly at a sharp high ridge as if there were no more road, and all beyond was sky" (436).

At this point Dickens no longer may shrink from the "region on which [from the beginning he] was little disposed to enter" (56). The region is death's, and its locus returns us to the stiflingly dark, murky, gaunt, decaying rust and dust of the first chapter. There Nell was the reverse of all about her; now Dickens is intent on reconciling her to it. "Why," he might be saying with Marlowe's Mephistophilis "this is the curiosity shop, nor are we out of it." Astonishingly, he devotes thirty-eight pages, chapters fifty-two to the end of fifty-five, to the last period in which we see Nell alive. Like the child, he is so "fascinated" with "the church, the ruin, the antiquated graves," that he can "turn to nothing else" (440).

The limitations he sets for himself intensify his concentration. The figures around Nell are specially recruited as functionaries and attendants; they are generic figures, old or very young, and mostly unnamed. Only the schoolmaster—also typical and already associated with death—is familiar. Nell is alone, or, more exactly, alone with the narrator and stand-ins like the bachelor. As earlier, her thoughts are interlarded with theirs.

The language of the four chapters draws heavily from the lexicon of decay and passing time; words betokening death and its stages number in the seventies. In this regard Dickens refuses to blink at what is happening; even so, there are surprises in what he insists upon. The word *old* is used therein a startling number of times; Nell's unblemished youth is caused to stand out all the more vividly as she is companioned by decrepit, senile, self deceiving age. The word *little*, appearing thirty-one times and every one a slight catch in the voice, betokens Dickens' emotional involvement, but there is no abatement.

In the midst of all this, Dickens reminds himself that "everything in our lives, whether of good or evil, affects us most by contrast" (493). And so contrasting oxymoronic elements appear: the beauty of the place, the peacefulness, the quietness are stated and reiterated. Words expressive of happiness and joy appear some thirty times, and the text recalls the reversed conceit that death unprisons the captives of time (485). There is humor, too: the sexton and gravedigger take comfort that the woman they are burying lied about her age and was considerably older than they. But even the jokes, as Kincaid has noted, "are by now clearly preparatory for death" (2). No truly relieving contrast is possible; the tide of the four chapters comes in irresistibly. The chapters are, like the house she is given by the sexton, Nell's place "to learn to die in" (482).

Aldous Huxley typifies readers who regard Nell at this point as beyond believability. He excoriates Dickens for being so emotionally blinded that "he didn't want to see anything" save "Little Nell's sufferings on the one hand and her goodness and innocence on the other" (155–56). Dickens stresses Nell's emotional suffering, yes, but he allows her even less physical self than she has had before. Forgetting that he had earlier written of "the sharp lineaments of rigid and unsightly death" (146), he pictures her at the end as "unaltered," without trace of sufferings and fatigue, while her "same sweet face . . . [has] the same mild lovely look" (654). He has not seen "the thin, pale, wasted hand, . . . the wasted, yellow face, . . . the enormous, feverishly glowing eyes," or heard her "broken voice" or "the rapid, hard breathing" through her "dry lips." The phrases are Dostoevsky's and come from a passage to which Huxley directs us, the scene in *The Brothers Karamazov* in which the child Ilusha lies mortally ill. To that bedside come a doctor, family relatives and friends, and frolicking school chums. Ilusha is a recognizable sick child; he is by turns quiet and voluble, petulant and then delighted by gifts, joyful and suffering. His pillows are mussed, the doctor is squeamish, and, most importantly, a great deal besides dying is going on in the room (Book 10, Ch. 5).

By contrast, Dickens' chapters are a marvel of single-minded concentration. With infinite, deliberate patience, they take us up to the point where the macabre sexton and Nell uncover the grave-like well. Then we shift back to London for thirteen chapters—eight weeks for the original readers—and when we return with her friends it is not to a death scene but to more delay before her death is confirmed in slow, widely spaced repetitions: "She was dead. . . . She was dead. . . . She was dead. . . . She had been dead two days." Dickens refuses to be hurried.[8] He carries on just as deliberately with the aftermath, but not to drape Nell's corpse in marmoreal folds of language. There is no taint of necrophilia here.

He has his purposes. He tests as far as he can the influence of Nell's death on the living; he does not let go until he has touched on every possibility of comfort. He patiently records the efforts to "soften" the grandfather's grief and open it to "old affections and old ties" (650).[9] His key word here is "soften," one he used several times in speaking of how death should be handled so as to affect the living properly.[10] Happily, he does not resort to signallings from the other shore. His method is to insist on any and all comfort we will take: Wordsworthian images, a Bible placed metonymically in Nell's hands, intimations of immortality from the natural world, the witnesses' sense of the figure of the child left with God, and at the end, in language that he cannot heighten enough to make its extraordinary claim he intones:

> "Oh, it is hard to take to heart the lesson that such deaths will teach, but let no man reject it, for it is one that all must learn, and is a mighty, universal Truth. When death strikes down the innocent and young, for every fragile form from which he lets the panting spirit free, a hundred virtues rise, in shapes of mercy, charity and love to walk the world, and bless it. Of every tear that mortals shed on such green graves, some good is born, some gentler nature comes. In the Destroyer's steps there spring up bright creations that defy his power, and his dark path becomes a way of light to Heaven"   (659).

Rather than softened, however, some modern readers are liable to be offended or, as in Oscar Wilde's case, to collapse into laughter. It strikes us as presumptuous and pseudo-sublime. Like Keats, we dislike work that has a palpable design on us. Here we feel at its height the pressures of authorial insistence that have increasingly marked Nell's fatal journey. As we have noted, the energy, variety, and openness of his freer ranging style have attended that journey from its beginning, and have gradually been narrowed, pressed down, and forced into a tight, monocular vision. In the London scenes, contrariwise, an unconstrained Dickens has kept on exceeding expectations with his free, various, invitingly fresh creative gambollings, and the contrast cannot but affect us. With Nell we are pushed past pitch of grief, and if we resort to tears they are likely to express frustration rather than sorrow.

We are enormously relieved to be "swivelled" away from such single-mindedness and back to the lively but lower-key doings in London for the last chapter. But there, too, we are likely to feel that the upbeat ending leaves us a bit downcast. In the manner of New Comedy, the young couples are married off in due time, and the helper figures, including Whisker, the Garlands' refugee from beast fable, are duly rewarded. Partially from the analogy with melodrama and partially, too, because Dickens had a strong vindictive streak in him, the villains feel the strong bite of his avenging lash. The severest strokes are saved for the Brasses, last seen as "cowering shivering forms, looking into the roads and kennels as they went in search of refuse food or disregarded offal" (665)—we would have thought them more resourceful in defeat. Quilp has already been reduced to the neuter pronoun "it" by the once-merry Thames. Well, we have stepped quite out of novel into moral tale.

The final illustrations carry the image of Nell even further than the text has done. Without language preparation she is pictured before an icon of the child Jesus in the arms of the Virgin Mary, and then as being assumed bodily to heaven like Mary herself. The illustrations force out the dubious implications of the earlier gothicized scenes and accord with his Chadband-like intonings. The visual send-off—some will say send-up—is a Dickensian last effort to despatch Nell into a quasi-religious immortality.[11]

What then are we to make of such an ending following such an extraordinary progress? The book of course is larger and richer than the segments I have concentrated on. In them it may simply be that Dickens tried to do more than a novel *can* do. Despite his wizardry, there is surely in those sections a too muchness of a much, the work of an extraordinarily confident, even cocky, young writer—a strong, brave, vulnerable writer, too, willing to persist, despite shrinkings of the spirit, even to the extremity of death, in an enterprise he felt drawn to by his genius and the imperious demands of his exploratory nature. We may object, but he has carried us along with him in a mixture of fascination and reluctance similar to his own.

By the last chapter we have had enough of innocent death and want Dickens to give his prodigious talent more room than he has taken for it here. Certainly he has done what he set out to do, to sound death's knell through the death of Nell and mark its bleak and unsatisfactory consolations. His last sentence grimly suggests that in writing the novel he has learned resignation to the death of everything, including the novel he has just written: "So do all things pass away, like a tale is told" (672).

NOTES

1. Jerome Meckier's perceptive article, "Suspense in *The Old Curiosity Shop:* Dickens' Contrapuntal Artistry," *Journal of Narrative Technique*, 2 (1972), 199–207,

shows how Dickens kept his readers uncertain as to whether Nell would die. Most modern readers know before they begin what will happen to Nell. The knowledge influences reading: suspense would likely have made us more patient and less critical.

2. For Dickens's conscious decision that Nell must die, see the note in the Pilgrim Edition of *The Letters of Charles Dickens,* ed. Madeleine House and Graham Storey (Oxford: Clarendon, 1965–) II, 125 (hereafter referred to as *Letters*).

3. She requires only so much particularity as to permit what Northrop Frye calls "the sense that a work of literature is expanding into insights and experiences beyond itself." See *The Secular Scripture: A Study of the Structure of Romance* (Cambridge, Mass.: Harvard UP, 1976), p. 59.

4. Among the rich evidence of Dickens's interest in curiosities is his possession of *Kirby's Wonderful and Eccentric Museum; or Magazine of Remarkable Characters. Including all the Curiosities of Nature and Art, from the Remotest Period to the Present Time, Drawn from Every Authentic Source. Illustrated with One Hundred and Twenty-four Engravings. Chiefly taken from Rare and Curious Prints or Original Drawings,* 6 vols. (London: R. S. Kirby, 1820).

5. Nell's thoughts come from the same Gothic sensibility as Jane Eyre's dream pictures. See *Jane Eyre,* Chapter 13.

6. Notably, Stephen Marcus in *Dickens from Pickwick to Dombey* (New York: Simon and Schuster, 1968), pp. 129–68.

7. Questions of the problems caused by the interfusion of novel, romance, and allegory in Dickens and others are interestingly considered by Edwin Eigner in *The Metaphysical Novel in England and America [:] Dickens, Bulwer, Melville, and Hawthorne* (Berkeley et al.: U. of California P., 1978).

8. Dickens's reasons, based on 18th-century ideas of sentiment, are admirably set forth in Fred Kaplan's *Sacred Tears [:] Sentimentality in Victorian Literature* (Princeton: Princeton UP, 1987).

9. Barbara Hardy says that Dickens "winds about in a disinclination to finish the story." *Forms of Feeling in Victorian Fiction* (London: Peter Owen, 1985), p. 67.

10. On 17 January, 1841 he wrote to Forster, "When I first began . . . to keep my thoughts upon this ending of the tale, I resolved to try and do something which might be read by people about whom Death had been,—with a softened feeling, and with consolation." *Letters,* II, 188, and see also I, 516; IV, 247; *American Notes and Pictures from Italy* (London, Oxford UP., 1957), p. 301; and *The Speeches of Charles Dickens,* ed. K. J. Fielding (Oxford: Clarendon, 1960), p. 10. Compare William Dodd, *Reflections on Death* (London: Carnas and N[?], 1769), pp. 9–10, which Dickens had in his library: "It is too commonly found, that a familiarity with death, and a frequent recurrence of *funerals, graves,* and *churchyards,* serves to harden rather than humanize the mind; and to deaden rather than arouse those becoming reflections, which such objects seem excellently calculated to produce."

11. See especially the review in *The Christian Remembrancer,* December, 1842, pp. 92–93. See also Eigner, *The Metaphysical Novel in England and America,* pp. 120–122. In a recent talk at the Dickens Universe meeting at University of California, Santa Cruz, Robert Polhemus has argued that Dickens intended Nell to be a sacrificial figure as well as a refiguration of the Virgin Mary.

WORKS CITED

Dickens, Charles. *The Letters of Charles Dickens*. Ed. Madeleine House and Graham Storey. Oxford: Clarendon, 1965–.

———. *The Old Curiosity Shop*. Ed. Angus Easson. Baltimore: Penguin, 1972.

Dostoevsky, Fyodor. *The Brothers Karamazov*. Trans. Constance Garnett. New York: Modern Library College Edition, 1950.

Eigner, Edwin. *The Metaphysical Novel in England and America: Dickens, Bulwer, Melville, and Hawthorne*. Berkeley: U of California P, 1978.

Frye, Northrop. *The Secular Scripture: A Study of the Structure of Romance*. Cambridge, MA: Harvard UP, 1976.

Graves, Robert. *The Real David Copperfield*. London: A. Barker, 1933.

Hardy, Barbara. *Forms of Feeling in Victorian Fiction*, London: Peter Owen, 1985.

Hood, Thomas. In *Athenaeum* 680 (7 October 1840): 887, Reprinted in *Dickens: The Critical Heritage*. Ed. Philip Collins. London: Routledge & Kegan Paul, 1971.

Huxley, Aldous. "The Vulgarity of Little Nell," reprinted in *The Dickens Critics*. Ed. George H. Ford and Lauriat Lane Jr. Ithaca: Cornell UP, 1961.

Kaplan, Fred. *Sacred Tears: Sentimentality in Victorian Literature*. Princeton: Princeton UP, 1987.

Kincaid, James. "Laughter and Pathos: *The Old Curiosity Shop*" in *Dickens the Craftsman: Strategies of Presentation*. Ed. Robert B. Partlow. Carbondale: Southern Illinois UP, 1970.

Kucich, John. *Repression in Victorian Fiction: Charlotte Brontë, George Eliot, and Charles Dickens*, Berkeley: U California P, 1987. "Forum" *PMLA* 95: 1980.

Marcus, Steven. *Dickens from Pickwick to Dombey*. New York: Simon & Schuster, 1968.

Meckier, Jerome. "Suspense in *The Old Curiosity Shop*: Dickens' Contrapuntal Artistry." *Journal of Narrative Technique* 2 (1972): 199–207.

Priestley, J. B. *The English Comic Characters*. New York: Phaeton Press, 1972.

Schlicke, Paul and Priscilla. *The Old Curiosity Shop. The Garland Dickens Bibliographies*, vol. 9. New York and London: Garland Publishing Inc., 1988.

Stewart, Garrett. *Dickens and the Trials of the Imagination*. Cambridge, MA: Harvard UP, 1974.

Walder, Dennis. *Dickens and Religion.* Boston: George Allen and Unwin, 1981.

Walton, Izaak, *The Lives of John Donne, et al.* London: Falcon Educational Books, 1951.

Welsh, Alexander. *The City of Dickens.* Oxford: Clarendon, 1981.

Whitehead, John. *Life of The Rev. John Wesley.* Boston: Hill and Broadhead, 1846.

Willmott, Robert A. Preface. *Jeremy Taylor: His Predecessors, Contemporaries, and Successors.* 2 vols. London: John W. Parker, 1847.

Little Nell and the Art of Holy Dying: Dickens and Jeremy Taylor

Marilyn Georgas

In chapter fifty-two of Dickens' *The Old Curiosity Shop,* Little Nell dreams by night of seeing "the roof opening, and a column of bright faces, rising away into the sky," and of hearing "music in the air, and a sound of angels' wings" all the while. And she goes by day (in chapter fifty-three) to the church, where one day, climbing up to the very turret top, she experiences:

> the glory of the sudden burst of light; the freshness of the fields and woods . . . all, everything, so beautiful and happy! It was like passing from death to life; it was drawing nearer Heaven.

But all too often Nell's readers have deserted her before she experiences this blissful transport, then moves past it. Few seem to want to finish with her this journey to death.

The critical history of *The Old Curiosity Shop* is legendary, the novel's passionate reception in its own day, with few dissenting voices in the throng, followed by a shift of opinion that brought about a predominating disdain for the novel which persists to the present day. Recent decades have seen a renewal and deepening of interest in Dickens, and readers of *The Old Curiosity Shop* have come to see great vigor in Quilp and great charm in Swiveller. Critics have looked with interest to the novel as a significant clue to the development of Dickens' thought or to the culture of his day. But the matter of Little Nell has continued to pose an obstacle to serious consideration of the novel as a work of art.

Criticism of Nell's plight has developed a body of preconceptions which make it difficult for readers to approach the work without ready-made judgments. The dominant critical preconceptions are based largely on biographical

35

and psychological interpretations of Dickens. Dickens' own descriptions of his intense grief over the death of his sister-in-law Mary Hogarth have survived to provide a convenient explanation for the novel: Dickens played out a binge of morbid and neurotic fantasy and grief in creating the delicate suffering virgin Nell. Add to this Dickens' money worries as he began to write the novel and it can be deduced that as Dickens began to realize that a sweet, pathetic child dying a protracted death could provide a money-making formula that would remedy the falling sales of *Master Humphrey's Clock,* he stretched and shaped the story for that purpose. While the child as protagonist and her prolonged dalliance with death formed a special attraction when the novel was published, these features pose great obstacles to today's sensibilities, and the commonplace assumptions about the novel's origins in Dickens' neuroses and greed seem to justify any disregard for Nell and her journey that readers may choose to give them.

It is not unlikely that the desire to make money along with a self-indulgent, possibly abnormal, binge of grief over the death of Mary Hogart figured in the complex of inspiration that produced *The Old Curiosity Shop*. Countless other personal and subjective elements probably figured in. But these are not at all an adequate, or ultimate, means of accounting for the novel. A wide range of objective materials, materials established independently of Dickens' personal psychology, were also at work in shaping Dickens' creativity, among them a rich field of literary tradition. But it is in a well-established literary tradition that one can find further, and very significant, explanations for the materials and the shaping of the novel. This source is the *ars moriendi* tradition, transmitted to Victorians by Jeremy Taylor's *Rule and Exercises of Holy Dying* (1651), which remained a standard work on the English bookshelf for the next two hundred years and beyond.

In taking the life and death of a child seriously, Dickens was doing something that had not been done before in prose writing except in works, usually religious tracts, which used the child as a didactic tool to provide grim warnings about death and to try to frighten audiences, particularly children themselves, into righteousness. It was Dickens who first created inner lives for children and used them as full-scale protagonists in full-length fictions. But while children may not long have been regarded as significant subjects, by the time death and the child came together in *The Old Curiosity Shop,* death had long been a significant subject, the subject for deep thought by ancient philosophers and, after the advent of Christianity, for Christian philosophers as well. It became, in fact, the center of a long tradition of *ars moriendi* writing.

Early in the Christian era lives of saints provided patterns for holy dying, but in the latter Middle Ages books of direct instruction and exhortation began to be written. Such writing continued past the Protestant Reformation and on into the seventeenth century in England. This *ars moriendi* genre culminated and ended with Taylor's *Rule and Exercises of Holy Dying,* which, quickly regarded as a companion to Taylor's *Rule and Exercises of Holy Living* (1650), joined that volume as a staple of English devotional reading.[1] While *The Holy Dying* was distinguished by many unique features of style and emphasis, the work was basically "an Anglican synthesis" of the insights on Christian dying from the previous two and a half centuries (Beaty 197), and as such, was a repository of biblical and classical adages and examples that had been kept current throughout the centuries in writing about death and dying.

While the divines produced no new work widely looked to as a significant source for deathbed accounts, Taylor's books continued to transmit the terms, images, and common expressions with which men contemplated death and dying. A biographer of Taylor in 1847 asserted that of the "elder writers" in England, Taylor was the only one who had "taken a firm and lasting hold of the popular mind." *The Holy Living and Dying,* he said, "is associated with the fireside pillow" (Willmott xi). George Eliot's concept of the breadth of the work's currency is apparent as she lists a copy among Adam Bede's books, names Taylor as a favorite author of Dorothea Brooke, and has Mr. Tulliver say of his copy, "I read in it often of a Sunday."

No other novel on death in the century succeeded like *The Old Curiosity Shop,* and this novel grew out of traditions embodied in the *Holy Dying.* The work provides a specific frame of reference, drawn from tradition and reinforced by the reality of a clergyman's practical experience, to account for some of the most maligned and misunderstood features of *The Old Curiosity Shop*—the virtuous child protagonist, the grotesque, gambling grandfather, the visit to the little scholar who dies, the extensive, and sometimes effusive, activities in cemeteries, and the minute attention to the last stages of Nell's process of dying. In recognizing the workings of the *ars moriendi* tradition in *The Old Curiosity Shop,* one finds a basis for taking Nell seriously as a fictional protagonist, for further understanding the novel's appeal to its first audiences, and for reconsidering Dickens' achievement in this novel.

I

"Bear up," says Taylor to the sick man, "for some man wiser and many a woman weaker . . . or the very children, have endured worse evil than is upon thee now.'' It is to the children that Taylor most often returns as a beneficial pattern for meditation on suffering and dying. ''Bear your sickness like a child,'' he says, without reflection, but by a ''direct sufferance . . . and as a pillar bears the weight of a roof'' (315). Children have ''never heard the sayings of old men, nor have been taught the principles of severe philosophy, nor are assisted with the results of long experience,'' and yet, ''by such aids as God is pleased to give them, children wade through the storm and murmur not'' (314).

Not only do children endure illness, they die, very frequently according to Taylor. His book's opening phrase reminds us that ''a man is a bubble,'' all life brief, but by the end of the first page he is talking about the death of children to impress upon us that life is often even briefer than we anticipate. He notes the frequent death of children seven years of age and under, and asserts that life brings an inevitable crisis every seven years (265). The first sure crisis is the loss of our first teeth, which ''fall and die before us, representing a formal prologue to the tragedy.'' Of every seven-year period he says, ''It is odds we shall finish the last scene'' (267).

Though emphasizing the brevity of life, Taylor cautions that a man cannot depend simply upon time, even though he be given a full life span, to bring him to maturity. Maturity is not an inevitable chronological achievement, beginning when one ''can feed himself, or walk alone, when he can fight, or beget his like.'' One is mature only ''when he comes to a certain steady use of reason according to his proportion, and when that is, all the world of man cannot tell precisely.'' Some are called at fourteen, some at one-and-twenty, and some never (277).

Wise or not, mankind has difficulty while in his prime, if he reaches it, in accepting the fact of the brevity of life and the inevitability of sickness and death. Taylor uses the image of the flower to condense the life cycle to the brief proportion which he strives to convey. He describes a rose ''newly springing from the clefts of its hood,'' which at first ''was as fair as the morning and full with the dew of heaven as a lamb's fleece,'' but ''by evening, had begun to put on darkness, and to decline,'' and then ''bowed the head and broke its stalk'' (271).

Taylor draws man's decline too, cataloging the physical debility that comes with age, the dim eyes, the trembling joints, the short breath and short memory (267), and describing the mental and moral decay that may come to men who die too late. Their ''clear reputation,'' ''good fortune,'' and ''honourable name'' are lost as they are ''tempted in their age to folly and vanity'' and fall under ''the disgrace of dotage'' (337).

Taylor differs somewhat from his predecessors in his genre in his focus on the whole life as preparation for death, rather than on the deathbed itself as the object for meditation. Dying well "is to be the work of our life, and not to be done at once; but as God gives us time, by succession, by parts and little periods" (294). It is achieved only through a lifetime of daily practice. "He that would die well must always look for death, every day knocking at the gates of the grave" (291). One should meditate daily upon one's own death, imagining it exactly as one thinks it will be. This practice will "make death safe and friendly," and we shall, when the time comes, "sit down in the grave as we compose ourselves to sleep" (292). Another excellent daily practice is visiting cemeteries and graves. All people have the "key of the churchyard" and "custom hath brought cemeteries and charnel houses into cities and churches, places most frequented, that we might not carry ourselves strangely in so certain, so expected, so ordinary, so unavoidable" an occurrence as death (345). Taylor even says that every night we should "make our bed the memorial of our grave" and make our evening thoughts "an image of the day of judgment" (297). These practices will bring one eventually to "look upon death with the same countenance as he hears a story" (283). If one adds to these practices a daily or frequent examination "of the smallest parts of our lives" (299) and bears his repentances "willingly and constantly" (294), he will come to "love tears, humility, solitude and repentance," and it is he who will die "holily and happily" (295).

Taylor tells of a young hermit who, after his beloved had been interred for a full two weeks, went secretly to her vault and "with the skirt of his mantle wiped the moisture from her carcass." In recognizing that what he saw was all that remained of the beautiful woman that he had desired, he found his cure, says Taylor, being much benefitted in accommodating himself to death. Taylor does not necessarily recommend such extremity, but he says that "severe counsel" such as this provides the object for "useful meditation," serving to "quench . . . the greedy passionate affections of this world" (292).

Most in danger of making a poor death is the man who thinks upon "far distant events" (272), devises "fantastic expectations" (283) or projects "long designs" or "crafty plots" (274). The life that is preparing for death will "seize upon the present, . . . because in it all our certainty does consist" (275). This person will "be busy near at hand" (275). Every day of his life he will "lay up against the day of death" (293), doing charitable deeds, learning to accept hardship with patience and thinking upon death. No virtue in life will be tried as much as patience. But let the sorely-tried person "ride in a storm; let his bones be broken in sorrow, and his eyelids loosened with sickness'' (327). It will be good training for him, preparing him to bear with patience those final and most terrible assaults sure to come upon his deathbed.

While all the sadnesses and miseries of daily life should be looked upon as a means ''to help sweeten the bitter cup of death'' (289), that period of sickness and suffering that usually forms the final passage to death should be looked upon as the great and ultimate opportunity for completing one's preparation for happy and holy dying. Sickness, Taylor says, allows the soul finally to ''dress herself for immortality'' (324). It is ''the agony in which men are tried for a crown'' (327). Sickness is ''sent with purposes of abstraction and separation, with a secret power and a proper efficacy to draw us off'' from the concerns of the world (317). If the whole course of life has served, as it should, to accustom one to ''a patient suffering of his injuries and affronts'' (293), then, in that final illness, he can come to the ultimate patience in the acceptance of his pain and suffering without murmur (313). Such a person can find the means of charity even on his deathbed. He can treat his nurses and servants sweetly (358). He can sing thanksgiving that his sickness will not last forever (321). Thus on his deathbed he can become charitable toward death itself, singing ''praises to God, even from the lowest abyss of human misery'' (313).

Taylor explains that God does not mean that we should not have fear or regret at dying. A sick man is not expected to ''act a part of patience with a countenance like an orator, or grave like a dramatic person'' (311). ''Our blessed Lord was pleased to legitimate fear to us by His agony and prayers in the garden'' (345). It is ''a great felicity'' to be withtout fear, but ''our dearest Saviour himself'' refused this felicity in order to suffer as most men suffer (345). It is only in doubting, complaining or blaspheming against God's will and man's destiny that one sins, or ''murmurs.''

Frequently Taylor describes the state of transport to which one will come as he achieves final readiness for dying. He will be ''in love with the felicities of saints and angels'' (342) and know that he goes to a place of greater joy than is provided by this world (343). The prepared soul ''goes forth full of hope,'' and ''instantly passes into the throngs of spirits, where angels meet it singing,'' while unprepared souls suffer ''terror of their abused fancies,'' ''feel the gripes of devils,'' and are cast at once into the ''eternal company of all the damned and accursed spirits'' (306–07).

For Taylor, the desirable life cycle consists of consecration by a ''forward baptism'' in childhood, ''seconded by a holy education and a complying obedience,'' followed by the ''ordinary returns of our prayers and periodical and festival solemnities'' (280). The life that results will practice the charity and learn the patience that brings him to readiness for dying. There is no mention of conversion, and scholarly opinion recognizes that Taylor throughout his works ''assumes that no man can achieve perfected love and obedience through a single dramatic conversion experience'' (Beaty 219). While Taylor's instructions assume the regular guidance of a clergyman in one's preparation and praying, one finds that Taylor does not hold that clergy is essential. He that ''means to have his sickness turn into safety'' must ''make religion the employment of his sickness,'' but God has, in the case of poverty, ''reduced this duty of man to an abbreviature.'' Martyrdom also allows ''abbreviature'' (350). God is not only to be found in ''a great prayer or, a solemn office.'' He is moved ''by a sigh, by a groan, by an act of love'' (357). Whatever the means, whether directed by clergy as Taylor assumes to be the norm, or achieved through some ''abbreviature,'' as he perceives possible, if the means are efficacious, the person will approach the brink of the grave with no more misgiving than he has always lain himself down in his bed to sleep at night.

Such representative passages from Taylor reveal a set of commonplace ideas which call attention to the special value of children as objects for meditation in the bearing of sickness and dying. Thirteen years old when *The Old Curiosity Shop* opens (and presumably still thirteen when the novel closes since no birthday is ever remarked), Nell provides concrete expression of a child called to wisdom early and her grandfather a case of the sort of which Taylor asks, ''Do not all the world say that it had been better this man had died sooner'' (377)? Taylor even provides a traditional explanation for the grandfather's seemingly bizarre characterization as a gambler. With his ''long designs'' and ''crafty plots,'' he becomes a commonplace figure of the type of person least prepared for holy dying[2] and therefore a particularly significant foil for Nell, who is always ''busy near at hand'' to exercise her charity and make her way. Taylor, then, provides a frame of reference that suggests that Nell may be seen as the protagonist in a fictional equivalent of the *ars moriendi* tradition, that she was to the novel's first readers a review and a reembodiment of deeply-embedded concepts and traditions.

II

The Old Curiosity Shop, perhaps to the surprise of the modern reader, was embraced by high churchman, broad churchman and unitarian, as well as by low churchman and dissenter, all of whom had the common frame of reference conveyed by Taylor's work. John Keble in 1817, as a young parish preacher just two years after his ordination, wrote to his brother Tom asking same favors and said, "as to books I should like Jeremy Taylor" (Battiscombe 45).[3] Thinkers as diverse as Samuel Wilberforce and Henry Manning came to be could continue to share an admiration for Taylor (Newsome 275–76). So practical a broad churchman as Dr. Thomas Arnold readily admitted, "I admire Taylor's genius," though he reveals his personal taste in judging *Pilgrim's Progress* more edifying than the works of the church fathers since it has "none of the rubbish of theologians mixed up with it" (Stanley 400–401). Edward Bickerstith, influential evangelical leader, praised Taylor's "practical and devotional power" (5: 223), and recommended him to readers in all walks of life in *The Christian Student* (6: 46, 47, 156), Bickerstith's popular guide to Victorian devotional reading.

Clergymen high and low, in addition to applying Taylor's teachings as recalled from their studies, often kept close at hand as a practical aid *The Clergyman's Companion,* in its tenth edition by 1805, and still being reprinted in the 1830s. The first section is a lengthy extract from Taylor recommended for use in visiting the sick. Here was a means of the steady inculcation of the traditional images and ideas of death, even among persons who might not have read Taylor themselves.[4] Another means of indirect transmission, a means that would have reached into the Church of England as well as throughout the realms of dissent, was in the influence of John Wesley. Biographers have demonstrated the impact of the *Holy Living and Dying* on Wesley, and have identified it as the work to which Wesley "ascribes his first religious impression" (Southey 25–30).[5] Thus, in embracing teaching derived from Wesley about death and dying, even readers who did not know Taylor directly were absorbing Taylor's precepts.

Bickerstith's biography (1851) emphasizes his repetition of specific scriptures during his final illness. It tells of his apology to his medical attendant for having given him such "troublesome office," and of his finding blessings to be thankful for even from the depth of misery, for example, the "pious children" attending his "dying pillow." Though he was in great pain, "no murmur ever escaped his lips," and he had some kind word "of counsel or of comfort" for all those who waited upon him (Birks 2: 384–409). The biography of Dr. Arnold (1844) reports that in his final illness, Dr. Arnold repeated "earnestly" the scriptures that his wife read to him, never complained, avoided disturbing his medical attendant at any early hour, asked his son to thank God for "giving me this pain," and found much else to be thankful for, for example, that "my head is untouched" (Stanley 618–19). These two deathbed accounts illustrate that evangelicals and high churchmen alike placed great value on achieving a death that demonstrated a virtual formula derived from Taylor.

One can easily find instances which fill out the formula in a manner far more extreme. Baptiste Noël, for example, popular evangelical clergyman, wrote exultantly in his *Meditations in Sickness and Old Age,* as he suffered what he thought would be his final illness, that death was a "conquered enemy," that he could "imagine myself cold and stiff, wrapped in my shroud, laid in my coffin, and lowered into my grave, without much repugnance" (144). This account echoes John Donne's preparation for death, well known from Walton's *Lives,* having himself arranged in his shroud as if dead and painted in life size in that condition, and keeping the picture at his bedside for the remainder of his life (58–59). In its direct focus on the corpse as an inducement to piety, Donne's story echoes Taylor's story of the young hermit who visited a body two weeks after interment.

A steady succession of books for devotional reading carried on the traditions deriving from Taylor. William Dodd's *Reflections on Death,* 1763, has been pointed out as "representative of hundreds of similar volumes whose depiction and evaluation of death Victorians read," and a scene from the work dramatizing the death of "a paragon of Christian virtue," a young mother who on her deathbed consoles her own parents, "wholly resigned" to her fate, pointed out as suggestive of such a character type as Nell (Kaplan 48–49). Dodd also gives extensive attention to the man who has lived too long. Such a one becomes "a burden even to our nearest friends" and talks "of nothing with satisfaction but the delusive mammon of unrighteousness" (139–41). While works such as this one may, in isolation, strike a reader as a possible source for Dickens's concepts in *The Old Curiosity Shop,* these works, in fact, derive from a long-established tradition, a tradition whose diverse elements were brought together and redispersed by Taylor's *Art of Holy Dying.*

III

The special value of "women . . . or the very children" as patterns for the bearing of suffering was extolled steadily from Taylor's day to Dickens'. But in the early nineteenth century, a renewal of puritan emphasis on the doctrine of original sin brought about a tendency to pressure, even frighten, children, and others, into immediate conversion lest early death take them to hell. While *The Old Curiosity Shop* is the first novel built on the death of a child, it came into a culture that was familiar with accounts of deaths of children through that body of religious tracts and compendiums which made up the main body of writing available to children at the time, all aimed at eliciting submissive piety from readers. Those works provide significant counterparts to Nell. Most famous of Nell's predecessors were Legh Richmond's heroines in his phenomenally successful autobiographical tracts ''The Dairyman's Daughter'' and ''The Young Cottager.''

Both the two tracts and Dickens' novel have female heroines who die prematurely, Elizabeth, the dairyman's daughter, at thirty-one, and Jane, the young cottager, at twelve. Neither has parental guidance in religion. Each undergoes a dramatic conversion and each is instrumental in converting other members of her family from her deathbed. Jane begins her conversion in the churchyard, scene of Richmond's instruction to young children, where he informs them ''that probably more than half of the bodies which were buried there were those of little children'' (162). The deathbed experience of each heroine is carried out in a long series of conversations with the clergyman, providing ''the prototype for the variety of catechetical exchange to establish the dying person's frame of mind'' (Jay 160), which evangelical readers virtually demanded of deathbed scenes. We are given details of Elizabeth's physical decay and taken for a ''last look at the remains'' where we are told in detail of the body's change in death,'' of the ''livid lips and sunken eyes of the clay'' (97–98). The account of Elizabeth's death concludes with a lengthy exhortation to the reader to be as sure of his own readiness as was the dairyman's daughter, while the story of little Jane opens with an exhortation to all readers ''to try to lead at least one little child by the hand'' to salvation. In each tract the conversion experience and the deathbed experience are the only episodes that are developed.

Richmond's tales reflect traditions derived from Taylor in the choice of the young female heroines, in the use of the churchyard as a scene for spiritual education, and in suggesting the direct contemplation of a corpse as a beneficial practice. They differ markedly from Taylor in their emphasis on conversion, their direct and extended focus on the deathbed, and their interest in demonstrating the deathbed as an opportunity for converting unsaved attendants. ''The Dairyman's Daughter'' is in line with Taylor in showing death as bringing finally a happy release from suffering for the prepared soul. ''The Young Cottager,'' however, in its urging the speedy conversion of children and showing the child's happy dying as an immediate fruit of conversion, follows puritan influences, in contrast to Taylor. Taylor extols the child's special ability in bearing suffering as coming naturally, without reflection, by a "direct sufferance," "like unto that of a pillar bearing the weight of a roof."

The story of Nell differs most from these two stories in having no account of conversion, in having a well-developed life filled with varied episodes, in allowing the accomplishment of holy dying without the aid of a clergyman, and in providing no dramatized deathbed scene. The novel follows Taylor in these respects, the varied episodes in line with Taylor's belief that the death scene took meaning only as the product of the experiences that had gone on in the life before. Nell, in line with Taylor and the tracts, learns much about death in a churchyard, though without the aid of a clergyman. And she does, in effect, accomplish the "saving" of her grandfather, though without "catechetical exchange." These accomplishments take place as activities growing naturally out of Nell's circumstances and personality, not as results of formal religious exercises. The "catechetical exchanges" of the tracts specified and often made lengthy quotations of specific scriptures. When Nell looks at the Bible we can only assume that she is looking at and paying attention to the passages that we think she should or would be looking at, for Dickens names no specific passages.

Dickens has one clergyman make an appearance during Nell's lifetime, a kindly and lovable old gentleman, but a child compared to Nell, showing no insight into her real needs as one nearing death. Though high church positions traditionally required the offices of a clergyman for deathbed rites, Taylor makes clear that one may die holily and happily on one's own, "by abbreviature." Evangelical doctrine held to the necessity of every person working out his own salvation, giving no priestly powers to the clergy, yet the evangelical depictions of the deathbed just examined included the constant guidance of a clergyman. We see that either group, high church or evangelical, could be at ease with Dickens' omission of a significant clergyman. Meanwhile broad churchmen and freethinkers could respond happily to Nell's plight as an account of the workings of natural, intuitive, even practical goodness.

Nell is depicted as conventionally pious, one who habitually prays (149, 304), one who says that she feels God's presence in the beauty of nature. But Nell's behavior is not shown to occur in response to religious training or ritual. Dickens does not portray Nell as formed by the instruments of formal religion. Even a few early readers noticed this, pointing out that though Nell might "haunt" the old church, "not a single Christian feature is introduced in the story," that though there might be a "picturesque sketch" of a Bible in the background, there was "no reference to the revelation it contains" (qtd. in Walder 75–76).[6] But most readers readily inferred Nell's orthodoxy according to their own definition.

One recent critic says that in creating Nell, Dickens "plucked a stock character from out of the world of religious tracts and shaped his narrative around her (Pickering 111). Another says that Nell "simply repeated a pattern which evangelical magazines had been using for decades" (Qualls 88). Such may be the case, but it is important to know that the woman and the child as patterns of special worth for the bearing of suffering and for dying existed as stock characters before the tracts developed them, and to know that the narrative that Dickens shaped differed in some important ways from the narratives of the tracts to which his story of Nell is so often compared.

While Richmond's tracts grew out of the evangelical environment in the early nineteenth century, the source of another of Nell's main predecessors, James Janeway's *Token for Children*, first appeared in 1671. This account of the "Conversion, Holy and Exemplary Lives, and Joyful Deaths of Several Young Children" had remained in print and been a family favorite for five or six generations by the time of Nell. Its first example is a little girl named Sarah Howley who between the ages of eight and nine is converted. The lengthy conversion experience is followed by a report of the child's immediate growth in industry and virtue. She now spends her whole time either in praying, reading or instructing at her needle, "at which she was very ingenious." Then at fourteen, "she brake a vein in her lungs" and "oft did spit blood," thus acting out, along with Richmond's little Jane, Taylor's adage that a crisis inevitably occurs at the end of every seven years so that "it is odds we shall finish the last scene." As she grew worse, she "carried it with wonderful patience," making a speech and repeating specific scriptures to relatives one by one. "Upon a Thursday she broke into a Divine Rapture" and "her soul was ravished with the love of Christ, and her tongue engaged in magnifying the lord." On Sunday she died. Little Sarah's story is followed by further stories of shortlived children, each brief life cycle following the same basic formula as that of Sarah.

The special place of this work with readers is illustrated in the *Family Memoirs* written by a Miss Houghton of Huddlesfield in 1846 as she recalls her girlhood among her sisters and brothers. "We were very fond of Janeway's *Token for Children*," she says, "it being almost the only history of children that we had" (45–46). This first child in the collection must have made a special impression, and she suggests a source of the near universal love for little Nell when she appeared—her readers finding little Sarah Howley or a close counterpart given a full life cycle, the new heroine Nell's patience and industry the same, yet her experience taking her among waxworks and showmen and through diverse adventures, her didactic function as exhorter left implicit. Critical discussions have established Nell rather thoroughly as an anemic little wraith, afraid of sex, in love with death, and totally unconnected with reality.[7] But to Nell's early audiences, as they met her in the context of innumerable pious and monotonously similar young heroines such as Elizabeth and Jane of the tracts and Sarah Howley of Janeway's *Token*, Nell must have seemed particularly vivid.

IV

The modern reader may be surprised that Nell, when we first meet her, actually is depicted as a pretty, healthy little girl—both Quilp and Swiveller note this—with a good sense of humor. There is delicacy, there is refinement in Nell's demeanor, but there is nothing to suggest debility or sexlessness. She is small, but this does not mean that she is weak, a point illustrated also by her small counterpart, or double, the "little" marchioness. Nell has cooked, cleaned, sewed and done errands on the street, even at night, hardly a routine in the grasp of a puny, lifeless child. She takes a tremendous amount of strain and exposure before her body breaks and before she gives up hope for peace in this life.

Though young, Nell is cast as one called to maturity early, and her adult role engages the reader's mature interest. The novel opens at the crisis of Nell's brief life, when she and her grandfather are forced to make a secret departure from London. The most sensible decision Nell could have made at this point was to stay with the Nubbleses and simply take the chances about her grandfather being cried mad and taken into custody. This, of course, would have required the hardness of a woman who could neglect or desert her own child, of an adult who could neglect or desert an aging parent. Despite her youth, Nell is being faced with the problems and responsibilities of an adult, and she responds to them, if not with practical wisdom, with great courage, hope and compassion, certainly not as a "pallid martyr."

A modern reader who thinks of Little Nell and her plight with a groan and neglects to read the book may hold among his assumptions that the puny little heroine has a morbid compulsion to go to cemeteries. One of the more helpful commentaries on this book includes the statement that Nell's itinerary seems

to include every churchyard in which some mute inglorious Milton lies buried'' (Marcus 146). Actually, Nell visits only two cemeteries, one on the
evening of her and her grandfather's second day out and the same one again
on the next morning; the other cemetery comes late in the book, when she
lives in a dwelling within the churchyard.

Nell walks through the first cemetery in the evening because the carter who
has given her and her grandfather a ride has to turn off the road and instructs
them to take a path passing through the nearby churchyard as the closest path
to the next town. It was not uncommon for paths to go through churchyards,
nor for people to stop to rest there, or to look around and tend graves, or, if
one was a child, to play there. Nor is it morbid that Nell goes walking there
the next morning while her grandfather still sleeps. The churchyard is just
out the door of the inn, with paths in it and objects of interest to look at.
Cemeteries were commonly regarded as places to be visited, serving people,
especially rural persons and persons uncultivated by reading, as "their book
of history, their biography, their instructor in architecture and sculpture, their
model of taste, and an important source of moral improvement" (quoted in
Morley 48).[8] Nell's visits to this cemetery do not in any way depict morbidity
or a desire for death on her part. She is healthily and typically curious, her
stroll and visit in keeping with common practices of the day.

Previous to Nell's entry into her second, and last, cemetery, where she
dies, comes the scene where the little scholar dies. Ready to go out for a
walk with the schoolmaster when a message comes that his most gifted student
is dying, Nell accompanies him to the sickroom (259). The child asks to hold
Nell's hand and dies holding it. Nell is not deliberately preparing for death
or in any morbid way seeking out death scenes and settings. But life is early
offering her experiences which can prepare her for death. Nell's microcosmic
life cycle shows her already laying up provision which sooner than nature
ordinarily dictates will be called to use.

While Nell is with Mrs. Jarley, Quilp is a constant nightmare to her, and
she sees her grandfather's growing debility. Yet there is an equilibrium at
this point—as much as most lives see probably, income and security ample
for the present, yet worry about the possibility of ruinous mishap in the future.
This is usually the adult parent's worry in relation to the child, but here it is
the child's fear and worry in relation to the aged parent. Nevertheless, with
Mrs. Jarley's benevolent protection and Nell's talent for her work, prospects
for survival seem good.

The reversal comes when Nell and her grandfather take shelter from a
sudden storm in the Valiant Soldier and the grandfather feverishly resumes

his gambling (296–97). The narrator identifies Nell as the "innocent cause of all this torture," and she herself must hear her grandfather repeatedly name her as the cause for his action (314). One is reminded that "In Adam's fall, we sinned all"—Nell is "innocent," yet is a part of the motivation for sin and crime. She certainly feels guilty, thinking, in a scene of self-examination, that if she had told the truth, he would be treated as a madman, that if she did not supply him with the money he would steal for it, and yet that in giving him money she "fed the fire that burnt him up, and put him perhaps beyond recovery" (314).

At this point, the novel goes to Kit and the Brasses for a ten-chapter interval. When it returns to Nell, there has been a drastic change. Until this time Nell has always been hopeful, determined to find a way for herself and her grandfather to survive. But we find her now, under the regimen of work and futile anxiety, virtually hopeless (397). And even the fragile equilibrium of this state is shortly overturned when Nell overhears her grandfather, in a highly stylized scene, agree to rob Mrs. Jarley's cashbox. Old Trent's implicit identity as a soul is peril made explicit as the narrator says that it is as if he has sold his soul to the devil. Nell hears him mutter her name as he makes his bargain, deluded that he will save her through his machinations. She cries out to herself for God's mercy, asking, "What shall I do to save him?" She has been all along trying to save her grandfather from the madhouse, but now, more like Faust's good angel than a little girl, she seems to recognize that he is in acute spiritual jeopardy as well, that he stands in danger of dying alone, afraid, powerless to find comfort, in effect, in danger of dying the death of a damned soul. Her life's work takes on urgency and weight in this scene. In comparison to Elizabeth and Jane and Sarah Howley's accomplishing the salvation of their loved ones on their deathbeds by mechanically repeating specified scriptures and declaring joy at the approach of death, Nell's significance becomes apparent. Her conflict relates far more to the complex anguish of actual human guilt and frustration when confronted with a desperate mission.

Nell is ready to make "instant flight," to "drag" her grandfather from that place, to die of want on the roadside, rather than risk the old man's further exposure to these "terrible temptations." Back in her room, "distraught by terrors," she cannot sleep. Finally, "half undressed, and with her hair in wild disorder," she goes to her grandfather's room and by feigning an account of a bad dream, moves him to get up and slip away, fleeing without thanks or farewell to her benefactress. Nell is maturing past the childlike state where she can bear burdens like Taylor's children who bear them like "pillars bear a roof."

The ordeals that follow their departure from the waxworks bring Nell to the point that more and more "to lie down and die" would seem a mercy (422). Coincidence finally takes the pair to their little home in the churchyard, setting for Nell's final "adornment of soul." Training for death becomes the explicit function of her experience as more and more sickness sets her apart from the pursuits of life.

On her first day here, the sexton shows her a frightening old well under the belfry of the church, likening it to a grave. Nell then goes into the church and sits among the graves and effigies, reads from the Bible for a while, and then thinks of the summer and springtime days that will come and of the "rays of the sun" that will "fall in aslant upon the sleeping forms." "Die who would," she thinks, this place "would still remain the same; these sights and sounds would still go on as happily as ever. It would be no pain to sleep amidst them" (494).

Nell is happy in the quiet routine that develops in her new home. Her physical decay is brought to the reader's mind only as the little boy who has become her friend tells her that people in the community say that she will not last until spring and implores her not to leave them (511). In response she weeps. She is not without sadness and questions here in her "garden" (501), but she is without complaint, and more and more each day without fear or dread. It is as if she knows what is neecessary to prepare herself and intuitively goes about attaining the final experiences that will assure that she can meet death unafraid. And in following these intuitions, she is acting out recommendations of Jeremy Taylor.

On what proves to be her last visit with the sexton, she follows him down into the old well, which is still "black and dreadful" to her, but as he talks, "the child still stood, looking thoughtfully into the vault" (283), able now, it would seem, to "look upon death with the same countenance" as she would "hear a story." That night, she leans upon her casement, from where, we know, she always looks out at the graves, and thinks, "The birds sing again in spring" (513). That is the last we see of Nell alive. It occurs at the end of chapter fifty-five, and the next chapter returns to Kit and his party. When the narrative returns to the village, in chapter seventy-one, Nell lies dead.

We have, then, no scripting of Nell's death. The subsequent chapter provides a brief flashback. All Nell's "utterings" in her last dreams had been of "those who had helped and used them kindly," with no reference to "painful scenes." She did not herself sing, as Taylor said one might, but she

heard "beautiful music" in the air, cheered her attendants, and never mur-
mured against her destiny. She is buried in the church, which had come even
before death to seem "another world," "a tranquil place of rest," (498)
buried in her old nook among the very tombs and effigies of which she had
said, "It would be no pain to sleep amidst them." And her life's work has
been accomplished. Her grandfather, comforted by the little boy who had
been Nell's companion, is peaceful at her death and soon, at her grave, makes
the peaceful death which she had hoped for him.

V

Before her death, Nell has dreamed of angels as they were on some "old
Scriptural pictures" she once saw. And the beauty of nature as she looks out
from the church tower has made her feel that she is coming closer to heaven.
Yet she has comforted herself with a fantasy that people left on earth perceive
the dead in the moon and the stars (501) and has received comfort from others
who say good deeds live on after one (503). Her one actual anticipatory
thought is that to be placed inside the old church where a slant of light came
across one's grave every afternoon would not be a fearful destiny.

Nell's companion, the little boy who follows her about and comforts her
in her last days, assumes her dead brother Willy to be both in heaven and
under the grave unable to turn up for a kiss (510). The schoolmaster and the
narrator hold as their major premise about immortality the idea that good
people live on after death as a result of their good deeds, though each also
conceives those good people living on after death as angels in heaven (503,
659). After Nell's death, Kit tells his young listeners that they will see Nell
in heaven if they follow her life as a pattern (671). The old and the infirm go
to her funeral (657–58), and old Trent recalls the way that Nell alone could
feed the birds and command even the wildest children, and he repeatedly
presses Nell's shoes to his lips (648–49). They all behave as if there might
be some miraculous power from Nell left on earth.

Back when Nell first arrives at the churchyard, the bachelor, "the universal
mediator, comforter and friend" in the village (486), is Nell's instructor as
she prepares for her duties as guide to antiquities. Though he does not figure
in her subsequent education, as he teaches her the legends related to the old
church, he repeatedly tells her that he would never "strip fair truth of every
little shadowy vestment in which time and teeming fancies love to array
her," that he would never have "brought to light" that which would trouble

comforting memories (496–98). Nell's meditations show her, like the bachelor, not denying or arguing against the traditional concepts—she imagines angels in terms of pictures she has seen, for example—but never once relying on them as a means to peace and quietness of spirit. She has quietly to work out for herself how to perceive what is happening, and that simply "to rest here" would not be painful. If she relies on any more afterlife, we never hear of it.

Taylor emphasizes a single view of what happens to the prepared spirit after death: he goes forth to a place of greater joy than is provided by this world and feasts and praises God throughout eternity. Dickens' only departure from the traditions transmitted by Taylor is in regard to the afterlife. In *The Old Curiosity Shop*, he provides a remarkable range of impressions and assumptions about the time after death yet affirms none as the actual case. Indeed he works out his main plot and theme in terms that reflect no assumption that there is a next life at all. Other readers have found Dickens to be "agnostic" (Stewart 15, n. 9), without "settled belief" (Larson 36), even to be plainly and simply without belief in supernatural powers (Welsh 116). My findings show him making no assumption of an afterlife or of any other supernatural element.

VI

The Old Curiosity Shop, especially the latter chapters, dealing with Nell's sojourn in the churchyard, has been judged as evidence that "something had horribly corroded Dickens's intelligence" (Carey 136), and the fact that readers in his day liked the story of Nell has been judged as evidence of nothing but their weakness for "gross and virtuous self-indulgence" (Leavis 225–26). But instead, Dickens was working within the framework of a distinguished literary tradition. The novel's first audience found in Nell a vivid recreation of type that reflected that tradition, a type familiar and significant to them from childhood reading and religious training. They saw, as today's reader may see in returning to the text in this light, a piquant, resourceful child, but one who was "called to maturity early," facing a conflict representative of the adult world and forced to play an adult's role. And they saw Nell live the type of life and garner the type of experiences they had been taught were needful in order to achieve a triumphant deathbed. Nell's experience gave a vision of every person's possibilities for achieving happy and holy dying, the compressed life cycle allowing the revelation of the intricate relationship between the experiences in a person's life and the manner in which he dies.

In claiming Nell's life cycle as a microcosmic version of every person's full, mature life, one may be inviting the counter-argument that she is not mature or representative because she is not sexually fulfilled. Taylor writes that maturity does not occur magically when "one can beget his kind," indicating that he did not see begetting as essential to maturity. Today's standards would hardly deny chaste saints and adoptive parents the potential to be mature, well-developed persons. Perhaps Kit can be imagined as being transformed by Nell's devotion had circumstances allowed, completing a doubling of the Marchioness-Swiveller pairing. But the masculine figure which circumstances associated and attached to Nell was a worn-out old male relative, so that Nell's prospect for fulfillment of duty and love took her into this inverted parent-child relationship.

Criticism recognizes that the novel as a genre emerged at "roughly the historical turning point where Western culture gave up looking systematically beyond death for religious meaning" (Stewart 8), that when Dickens wrote, "the impetus of theological controversy" was moving away from "discussion of the fate of a man's soul . . . and towards the first question of proving that a man was actually possessed of an immortal soul" (Jay 167). The implications of such questions and their consequences to the concept of happy, holy dying are not expressed explicitly in *The Old Curiosity Shop*, but, as is characteristic with Dickens' expression of his beliefs, are "embodied in the texture of the work" (Walder 78). He shows us in *The Old Curiosity Shop* reasons to be consoled about death and ways to accomplish a satisfactory death, a death "holy" in the sense of being infinitely good, worthy of reverence. He affirms the abiding, practical worth of traditional teachings about death, but he quietly disengages the traditions from their ecclesiastical framing. Dr. Arnold might have said of the work that "it has none of the rubbish of theologians mixed up with it." The novel's vision of the achievement of happy and holy dying requires for its fulfillment only human potential availing itself of the opportunities presented within life's routine. The happy and holy death is presented as being achieved without any supernatural elements interacting with the natural, verifiable facts of human possibility. Dickens' handling of his materials in this way allows the novel to continue to have meaning even in a time when it has become common to define life's meaning and its ending without reference to a life "beyond death or to the actuality of an "immortal soul."

A final point remains. *The Old Curiosity Shop* has been thoroughly maligned for making perverted use of the deathbed tradition, its latter chapters even being called "spiritual necrophilia" (Marcus 146). But in choosing not to depict the deathbed scene, to let the shape of Nell's life serve as the index to her death, Dickens was in line with Taylor's avoidance of emphasis on the deathbed, but different from most other literature on dying in his own time. If Dickens' imagination had been in service to stock situations that were sure to please readers, surely the deathbed scene would have been a major episode and various aspects of Nell's training for death and of her physical deterioration would have been described with sensational detail. Even Taylor had shown value in the contemplation of a disintegrating corpse, and at about the same time that Taylor wrote, Isaak Walton was recording John Donne's enactment of the role of the corpse. A century later Richardson's Clarissa makes final preparation for dying by selecting her own coffin and shroud and having them placed in her bedroom, after which she claims to sleep more soundly than before. Taylor would have approved of such practices. Nell's visits to the church and the graves and the tombs, representing one more century's modification of the traditions, are mild compared to these earlier examples. They are, in fact, as we have seen, mild, restrained, compared with depictions in works which were popular in Dickens' own day.

NOTES

1. *Holy Living* achieved no extraordinary popularity, but Stranks, p. 93, says that *Holy Dying* "achieved the greatest popularity" of any book ever written on the subject of death in English.
2. Pickering, p. 114, illustrates uses of the gambler as a stock figure of the soul in peril.
3. Authorities, e.g., Battiscombe 45 and Stranks n. 4, pp. 93–94, recognize that Taylor was always to be a favorite author and an obvious influence upon Keble. Keble and Newman's *Correspondence,* pp. 263–64, shows Taylor as a working part of their mutual frame of reference throughout their lives.
4. Though the *Companion* seems to have been by far the most popular, there were other such handbooks in use as well. Bickerstith, 6: 216, for example, recommends *The Clergyman's Instructor and Assistant* for use in pastoral care, naming Taylor as the first contributor in the volume.
5. See also Whitehead, 1: 238–45.
6. Walder is quoting *Christian Remembrancer,* vol. 4, December, 1842, and *North British Review,* vol. 3, May, 1845.
7. Sanders, p. 65, gives a representative catalog of negative epithets applied to Nell and her story. MacPike gives a detailed tracing of Nell's status.
8. Morley is quoting J. C. Loudon, *On the Laying Out, Planting and Managing Cemeteries . . . ,* 1843.

WORKS CITED

Battiscombe, Georgina. *John Keble.* New York: Knopf, 1964.

Beaty, Nancy Lee. *The Craft of Dying: A Study of the Literary Tradition of the Ars Moriendi in England.* New Haven: Yale UP, 1970.

Bickerstith, Edward. *The Christian Student,* 2 vols., printed as Vols. 5–6, *The Works of the Rev. Edward Bickerstith.* 5th ed. Fleet Street: Seeleys, 1853.

Birks, T. T. *Memoir of the Reverend Edward Bickerstith.* New York: Harper and Brothers, 1851.

Carey, John. *The Violent Effigy.* London: Faber and Faber, 1973.

Correspondence of John Henry Newman with John Keble and others, 1839–1845, edited at the Birmingham Oratory. London: Longmans, Green, 1917.

Dickens, Charles. *The Old Curiosity Shop.* Ed. Angus Easson. Harmondsworth: Penguin, 1972.

Dodd, William. *Reflections on Death.* Philadelphia: R. Johnson, 1806.

Janeway, James. *A Token for Children: An Account of the Conversion, Holy and Exemplary Lives, and Joyful Deaths of Several Young Children.* London: Dorman Newman, 1676. Rpt. New York: Garland, 1927.

Jay, Elisabeth. *The Religion of the Heart.* Oxford: Clarendon, 1979.

Kaplan, Fred. *Sacred Tears.* Princeton: Princeton, UP, 1987.

Larson, Janet. *Dickens and the Broken Scripture.* Athens: U of Georgia P, 1985.

Leavis, F. R. and Q. D. *Dickens the Novelist.* London: Chatto and Windus, 1970.

MacPike, Loralee. " 'The Old Cupiosity Shape'': Changing Views of Little Nell,'' Parts I and II, *Dickens Studies Newsletter* 12 (1981), June, 33–38, September, 70–76.

Marcus, Steven. *Dickens from Pickwick to Dombey.* New York: Basic Books, 1965.

[Miss Houghton]. *Family Memorials of the Late Mr. and Mrs. Houghton of Huddlesfield and of Several of their Children.* London: Tyler and Read, 1846.

Morley, John. *Death, Heaven and the Victorians.* Pittsburgh: U of Pittsburgh P, 1971.

Newsome, David. *The Wilburforces and Henry Manning.* Cambridge, Mass.: Harvard/Belknap Press, 1966.

Noel, Baptiste. *Meditations in Sickness and Old Age.* Philadelphia: Henry Perkins, 1839.

Pickering, Samuel. *The Moral Tradition in English Fiction.* Hanover, N. H.: U P of New England, 1976.

Qualls, Barry. *The Secular Pilgrims of Victorian Fiction.* New York: Cambridge U P, 1982.

Richmond, Legh. *Annals of the Poor.* New York: J. and H. G. Langley, 1841.

Sanders, Andrew. *Charles Dickens, Resurrectionist.* New York: St. Martin's, 1982.

Southey, Robert. *Life of Wesley.* 1820. London: Oxford U P, 1925.

Stanley, Arthur Penrhyn. *The Life and Correspondence of Thomas Arnold, D. D.* 6th ed. London: B. Fellows, 1846.

Stewart, Garrett. *Death Sentences.* Cambridge, Mass.: Harvard U P, 1984.

Stranks, C. J. *Anglican Devotion.* London: SCM Press, 1961.

Taylor, Jeremy. *The Rule and Exercises of Holy Living and Holy Dying.* London: Longman, Brown, et al., 1850, Vol. III of *The Whole Works,* edited by Reginald Heber, 1822. Rpt. Hildesheim: Olms, 1969.

Walder, Dennis. *Dickens and Religion.* Boston: George Allen and Unwin, 1981.

Walton, Izaak. *The Lives of John Donne, et al.* London: Falcon Educational Books, 1951.

Welsh, Alexander. *The City of Dickens.* Oxford: Clarendon, 1981.

Whitehead, John. *Life of The Rev. John Wesley.* Boston: Hill and Broadhead, 1846.

Willmott, Robert A. Preface. *Jeremy Taylor: His Predecessors, Contemporaries, and Successors.* 2 vols. London: John W. Parker, 1847.

"My Most Unwilling Hand": The Mixed Motivations of *David Copperfield*

David Kellogg

This paper's subtitle reveals some of its basic oppositions. The word *motivations* implies a human subject, impelled by external forces toward some specific end; naturally we assume this subject to be, as the novel's larger title says, "David Copperfield the Younger, of Blunderstone Rookery"—a person tied to a time and place. Yet we know this to be false, for *David Copperfield* is a fiction "By Charles Dickens, With Illustrations by H. K. Browne." This paper touches on *David Copperfield* in both major roles: as unique psychic identity, and as endlessly reproducible words on a page, socialized and socializing text. Still, this name that is also title could lead to confusion. Add to the book's dual identity the widely shared conviction that *David Copperfield* is Dickens' "autobiographical" novel, packed with clues about its author and even in some sense derived from an abandoned autobiographical project, and it is easy to see how this text has become vulnerable to the kinds of suggestive but perhaps overly speculative psychological readings that have dominated *Copperfield* criticism in this century.

Recently, however, critical response to *David Copperfield* has decisively turned toward social concerns. This is as it should be. Edmund Wilson's well-known reading of the novel in terms of the young Dickens' ordeal at Warren's Blacking has been attacked on a number of fronts;[1] and though others, notably Stephen Marcus, have attempted ingenious psychoanalytic readings of the "autobiographical fragment" that records the warehouse experience and informs so many responses to *David Copperfield,* recent trends in literary theory have allowed more sophisticated analyses of the novel, analyses which refuse to reduce it to an elaborate response to a single experience that "produced in Charles Dickens a trauma from which he suffered all his life" (Wilson 6).

Indeed, we have come to understand *David Copperfield not* as a novel divorced from political concerns but rather as one with a deeply embedded social subtext.

One of the best of these new readings argues that "anxiety about social class infects David's narrative and produces significant displacements, distortions, and omissions in his self-presentation and in his accounts of other people" (Jordan 63). For this critic, David Copperfield as narrator submerges his own anxiety about social mobility, class anger, and aristocratic privilege into his representations of the people around him, thus legitimating his own social position. "[T]he search for social legitimacy . . . constitutes the course of [David's] career" also for Chris R. Vanden Bossche (87), who believes that the very profession of author is attractive to David partly because of its gentility; it can never be confused with the kind of alienated labor performed at Murdstone and Grinby's (103).

But the mention of Murdstone and Grinby's brings us back to childhood and models for self-development; and in fact political and psychoanalytic readings overlap considerably.[2] Differences in (social and "public" vs. psychological or private) emphases produce different assessments of the narrator: biographical critics such as Alexander Welsh maintain that "*David Copperfield* was written from the assured perspective of a relatively stable sense of identity . . ." (108), while political critics emphasize David's lingering insecurity about his own rise in social and monetary status (Jordan 66). Though some psychoanalytic readings will admit that David's "personal development is conspicuously mixed, partial, and incomplete" (Hirsh 92), most would agree with Lawrence Frank that David writes in order to heal his psychic wounds, and that this healing is (fairly) successfully realized (75).

If these forms of reading conflict and intersect, it may be because *David Copperfield* tracks the collisions of self and society. This paper will examine some of these collisions, specifically those involved in Copperfield's act(s) of writing. David Copperfield is wounded both psychologically and socially; he writes both for psychic healing and for social and financial advancement. However, the very existence of *David Copperfield* the unpublished autobiography may imply that these motivations for writing conflict, that writing fiction for a large consuming audience improves David's position in society but does not deal. David thus writes his autobiography in order to achieve the psychic healing that the novels could not give. However, novel-writing may have accomplished its goal of social and financial respectability so well that David can no longer retrieve a position of innocence with respect to his public life; his entrenchment in the middle class may be so complete that

David is blind to his own implication in that entrenchment. In this reading, *Copperfield* as autobiography attempts to reprivatize, by writing, a life which has become publicly implicated through that selfsame writing. Though David says of his book that "this manuscript is intended for no eyes but mine" (42.671), honesty does not necessarily follow.[3]

When David's aunt Betsy Trotwood adopts David, she asks Mr. Wickfield for advice on his education. David has just met Uriah Heep, on the representation of whom he "heaps" all his own pecuniary interests, and he is about to meet Agnes, his "better Angel" and the representative of all his purer motivations. In the gap between these encounters Mr. Wickfield inquires into Miss Trotwood's motives for educating David; and when she becomes indignant, Mr. Wickfield, "shaking his head and smiling incredulously," declares that "It must be a mixed motive" (15.277). His answer indicates that Miss Trotwood has not admitted mixed motives; yet her motives, while "on the surface," need not be pure: "to make the child happy and useful" (15.277). Happiness and utility hardly walk hand in hand, and indeed may conflict: *happy* implies a psychological state independent of others, while *useful* connotes an existence the worth of which depends on the value others assign. Happiness is essentially personal or private, utility social, public, and economic. *David Copperfield* explores and is caught up in their collision.[4]

1

> But under this difficulty, and under all the other difficulties of my journey, I seemed to be sustained and led on by my fanciful picture of my mother in her youth, before I came into the world.   (Dickens 13.243–44)

The "difficulties of [David's] journey" should be neither downplayed nor inflated. That the book urges us to read it in terms of Dickens's life—that, as Welsh says, "alert readers . . . , without any special knowledge, could realize that certain games were being played" with the Dickens biography (115)—presents a number of dangers, encouraging diverse biographical readings and misreadings. This quality of oblique confession has some importance for this paper, and I will discuss it later. For now we must recognize that, though it is impossible to place ourselves in a position where we do not know that *David Copperfield* is Dickens' autobiographical novel, we must resist a Dickens-centered analysis if we are to understand the strained and contradictory motivations of the text.

David suffers a number of real and significant losses early in the story of his life, with the second half of the book enacting a drama of recovery from the losses experienced in the first. Gordon Hirsh believes that "the plot is actually *based* on recurring experiences of separation and loss" (85; emphasis added), though I would argue that the major losses of the second half, the deaths of Steerforth and of David's "child-wife" Dora, rather *close* wounds opened in the first half—the loss of Steerforth's friendship and the death of David's mother. This dual function of death as both wound and healing casts new light on what have become commonplaces of *Copperfield* criticism: Steerforth as David's alter ego, Dora as a recreation of David's mother, and David as fluctuating, insecure identity. In "The Beginning of a Long Journey," which effectively opens the second half of the novel, David refers to Steerforth as "a cherished friend, who was dead" (32.516); but when he finally sees the body, Steerforth is "lying with his head upon his arm, as [David] had often seen him lie at school" (55.866). Thus his death brings on for David not merely an attack of nostalgia but the imaginative recreation of an earlier, better time before Steerforth's moral and social fall.

This partial temporal reversal must be made complete, so David takes the responsibility for Steerforth's body: "I knew that the care of it, and the hard duty of preparing his mother to receive it, could only rest with me; and I was anxious to discharge the duty as faithfully as I could" (56.867). David is anxious faithfully to discharge his duty not merely because of his former closeness to Steerforth but also because of his earlier faithlessness regarding Little Em'ly. His implication in her fall has brought on the guilt and anxiety he feels at this point; in burying Steerforth, David performs a purgation or even an exorcism, a symbolic burial of his own guilt in effigy as Steerforth. Furthermore, that David in the midst of all this takes on "the hard duty of preparing [Steerforth's] mother" only underscores the connection in the text between the expurgation of guilt and the restoration of proper parent-child relationships. As we shall see, both this expurgation and this restoration are entangled in uneasy questions of personal identity.

Indeed, as has often been observed, David's own mother reenters the novel in another form soon after Steerforth's death. When he first loses Steerforth, David finds comfort in loving Dora: "Her idea was my refuge . . . and made some amends to me, even for the loss of my friend" (33.534). Her "idea" serves as refuge partly because Dora reminds David of his mother, and of a time of seeming innocence. Connections between David's mother and Dora are easily established. Both women are children in the home; neither has a

sense of domestic economy; both defer to their husbands and to more dominating women. In these contexts, Betsy Trotwood calls David's mother "the
Baby" (1.55) and Dora "Little Blossom" (44.705). David, blindsided by
the double losses of Steerforth and Little Em'ly, creates in Dora a "fanciful
picture" (13.244) of his mother, never fully seeing his wife at all. In marrying
Dora, David refuses to recognize the death of his mother, creating a substitute
for her in his wife. Dora's death devastates David not because of his love for
Dora but because he has recreated his mother *in* Dora. The loss of a parent
is likely to destabilize anyone's identity; but for David, whose sense of self
is repeatedly threatened from a number of quarters, the death of Dora comes
as the last in a series of severe traumas.

We must recognize, in addition to other losses in the book, David's own
repeated loss of identity. David holds, as has often been noted, multiple
names and identities. Even before his birth, his aunt names him Betsy Trotwood, after herself (1.55), and when he runs to her later she refrains from
calling him David, referring to him rather as "David's son" (13.254). Only
after she adopts David does she call him by name—and then she renames
him Trotwood (14.271) and persists in calling him "Trot" to the end of the
book (62.938). Earlier, when his mother remarries, David receives a new
name and is understandably uncomfortable with it. On his way to school he
has a hard time getting a meal because of his confusion of identity:

> "What name?" inquired the lady.
> "Copperfield, ma'am," I said.
> "That won't do," returned the lady. "Nobody
> dinner is paid for here, in that name."
> "Is it Murdstone, ma'am?" I said.
> "If you're Master Murdstone," said the lady, why do you go and give
> another name, first?"   (5.116)

Thus David's identity crisis is also a crisis of finance.

David must constantly adjust himself to the different names he receives
and their varying social implications—David, Davy, Brooks of Sheffield,
Mas'r Davy, Daisy, David Murdstone, Trotwood Copperfield, Master Copperfield, and my particular favorite, *Doady*—"which was a corruption of
David" (41.667). Part of the drama of recovery, then, is a repeated fantasy of
reestablishing his true name and identity in the face of recurring corruptions.

But true identity can be imagined apart from social class neither in *David
Copperfield* nor in the Victorian society it represents. Despite increasing
potential for social mobility, stratification remains powerful and pervasive.

Personal worth in *David Copperfield* is bound up largely with personal *wealth* or station, with questions most often answered by reference to one's own (or one's father's) occupation. At school, however, David finds his identity (pre)determined largely by his earlier hostility to his stepfather, his own father having died before the son was born, making David "a posthumous child" (1.50). The traditional avenue of establishing identity through lineage is blocked off at the start. Nevertheless, David maintains throughout the novel a sense of personal nobility in spite of his own alienation from the usual paths to gentility.

When David runs away from Murdstone and Grinby's, he conjures the image of his mother as an aid. That he does so evidences how destabilized he is, since personal as well as public identity "naturally" (in David's mind and in British law) spring from the father. As we have seen, this line of descent is impossible for David. So he imaginatively fills the gap in an act which both prefigures his later imaginative writing and nullifies another script which had announced his severance from the father.

Earlier, when David goes off to school, he receives a placard to wear on his back: *"Take care of him. He bites"* (5.130). His stepfather Mr. Murdstone thus deprives him of a name and reduces him to a beast; and in spite of his own sense of having been wronged, David even begins to fear himself "as a kind of wild boy who did bite" (5.131), thus coming to inhabit the text that socially locates him. But most of all he fears what the other boys will think. Waiting for the others to return, David reads *their* names carved in a door, and he notices in particular that "there was one boy—a certain J. Steerforth—who cut his name very deep and very often . . ." (5.131). Such conviction frightens the truly self-less David, and later both this assurance of identity and Steerforth's social power become deeply attractive to David. David's realization that Steerforth's "great power," which "was, of course, the reason of [David's] mind running on him" (6.140), comes from his mother, who "was a widow, and rich, and would do almost anything . . . that he asked her" (7.154), may spur David's later resurrection of his own mother. In any case, Steerforth provides for David a close model of seemingly self-authorized identity and power.

Thus David experiences, in his schooling as elsewhere, both true decenterings of psychological identity and losses of social position and privilege. At Murdstone and Grinby's these losses come together. Surely the awfulness of the warehouse experience owes as much to David's own disoriented psyche, what with the recent death of his mother and his stepfather's utter neglect of him, as it does to the warehouse itself. At home he was lonely, at school decentered, but at Murdstone and Grinby's he is deprived even of the comforts of his books, without which he "should have been perfectly miserable" (10.215). We might think that a boy in David's position would jump at the chance for friends; David, however, dismisses his potential friends at Murdstone and Grinby's, Mick Walker and Mealy Potatoes, with a disparaging mention of their fathers' working-class occupations (11.209–10). It seems that the sons of, respectively, a bargeman and "a waterman, who had the additional distinction of being a fireman" (11.210), are not good enough for David's society. They offend his "natural" gentility.

David compares "this companionship" with his "happier childhood—not to say with Steerforth and Traddles, and the rest of those boys." He "felt [his] hopes of growing up to be a learned and distinguished man, crushed in [his] bosom" (11.218) David himself locates this crush of hope in the shame in his "position," the loss of which leaves him "utterly without hope." David, however, if he is to keep a sense of self, must represent gentility to himself as well as to others throughout. He succeeds so well that the other workers call him " 'the little gent', or 'the young Suffolker' " (11.218), in spite of the fact that "[he] worked, from morning until night, with common men and boys, a shabby child" (11.216). Among the few comforts David takes at Murdstone and Grinby's is that he held "some station" there (11.216). This maintenance of gentility in the midst of hardship culminates in the magnificent image of the shabby young David walking into a pub and asking for "your best—your *very best*—ale" to the amusement of the pub owner and his wife (11.216).

David, then, maintains his identity in the midst of the trauma of Murdstone and Grinby's by remembering *who he is*. And remembering who he is means representing an "original" place in genteel society which he imagines was his; this original space, created after the fact and by imaginative fiat, much of the novel will try to regain. Thus the first sentence of the novel, which couples David's potential heroism with his social station, as John O. Jordan has argued (64–65), also engages the act of writing:

> Whether I shall turn out to be the *hero* of my own life, or whether that *station* will be held by anybody else, *these pages* must show. (1.49; emphasis added)

Writing then turns out to be an act of personal recovery and an affirmation of privileged social standing. David Copperfield will take it a step further, actually using writing as the means to (re)gain what he conceives as his rightful place. But the economic motive for writing undercuts and subverts the psychological one, which is to (re)create from an irrecoverable past an absent identity already fixed and located "before [he] came into the world (13.243–44).

2

I wallow in words.
(Dickens 43.692)

Even in youth David has a touch of the artist about him; when he goes with Peggoty to visit Yarmouth for the first time, he remarks that:

> a mound or two might have improved it; and also that if the land had been a little more separated from the sea, and the town and the tide had not been quite so much mixed up, like toast and water, it would have been nicer. But Peggoty said, with greater emphasis than usual, that we must take things as we found them, and that, for her part, she was proud to call herself a Yarmouth Bloater.
> (3.77–78)

Peggoty's somber tone and sharpness rise mainly from her knowledge that David will soon change his identity when his mother marries Murdstone. We can also possibly detect elements both of class and of regional pride in her voice. In any case we find here David "improving" the scene through imagination, a pattern of both imaginative creation and a tendency toward self-deception that will occur throughout the book.

I have mentioned how David found reading a comfort after his mother's death. Even before that event, though, he takes refuge in his father's book collection, which consisted mainly of eighteenth-century novels. "They kept alive my fancy," David says, "and my hope of something beyond that place and time" (4.105). "[T]hat place and time," however, is not without reading at all, but rather filled with "solemn lessons," "the death-blow of [David's] peace, and a grievous daily drudgery and misery" (4.103). This marks David's first awareness in the novel of an important split between two divergent uses of signs. David reads to escape or transcend his social imprisonment, while Murdstone oversees his stepson's lessons in order to see that social place confirmed. We might dub these two (to the young David) opposing functions of signification as private and public, or possibly happy and useful, or perhaps best of all *alphabetic* and *numeric*. David associates the alphabet with his mother, with the pleasure of a "puzzling novelty," and with an "easy good-nature"—thus letters take on life and personality (4.103). He calls Murdstone's lessons, however, "very *numerous*" (4.103; emphasis added)—a modifier which might refer to content as well as form—and writes of their culmination in "an appalling sum" which is "invented" by Murdstone especially for David (4.103).

It should, then, come as no surprise to the reader to see David's control over alphabetic signs collapse under the numeric weight of Mr. Murdstone. Whereas with his mother David had learned well and happily, "the very sight of [the Murdstones] has such an influence over me, that I begin to feel the words . . . all sliding away, and going I don't know where" (4.103). In their place, significantly, rise involuntary reflections on number and finance:

> . . . I can't think about the lesson. I think of the number of yards of net in Miss Murdstone's cap, or of the price of Mr. Murdstone's dressing-gown, or any such ridiculous problem that I have no business with, and don't want to have anything at all to do with.   (4.104)

But David has more business with such reflections than he yet knows, and these new problems hit closer to the ethical source than those his stepfather invents. It is easy to see how practical subjects—history, geography, and especially math—offend young David's imaginative sensibility. But it is far more important to note how the discourse of mathematics and numbers, especially financial calculation, serves throughout the novel as a form of *reading* opposing imaginative literature and alphabetical signification in general. The great force of this type of signification reduces David to financial metaphors even when he describes his own loss of language; his missed lessons become "a pile of arrears," the size of which is inversely proportional to David's intelligence: "The bigger it gets, the more stupid *I* get" (4.104). The Murdstones, practical as they are, threaten David's imagination and grasp over language as they destabilize his identity.

David's power over language continues to fail until he finds, he says, "the words of my lessons slipping off, not one by one, or line by line, but by the entire page" (4.107). When confined to his room for five days, he becomes desperate for any form of communication: "I listened to all the incidents of the house that made themselves audible to me" (4.109), he writes, and refers to "the strange sensation of never hearing myself speak" as a special torture (4.109–10). We must assume that, since David does not have access to his father's room, he has no books either, which is probably why the period "appears to have gone round and round for years instead of days" (4.110) in his mind.

All this is to say that David takes refuge in the imagination—a natural response for any child, one supposes, yet crucial to David's understanding of his own identity and gentility. In these early days, David occasionally creates imaginatively, but his youthful imagination is far more receptive than expressive. The older David Copperfield, the one who narrates, is aware of the social power of imaginative creation. In a suggestive metaphor, the narrator illustrates the limits of his youthful imagination, as well as its later force:

> I could observe, in little pieces, as it were; but as to making a net out of a number of these pieces, and catching anybody in it, that was, as yet, beyond me.   (2.70)

The vehicle of this metaphor images the power inherent in imagination, which might catch and restrain hostile persons or forces, in this instance specifically Murdstone. As both protection and power, shield and sword, metaphor has as many social as aesthetic implications.

In school David first learns the public power of his imagination. In Chapter 7 we find an interesting contest of observation between the young David and Mr. Creakle, in which first David is "humbly watching his eye" and then "eyeing him" (7.142). The center of perspective power shifts from Creakle to David, who "blink[s] at him like a young owl" (7.142) and then even "eyes" him through walls. Later, Copperfield gains admittance to Steerforth's inner circle through telling stories—the first instance of Copperfield gaining public rather than merely psychological power through his imagination (7.144). David's justification of his motive is worth noticing:

> I was moved by no interested or selfish motive, nor was I moved by fear of him. I admired and loved him, and his approval was return enough.   (7.145)

Of course that approval itself carries perks, and Steerforth's public position clearly implicates David's own supposedly uninterested love and admiration.

The death of David's mother soon overwhelms and indeed suppresses the public functions of his imagination, and again David turns inward. Such turning is, of course, "social" through and through, as is any act of signification; however, we need to stress here that imaginative escape has its own reality for a Victorian society in which even the social space of the domestic is considered "private." Again David takes solace in books, both his father's books at home and Foxe's *Book of Martyrs* at the Barkis' (10.203). In fact, David has begun to see himself self-consciously as a victim, as martyr:

I considered, after some hours were gone, if my tears were really hard to flow now, as they seemed to be, what, in connection with my loss, it would affect me most to think of when I drew near home—for I was going home to the funeral. I am sensible of having felt that a dignity attached to me among the rest of the boys, and that I was important in my affliction.   (9.177)

Later, as he runs away from Murdstone and Grinby's, he "began to picture to myself, as a scrap of newspaper intelligence, my being found dead in a day or two, under some hedge" (13.236). *Under some hedge*; already David embellishes with the touch of the born novelist. Later he sits "looking at the moonlight on the water, as if I could hope to read my fortune in it, as in a bright book" (13.255); still later at his aunt's he will learn about Mr. Dick's Memorial, and will hear that some people "are paid to *be* memorialized" (14.261).

Clearly imagination and fortune are connected; small wonder, then, that the first of the present-tense imaginative retrospectives that puncture the book relives his rise in the school to head-boy, and the imaginative killing of his own youth: "I am the head-boy, now! I look down on the line of boys below me, with a condescending interest in such of them as bring to my mind the boy I was myself, when I first came there" (18.325). However, his newly found social superiority flies quickly; almost as soon as he leaves school and enters the world, he meets Steerforth again, who considers "Daisy" his property and who makes David painfully aware of his own youth (20.348). In an interesting exchange, David subconsciously offers the working-class Em'ly to Steerforth, while Steerforth's indifferent attitude toward Rosa encourages David to dream of her (Jordan 69). Steerforth, David learns, gave Rosa the scar upon her lip—David imaginatively recreates the scar on a painting of Rosa in his room:

The painter hadn't made the scar, but *I* made it; and there it was, coming and going; now confined to the upper lip as I had seen it at dinner, and now showing the whole extent of the wound inflicted by the hammer, as I had seen it when she was passionate.   (20.356)

"Passionate" must be taken in its sexual as well as its emotional sense; David remakes Rosa's wound, rewounds her in fact, and so participates in Steerforth's sexual domination of her (Jordan 69–70).

Later David visits Yarmouth with Steerforth and so ushers in Em'ly's fall. But while Steerforth orchestrates that, David haunts his parents' grave, and the themes of identity and ambition conflate:

My reflections at these times were always associated with the figure I was to
make in life, and the distinguished things I was to do. My echoing footsteps
went to no other tune, but were as constant to that as if I had come home to
build my castles at a living mother's side.   (22.378)

We can read *figure* here in three senses: as social station, as writing itself
(alphabetic signification or figuring), and as income (numeric signification).
When David begins to write, these figurations of *figure* conflate.

The period of David's relation to Dora seems to cover roughly one period
in his career, that of writing for financial gain. David tells of taking "with
fear and trembling to authorship" in the same paragraph that he tells us that
because of his authorship, "I am quite well off; when I tell the income on
the fingers of my left hand, I pass the third finger and take in the fourth to
the middle joint" (43.692–93). In this context of financial gain through writing, as well, he tells us that he is to be married to Dora. Significantly, his
own hand measures his worth. Counting by knuckles was common in Victorian England, but such a bodily measurement may also indicate that David is
selling his self in his fiction. While he composes with his right hand, he ticks
off the profits on his left; while the right hand spins out, the left takes in. We
are perhaps reminded of the first chapter in the novel, of young David watching his own caul raffled off "at half-a-crown a head" (1.50). While at the
time David was "uncomfortable and confused, at a part of myself being
disposed of in that way" (1.50), he seems not at all uneasy at this later selling
of the self in fictional bits and pieces.

Alexander Welsh has noted that David presents his new career so quickly
that "as readers we are a little taken aback and have to remind ourselves that
this is a novel about a novelist" (109). This reaction is part of the nature of
the retrospective chapters, all of which telescope years into a few pages
through the use of selected present-tense scenes. Additionally, they all cover
times of social advancement for David; they allow David briefly to review
his own social climb in the present tense, without the potential complications
of reflection and judgement. Also, they present scenes quickly, in a kind of
fluid succession. Even in other chapters, David talks about his success only
in passing, always quickly and with some humility; but his references often
reveal the way the novel is quite literally for David a socializing form: "my
success had steadily increased with my steady application, and I was engaged
at that time upon my first work of fiction" (46.733), he says, as though writing
were a business like any other. Or again: "I have been very fortunate," he
tells Mrs. Steerforth, "and find my name connected with some praise"

(46.742). As in childhood, again the solidity and validity of the *name* become allied with social position and status.

But while David acquires a name, financial stability, and social/economic recognition as a gentleman, he remains psychologically battered and scarred. What might be called the Agnes-period of David's writing career begins while David is in Switzerland, recovering from his many wounds: the deaths of Steerforth, Dora, and Ham, the emigration of the Peggotys and the Micawbers. His "third work of fiction" seems written almost purely for the purposes of healing; David admits that the story rises "not remotely, out of . . . experience," and indeed "[i]t was not half written, when, in an interval of rest, I thought of returning home" (58.889). Immediately he speaks of his love for Agnes and his desire "to cancel the mistaken past" (58.890). Agnes has purified his motives for writing. Now, for instance, when he meets Chillip and Chillip wants to talk about his writing, David resists the narcissistic urge and "divert[s] [Chillip's] attention . . . to his own affairs" (59.907). Fiction has done for David what the sorrows of the Peggotys did for Mrs. Gummidge: it has released him from self-pity.

3

"Has that Copperfield no tongue?" muttered Uriah. "I would do a good deal for you if you could tell me, without lying, that somebody had cut it out."
                                                                    (Dickens 52.827)

And yet we have these two strikingly different *David Copperfields*: the autobiography, which the author "never meant to be Published on any Account," and the public fiction by one Charles Dickens, whose life bears remarkable resemblance to David Copperfield's and who seems to have encouraged the search for correspondences both in the text itself and outside it, in letters to Forster and in the Preface to the Charles Dickens edition of the work, calling it his "favorite child" (47). Thus we either talk about the novel from David's perspective, as fictional autobiography, or from Dickens' perspective (if we can find it), as autobiographical fiction. Interrogating the first perspective, John O. Jordan questions David's "reluctance to publish" and finds the answer in "a sense of social shame." "David's reluctance to publish his autobiography comes from his knowledge that to do so is to make his secret public" (66). "[H]is secret" is nothing less than his identity—to

publish would be to admit that David has made his own name, an admission
which conflicts with the apparent givenness of gentility itself. But perhaps a
more relevant question than, Why didn't David publish his Autobiography?,
is the question, Why did he write it in the first place?

First of all, because fiction conceals.

> I have made [the autobiography], thus far, with no purpose of suppressing any
> of my thoughts; for, as I have elsewhere said, this narrative is my written
> memory. I have desired to keep the most secret current of my mind apart, and
> to the last.   (58.889).

The narrative voice here assumes that fiction is unable to accomplish this.
Fiction always conceals, possibly because of its wide availability. In fact,
one might say that fiction conceals because it is so revealed. In any case,
though it will perhaps be inevitable that fiction take itself from the life—it
might be impossible for Mr. Dick ever to keep the severed head of King
Charles from rolling into his memorial—autobiography has the advantage of
attempting to represent truth without regard to an audience other than the self.
Fiction scatters the self; autobiography gathers.

On the other hand, if the social subtext of *David Copperfield* includes
ambivalence over the motives for public writing, then perhaps the writing
takes autobiographical form not only to gather the self but to keep it from
participating in an economic system in which writing—and by implication
self-healing and indeed self-creation—are commodities, bought and sold like
any other for public consumption. Uriah Heep, David's shadowy double, to
some extent embodies all of David's baser ambitions. He realizes David's
love for Agnes even before David does, and he recognizes the parallel in their
public situations almost immediately. In the explosion chapter we are made
aware both of the parallels between the two and of David's position of power
relative to Uriah. Uriah is aware of it, too, and speaks of his desire that
David's tongue be cut out. But David hasn't spoken a word. He doesn't have
to; Micawber and Traddles vocalize him. His power is manifest not in his
speech but in his silence, in others' doing his dirty work. All through the
chapter we are aware of Uriah Heep's body (as throughout the novel we are
made aware of it by its twisting and writhing) and of David's power—his
social voice made louder in its silence—through his mouthpieces, Traddles
and Micawber. The entire chapter repudiates David's dark, money-grubbing
side.

But David has gained a voice in society through his social rise, which itself
results from his writing but does not equal it. In fact, David has gained his

position, his voice, through an ambitious personality similar to Uriah's. The distance between Uriah Heep and David Copperfield might then be summed up, in a (perhaps too) neat division of labor, in the difference between body and voice. Copperfield's public, fictional voice, then, is not innocent, pure, or stable, but is implicated in the capitalist system by which it is established as a public commodity, being made by its relation to the audience even as it makes fictions out of life.

Early in *David Copperfield* we see the private, innocent Mr. Dick, flying kites made out of bits of his Memorial; late in the book we find a more peaceful but less conscious Mr. Dick.

> My aunt informed me how he incessantly occupied himself in copying every-thing he could lay his hands on, and kept King Charles the first at a respectful distance by that semblance of employment; how it was one of the main joys and rewards of her life that he was free and happy; and now (as a novel general conclusion) nobody but she could ever fully know what he was.   (60.909)

Is it too much to see a pun in "novel general conclusion," and to read in this passage a dispersal and loss of the auctorial self in the conclusion, generally speaking, of novels? Is it too much to see the novelist's selling of the self foreshadowed in the earlier disposal of the caul (1.50)?

If not, then *David Copperfield* the autobiographical *bildungsroman* attempts to bridge the gap between public and private worlds, between happiness and utility, between this new, public Mr. Dick, slavishly copying words, and the sadder (but more self-conscious) Mr. Dick of the earlier novel, flying lonely kites constructed of bits of his Memorial. In Mr. Dick's case we see happiness and utility combine, but the result, it seems, is a loss of conscious-ness. The disappointing end of *David Copperfield* as autobiography, as well, seems to admit a similar loss of awareness; the author who desires "to linger yet" on his life (64.950) at the end seems a far cry from the tortured and lonely autobiographer whose "most unwilling hand" (31.509) attempts, for a while at least, to expose the depths of the self. David's social rise through writing, then, subverts this quest; the autobiography of David Copperfield ends with the very burial or suppression of the conscious self that had been feared. On the other hand, the *novel David Copperfield* seems a highly self-aware literary hall of mirrors, with on the one side happiness and on the other side utility, confession and fiction in infinite regress. By keeping these elements in perpetual play, it tastes of both worlds.

NOTES

1. Recently an entire book, Alexander Welsh's *From Copyright to Copperfield: The Identity of Dickens,* was written "as an assault on Warren's Blacking Warehouse . . . expressly denying that a trauma in childhood provides the best ground for biographical criticism" (vii). Welsh's book is a curious mix of social and biographical reading, arguing that Dickens' first visit to America was far more important for his development as a writer than anything in his childhood. But though society constantly impinges on Welsh's book, Welsh offers nothing like a political reading, remaining solidly biographical in emphasis.
2. John O. Jordan, for example, acknowledges his debt to Fredric Jameson's *The Political Unconscious* (Ithaca, N.Y.: Cornell UP, 1981) for its (political) view of textual repression (Jordan 90).
3. All references to *David Copperfield* are by chapter and page number and cite the edition edited by Trevor Blount (London: Penguin, 1966).
4. As usual with binary oppositions, these distinctions are less clear-cut than they seem and might well be challenged. We are hardly able, at this late date, to posit a "personal" identity which is not already "social" or public. I have no intention of recovering an uncontaminated privacy which never existed; but, however unsatisfactory and imprecise in the final analysis, public/private distinctions of many varieties weightily obtain in Victorian society and are thus worth keeping in *Copperfield,* if only as well-defined *strategies* to help us locate inevitable sites of struggle in the text.

WORKS CONSULTED

Dickens, Charles. *David Copperfield.* Ed. Trevor Blount. London: Penguin, 1966.

Frank, Lawrence. *Charles Dickens and the Romantic Self.* Lincoln: U of Nebraska P, 1984.

Hirsh, Gordon D. "A Psychoanalytic Reading of *David Copperfield.*" *Charles Dickens: New Perspectives.* Ed. Wendell Stacy Johnson. Englewood Cliffs, NJ: Prentice-Hall, 1982. 83–93.

Jordan, John O. "The Social Sub-Text of *David Copperfield.*" *Dickens Studies Annual* 14 (1985): 61–92.

Marcus, Stephen. "Who is Fagin?" *Dickens: From Pickwick to Dombey.* London: Chatto and Windus, 1965. 369–78.

Moretti, Franco. *The Way of the World: The* Bildungsroman *in European Culture.* London: Verso, 1987.

Musselwhite, David E. "Dickens: The Commodification of the Novelist." *Partings Welded Together: Politics and Desire in the Nineteenth-Century English Novel.* London: Methuen, 1987. 143–226.

Thompson, F. M. L. *The Rise of Respectable Society: A Social History of Victorian Britain, 1830–1900.* Cambridge: Harvard UP, 1988.

Tracy, Robert. "Stranger than Truth: Fictional Autobiography and Autobiographical Fiction." *Dickens Studies Annual* 15 (1986): 275–89.

Vanden Bossche, Chris R. "Cookery, not Rookery: Family and Class in *David Copperfield*." *Dickens Studies Annual* 15 (1986): 87–109.

Welsh, Alexander. *From Copyright to Copperfield: The Identity of Dickens*. Cambridge: Cambridge UP, 1987.

Wilson, Edmund. *The Wound and the Bow*. New York: Oxford UP, 1959.

The Endless Memorial: Dickens and Memory/Writing/History

Malcolm J. Woodfield

All narrative may be in essence obituary.
Peter Brooks, "Fiction the Wolfman" (35)

1

"It don't signify; it keeps him employed," says Betsey Trotwood of the mad Mr. Dick's Memorial in *David Copperfield* (14: 175). In spite of her disclaimer, she offers to interpret the significance of the figure of Charles I, whose bodiless head frequently interrupts work on the Memorial: "He connects his illness with great disturbance and agitation, naturally, and that's the figure, or the simile, or whatever it's called, which he chooses to use." I shall examine the significance of this diagnosis, of how and why Dickens "chooses to use" the figure of Mr. Dick in his own fictional memorial, and with what disturbances, personal or historical, the character and the historical project are connected.

Dickens' contemporary G. H. Lewes could not find "a single thoughtful remark on life or character throughout the twenty volumes of Dickens' work"—while admitting that "all the resources of the bourgois epic were in his grasp" (151). Since Lukács, in effect, answered Lewes with his dictum that "the novel is the epic of a world abandoned by God" (88), a great deal of attention has fixed on the role played by narrative in the human response to ethical, historical and epistemological change, as a form of control, comprehension and communication.[1] Of the many late-nineteenth-century delimitations of Dickens, however, one of the most revealing comes from an unexpected quarter. For Strindberg the "bourgeois" literary character "became a man fixed in a mould . . . to establish whom it was only necessary to equip with some physical defect . . . or else some oft-repeated phrase, such as "Barkis is willin'." He contrasts his own work: "My souls (or characters) are agglomerations of past and present cultures, scraps from books and newspapers, fragments of humanity, torn shreds of once-fine clothing" (102–103). Although Strindberg claims to be writing about the transfer of characters to the stage, his example of contemporary characterization ("Barkis is willin' ") comes from *David Copperfield*. This may unwittingly represent a perception, of great interest in recent years, of Dickens as dramatist and a sense of the tension in Dickens between the written and the spoken word. The comment suggests that Dickens, just as much as Strindberg, is caught between cultures, between social classes and between modes of representation. Strindberg's torn shreds of once-fine clothing are characters whose autonomy derives from a memory of, even a nostalgia for, a time when the culture was characterized by wholeness (see J. Hillis Miller 23). This is also true of Dickens' characters. They are scraps from books and newspapers, parts only tenuously related to wholes, neither located in popular culture nor moulded to a fixed role in life.

It is significant that David Copperfield, on the run to Dover, finds comfort in depicting himself as a scrap of newspaper: "I began to picture myself, as a scrap of newspaper intelligence, my being found dead in a day or two, under some hedge" (13: 154). Of course, the character David *is* a scrap of newspaper intelligence disseminated in parts by the periodical press. The character seems to glimpse the truth that he is not the truth, but merely its "picture" and simulacrum: an early realization of what D. A. Miller calls David's "ambition to be vicarious" (33). Simultaneously, Dickens shows us the truth that his narrative is only a picture, an ephemeral scrap of intelligence. This fracture and simultaneity is achieved in narrative itself, and is embodied in, not merely glimpsed at by, the figure of the mad narrator Mr. Dick. His Memorial, as Murray Baumgarten suggests, "teases us into a comparison with Dickens' own obsessive writing and his equally obsessive preoccupation with theatrical modes of presentation" (42). Mr. Dick is the paster-together of scraps, the disseminator of fictions. Baumgarten's Mr. Dick shows signs of Strindberg's modernity, caught at "the moment of transition from oral to literate culture," between the two social classes characterized by those modes of representation, able neither to speak directly nor write plainly of his difficulty. Even this, though, is too optimistic a reading of the character for whom there is no real transition or progress, who is both a prisoner and a spectator of the social system, not an aspiring participant in it (as David is). Neither does it explain the part played by the historical figure of the King in his project. For Mr. Dick, writing history is not transitional nor linear, it is the *Pharmakos* which simultaneously cures and poisons, which drives him to remember and enables him to forget (see Derrida 95–117 and McCormack).

After escaping to his Aunt Betsey's in Dover, the first person seen by David is this enigmatic figure, a shred of once-fine clothing who employs himself in pasting together scraps of manuscript. He seems both to embody and to be the personal victim of cultural breakdown. In spite of, or because of this status, Betsey Trotwood, however, treats Mr. Dick as a repository of wisdom, the source of "sound advice," and one possessed of a mind "as sharp as a surgeon's lancet."

She turns to him when David arrives, in chapter thirteen:

> "Now, here you see young David Copperfield, and the question I put to you is, what shall I do with him?"
> "What shall you do with him?" said Mr. Dick, feebly, scratching his head. "Oh! do with him?"
> "Why, if I was you," said Mr. Dick, considering, and looking vacantly at me, "I should—" The contemplation of me seemed to inspire him with a sudden idea, and he added, briskly, "I should wash him!"   (13: 165)

The pattern of this exchange is repeated at the end of the chapter after David has been washed: "What would you do with him now?" . . . "Do with—I . . . I should put him to bed." Mr. Dick does not address himself to the teleological issue raised by the question "what shall I do with him?" He has no regard for the long term aim or the sense of a projected whole life—he embodies a "comic" version of modernity. Mr. Dick has no preexisting center, no organizing principle, he is "vacant" until the evidence of his own senses (in this case, the appearance of David) "inspires him with a sudden idea." Mr. Dick is therefore considered out of his senses, "*called* mad" as Betsey Trotwood says with emphasis, though she knows the secret connection of the story which might explain him. She also suggests that there is a possible world elsewhere in which Mr. Dick would be regarded as quite sane and the rest of the world as quite mad.

One of the consequences of Mr. Dick's "vacancy" is that he is "open" to interpretation—by other characters, by readers, and by the writer himself. Readers have found him magical, charming: William Thackeray thought the

character "a charminng bit of insanity" (2: 588).[2] The idea that such a
character is "charming" is questioned by D. A. Miller: "What charm is there
in the spectacle of such pathetically reduced beings?" (28). He answers
his own question, inadvertently also answering Strindberg's accusation of
meaningless "fixity" in Dickens: "the charm we allow to Dickens' characters
is no more than the debt of gratitude we pay to their fixity for giving us, by
contrast, our freedom." I submit we can see this play of contrasting freedom
and fixity, debt and payment, in the "reading" of Mr. Dick undertaken by
David (who literally "borrows" from Mr. Dick but refuses to spend the
money). Moreover, as his own first reader and interpreter Dickens revised
his original conception in which Mr. Dick was an "unfixed" and threatening
madman and rendered him charming on second thoughts, on mimetic reflection.

In the published version David sees, on approaching the house, "a florid,
pleasant-looking gentleman, with a grey head, who shut up one eye in a
grotesque manner, nodded at me several times, shook it at me as often,
laughed, and went away." Originally, Dickens had described (after the word
"with a grey head") Mr. Dick's "putting his tongue out against the glass,
and carrying it across the pane and back again; who, when his eye caught
mine, squinted at me in a most terrible manner."[3] This slobbering lunatic
was rendered considerably less nightmarish when Dickens came to lick his
chapter into shape. The first version represents what Dickens knew an inmate
of an asylum might look like: he had a deep interest in the causes and treatment
of insanity, and two visits to asylums are vividly described in *Household
Words* essays: "A Curious Dance Round a Curious Tree" (1852) and "Idi-
ots" (1853). In the former, he compares (anticipating D. A. Miller's idea of
the patronizing spectator who pays for his or her own freedom) the madhouse
to the playhouse: "that jocund world of Pantomime, where there is no calamity that leaves the least impression . . . where everyone is so superior to all
the accidents of life that I suspect this to be the secret of the general enjoyment
which an audience of vulnerable spectators find in this class of entertainment"
(*Uncollected Writings* 2: 384; cited by Lettis 153). In the latter piece he
speculates on the association of "idiocy" with "mental suffering, fright, or
anxiety, or with a latent want of power, in the mother" (*Uncontrolled Writings* 2: 499). His speculations are brief and tentative, but suggests a connection between Mr. Dick's anxiety and David's suffering as a child, unprotected
by his mother. Both of these child-men are now under the protection of Aunt
Betsey, empowered by her suspicion of men and sexuality. As if to cement

the discomforting connection between playhouse, madhouse, and nursery-room, Edwin Eigner has shown how the character of Betsey Trotwood has roots in the magical but sinister Pantomime Dame of stage and nursery rhyme. The figure is sexually ambivalent and aggressive: she is, to this day, always played by a man.

In the second essay Dickens—in a manner typical of David the narrator—blends personal memory and cultural taxonomy in depicting the Idiot:

> As a remembrance of our own childhood in an English country town, he is a shambling, knock-kneed man *who was never a child,* with . . . a tongue too large for his mouth, and a dreadful pair of hands that wanted to ramble over everything—our own face included. . . . And if he be further recalled as under restraint in a workhouse or lunatic asylum, he will still come upon the imagination as wallowing in the lowest depths of degradation and neglect: a miserable monster, whom nobody may put to death, but whom every one must wish dead, and be distressed to see alive.   (*Uncollected Writings* 2: 490)

Dickens fulfilled this latter wish in the revision of *David Copperfield,* immediately killing off the monster he had created: the crazy old man, restrained behind glass but physically and sexually uncontained and incontinent, becomes the harmless child he had never been. The alien laugh and squint become a collusive nod and a wink. He is no longer one of them, but one of us, both knowing and known. Mr. Dick is no longer a real lunatic, but characterizes the metaphorical madness of modern culture in which all take part. As Deborah Cook comments, citing Foucault, "the truth of the madman is the truth about the world itself" (142). The "telling" of this truth for Dickens is projected in his vision (and revision) of Mr. Dick and its relationn to reason, writing and history.

When David speaks alone for the first time with Mr. Dick, at the beginning of the next chapter (14), Mr. Dick begins by taking David into his confidence:

> "Ha! Phoebus!" said Mr. Dick, laying down his pen. "How does the world go! I'll tell you what," he added, in a lower tone, "I shouldn't wish it to be mentioned, but it's a—" here he beckoned to me, and put his lips close to my ear— "it's a mad world. Mad as Bedlam, boy!" said Mr. Dick, taking snuff from a round box on the table, and laughing heartily.   (14: 172)

The madman glimpses the truth that the modern world is mad, he pictures himself (a symptom of his madness) as the only sane person in such a world and looks for a context and continuity for his life in a history which is fused with his story. Mr. Dick's paradoxical claim to be the only sane person in an insane world is typical of the modern agent who tries to render himself or herself certain in an uncertain world, partly by denouncing or unmasking this general uncertainty from behind the mask of individual and exceptional certainty. "We are involved," says MacIntyre, "in a world in which we are simultaneously trying to render the rest of society predictable and ourselves unpredictable" (*After Virtue* 99). Alexander Welsh has characterized Victorian novelists and thinkers (principally John Stuart Mill) as obsessively interested in the analogous tension between the simultaneity of individual liberty and public accountability, the need to be simultaneously "open" and "closed." Indeed, he has described the entire Victorian bourgoisie in such terms: "the middle class protected themselves from view . . . and strove to keep watch on the servants and working class" (*Blackmail* 75). As several recent commentators (following Foucault and Jonathan Arac) have suggested, the novel as "bourgeois epic" contributed to this panoptical project.

The modern agent whose actions are characterized by simultaneity plays a vital role in this analysis. We need to be, if sanity is to be preserved in a "mad" world, both "determinate" and "open." This need drives Dickens' characters: they perceive themselves to be autonomous agents who are yet utterly transparent and predictable to the reader. They provide, indeed, satisfying objects for those very predictive practices which are constitutive of modernity.

Mr. Dick's observation is a search for the origins of this species of madness, the secular genesis of cultural "disturbance" (Beer 14). He asks David the date of the beheading of Charles I. David replies that he believes it was 1649, to which Mr. Dick replies: "how could the people about him have made that mistake of putting some of the trouble out of *his* head, after it was taken off, into *mine?*" This is not only, as Philip Atteberry argues, a disturbing metaphor, it is also an insistent question about disturbance, about the relation of the inside of experience to its outside manifestation.

This question asked by Mr. Dick is also the product of revision and supplementation by Dickens. Just as the entry of Charles I forces constant revision onto Mr. Dick, so Dickens himself came to use the idea of the intrusive royal decapitee only on second thoughts. Dickens routinely revised after the proof stage and his friend and biographer John Forster, having read in proof the Mr. Dick episode, suggested some changes. In the original text Mr. Dick does not ask David the date of the execution, but rather asks: "Do you recollect the date when the bull got into the china warehouse and did so much mischief?" Forster could not recollect exactly what he had said to Dickens, but had expressed "doubts having reference to the propriety of the kind of delusion . . . which appeared to be a little too farcical for that really touching delineation of character" (2: 54). It is likely that what suggested farce and impropriety to Forster was the connection of Mr. Dick's question with popular culture, with the stage and the stock figure of the Idiot. David's response to the question originally gave the game away, revealing the world of popular song from which Mr. Dick is himself a "quotation: "

> I was very much surprised by the inquiry; but remembering a song about such an occurrence that was once popular at Salem House, and thinking he might want to quote it, replied that I believed it was on St. Patrick's Day.

Forster records the erased text in his biography, so that Victorian and Edwardian readers, charmed by Mr. Dick, tracked down the very song, "The Bull in the China Shop," composed by Charles Dibdin and made famous in 1807 by the great *farceur,* Grimaldi (Kidson 44; Lightwood 110–11). Another *Dickensian* registers the existence of "a much admired old song" titled "Happy Dick" (Rushton 223–24). These origins leave their traces behind as former sources of authority, just as the figure of the king is a lost but remembered authority for Mr. Dick. They are sources which both writers "might want to quote."

There is great significance in Dickens' initial deployment and subsequent repudiation of these memories of popular culture. They are replaced by the political and historical figure of Charles I and the associations of popular revolution and civil war. A memory of childhood song is not so much rejected as displaced by the representation of the disturbance which the original memory signified. "At odd dull times, nursery tales come up into the memory, unrecognized for what they are," says Steerforth to David, "I have been confounding myself with the bad boy who 'didn't care,' and became food for lions—a grander kind of going to the dogs, I suppose" (22: 274). Mr. Dick's memories of Charles I must be "recognized for what they are": displacements and representations of his story and history. As such, the figure looks before and after, is both a relief of and reimposition of what Mundhenk cites as "the oppression of remembrance" in Dickens. The memory resists linear narrative rationalization into what Eigner and Bruffee perceive as Dickens' "elegiac romance." It is, in particular, the relation of this memory to *narrative,* to *reason* (and unreason), to *history* and to *modernity* which is raised by the texts and memories of Mr. Dick and Dickens.

2

The initial exchange between Mr. Dick and David is left mysterious and David is about to leave when his attention is directed to a kite in the room:

> He showed me that it was covered with manuscript, very closely and laboriously written; but so plainly, that as I looked along the lines, I thought I saw some allusion to King Charles the First's head again, in one or two places. "There's plenty of string," said Mr. Dick, "and when it flies high, it takes the facts a long way. That's my manner of diffusing 'em. I don't know where they may come down. It's according to circumstances, and the wind, and so forth; but I take my chance of that." (14: 173)

The meaning of the manuscript which is always being started but never finished, and of the flights of fancy which disseminate Mr. Dick's scraps, is unfolded by Betsey Trotwood when David leaves the room and goes downstairs. She recounts the story of Mr. Dick's incarceration by his brother and his sister's ill-treatment at the hands of his brother-in-law. This is the context for the "diagnosis" I have already cited:

> "That was before he came to me, but the recollection of it is oppressive to him even now. Did he say anything to you about King Charles the First, child?"
> "Yes, aunt."
> "Ah!" said my aunt, rubbing her nose as if she were a little vexed. "That's his allegorical way of expressing it. He connects his illness with great disturbance and agitation, naturally, and that's the figure, or the simile, or whatever it's called, which he chooses to use. And why shouldn't he, if he thinks proper?"
> I said: "Certainly, aunt."
> It's not a business-like way of speaking," said my aunt, "nor a worldly way. I am aware of that; and that's the reason why I insist upon it, that there shan't be a word about it in his Memorial."
> "Is it a Memorial about his own history that he is writing, aunt?"
> "Yes, child," said my aunt, rubbing her nose again. "He is memorializing the Lord Chancellor, or the Lord Somebody or other—one of those people, at all events, who are paid to *be* memorialized—about his affairs. I suppose it will go in, one of these days. He hasn't been able to draw it up yet, without introducing that mode of expressing himself; but it don't signify; it keeps him employed." (14: 175)

Alexander Welsh explains that the Memorial is "a petition, an appeal to the Lord Chancellor or someone in authority" (*Copyright* 117). This also explains the reference to Mr. Dick's "affairs" as the real subject of the Memorial: it is both an account of his past and an appeal which will undo the past and enable him to begin again (Welsh suggests that it is an appeal for release from his obsession, Baumgarten a petition for the restoration of his rights: two sides of the same coin). When he reaches the point at which he has to speak of his incarceration and the abuse of and by his family, he has to have recourse to the simile of the king, though it *feels* like an interruption from inside, not a formal narrative device. In composing the narrative, he composes himself, only to be discomposed by the interruption; the memory of the execution enables and disables the execution of the task. Composition is then begun again, the rejected fragments being pieced randomly together to form the kite. The interruption is rejected but inevitable, indeed necessary—it is the crucial part of the story. Writing is both calming and disturbing, both remedy and poison. "Contrary to life, writing—or, if you will, the *pharmakon*—can only *displace* or even *aggravate* the ill. Such will be the objection the king makes to writing: under pretext of supplementing memory, writing makes one even more forgetful; far from increasing knowledge, it diminishes it" writes Derrida, recalling Plato (100). For Mr. Dick the manuscript is simultaneously manumission and manacle, expressing the ambivalence Dickens felt about the function of writing and its relation to memory. Fred Kaplan finds in Dickens a similar sense of being imprisoned by the freeing of memory in writing. He cites the image (further discussed by Jean Ferguson Carr) with which Dickens described his struggle to write autobiography: "like a wild beast in a caravan describing himself in his keeper's absence" (Kaplan 338). Dickens is both beast and keeper, both absent and present: a simultaneity which fails fully to satisfy his own "ambition to be vicarious."

Betsey Trotwood is the benevolent keeper who ensures the Memorial will continue by refusing to admit into it the epistemologically "false" supplement of the simile: the figure of Charles I tells the truth but in an "improperly" lying form.[4] Hence her refusal of significance to the Memorial beyond its function in keeping Mr. Dick employed. This, however, is a serious function. By committing his thoughts to paper, he avoids being committed to a real asylum, although the regime is analogous. As Foucault writes of the function of "meaningless" labor in the nineteenth-century treatment of the insane: "In the asylum, work is deprived of any productive value; it is imposed only as a moral rule; a limitation of liberty, a submission to order, an engagement of responsibility, with the single aim of disalienating the mind lost in the excess of a liberty which physical constraint limits only in appearance" (248). Betsey Trotwood's house is for Mr. Dick an asylum from the disturbances of the world, and his Memorial a meaningless employment maintained by his benevolent Keeper both to express and contain the contingencies of freedom, the excesses of liberty (which in the unrevised text were physical, evidenced

by the "dreadful pair of hands" which "wandered over everything") represented now by the disseminating kite.

The image of the kite-flying man is moving and also motionless, it allows
the madman expression and renders him magical, charming, a captivating
captive. The Trotwood household in general envelops Mr. Dick in, as Foucault describes it, a paradoxical "parental complex" where he is treated
simultaneously as child and adult. This has the effect, carefully contrived by
Dickens in the whole novel, of defining a parallel simultaneity in David: he
is the adult to Mr. Dick as child, but the child to him as adult. David looks
up to Mr. Dick and listen to him with the respectful attention due to a snuff-
taking male adult by a fatherless child, especially one whose utterances are
authorized by the female but not motherly Betsey Trotwood. On the other
hand, David watches and interprets the hopeless kite-flying with the patience
and pity of an adult, even a father. This threesome is part of a repeated pattern
of what Virginia Carmichael (employing Lacan) calls the "triangulation of
desire" in the novel. The recognition of David of the otherness of the child
in Mr. Dick is an important part of his own education into adulthood, that he
is not this other thing, the child. Again, this is a normative version of a
parallel process in Mr. Dick, who defines himself against the otherness of a
world which is "Mad as Bedlam." This self-definition is the result of a phase
in the Victorian treatment of the insane which Foucault calls "exaltation":
"Madness is made to observe itself, but in others: it appears to them as a
baseless pretense—in others words, as absurd" (263). Mr. Dick believes
himself to be observing madness in others, and not in any specific other, but
in the whole world as otherness. Nevertheless, in this perception of madness
in others he justifies himself and his own ability, in spite of constant disap-
pointment, to write the Memorial. Mr. Dick is enabled to become a biographer
by denouncing the rest of the world as truly mad and claiming its reason as
his own. He tells David the truth about the world by whispering it into his
ear ("Mad as Bedlam, boy!") as if it were a secret only perceived by him.
Mr. Dick's belief in his ability to distinguish what "is" from what "seems,"
to perceive the madness of the world, is the source of his comic "wisdom"
to Betsey Trotwood. But David's suspicion of the reliability of Mr. Dick is
the souce of David's authority, it is what makes *him* the reliable narrator.
The evaluation of Mr. Dick's Memoir as incomplete and incompletable allows
the narrator David to configure and continue his own. The unmasking of the
child-like Mr. Dick thus confirms the right of David to assume the mask of
the adult narrator. His "good" writing is designated through the metaphor of
the failed writing of Mr. Dick; the potent writer and man is defined against

the kite-flying child-man whose ideas are in the air but not on paper; in David's growing ability to write is articulated the culture's preference "for a seed that engenders because it is planted inside over a seed scattered wastefully outside" (Derrida, 49).

3

Dickens uses the character of the mad historian to dramatize or simulate matters of which he can neither speak directly nor write without dissimulation. They are matters which have to do with the idea of epistemological crisis in general and with the success or failure of narrative stories or histories to resolve that crisis. Dickens' reluctance to write of such matters other than through drama or simile is responsible for the absence from his novels of generalization, or what Lewes called "serious thoughts." Compared with the narratives of George Eliot or Thomas Hardy, say, we find in Dickens little explicit reflection of the difficulties of inferring from the behavior of others, and of the past, to conclusions about general human nature or behavior in the future. In *David Copperfield* the eponymous narrator avoids the epistemological problems associated with generalization and prediction by constantly constructing narratives which explain and enlarge upon earlier narratives: the narrative by which David understands himself constantly becomes, itself, the subject of a narrative, with appropriate changes of character ("Daisy," "Trotwood," "Mas'r Davy," and so on). Mr. Dick's project, composed of overlapping fragments, is a failed version of such a story. This constant narrating is what Louis Mink calls the "configurational mode" of story, an attempt at least to appear to solve the problem of the need for simultaneity and to bridge the gap between part and whole. Elements of knowledge, says Mink, are converted into understanding by overlapping, approximating to "the *totum simul* which Boethius regarded as God's knowledge of the world" since "the human project is to take God's place" (50–53).

If such narrative constructions represent epistemological progress, then Mr. Dick's madness is occasioned by his failure to move towards completing and constructing an adequate narrative. His configured narrative is constantly interrupted by a figure who represents a lost wholeness, the divinely authorized objectivity of the pre-revolutionary king. Memory forces a rejection of writing and severs the rational continuity which the Memorial was constructing. Mr. Dick's breakdown demonstrates the consequences of a self-questioning which simultaneously rejects the (post-revolutionary) narrative means of communication and comprehension. As Alasdair MacIntyre says, connecting self-questioning, narrative and madness: "To say to oneself or to someone else, 'Doubt all your beliefs here and now' without reference to historical or autobiographical context is . . . an invitation not to philosophy but to mental breakdown." The ability to provide such an articulated narrative context is what we understand by sanity, while "to be unable to render oneself intelligible is to risk being taken to be mad, as if taken far enough, to be mad" ("Epistemological Crises" 462, 455). Mr. Dick is ultimately saved from such isolation by being given a role in the story, just as Mrs. Gummidge, who appears to have gone mad with grief and been reduced merely to repeating "I'm a lone lorn creetur," is given new life and meaning in the altered history of her family. Such returns to narrative, however, cannot resolve but only displace the lingering question of the relation of self-questioning to autobiography, and the place of the history of the self in the history of the world.

Peter Brooks writes: "With the decline in belief in a sacred masterplot, the life-history of societies, institutions, and individuals assumed new importance. The interpretation of human plots, especially the understanding of their generalizable patterns, became a task of prime urgency" (*Diacritics* 72). There are many well-documented nineteenth-century cases of such anxiety about the past and about the generalizable meaning of one life in the totality of lives. John Stuart Mill felt himself threatened by mental breakdown as a result of being omitted from the social narrative, of feeling that he played no part in any larger worthwhile whole. His account is well-known but important enough to repeat:

> From the winter of 1821, when I first read Bentham, and especially from the commencement of the *Westminster Review,* I had what might truly be called an object in life; to be a reformer of the world. . . . But the time came when I awakened from this as from a dream. It was in the autumn of 1826. I as in a dull state of nerves, such as everybody is occasionally liable to; unsusceptible to enjoyment or pleasurable excitement; one of those moods when what is pleasure at other times becomes insipid or indifferent; the state, I should think, in which converts to Methodism are, when smitten by their first "conviction of sin." In this frame of mind it occurred to me to put the question directly to myself, "Suppose that all your objects in life were realized; that all the changes in institutions and opinions which you are looking forward to, could be completely effected at this very instant: would this be a great joy and happiness to you?" And an irrepressible self-consciousness distinctly answered, "No!" At this my heart sank down within me: the whole foundation on which my life was constructed fell down. All my happiness was to have been found in the continual pursuit of this end. The end had ceased to charm, and how could

there ever again be any interest in the means? I seemed to have nothing left to live for.   (279–80)

Mill's self-questioning threatens his mind because it touches, though never raises, the possibility that he is already mad and merely "employed" an projects which do not "signify." How would he know? Is this questioning a form of signification or merely a repetition of the problem—does it refer to anything outside itself? He attains the perspective, the "view from nowhere," which enables him to make empirical sense of his crisis by putting it in an autobiographical narrative: that is his reliable paradigm. It enables him to give an account of a radical shift from one such paradigm to another, from one situation to another with which it has no rational continuity ("Epistemological Crises" 453–72). It is crucial to notice that Mill considers two other models, first the dream ("I awakened from this as from a dream"), then the religious conversion or "awakening" ("the state in which converts to Methodism are"), which he tacitly rejects in favor of secular narrative. As a philosopher, Mill's reaction to the collapse of his teleological system, the ends which he had set himself, and the teleological scheme of things in general (he says later: "I felt that a flaw in my life must be a flaw in life itself") was to mount a secular defence of human character as something which should be free from custom, tradition and habit. Breakdowns such as Mill's are not associated with exclusively religious doubt, but with self-questioning of any kind. The very practice of putting in question accepted habits, customs or traditions requires, if sheer mental breakdown is to be avoided, a narrative tradition of its own: the Puritan tradition of confession and self-surveillance. Mill's self-questioning is, like his "inner voice," cast in the very form which will answer it. However, in the figure of Mr. Dick and his figure of Charles I, Dickens expresses deep anxiety about the relation of narrative to confession. Mr. Dick's project, in contrast to those of Mill (including Mill's memoir) simply keeps him going, gives him the sort of sense of an end in life which Mill felt he had lost. As Thomas Leitch implies, Dickens virtually replaces teleology with narrative, while Mill (false, for Dickens) feels he has successfully used narrative to signal an absent teleology. The Memorial lends a madman a sense of sanity, while Mill's memoir gives a sane man a glimpse of madness. Mill wants to construct a place for his life in history, while Mr. Dick needs a place for history in his life. Mr. Dick's project disturbs and contains disturbance, it gives form, albeit a repetitious form, to a life which would otherwise be a continuum of unpunctuated epiphanies, a mad, meaningless chaos: in a word, Bedlam.

Murray Baumgarten suggests that Mr. Dick's kite-flying is "an act of great joy" and a "liberation of language." This is, on one level, quite true. But if Mr. Dick is made happy by his employment it is the sort of happiness criticized by Victorian commentators like W. H. Mallock and feared by Mill: the happiness of imprisoned repetition. For Mallock, the *telos* of human happiness offered by secular ethics (such as Mill's Utilitarianism) did not really offer an end in life but merely a vicious circle of virtuous repetition: "There is no real escape in saying that we must all work for one another, and that our happiness is to be found in that. . . . "I am so glad that you are glad that I am glad" . . . but all this gladness must be about something besides itself" (*Is Life* 52–3). Mr. Dick is the victim of such happiness: he is not happy about anything but the fact or feeling of his own exalted happiness. His incomplete Memorial betokens a deep skepticism of the possibility of what Mallock calls "real escape," of reaching knowledge through narrative, a suspicion that the narrative is mere sophistry: "The sophist sells the signs and insignia of science: not memory itself, only monuments, inventories, archives, citations, copies, accounts, tales, lists, notes, duplicates, chronicles, genealogies, references. Not memory but memorials" (Derrida 107).

As Philip Atteberry observes, Dickens is preoccupied with the impossibility of rendering the "exact truth" in David Copperfield, though the concern was more forcefully and directly expressed by his close friend Carlyle. In the opening to his *Oliver Cromwell's Letters and Speeches,* Carlyle characterizes modern historical writing as opposed both to true memory and to speech: "the documents and records of it, scattered waste as a shoreless chaos, are not legible. . . . The sound of them is not a *voice,* conveying knowledge or memorial of any earthly or heavenly thing" (2–3). A previous biography is "not properly a Book, but rather an Aggregate of bewildered jottings; a kind of Cromwellian Biographical Dictionary" (16). For Carlyle there is an unbridgeable gap between divine omniscience and the mere insignia of science offered by the sophist's narrative: "Narrative is, by its nature, of only one dimension; one travels forward towards one, or towards successive points: Narrative is *linear,* Action is *solid*" (*Essays* 2, 89). We comprehend, he argues, human activity by rendering it linear but sacrifice truth in doing so. While working on *The French Revolution,* he writes of "the chaos which I am to re-create." This chaos, Bedlam, is what history is really like, though only Omniscience would see this and, in seeing it, render it orderly (*Letters* 8: 209)—as Michael Timko points out, even the repeated "Chaos" is a reopened Biblical simile. Elsewhere Carlyle writes of the human impossibility of access to "the secret of being at once determinate (*bestimmt*) and open" (*Two Notebooks* 77). This difficulty goes to the heart of the Victorian crisis in epistemology and in political and moral freedom—the question of the relation between a person's inner life and outer life, between privacy and public intervention, between the individual, temporal part and the social, historical whole. Indeed, the problem of narrative was that of relating the part to the whole, the individual to his or her story or history, and of relating such history while preserving the "truth" of the simultaneity, synchronicity or "solidity" of human activity. Narrative writing is the great *pharmakos* of the nineteenth century, its cure and its plague, dangerously inadequate but obsessively practiced. Mr. Dick is a product of Carlyle's despair of the possibility of representing history in a complete narrative. He represents the consequences of becoming, in Carlyle's phrase, "cut off from Narrative," a true state but comprehensible only through the lie of metaphor.[5]

Mr. Dick is not the only character of Dickens thus cut off, and whose alienation is both treated and aggravated by obsession and repetition. Miss Havisham is trapped in a timeless present in which the past is endlessly reproduced while she remains, in Strindberg's term, "fixed." Her obsession with time cuts her off from narrative. When, in Chapter 49, Pip tries to tell her "the secret history" of his partnership with Herbert he realizes "she was thinking in a discursive way of me, rather than of what I said" (p. 408). She can understand discourse but not story. In Dickens' novels, sanity, generalization, and comprehension are always associated with narrative. Fixation with the written, however, pervades *Bleak House,* a fixation which finds its most extreme representation in Krook, to whom the marks are not even legible: "it's a monomonia with him, to think he is possessed of documents" (32: 508). Similarly, *A Tale of Two Cities* eventuates in a crucial document, Doctor Manette's hidden memoir which condemns Darney. Manette displays obsessive employment of a kind somewhat similar to Mr. Dick's. He had plainly preserved his sanity while imprisoned by laboriously and repetitively making ladies shoes, an action which kept him in mind of his daughter while simultaneously keeping thoughts of her and of his imprisonment out of his mind. He later keeps the tools in his room and reverts to the behaviour when under stress. Though the reversion is not conscious he is able to interpret it: "There has been a violent stress in one direction, and it needs a counter-weight," he explains, though only by speaking of himself in the third person, "it relieved his pain so much, by substituting the perplexity of the fingers for the perplexity of the brain" (19: 234). He does not, though, allow himself to face the discomforting fact that he reverts to the "meaningless" employment when is daughter marries Darney, returning to "normal" behaviour days after the wedding, having completely lost track of time. The motion of fabricating the shoe (there are no real materials involved, only his false memory of them) "relieves" the pain of fatherhood but also aggravates it, displaces it and avoids its recognition—the process is one of defamiliarizing the intimate and the sexual. Mr. Lorry, however, intervenes to remove the means by which Manette reproduces (without truly remembering) his past and Dickens constructs an historical narrative in which Manette will play an "historic" part (the sort desired by Mill). Dickens shows, by turn, Mannette's effect on history, but history's effects on Mr. Dick—he bears the marks of history on his mind and body. In all these cases monomania evidences insanity but simultaneously maintains continuity with the world and prevents complete breakdown. Mr. Dick's is the most "truly" monomaniacal of these examples because it is "barred to common sense by its very semblance of sanity" (During 87) and its sanity is its resemblance to the life of writing the past.

4

Carlyle's project, in his *Oliver Cromwell's Letters and Speeches*, was to "reconnect" early Victorian England with the true spirit of Puritanism, to show his audience "that Puritanism is not of the Nineteenth Century, but of the Seventeenth; that the grand unintelligibility for us lies *there*" (8). His project is to show "how the Memory of Cromwell, in its huge inarticulate significance, not able to *speak* a wise word for itself" has nevertheless been "steadily growing clearer in the popular English mind" (16). The seventeenth century is for Mr. Dick, by contrast, a site of fracture and loss. His memorial is opposed to memory, and his biography is interrupted by the opposing figure of Charles I. His allusion to the "disturbance" of the seventeenth century is an allusion to the roots of modernity, to the genealogy of writing (especially confessional writing) and of morality (especially of Victorian "Puritanism"—itself an allusion to, not a recreation of, Puritanism).

Mr. Dick is composing two Memorials: the first, the appeal, is Mr. Dick's account of his life, the second, which interrupts the first, is the life and death of the king (two further, related, memoirs are being composed, of course: David's and Dickens'). The two are closely connected in that the figure of the king was the highest authority to whom appeal could be made. It is the memory of the loss of such authority which brings Mr. Dick to a halt, but the invention of human omniscience which, by contrast, simultaneously allows the narrator David/Dickens to continue.

As the older narrative voice implies at the end of David's exchange with Mr. Dick, human history is a lie:

> "Did you get that date out of history?"
> "Yes, sir."
> "I suppose history never lies, does it?" said Mr. Dick, with a gleam of hope.
> "Oh dear, no, sir!" I replied, most decisively. I was ingenuous and young, and thought so.   (17: 214)

To Dickens the historical figure of Charles I was, above all, a writer and a liar. "The King," he wrote in his *A Child's History of England*, "never could be straightforward and plain, through one single day or thorugh one single sheet of paper" (461). Mr. Dick uses the figure or simile of Charles I because he, similarly, cannot write plainly; in opposing Cromwell to Charles, both Dickens and Carlyle reflect what Katherine Van Eerde has shown to be the popular appeal of the myth of Cromwell's "sincerity." Cromwell is the authentic hero, Charles the anti-hero; Cromwell is the memory, Charles the history, the lying counter-memory. For Carlyle, Cromwell was "the inarticulate Prophet; Prophet who could not *speak*. Rude, confused, struggling to utter himself, with his savage depth, with his wild sincerity. . . . A kind of chaotic man" (*On Heroes* 217). It is precisely this tension between chaos and re-creation, the inarticulate voice and the sophistry of writing, which located for Carlyle, reflecting on the composition of *The French Revolution*, the problem of telling truth in narrative.

Mr. Dick is a Cromwellian "chaotic man" and the interruption of Charles I, though provoking disorder, represents the memory of order. History is not memory, and Mr. Dick's "Cromwellian" Memorial is plagued by the fear that it may turn out to be a history, and therefore a lie, after all. Mr. Dick is preoccupied with Charles I who died in memory of his own ancestors: the tradition that "Remember" was his last word on the scaffold is repeated by Dickens the historian (*Child's History* 217). Just as Miss Flyte, the mad woman in *Bleak House*, believes against reason that the old aristocratic order, the once-fine clothing is still intact, so Mr. Dick is connected with the vanished old world of inevitable "succession" when God was in his heaven and each was fixed in his or her proper place. The break in lineage and succession (the beheading of Charles) breaks his linear narrative line. He is socially unconnected (Betsey Trotwood calls him a "distant connection"), he lives in the present, without history but with the imperative need to remember and to forget. When he flies his kite, Mr. Dick spreads the word—in effect, the word "Remember"—randomly from the end of a vertical string: the past seems to have no horizontal, linear narrative connection to the present.

Mr. Dick's memory of seventeenth-century disturbance prevents the writing of a coherent narrative; it allows partial expression but avoids complete revelation. The Memorial is a "bad" version of David's/Dickens' memorial, his autobiographical fiction, which, in turn, is a version of the realistic novel with its roots in Puritan autobiography. In Mr. Dick, Dickens alludes to the connection between modernity and his own narrative construction. "The history of the novel," wrote Ian Watt, "is directly connected with . . . the struggle between Puritanism and the tendency to secularization which was rooted in material progress" (83). If Dickens were to place himself in the tradition of the English novel, to define himself in relation to literary history, he would have to recognize his debt to the Puritan autobiography. He would also have to recognize, contrary to Watt's binary opposition, the strange *alliance* of Puritanism with secularization, its dissent from the traditional values of the Church and the State headed by the person of the King. The presence of his complex and disturbing genealogy—both of morals and of writing—is alluded to by the history of Charles I. The values and memories of the traditional order constantly interpose to prevent the narrative making progress and taking on the shape of a whole secular autobiography. Mr. Dick's is therefore decidedly no sort of pilgrim's progress; indeed progress is exactly what it lacks. David's journey, as Barry Qualls shows, is rendered positively Bunyanesque by the contrast. Dickens, similarly, confesses his anxiety about confession while avoiding the insane endless regression of that tautology.

The "Puritanical" roots of the novel identified by Watt and figured by Mr. Dick are of central importance to the narrative and conceptual schemes of the nineteenth century. Indeed, Dickens cannot allude to modernity from any other point of view: secularization *is* the narrative of the nineteenth century. Watt writes: "As secularization increased, there arose a widespread tendency to ethical rigorism for its own sake, a tendency which is Puritan only in the sense that Victorian morality was Puritan: resistance to the desires of the body became the major aim of secular morality; and chastity, instead of being only one virtue among many, tended to become the supreme one, and applied to men as well as to women" (156). Since Watt wrote this, scholars like Stephen McKnight have pushed back the origins of modernity; others have run the argument in the other direction, arguing that Victorian morality is an attempt to sacralize repression rather than secularize religion; others, notably Lyotard and Vattimo, suggest that this very reversability and fluidity of argument, the ability to see the conceptual schemes and terminology of one age as the quotations from an earlier age, is itself the principal characteristic of modernity.

This crisis is what renders Mr. Dick "cut off from Narrative," severed from and yet dependent upon available history to explain his mental and physical suffering, his social and sexual alienation. He is a victim of the characteristics identified by Watt—the self-referring nature of ethics of the practice of "ethical rigorism for its own sake" (like Mallock's vicious circle of repetition, with no higher authority to whom one might appeal) and the identification of moral judgement with sexual conduct. In Mr. Dick, Dickens is expressing anxiety about the irrational, about the interruptions of traditions and of the counter-claims of a reality that cannot be narrated. For both Mr. Dick and Dickens, what cannot be directly told or accounted for is love and its associated sources and objects of pain: father, mother, family, wife, sexuality. The interruption of the king stands for the non-"Puritanical," for intimate familial and sexual relations which are simultaneously sacred. The "Puritanical" disturbance severs such ties and conventions: family relationships are metaphorically sacred but actually transformed into what Robert Barickman calls "corrupt relations," and writing eventuates in meaningless documents which serve only to keep the writer/reader employed but "don't signify." In repeatedly denying the figure of the king, first by rendering him bodiless, then by disseminating his seed in the ritual kite-flying, Mr. Dick makes himself the only acceptable male to the otherwise man-hating Betsey Trotwood. He is for her an emasculated male who helps drive off the sexually symbolic donkeys which threaten to invade her patch of green. Mr. Dick is the only man, in contrast to the donkeys and their boys (who, as Ian Crawford shows, are distinguished from David) who is allowed on "those sacred precincts" and to "trespass over that immaculate spot" (13: 159).

As a means of dealing with mental disturbance, Mr. Dick's project is clearly extremely effective. Judging by his behavior and language, his madness has been mastered. In particular, his behavior is noticeably non-violent and his language free from "typically" lunatic profanations and blasphemies, or attacks on the cause or object of his disturbance, his own family. Neither the sacred nor the secular Father is confronted by Mr. Dick, although it seems that the decapitation of Charles I represents the loss of the head of both Church and State, of the Christian and the social community. Mr. Dick is alienated from both of those worlds. Indeed the world of family values came to fulfill the function of the Christian community in the nineteenth century, and madness to represent, as it became the object of psychoanalysis, "the secret thrust of instincts against the solidity of the family" (Foucault 254). Dickens' completed narrative testifies to the sacrality of social virtues, but Mr. Dick (his name an incomplete Dickens) powerfully testifies to the reality of their breakdown.

5

Suppressed and re-located though they may be, religious concerns are present in both Mr. Dick's project and David's account of it: Charles I is frequently referred to in the text as a martyr, as if this perpetually cancelled Memorial is a secular hagiography. The saint and martyr is the figure who, on Ricoeur's model, disturbs the world, "tumbles" one's history "out of all shape" in order that it might be re-described: the model for such a transfer is, as for Mill, that of conversion (*Metaphor* 149). The Memorial represents a memory of the use of religious metaphors, figures or similes much as Jeffrey Stout describes their use by Milton and Descartes: "to create an inner refuge from the turbulence of seventeenth century Europe" (72). Stout continues, tracing the genealogy of modernity: "they [Milton and Descartes] were, in effect, taking Protestant inwardness a step further, widening the gap between inner and outer reality, and radicalizing the solipsistic tendencies of various metaphors whose roots can be traced deep into our Greek and Christian past." Radicalizing the tendency of metaphor, detaching it from reality, is precisely how Dickens achieves much of his comedy—as in Wemmick's home-as-castle in *Great Expectations,* or Mr. Dick's word-as-seed ritual. As metaphor, the decapitation of King Charles is both a refuge from and an expression of what the Victorian James Baldwin Brown called, in 1871, "the revolution of the last quarter of a century."

Religion is always thus "comic" for Dickens. To put this another way, he is a modern writer in his suspicion of the religious roots of ethical terms, Biblical language and even story-telling itself: they tend to become allusive and metaphorical, scraps of once-fine whole cloth.[6] As Carlyle says: "The old names and similitudes of belief still circulate from tongue to tongue" (*Oliver Cromwell* 4). When David arrives on her doorstep, his aunt observes: "He's as like Cain before he was grown up, as he can be" (168; ch. 13). The Biblical allusion is casually circulated on her part but deliberately on Dickens', valued for its function as simile. More so than any other metaphorical language, Biblical simile simultaneously suggests likeness and unlikeness:

to understand the full significance of Betsey's allusion we need to know the sacred text, but not as sacred text.

The metaphorically sacred status of Mr. Dick's project and its secular, ethical importance to David's progress is signaled by the opening of chapter fifteen, which the narrator titles, "I Make Another Beginning: "

> Mr. Dick and I soon became the best of friends, and very often, when his day's work was done, went out together to fly the great kite. Every day of his life he had a long sitting at the Memorial, which never made the least progress, however hard he laboured, for King Charles the First always strayed into it, sooner or later, and then it was thrown aside, and another one begun. The patience and hope with which he bore these perpetual disappointments, the mild perception he had that there was something wrong about King Charles the First, the feeble efforts he made to keep him out, and the certainty with which he came in, and tumbled the Memorial out of all shape, made a deep impression on me. What Mr. Dick supposed would come of the Memorial, if it were completed; where he thought it was to go, or what he thought it was to do; he knew no more than anybody else, I believe. Nor was it at all necessary that he should trouble himself with such questions, for if anything were certain under the sun, it was certain that the Memorial never would be finished.

Mr. Dick, in David's remembrance, flies (with) the kite as in a dream ("he seemed to wake gradually out of a dream," says David). This is the first model to which Mill was drawn, since dreams are figurative and escape language: our narrative accounts of them, like the fictional autobiography, are secondary elaborations, false rememberings. The break in the novel is also like Mill's second paradigm of conversion, confession, and redemption. Dickens tries to avoid this narrative model by proposing that the text is "drama." In well-known lines, Dickens/David speaks of lifting the curtain on his past: "I have lifted it for a moment, even in this narrative, with a reluctant hand, and dropped it gladly . . . I only know that it was, and ceased to be; and that I have written, and there leave it." It is not, of course, quite as simple as that, and Mr. Dick subverts this metaphor of life-as-theater: rather than revisiting the past in order to speak of it, Mr. Dick's past and "the past" revisit him, overturning his narrative and his speech.

This redemptive re-starting is one of many points where the reader is subtly invited to weigh David's progress, to ask what *kind* of progress is being made, and to do so, as Carla Peterson observes, in terms of the narrative genres of popular fiction being made available: will he be a "picaresque hero who successfully outwits and replaces the father," or a "Hop o' My Thumb who successfully tracks his way home again" or the young man "sorely tried by God but always trusting in Divine Providence"? (102). The Chapter heading, "I make another Beginning" is an allusion to the figurative re-startings of Mr. Dick, and the figure of life, especially on the Christian model, as a succession of new beginnings. And to writing as a series of beginnings: the "I" is both David the narrator and Dickens the maker.

The writing of the Memorial teaches Christian virtues ("the patience and hope with which he bore these perpetual disappointments"). Sylvère Monod has suggested that the "essential message" of the novel lies in its "insistence on the value of perseverance" (365), but in this instance perseverance is displayed in an employment without signification, without teleology. It provides a sense of certainty but not a sense of an ending. The certainty, in a world engulfed by uncertainty, is that the task of re-description will go on endlessly: "if anything were certain under the sun, it was certain that the Memorial never would be finished." Mr. Dick's interrupted Memorial gives shape, though endlessly revised shape, to a world whose significance has endlessly to be revised: it is not so much a history as an allusion to history itself. The character of Mr. Dick, on the other hand, is quite the contrary: he is a satisfying object for our predictive practices. Almost all Dickens' characters are in this sense and for this reason eminently foreseeable (Heep will always be humble, and so on), their characters have a unity to which any individual action can be referred for justification. They live, though, in a world which is unforeseeable: Mr. Micawber emobodies this—he predictably expects something unpredictably to turn up and change the shape of his life.

Mr. Dick is "saved" by being employed not on a project of his own, but on that of another—on Dr. Strong's Dictionary. Just as Mr. Dick could not get "beyond" Charles I, so Dr. Strong could not get beyond the letter "D" (Garrett Stewart suggests this is because it stands for Death). Mr. Dick is still plagued by interruptions from the kingly figure, but separates those from his lexicographical work: the problematic figure who represents the origin of the Word (the king, the father) is finally split off from the consideration of the origins of and human deployment of individual words. Mr. Dick is never forced into the stage of abasement, or made to identify himself with the object of his madness. David, however, does come close to this self-demystification, this self-knowledge. It is not thorough-going, since this would demand the impossible: an exact self-portrait, from no vantage-point, a view from nowhere, a narrative without secrecy. Mr. Dick remains in his state of exaltation, strung out like his kite. If David the narrator, writing his Memorial, is to progress in a secular world, he must risk abasement and demystification.

There is a further element of demystification in the account of the Memorial, as if the essence of narrative is being laid bare. As Peter Brooks writes:

"narrative always makes the implicit claim to be in a state of repetition, as a going over again of ground already covered. . . . It is the role of fictional plots to impose an end which yet suggests a return, a new beginning, a rereading" (97, 109). That writing is a series of new beginnings is especially true of historical writing, whether the history is of the self or of others, or of others as a version of oneself, as is the case with Mr. Dick's memory of the historical King Charles and with Dickens' memory of David Copperfield. In the case of both writers, their histories are means of both memorializing and displacing. David is Dickens' Charles I, constantly interrupting the narrative, forcing a new beginning which questions the role of the past in the present. Dickens resists making generalizable patterns explicit, but this interruptive question is at the very heart of his anxiety about "the age." Modernity for him is characterized by the suspicious confession, by the distortion of history by memory and the intrusion of history into memory: "Memory and history," writes Pierre Nora, "far from being synonymous, appear now to be in fundamental opposition" (8).

NOTES

An earlier version of this paper was given to the University of Chicago History and Literature Workshop. My thanks are owed to the generous and careful readings of James Chandler, Frances E. Dolan, Margot Finn, Elizabeth K. Helsinger, and to the conversation of Lynn M. Poland and Beth Ash.

1. On narrative in religion and theology, see Frei, Goldberg and Wright. On narrative, ethics and history, see Mink, Danto, Handwerk and Booth. This essay is also indebted to the thoughts on writing, modernity and the history of institutions of containment and control in Derrida, Bender and Foucault. I also refer readers to the excellent recent series of three essays by J. Hillis Miller on Ruskin's religion and his unfinished and "in principle unfinishable" (Lockridge, 132) autobiography, *Praeterita,* and to the two seminal pieces by de Man, on self-effacement and de-facement in writing which "kills the "I" who writes" (Lockridge, 136).

2. For more recent readings on Mr. Dick, see Hutchings, Tick, Westburg (who traces Dickens' interest in Charles I from his celebration, with Forster, of the bicentennial of 1649 while writing *David Copperfield,* to the depiction of Charles in his 1853 *A Child's History of England*), Spengeman, Baumgarten and Eigner. On proper names, signatures, and dates, see Derrida (1986).

3. The corrected proofs of this section of the novel are held in the Forster Collection at the Victoria and Albert Museum, London (MS 48. B. 14.)

4. She is also reflecting the contemporary desire for literal and legible public monuments. As J. G. Lough wrote in submitting his design for Nelson's Memorial in 1839: "My idea of a monument being to make it national and intelligible to all classes, I have studiously avoided allegory" (Stein 255).

5. The phrase is from "On History": "Cut us off from Narrative, how would the stream of conversation, even among the wisest, languish into detached handfuls" (*Essays* 2; 84).

6. Contemporary discussions of Dickens and religion are typified in the three approaches by Qualls, who constructs a religious tradition which Dickens manipulates, Larson, who sees religion as a system of symbols which manipulates Dickens, and Walder, who identifies religion in Dickens with piety (especially in women) and the institutional church (especially the figure of the clergyman).

WORKS CITED

Arac, Jonathan. *Commissioned Spirits: The Shaping of Social Motion in Dickens, Carlyle, Melville and Hawthorne.* New Brunswick: Rutgers UP, 1979.

Atteberry, Philip. "The Fictions of *David Copperfield.*" *Victorians Institute Journal* 14 (1986): 67–76.

Barickman, Robert, Susan MacDonald and Myra Stark. *Corrupt Relations: Dickens, Thackeray, Collins and the Victorian Sexual System.* New York: Columbia UP, 1982.

Baumgarten, Murray. "Writing in *David Copperfield.*" *Dickens Studies Annual* 14 (1985): 39–59.

Beer, Gillian. "Origins and Oblivion in Victorian Narrative." *Sex, Politics and Science in the Nineteenth Century Novel.* Ed. Ruth Yeazell. Baltimore: Johns Hopkins UP, 1986.

Bender, John. *Imagining the Penitentiary: Fiction and the Architecture of Mind in Eighteenth-Century England.* Chicago: U of Chicago P, 1987.

Booth, Wayne C. *The Company We Keep,* Berkeley: U of California P, 1988.

Brooks, Peter. "Fiction of the Wolfman: Freud and Narrative Understanding." *Diacritics* 9(1979): 72–81.

———. *Reading for the Plot: Design and Intention in Narrative.* London: Oxford UP, 1984.

Brown, James Baldwin. "The Revolution of the Last Quarter of a Century." *First Principles of Ecclesiastical Truth.* London: n.p. 1871.

Bruffee, Kenneth. *Elegiac Romance: Cultural Change and the Loss of the Hero in Modern Fiction.* Ithaca: Cornell UP, 1983.

Carlyle, Thomas. *Collected Letters of Thomas and Jane Carlyle.* Ed. C. R. Sanders, et al. Durham: Duke UP, 1970–.

———. *Critical and Miscellaneous Essays.* 5 vols. New York: Charles Scribners, n.d.

———. *Oliver Cromwell's Letters and Speeches: With Elucidations.* 4 vols. London: Chapman and Hall, 1897.

————. *On Heroes, Hero-Worship and the Heroic in History*. London: Chapman and Hall, 1897.

————. *Two Notebooks of Thomas Carlyle: From 23rd March 1822 to 16th May 1832*. Ed. Charles Eliot Norton. New York: The Grolier Club, 1898.

Carmichael, Virginia. "In Search of *Beein'*: Nom/Non du Père in *David Copperfield*." *ELH* 54 (1987): 653–68.

Carr, Jean Ferguson. "Dickens and Autobiography: A Wild Beast and His Keeper." *ELH* 52 (1985): 447–69.

Cook, Deborah. "Nietzsche, Foucault, Tragedy." *Philosophy and Literature* 13 (1989): 140–50.

Crawford, Ian. "Sex and Seriousness in *David Copperfield*." *Journal of Narrative Technique* 16 (1986): 41–54.

Danto, Arthur C. *Narration and Knowledge*. New York: Columbia UP, 1985.

De Man, Paul. "Autobiography as De-Facement", *Modern Language Notes*, 94 (1979), 919–30, reprinted in *The Rhetoric of Romanticism*. New York: Columbia UP, 1984.

De Man, Paul. "Hypogram and Inscription," *The Resistance to Theory*. Minneapolis: U of Minnesota P, 1986.

Derrida, Jacques. *Dissemination*. Trans. Barbara Johnson. Chicago: U of Chicago P, 1981.

Derrida, Jacques. *Schibboleth/pour Paul Celan*. Paris: Editions Galilée, 1986.

Dickens, Charles. *Charles Dickens' Uncollected Writings from 'Household Words', 1850–1859*. Ed. Harry Stone. 2 vols. Bloomington: Indiana UP, 1968.

————. *A Child's History of England*. London: Oxford UP, 1958.

————. *David Copperfield*. Ed. Nina Burgis. London: Oxford UP, 1981.

————. *Great Expectations*. Ed. Angus Calder. London: Penguin Books, 1985.

————. *A Tale of Two Cities*. Ed. George Woodcock. London: Penguin Books, 1988.

During, Simon. "The Strange Case of Monomania: Patriarchy in Literature, Murder in *Middlemarch*, Drowning in *Daniel Deronda*." *Representations* 23 (1988): 86–104.

Eigner, Edwin M. "*David Copperfield* and the Benevolent Spirit." *Dickens Studies Annual* 14 (1985): 1–15.

Eigner, Edwin M. "Death and the Gentleman: *David Copperfield* as Elegiac Romance." *Dickens Studies Annual* 16 (1987): 39–60.

Forster, John. *The Life of Charles Dickens*. Ed. A. J. Hoppé. 2 vols. London: J. M. Dent, 1966.

Foucault, Michel. *Madness and Civilization: A History of Insanity in the Age of Reason*. Trans. Richard Howard. London: Tavistock, 1982.

Frei, Hans. *The Eclipse of Biblical Narrative*. New Haven: Yale UP, 1974.

Gilead, Sarah. "Liminality, Anti-Liminality and the Victorian Novel." *ELH* 53 (1986): 183–97.

Goldberg, Michael. *Theology and Narrative: A Critical Introduction*. Nashville: Abingdon, 1982.

Handwerk, Gary. *Irony and Ethics in Narrative*. New Haven: Yale UP, 1985.

Hutchings, Richard J. *Dickens on an Island*. Bath: James Brodie, 1970.

Kaplan, Fred. *Dickens: A Biography*. New York: William Morrow, 1988.

Kidson, Frank. "The King Charles's Head Allusion in *David Copperfield*." *Dickensian* 2 (1906): 44.

Larson, Janet. *Dickens and the Broken Scripture*. Athens: U of Georgia P, 1985.

Leitch, Thomas. "Closure and Teleology in Dickens." *Studies in the Novel* 18 (1986): 143–56.

Lettis, Richard. "Dickens, Drama, and the Two Realities." *Dickens Studies Annual* 16 (1987): 149–87.

Lewes, George Henry. "Dickens in Relation to Criticism." *Fortnightly Review* ns 11 (1872): 141–54.

Lightwood, James T. *Charles Dickens and Music*. London: Haskell, 1912.

Lukács, Georg. *The Theory of the Novel*. Trans. Anna Bostock. Cambridge: M.I.T. Press, 1973.

Lyotard, Jean-Francois. *Peregrinations: Law, Form, Event*. New York: Columbia UP, 1988.

McCormack, Kathleen. "George Eliot and the *Pharmakon*: Dangerous Drugs for the Condition of England." *Victorians Institute Journal* 14 (1986): 35–66.

MacIntyre, Alasdair. *After Virtue: A Study in Moral Theory*. London: Duckworth, 1981.

———. "Epistemological Crises, Dramatic Narrative and the Philosophy of Science." *Monist* 60 (1977): 453–72.

McKnight, Stephen A. *Sacralizing the Secular: The Renaissance Origins of Modernity*. Baton Rouge: Louisiana State UP, 1989.

Mallock, W. H. "*The Impressions of Theophrastus Such*." *Edinburgh Review* 150 (1879): 557–86.

————. *Is Life Worth Living?* New York: Putnam, 1879.

Mill, John Stuart. *Autobiography. John Stuart Mill: A Selection of his Works.* Ed. John M. Robson. New York: Macmillan, 1986.

Miller, D. A. "Secret Subjects, Open Secrets." *Dickens Studies Annual* 14 (1985): 17–38.

Miller, J. Hillis. *The Disappearance of God; Five Nineteenth Century Writers.* Cambridge: Harvard UP, 1963.

————. "Catachresis, Prosopopeia, and the Pathetic Fallacy: The Rhetoric of Ruskin". *Poetry and Epistemology.* Ed. Roland Hagenbüchle and Laura Skandera. Regensburg: Verlag Friedrich Pustet, 1986.

————. "Prosopopoeia and *Praeterita*". *Nineteenth Century Lives.* Ed. Laurence S. Lockridge et al. Cambridge: Cambridge UP, 1989.

————. "*Praeterita* and the Pathetic Fallacy". *Victorian Connections.* Ed. Jerome J. McGann. Charlottesville: UP of Virginia, 1989.

Mink, Louis. *Historical Understanding.* Ed. Brian Fay, et al. Ithaca: Cornell UP, 1987.

Monod, Sylvère. *Dickens the Novelist.* Norman: U of Oklahoma P, 1968.

Mundhenk, Rosemary. "*David Copperfield* and 'the Oppression of Remembrance'." *TSLL* 29 (1987): 323–41.

Nora, Pierre. "Between Memory and History: Les Lieux de Mémoire." *Representations* 26 (1989): 7–25. Special Issue—"Memory and Counter-Memory." Ed. Natalie Zemon Davis and Randolph Starn.

Peterson, Carla L. *The Determined Reader: Gender and Culture in the Novel from Napolean to Victoria.* New Brunswick: Rutgers UP, 1986.

Qualls, Barry. *Secular Pilgrims of Victorian Fiction: The Novel as Book of Life.* New York: Cambridge UP, 1982.

Ricoeur, Paul. *The Rule of Metaphor: Multidisciplinary Studies of the Creation of Meaning in Language.* Trans. Robert Czerny. Toronto: U of Toronto P, 1975.

Rushton, Joseph. "Bill Sikes and Mr. Dick." *Dickensian* 7 (1911): 223–24.

Shelston, Alan. "Past and Present in *David Copperfield.*" *Critical Quarterly* 27 (1985): 17–33.

Spengeman, William C. *The Forms of Autobiography.* New Haven: Yale UP, 1980.

Stein, Richard L. *Victoria's Year: English Literature and Culture, 1837–1838.* New York: Oxford UP, 1987.

Stewart, Garrett. *Death Sentence: Styles of Dying in Victorian Fiction.* Cambridge: Harvard UP, 1984.

Stout, Jeffrey. *Ethics After Babel: The Languages of Morals and Their Discontents.* Boston: Beacon, 1988.

———. *The Flight from Authority: Religion, Morality and the Quest for Autonomy.* Notre Dame: U of Notre Dame P, 1981.

Strindberg, August. *Miss Julie. The Plays of Strindberg.* Trans. Michael Meyer. New York: Random House, 1964.

Tambling, Jeremy. "Prison-bound: Dickens and Foucault." *Essays in Criticism* 36 (1986): 11–31.

Thackeray, William Makepeace. *Letters and Private Papers of William Makepeace Thackeray.* Ed. Gordon N. Ray. 4 vols. Cambridge: Harvard UP, 1945.

Tick, Stanley. "The Memorializing of Mr. Dick." *Nineteenth Century Fiction* 24 (1969): 142–53.

Timko, Michael. "Dickens, Carlyle and the Chaos of Being." *Dickens Studies Annual* 16 (1987): 1–15.

Van Eerde, Katherine. "The Uses of History: Cromwell and the Victorians." *Victorians Institute Journal* 15 (1987): 81–92.

Vattimo, Gianni. *The End of Modernity: Nihilism and Hermeneutics.* Johns Hopkins UP, 1988.

Vogel, Jane. *Allegory in Dickens.* University: U of Alabama P, 1977.

Walder, Dennis. *Dickens and Religion.* London: George Allen and Unwin, 1971.

Watt, Ian. *The Rise of the Novel: Studies in Defoe, Richardson and Fielding.* Berkeley: U of California P, 1967.

Welsh, Alexander. *From Copyright to Copperfield: The Identity of Dickens.* Cambridge: Harvard UP, 1987.

———. *George Eliot and Blackmail.* Cambridge: Harvard UP, 1985.

Westburg, Barry. *The Confessional Fictions of Charles Dickens.* Dekalb: Northern Illinois UP, 1977.

Wright, T. R. *Theology and Literature.* Oxford: Basil Blackwell, 1988.

"I Never Knew My Lady Swoon Before"; Lady Dedlock and the Revival of the Victorian Fainting Woman

Douglas Thorpe

Long before feminism became a force in literary criticism, Dickens was being criticized for his fictional treatment of women. In 1857 Anna Maria Hall wrote of Dickens that "with all his liberality [he] has done more than any other writer to lower us women in the intellectual scale" (Slater 434). Dickens' women characters, says Hall, "are dots, or drolls, and when he attempts to change the construction, he turns us into Lady Macbeths!" (Slater 219). Recent criticism has qualified this charge, with a general willingness to see a more serious portrayal of women emerging in the later novels, though this portrayal has its severe limits. Michael Slater's *Dickens and Women* states a by now common position, that Dickens "seems compelled to show [female passion] as finally punished or at least neutralized" (265). The charge is only partially diffused by subsuming Dickens' portrayal of women in a general backwardness in the understanding of sexuality, as John Carey does, himself echoing Angus Wilson: ". . . the biggest gap in [Dickens'] achievement consists in his failure to portray even once, with any kind of fullness or understanding, a normal sexual relationship. There is no one, in the whole of Dickens' massive output, who, to quote Angus Wilson, 'gives woman the true dignity of a whole body and a whole mind' " (Carey 154). A feminist biographer, Phyllis Rose, echoes the judgment by way of registering Dickens' own emotional needs: "Dickens was moved by dependency and weakness in women—but it had to be an active, quivering, sensitive weakness, a weakness which could testify to his strength. . . ." (173). Thus, in his later writings especially, Dickens increasingly shows "an understanding of repression in men and of complex erotic appeal in women'' (Rose 189). Often the best that defenders of Dickens' reputation can do is to contextualize the charge by pointing out how such limitations, both of personal character and of literary range, are common in Victorian men.

It is not my intention in this article to dispute the charge, but to reframe the issue in a less biographical and more literary way. After all, patriarchy is not a person, though it absorbs persons (both men and women), but an institution, an ideology, a use of language, and a tradition of literary representation.[1] That tradition largely denies female independence by either constraining the woman's powers of action, or marginalizing what activity she has. To understand how this works I propose to examine the motif of the fainting woman. Once one of the commonplaces of literature, this figure was, in the nineteenth century, slowly disappearing. At first glance one might be tempted to simply correlate this disappearance to the growing stature of women in both society and literature. An increasingly serious preoccupation with a woman's place in the world, with various forms of female action, and with the psychology of being female, would presumably preclude the use of a swooning heroine. By the same token, one might ascribe the persistance of the motif to the reluctance of male authors to part with it. It is hard to imagine George Eliot's Dorothea Brooke fainting, yet at about the same time, Dickens has Rosa Bud swooning under the withering gaze of John Jasper. In narrative terms one might think it is a device which maintained the woman's prominence in the narrative yet robbed her, at least temporarily, of her power of action. To a culture which felt threatened by the prospect of female action, the device had the appeal of stabilizing the woman's significance as someone incapable of acting, perhaps even waiting to be acted upon. Yet this significance was never all that stable, and on closer inspection the fainting woman proves to be a very problematic figure. My argument is that while the motif is inherently patriarchal and patronizing, Victorian authors, both men and women and including Dickens, were increasingly drawn to it for its very instability, and their struggle to alter the purpose of the motif shows their ambivalent fascination with the emergent type of the independent woman. By focusing on Lady Dedlock in *Bleak House,* my argument has the added purpose of shedding some light on a character whom literary criticism has never given the attention she deserves.[2]

In the second chapter of *Bleak House* we are introduced to the Dedlocks and their world. The chapter works by the repeated trope of anti-climax. Sweeping overviews of the scene are punctuated by apparently insignificant details; exalted rhetorical claims for importance are deflated by non-events;

mud and fog, as every critic has noted, are not only the dominant images of the novel's opening, they are the condition of the narrative itself. Thus, the second chapter opens with the vantage point of the fashionable press, which, we are told, places the Dedlocks at the very pinnacle of the social heap, and follows the every movement of Lady Dedlock in particular with eager attention. Despite this status, and the expectation that it raises, Chapter 2 shows us a Dedlock household defined by its lack of movement, interest, or action. The only event in the chapter is the routine visit of the Dedlocks' lawyer, Tulkinghorn, who summarizes some legal documents, like hundreds of others he has presented in this way. Sir Leicester Dedlock shows no interest whatever, and Lady Dedlock appears to do the same, until, in the last half-page of the chapter, she is struck by the handwriting of one document. She then swoons, and the scene and chapter abruptly end. The next chapter transplants us to Esther's narrative and other matter entirely, and it is not until ten chapters later that we pick up on the strange matter of Chapter 2.

Dickens clearly wants us to brood on the question of why Lady Dedlock faints, despite offering the immediate explanation that she has been sitting too close to the fire and the heat has overcome her. Since characters in fiction rarely faint for physiological reasons, we naturally sense a mystery, and Dickens obligingly feeds us a series of clues, so that even the most obtuse of readers has guessed the truth long before Guppy spells it out in Chapter 29. Lady Dedlock has recognized the handwriting of her former lover, presumed dead twenty years ago, and the shock apparently leaves her faint. Yet even this answer, scarcely less simple than the heat of the fire, while it may gratify the mystery-reader's thirst for connectedness and causality, is still inadequate, for *Bleak House* eludes the simple gratifications of the mystery story. The mystery is effectively cleared up (for the reader, at least) when there are still five hundred pages of story left. The whole question of why Lady Dedlock reacts as she does bears closer scrutiny. The search for a full answer will take us into the novel's rich metaphoric texture, and will show Lady Dedlock to be a more subtle and complex character than is usually allowed. This complexity is a sign of Dickens's ambivalence towards not only the motif of the fainting woman, but towards women in general.

To contextualize the moment we need to look briefly at the history of the device, to see what range of responses Dickens is drawing on in his readers. The familiarity of the motif makes it available to Dickens, yet if his novel is in part a critique of causality we should not be surprised to find Dickens engaging in an exposure of the deceptively simple significance of swooning. We need only look six years earlier, to *Dombey and Son,* to find Dickens invoking the motif only to subvert it by framing it in a reflexive critique of its own claims for significance. When Miss Tox passes out, Dickens remarks of Mrs. Chick's reaction:

> But none of that gentle concern which usually characterizes the daughters of Eve in their tending of each other; none of that freemasonry in fainting, by which they are generally bound together in a mysterious bond of sisterhood; was visible in Mrs. Chick's demeanour. Rather like the executioner who restores the victim to sensation previous to proceeding with the torture . . . did Mrs. Chick administer the smelling-bottle, the slapping on the hands, the dashing of cold water on the face, and the other proved remedies.   (403)

The very self-consciousness about literary types that Dickens shows here is his admission that such scenes can only be appreciated inter-textually. He is not so much creating a scene as appropriating a pre-written scene, the effect of which he wants to twist from something caring into something hostile. What then, in Dickens' terms, "usually characterizes" such scenes? Fainting women are legion in literature before Dickens, and any response to Dickens' scene is partly pre-formed (as he clearly expects) by similar scenes that both he and his readers were familiar with.

Dickens appeals to a tradition here for comic negation, yet that tradition had its own built-in negations already. The traditional swooning woman appears in two guises, one active and one passive, i.e., one an agent of action and the other an object. The passive woman faints out of fear, strain, or out of the sheer over-refinement of her sensibility. On the other hand the active woman uses the swoon as a weapon, out of guile and manipulative ambition. Paradoxically though, in order for the weapon to work the active woman must assume the mask of the passive woman, so that the figures share in the visual iconography of female prostration. Also, the weapon works only if the spectator, usually a male character, can't tell the difference. Thus, in some cases, the two figures seem to blur into one, and we can pose rival interpretations of the same figure.

The passive figure is prominent in the novel of sensibility, in the Gothic, in melodrama, and in the penny dreadful. The faint leaves her vulnerable to the nefarious designs of the villain and dependent on the providential energies of the hero. One particularly noxious example will suffice, from the mid-Victorian thriller *Varney the Vampyre: or, the Feast of Blood*. It describes the vampire's conquest of his first victim:

> The glassy, horrible eyes of the figure ran over that angelic form with a hideous satisfaction—horrible profanation. He drags her head to the bed's edge. He

forces it back by the long hair still entwined in his grasp. With a plunge he seizes her neck in his fang-like teeth—a gush of blood, and a hideous sucking noise follows. *The girl has swooned, and the vampire is at his hideous repast!*

(Rymer I: 4)

Despite the righteous parenthesis about profanation, the intent of such a passage is clearly pornographic. The narrator dwells on the woman's body just as the vampire does. Indeed, amid such excess, the final swoon is gratuitous, for the woman is already incapable of genuine resistance or flight. Dickens' writing is of a different quality from this, yet we should not lose sight of the fainting woman's association with sexual vulnerability. Whatever his aesthetic intent, he is alive to the associations.

The other guise of the fainting female, the active guileful one, was epitomized by Swift in "The Furniture of a Woman's Mind." For Swift, a swoon can reveal a woman's duplicity:

Can dext'rously her Husband teize,
By taking Fits whene'er she please:
By frequent Practice learns the Trick
At proper Seasons to be sick;
Thinks nothing gives one Airs so pretty;
At once creating Love and Pity.   (329)

In literature, feigning of this sort became a stock device in satire. The fourteen-year-old Jane Austen parodied the fainting art with glib nonchalance in "Love and Freindship," leaving us with, among others, the following unforgettable sentence. The female narrator says at one point: "It was too pathetic for the feelings of Sophia and myself— We fainted alternately on the sofa" (VI: 86).[3] Dickens is one of the main inheritors of this comic tradition. Thus, in *Nicholas Nickleby*, when the Kenwigs family learns that the inheritance it has been fondly anticipating will never materialize, young Morleena Kenwigs falls "all stiff and rigid, into the baby's chair, as she had seen her mother fall when she fainted away," springing up unharmed a page later when she finds that no-one has noticed her performance (II: 351–52).

To "faint" in this sense is also to "feint" or to "feign." All three English verbs come from the Old French "faindre," meaning to contrive, which in turn comes from the Latin "fingere," the root of our word "fiction." The act was thus both a means of fictionalizing one's own life, and, for a woman whose situation might otherwise be powerless, a way of gaining control over a man, as Swift acknowledges. At the end of the eighteenth century, Mary Wollstonecraft saw the political implications of the fainting female:

> . . . must a wife . . . condescend to use art, and feign a sickly delicacy, in
> order to secure her husband's affection? Weakness may excite tenderness, and
> gratify the arrogant pride of man; but the lordly caresses of a protector will not
> gratify a noble mind that pants for and deserves to be respected.   (112)

What Wollstonecraft protests here is that women have defined a sphere of
influence for themselves, but made it a marginal one, one that can only be
claimed by a negation of activity.

The swoon's very doubleness as a sign, i.e., a sign for both genuine and
for feigned vulnerability, complicates the issue of the reader's response in an
intriguing way, for the doubleness means that a blurring of signification itself
becomes available as a literary effect. Perhaps the most interesting such case
is in Richardson's *Pamela*. Mr. B., with the aid of the housekeeper Mrs.
Jewkes, disguises himself as the maid Nan, and gains access to Pamela's bed.
Threatened with rape, Pamela responds as follows: "With struggling, fright,
terror, I fainted away quite. . . ." When she comes to, she finds that Mr. B.
has been intimidated by the spectacle, for which the conniving housekeeper
berates him: "And will you, sir, said the wicked wretch, for a fit or two,
give up such an opportunity as this?— I had thought you had known the sex
better." Seeing that Mr. B. is ready to follow this advice, Pamela promptly
faints again (212–14).[4] How do we interpret these two swoons? The first is
interpreted by Pamela herself in terms of vulnerability and victimization and
by Mrs. Jewkes as calculated evasive action, a hermeneutic impasse that the
reader resolves only by implicating his or her own bias. With the second
faint, however, it seems clear that Pamela has, in Swift's terms, learned the
proper season to be sick. In doing so she has realized a valuable source of
power over Mr. B., even at the cost of substantiating Mrs. Jewkes' cynical
judgment of her. However unconscious Richardson may have been of such
complexity, Pamela's swoon manages to encode simultaneously the assertion
of male power and the realization of female power (however marginal), and
to establish a dialectical relationship between the two. Indeed, it seems clear
that the swoon does not simply register character, but helps reveal the twin
male courses of patronization and victimization, and the twin female recourses
of submission and deception.

Nineteenth-century novelists pick up on this drama of interpretation, drawing on the familiarity of the swoon in both of its guises in order to defamiliar-
ize it. A culture increasingly critical of the traditional representation of female
nature is drawn to the fainting motif not for its apparent reduction or margin-
alization of female action, but for its narrative suspension, for the way in
which it provides an opportunity for the scrutiny of signs. The reader's interest

is thus directed increasingly not at the act itself but the drama of conflicting reactions. In the third chapter of the third volume of Jane Austen's *Emma*, for example, Emma sees Harriet Smith faint:

> . . . they were all three soon in the hall, and Harriet immediately sinking into a chair fainted away.
> A young lady who faints, must be recovered; questions must be answered, and surprises be explained. Such events are very interesting, but the suspense of them cannot last long. A few minutes made Emma acquainted with the whole.   (333)

Note how quickly the narrator reminds us that this is not an individual event taking place, but a general pattern being exemplified. With typical Austen economy the motif is used simultaneously as a traditional sign of Harriet's feminine helplessness, but also, and more intriguingly, as a sign of Emma's own predisposition to see such a sign. It is the swoon's status as a literary type that the scene explores. The motif shapes the way Emma sees events, so that she turns life into narrative, trying to control the unruly and unpredictable world of sense by assimilating it to a familiar fictional order. A few paragraphs later the issue of the generality of such scenes is again raised:

> Such an adventure as this,—a fine young man and a lovely young woman thrown together in such a way, could hardly fail of suggesting certain ideas to the coldest heart and the steadiest brain. So Emma thought, at least. Could a linguist, could a grammarian, could even a mathematician have seen what she did, have witnessed their appearance together, and heard their history of it, without feeling that circumstances had been at work to make them peculiarly interesting to each other?— How much more must an imaginist, like herself, be on fire with speculation and foresight!   (334–35)

Emma connects the spectacle of feminine vulnerability with the prospect of romantic union, a telltale lapse in one so discriminating. Her attempt to make the connection seem available to even the most hard-headed thinkers breaks down with the admission that an "imaginist" will see "much more." Harriet's faint, then, must be a sufficiently common device to make Emma's response seem inevitable, yet a device whose status as an artificial fictional convention is sufficiently well-recognized as to taint Emma's response for the reader attuned to the emerging critiques of feminine subjection. It would be too simple to read the scene's effect in terms of an intention of Austen's, whether satiric, polemical, or conservative. A novelist so centrally preoccupied with consolidating romantic attachments into marriage can hardly avoid the traditional devices for forming attachments, however much her intelligence insinuates a vital critique of the conventions she is using. A device such as a woman's swoon conveniently registers for us both the plot's central concern with complementing a woman with a man, while allowing for an exposure of the problematic relations such plots entail.

The scene in *Bleak House* can best be seen as a complex embodiment of the drama of interpretation that had grown up around the motif. Against such complexity, some might argue that the scene first suggested itself to Dickens for the sheer availability of the swooning woman as a device which exposed a woman to a man's hostile designs. Dickens was, indeed, capable of using the Gothic conventions in unabashed fashion. When he was partway through the writing of *Bleak House,* for example, he published (in *The Keepsake*) a short story called "To Be Read at Dusk," in which a woman is haunted by the nightmarish vision of a certain face. When she eventually meets a man with the same face, she promptly swoons. That act points clearly to the story's end, when the man mysteriously abducts the woman.[5] Though the traditional vulnerability of the swooning woman is unmistakeably invoked in the *Bleak House* scene, I will argue that the scene transforms this traditional effect by shifting our attention to Tulkinghorn's interpretation of the faint. As in *Emma,* the scene draws simultaneously on the motif's familiarity and artificiality in order to expose a character's problematic reaction. Just as Emma did, Tulkinghorn mis-reads the significance of the swoon (and many readers have followed him in this), resulting in a fascinating tension between the lawyer's desire for mastery and Lady Dedlock's surprising firmness. The swoon opens up the exploration of Lady Dedlock's character for us, yet it simultaneously lays open the author's ambivalence about the kinds of power he gives his female characters. Tulkinghorn is in this respect an extension of Dickens himself. They scrutinize Lady Dedlock with an eye at times respectful, at times cruel, yet the female image they see is opaque and elusive. In the end, neither can do anything with her, as she seems to elude their attempts to stabilize her significance.

Let us now look closely at the narrative details that make up this complex pattern, beginning with the scene in Chapter 2 itself. Note first of all Sir Leicester's reaction to the faint, which forms part of my title: " 'I never knew my Lady swoon before' " (Chapter 2: 17). The swoon is an anomaly; it reveals character only by exception. Indeed, Lady Dedlock is first characterized for us in terms of her stature and self-possession: ". . . she had beauty, pride, ambition, insolent resolve, and sense enough to portion out a legion of fine ladies" (2: 12). She has used these assets to her best advantage and won a place at the top of society. Unlike Edith Dombey, whom she resembles in some other respects, Lady Dedlock was not pushed into the marriage market against her will; rather, she has baited herself. Dickens describes the price Lady Dedlock has paid:

> My Lady Dedlock, having conquered *her* world, fell, not into the melting, but rather into the freezing mood. An exhausted composure, a worn-out placidity, an equanimity of fatigue not to be ruffled by interest or satisfaction, are the trophies of her victory. (2: 13)

The terms are deftly managed: her social rise has been accompanied by an inward fall. Though Dickens continually sounds "boredom" as Lady Dedlock's leitmotiv, we are frequently invited to see that the boredom springs not from lack of interest but rather is a refuge from interest. Earlier on in the chapter, the narrator notes why Lady Dedlock has left her country home for the city home. He describes her sitting in Chesney Wold as follows:

> My Lady Dedlock (who is childless), looking out in the early twilight from her boudoir at a keeper's lodge, and seeing the light of a fire upon the latticed panes, and smoke rising from the chimney, and a child, chased by a woman, running out into the rain to meet the shining figure of a wrapped-up man coming through the gate, has been put quite out of temper. My Lady Dedlock says she has been "bored to death." (2: 11)

Here it is the boredom itself that seems feigned; it masks an inner distress. The subtext of the passage tells us that far from having no interest in children, Lady Dedlock is clearly both fascinated and unsettled by the sight of them. Her response to the threat of such feelings is to deaden and freeze all the channels of feeling preventatively.

The ensuing scene, in the city house, positions Lady Dedlock "on a sofa near the fire, shading her face with a hand-screen" (2: 15). This setting creates a visual oxymoron: a block of ice is placed near a roaring fire and does not melt. Fire is a traditional emblem, not only of passion, but also of consumption and change, and Lady Dedlock's defensive posture towards it (screening her face, shifting her chair further away) signifies that it is an alien element to her. The fainting scene itself is remarkably indistinct:

> Mr. Tulkinghorn reads again. The heat is greater, my Lady screens her face. Sir Leicester dozes, starts up suddenly, and cries "Eh? what do you say?"
>
> "I say I am afraid," says Mr. Tulkinghorn, who has risen hastily, "that Lady Dedlock is ill."
>
> "Faint," my Lady murmurs, with white lips, "only that; but it is like the faintness of death." (2: 16)

The sight of the woman fainting is entirely missing, as we get instead the belated reactions of Sir Leicester, who has missed it completely, and Tulkinghorn, who seems incapable of interpreting the sight adequately. Indeed, the faint is almost non-referential. The root word "faint" is used only as adjective and noun, so that it signifies not an act but a quality of consciousness that is now associated with Lady Dedlock. And this is ultimately the most striking aspect of this "fainting" scene: it marks neither a loss of consciousness nor a loss of power to act, but rather an intensification of both (usefully counterpointed by Sir Leicester's falling asleep at the same moment).

Dickens eliminates the conventional image of the woman's swooning form and in doing so opens up a fictional space for Lady Dedlock. The moment itself is indeterminate, a blank, yet it manages a transition from one state to another. Lady Dedlock's own explanation, in words both figuratively and literally cryptic, refers not to the act, but reveals her sudden consciousness or portentous transitions. She shrouds the moment with the analogy to an ultimate loss of consciousness, death. The analogy is a suggestive one. As Garrett Stewart has shown in his recent book *Death Sentences: Styles of Dying in British Fiction,* Dickens uses what Stewart calls "the rhetoric of evasive intervals," often suppressing reference to the moment of death only to heighten the sense of passage to a revelation in which the character's identity is given the centrality and stature that eluded it in life. Thus, to use Stewart's *Bleak House* example, the death of Jo is marked only by an incomplete sentence, a blank which is then covered by the narrator's oration on the meaning of Jo's life. "Again and again in Dickens, death plays both sides against the excluded middle." (Stewart 63, 59)

With the "middle" of the fainting scene effectively excluded, a special intensity is given the aftermath, which initiates a contest between Tulkinghorn and Lady Dedlock for control over her actions. Tulkinghorn's feeling of mastery is based on a "reading" of an act the reader hasn't seen. This reading stabilizes Lady Dedlock in the position of victim, yet the narrator shifts our attention to the more obscure and metaphoric revelations that Lady Dedlock herself seems to promise. The swoon has not so much shown her betraying a weakness, as Tulkinghorn judges, as being enveloped by an atmosphere; a quality of consciousness is now available to her. The woman who had striven to keep herself in an antiseptic, frozen state, perpetually denying life, has become infected with personal associations that cannot be evaded. The swoon marks the beginning of the melting of Lady Dedlock. It is thus a kind of rebirth, though couched in the language of a different passage, that of death. Her phrase "the faintness of death" generalizes her feeling, embodying all the feelings associated with the thought and experience of mortality. In narrative terms, her presence in the novel expands, and she becomes a central link in the intricate pattern of interwoven lives and deaths that is *Bleak House*.

The link between the fainting scene and this patterning becomes more pronounced as the phrase "the faintness of death" echoes later in the novel. When Tulkinghorn arrives at Nemo's lodging to find the law-writer dead, the narrator dwells on the room's atmosphere: ". . . through the general sickness and faintness, and the odour of stale tobacco, there comes into the lawyer's mouth the bitter, vapid taste of opium" (10: 124). As with the earlier scene, Dickens offers both a physiological and a metaphorical comment. Opium explains the death; but the faintness of death is what is memorable, since Lady Dedlock's comment now assumes the status of a premonition, though she had thought she was recalling a death twenty years in the past. Lest we should miss the connection, Dickens repeats the motif in the scene where Lady Dedlock confronts Esther in the park at Chesney Wold. As Lady Dedlock approaches, Esther is disconcerted by

a something in her face that I had pined for and dreamed of when I was a little child; something I had never seen in any face; something I had never seen in hers before.
A dread and faintness fell upon me, . . .   (36: 448)

As with Lady Dedlock earlier, Esther's experience of the "faintness" involves a mixed consciousness of the living and the dead. Esther has already told us that Lady Dedlock's face is strangely associated in her mind with that of her godmother, whose death Esther witnessed in an especially traumatic way. That recollection in turn is a kind of portent for the living mother that now reveals herself to Esther. What now binds them is a shared sense of being haunted by the dead past. Dickens' variations on the "faintness" of death tie together a nuclear family of the sort that put Lady Dedlock out of temper in Chapter 2. All three of them are alive when the novel opens, yet they are not united until Chapter 59, when Esther is forced to see her dead parents divided only by the gate of a pestilential graveyard. That graveyard is ultimately the source of the "faintness." Lady Dedlock's swoon in Chapter 2 is a sign that the atmosphere has reached and possessed her. Her cryptic explanation shows that she is somehow aware of where she is inevitably headed.[6]

Such a morbid progress should not distract us from the more immediate effects of her rekindled memories. She does not sink into a languorous waiting for death. If anything, she is stirred into motion. Her next appearance after

Chapter 2 shows her returning from Paris. Sir Leicester reads a letter from Tulkinghorn which raises again the issue of the mysterious handwriting. Upon hearing this Lady Dedlock abruptly has the carriage stopped and walks resolutely through the fields in a kind of ritual demonstration of self-possession and active response. When Lady Dedlock and the lawyer next discuss the matter in person, the narrator remarks that they both "without any other alteration in their customary deportment, have looked very steadily at one another . . ." (12: 150). This unflinching ability to face threatening truths is one of Lady Dedlock's impressive qualities. Mrs. Rouncewell, in telling the legend of the Ghost's Walk, remarks that " 'My lady, who is afraid of nothing, admits that when it is there, it must be heard' " (7: 85). True to this reputation, Lady Dedlock does not flinch when Tulkinghorn eventually confronts her with his knowledge of her past. In fact, she astounds him by offering to sign a document, "certifying" his discovery: "I will write anything, here and now, that you will dictate. I am ready to do it" (41: 509).

We need to be wary of imposing a more conventional reading of Lady Dedlock's character than the novel actually warrants. Like the fainting woman, the woman with a past is a stock figure in Victorian literature, and the conventions often demand that we share her fear of exposure, for exposure spells ruin.[7] Though Dickens' conception is conventional in that Lady Dedlock is eventually exposed and ruined, she does not fear this, nor does she seem to have any particular desire to avoid it. In her encounter with Esther, Lady Dedlock reiterates the metaphor of "the dark road" as a forecast of her life ahead: " 'I follow it alone to the end, whatever the end be. It may be near, it may be distant; while the road lasts, nothing turns me' " (36: 451). Even before her confrontation with Tulkinghorn, then, Lady Dedlock is bent on casting herself out. The plot twist of having her falsely accused of Tulkinghorn's murder finally precipitates her flight, but that simply actuates a resolve clearly made much earlier.

What Lady Dedlock implies, but does not state, is that the end of the road is a re-union with her dead lover. She who has lived for prestige and material influence will now try again to live for love. We learn little of the past affair with Captain Hawdon, but we assume that for her at least it was an affair of the heart. Her present life has alienated her from her own heart, so that it is not the scandal which she dreads at all, but the necessity of continuing her life of fashionable deception. With all this in mind it is scarcely surprising that she is so little moved when Tulkinghorn plays his trump card, or that she so soon breaks the rules of the game he has set up. His only threat is to expose truths about her which she has already accepted for herself, and indeed come to cherish as a last desperate bid to salvage some meaning for her life. Her apparently wandering flight is designed to throw off pursuit, for her planned destination is clearly her lover's grave. Her two trips there, one to find the spot and the other to die there, are both accomplished in borrowed humble clothing, expressing her voluntary dislocation in identity. Coming to the graveyard to die is fitting, for, as she says in her final note, the place "has been often in my mind" (59: 710). As with the conclusion of Joyce's "The Dead," the dead have become more vibrant and alive than the living, and in both stories the snowy graveyard scenes pass a chilly benediction on the lives contained there.

Thus, despite the interpellation of Lady Dedlock into two traditional fictional guises, the fainting woman and the ruined woman, Dickens strains to give her stature and a measure of self-possession and control, however destructive the results. Other signs of this stature can be found in the subplot involving her companion Rosa. Lady Dedlock's dismissal of Rosa, freeing the girl to marry Watt Rouncewell, is ostensibly what provokes Tulkinghorn to make Lady Dedlock's secret public. Most critics have followed Tulkinghorn's lead in judging that the dismissal is motivated by Lady Dedlock's desire to free Rosa from any association with the coming scandal. Again, though, there are signs that this resolve was formed earlier, before Tulkinghorn's terms were set. Lady Dedlock first meets Rosa back in Chapter 12. When Rosa says that she is nineteen, Lady Dedlock repeats the figure "thoughtfully," then adding: "Take care they don't spoil you by flattery." (12: 141). A double identification is at work here. The lesson on flattery shows that Lady Dedlock sees a young version of herself in Rosa's beauty. The reference to the age, however, signifies Lady Dedlock's awareness that her own child, had it survived, would now be nineteen. For both reasons, Lady Dedlock takes a special interest in Rosa, and it becomes apparent that part of Lady Dedlock is living vicariously through Rosa. The narrator pictures

> . . . Lady Dedlock standing beside the village beauty, smoothing her dark hair with that motherly touch, and watching her with eyes so full of musing interest. . . .   (28: 355)

The scene ends with Lady Dedlock promising to make Rosa happy, "if I can make anybody happy on this earth" (28: 356). The speech has a valedictory air, like Edmund's "Some good I mean to do" near the end of *King Lear*. She imagines herself freeing Rosa to follow her heart, which she herself has failed to do. There is a foil for Lady Dedlock in this theme of transferred emotional life. The humble Jenny, whose baby has just died, compensates for caring for her friend's baby, saying ''It's my dead child . . . that makes me love this child so dear . . .'' (22: 280). When Jenny and Lady Dedlock exchange clothes later on, it signifies not only the latter's social fall, but also their kinship as mothers whose children are lost to them, as well as their kinship as women who radiate a self-possession at odds with their positions as victims.

The swoon in Chapter 2 thus marks a crucial turning point for Lady Dedlock. Although the turn may appear negative in that her ''impulsive'' reaction exposes her to the hostile machinations of Tulkinghorn, in several more important ways it is a positive turn. It liberates her from her ''freezing mood,'' calling into life feelings that had been long stifled and denied. It brings her in touch with her daughter, with a symbolic daughter, and with a symbolic sister. It leads her to re-experience a past that she thought had died, while freeing her to throw off a present life that had become deadly and intolerable to her. Though her social standing diminishes, her status as a person is enhanced, thus reversing the rise and fall motif noted earlier.

A most intriguing aspect of the novel in this respect is the way in which male scrutiny responds to this continually expanding picture of female life. In a series of scenes among the most subtle in the novel, though little noticed by critics,[8] Tulkinghorn is the one who continually registers Lady Dedlock's complexity and independence for us. Despite his position of power over her, and her apparent paralysis in the face of this power, he seems perpetually incapacitated by his inability correctly to assess her nature and predict her responses. Throughout their confrontation scene in Chapter 41, Tulkinghorn marvels at Lady Dedlock: ''The power and force of this woman are astonishing!'' (41: 508). Later, when he realizes that she is determined not to play his game, he is again impressed by her sense of resolution and can only conclude to himself, ''This woman . . . is a study'' (48: 581). The quest for mastery over her has been blunted into an incredulous curiosity about the sources of her own mastery of him. To himself, he confesses that ''This woman understands me'' (48: 581). The ultimate compliment from someone who prides himself on his mastery of people's minds.

Tulkinghorn can be compared usefully to a character who is a walking emblem of male certainty and dominating intelligence, Inspector Bucket. Bucket's scrutiny of Esther during the search scenes is strangely similar to Tulkinghorn's attention to Lady Dedlock. Outwardly affable, yet ultimately determined to push the search to its exhausting limits, Bucket is to Esther an awesome controlling presence. We first meet Bucket, in fact, as Tulkinghorn's man, and they are in cahoots for much of the novel. They share the ability to gather and assess knowledge, and take pleasure in the hold this knowledge gives them over people. We sense sexual overtones in Tulkinghorn's fascination with Lady Dedlock, while John Carey has pointed out that Bucket's penetrating detective action is also quite sexual, and it gives him a mastery over Esther during the search.[9] At the mid-point of the search, Bucket realizes the deception of the exchanged clothes, and turns the search back into London. For some reason he does not give Esther a full explanation, speaking instead in riddles. He demands that she trust him, depend on him. When she complies, he launches into a speech in praise of her: "You're a pattern, you know, that's what you are . . . you're a pattern . . . when a young lady is as mild as she's game, and as game as she's mild, that's all I ask, and more than I expect. She then becomes a Queen, and that's about what you are yourself" (59: 704). It's hard to avoid the conclusion that mother and daughter—the "study" and the "pattern"—form Dickens' composite portrait of feminine fortitude and endurance. Bucket's encomium is just the first of a series of rewards that Dickens showers on Esther, modulating the novel towards the tone of its coda, even while the doomed mother is still being pursued.

"Mild" and "game" are a somewhat uneasy pair, reflecting Dickens' ambivalent attitude to active women. Esther's "gameness," after all, means for Bucket her willingness to go along with anything he suggests. Lady Dedlock lacks Esther's mildness, and is not rewarded with survival as Esther is. There is a jarring discontinuity when the death of Lady Dedlock is accomplished, and fades quickly into the background while Esther's nature is allowed to flower. This too may reflect Dickens' unease with the kind of stature he has given Lady Dedlock. Dickens is fascinated with Lady Dedlock's passion but he won't let it lead anywhere but to the end of the "dark road." Lady Dedlock's journey through the snow to the graveyard completes the metaphoric configuration established in Chapter 2. There, she was all ice within, yet exposed to the consuming fire without. In her death, the passion within her has driven her on, exposing her to the icy chill of the weather. Her frozen body belies her final essential state. In the end, the vulnerability of the woman with a past reclaims her, and she becomes, despite all her stature, indistinguishable from the many other ruined women that crowd in Victorian novels, plays, and paintings. She is given the power to act, but there is no narrative action available for her. She is given a large nature, but only an illusory freedom.

The faint in Chapter 2, then, enacts not only a traditional process of female vulnerability and victimization, but exposes as well the male fallacy of taking this process for granted. Tulkinghorn triumphs, but is somehow denied any satisfaction in his triumph. Appropriately, he dies at the hand of another of Lady Dedlock's doubles, the passionate and resentful Hortense. Any interest in Lady Dedlock is with her death deflected onto the safer, though in some ways just as ambivalent, figure of Esther. "Game" as she is, Esther at one point faints from the strain of tracking her mother with Bucket. Of her recovery from this swoon, Esther has a suitably reflexive comment:

> I was frightened when I found them all about me, but I remembered that before
> I fainted I tried very hard not to do it; and that was some little comfort.
> (57: 688)

Dickens speaks for himself here, partly, in taking "some little comfort" in his attempt to create a fictional space for female action, however confined it is by a narrative frame that marginalizes and even excludes such action.

Returning to the charge against Dickens that I opened with, we can see that the ambivalent handling of the swooning woman motif, while not exculpating Dickens of the charge, shows us that it is not an individual we are charging, but a literary culture which individual authors cannot remake at will. In this regard, it is not surprising that female authors contemporary with Dickens struggle with fictional convention in much the same way he does, though with arguably variable results. Of the traditional marginalizing of the fallen woman, for example, Nina Auerbach, in her book *Woman and the Demon*, offers a balanced perspective. She points out that the myth of the fallen woman is both conservative and pervasive. Even authors more progressive and sympathetic than Dickens punish their heroines in the same way (Auerbach cites Gaskell's *Ruth*, Eliot's *Adam Bede*, and Hardy's *Tess*). What ultimately interests all these authors, Auerbach says, is

> . . . the tension between social possibility, in which the community, more
> elastic than it seems, absorbs the fallen woman comfortably, and a social myth
> that aggrandizes the outcast.   (170)

Dickens, too, fits this profile. His community promises tolerance when Sir Leicester says that all is forgiven. Bucket is pursuing Lady Dedlock, after all, to restore her to her home, not to punish her. Her death is in the main, as we have seen, of her own choice. Somewhat like Tess, she has become disenchanted with this life and finds in flight a last gesture of self-determination. That she anticipates this gesture is clearly marked throughout the novel.

In addition to talking of the "dark road" she is continually seen looking thoughtfully out of windows, a familiar emblem for yearning dissatisfaction. In this she avoids the fate of a Miss Havisham, who is also in the freezing mood, and has shut all her windows permanently. Her passion finds no outlet at all, and she is eventually consumed by a combustion no less spontaneous than Krook's. Lady Dedlock's fire also threatens her, but it is no match for the fire within her, and she becomes defined for the rest of the novel by her motion, and her steadfast course. It is her fainting scene that first manifests this renewed motion and life, but the faint is itself a paradoxical emblem, showing both the impulsive nature and the dead end it will lead to.

That the motif of the fainting woman could prove just as attractive, and yet intractable, for one of Dickens' female contemporaries may be seen by considering the case of Margaret Hale in Gaskell's *North and South*. In this novel we find a familiar tension between the conservative tendency of the plot, which consummates a marriage between Margaret Hale and the principal male character, Mr. Thornton, and the thematic interest in Margaret's pride, intelligence and spirit of independence. Some modern readers are dismayed to find (as in the similar case of *Jane Eyre*) that a sudden inheritance for the heroine has the effect, not of enabling a life of independence, but of smoothing the way to the marriage. Gaskell's partial break from patriarchal narrative conventions manifests itself in her use of the fainting woman motif. At a crucial juncture in the ninth chapter of the second volume, Margaret lies to a police inspector in order to save her brother from arrest. Such is the strain on her of this event that she swoons:

> Then she went into the study, paused—tottered forward—paused again — swayed for an instant where she stood, and fell prone on the floor in a dead swoon.   (*North and South* 275)

Rather like Esther Summerson, she tries very hard not to, somehow having the composure both to wait until the inspector leaves, and then to retire to a private room in order that her moment of weakness be unobserved. Curiously, the potential marriage partner, Mr. Thornton, is in the house, so it is partly exposure to his scrutiny that she avoids. While this spatial proximity at a vulnerable moment may symbolize the end of her independent refusal of Mr. Thornton and prefigure her assimilation to him through marriage, Gaskell is evidently anxious that this particular moment of weakening not precipitate the change. As with the case in *Emma* and *Bleak House* the swoon seems used in a way which undercuts its sense of narrative promise. Gaskell dwells on Margaret's private recovery:

> . . . Margaret lay as still and white as death on the study floor! She had sunk under her burden. It had been heavy in weight and long carried; and she had been very meek and patient, till all at once her faith had given way, and she had groped in vain for help! . . . The first symptom of returning life was a quivering about the lips—a little mute soundless attempt at speech; but the eyes were still closed; and the quivering sank into stillness. Then, feebly leaning on her arms for an instant to steady herself, Margaret gathered herself up, and rose. Her comb had fallen out of her hair; and with an intuitive desire to efface the traces of weakness, and bring herself into order again, she sought for it, although from time to time, in the course of the search, she had to sit down and recover strength. (276–77)

Though Thornton does not see this, Margaret is still scrutinized by the narrator, whose language shows a mixture of impulses. While Margaret's swoon is ennobled by the metaphors of Christian struggle ''She had sunk under her burden''; ''her faith had given way''), her unconscious body becomes the object of a detailed physical description that reminds us of her status as the object of Thornton's desires. Margaret is simultaneously, though privately, the struggling Bunyanesque pilgrim and the passive Gothic heroine.[10] Her way out is to ''efface the traces of weakness,'' an opportunity usually denied swooning women, and the phrase could act as a description of what authors such as Dickens and Gaskell are doing with this traditional motif.

One final case points to a further shift in the history of the motif by the end of the century. Thomas Hardy's Tess Durbeyfield has always been a controversial character, and recent feminist criticism has intensified the controversy. The key issue focuses on how a character made to utter so many progressive-sounding speeches, made to embody ''the ache of modernism,'' can nevertheless be so consistently passive and powerless. Hardy's portrayal of character generally has alternately been praised for its psychological acuity and rebuked for its stiffly Gothic staginess. Rather like Dickens, Hardy sympathizes with the abused woman, and can give her both a proud spirit and a sharp tongue, yet he can find no way to set her free. His struggle with this problem can be seen in how he wrestles with the problem of how Tess loses her virginity. Hardy seems to have wanted to buck the century's trend of punishing women of a passionate nature. Accordingly, the early versions of this episode allow for Tess's participation in the event as an active, desiring woman. When it became clear that the novel-reading public (as personified by shocked and reluctant editors) would not accept such a figure as a sympathetic heroine, Hardy then substituted the version we now know (though even it was too strong for the initial serial publication) in which Tess seems to be a victim of Alec's hostile sexual aggression. ''Seems'' is the operative word here, for Hardy saw no explicit way of victimizing Tess without denying the essential truth of her sexual nature. Kristin Brady has summarized his dilemma well:

> If [Hardy] had clearly described a rape, then his readers could have concluded that Tess did not herself have any sexual response to Alec; if he had described Tess as submitting completely to Alec's sexual attentions, then they might have dismissed her as unworthy of their sympathies. Instead, Hardy retains their interest and consummation in The Chase engulfed in fog, darkness, and silence.[11]
>   (145)

What is interesting in this for my argument is the exclusion of the narrative device of rape since it would make Tess too passive. But do we find that, by the same token, Hardy also excludes the faint as a way of rendering Tess vulnerable? Only partly. A few pages before the climactic scene, Alec saves Tess from the hostility of her co-workers. Note her first reaction to his offer of assistance:

> She felt almost ready to faint, so vivid was her sense of the crisis. At almost any other moment of her life she would have refused such proferred aid and company, as she had refused them several times before. . . .   (94)

Her dependence on Alec here, like the faint that almost happens, is again made anomalous, a betrayal of character for the sake of precipitating a narrative crisis. With the moment of crisis itself, Hardy experimented with various devices for rendering Tess insensible, and successive versions of the manuscript refer to Alec giving Tess some medicinal spirits, a gesture altered in the first edition to the use of a druggist's cordial. Beginning with the 1892 edition Hardy excluded all such outside aids, and we are left with the description of Tess falling asleep in the forest, and no description at all of her consciousness when the "coarse pattern" is "traced" on her (100–103).[12] Hardy's recourse to obtuse euphemism shows his inability to solve the narrative dilemma of how to portray a scene of sexual intercourse given the narrow range of responses available from his audience. Yet it seems clear that apart from the one brief reference to the possibility of Tess fainting, he never considered that motif a meaningful resolution to the problem. The motif had apparently lost even that ambivalent usefulness it had at mid-century.

Recent feminist criticism on Victorian fiction has analysed the myriad of ways in which even well-intentioned authors find it hard to "efface the traces of weakness" from their female characters. While narrative conventions prove stubbornly conservative, their very continued presence can be destabilized by an increasingly antithetic rhetorical context. Thus, for example, Ellen Moers has argued convincingly that the women of *Bleak House* actually dominate that novel. Moers points out how the images of energy, motion, and forcefulness are associated with women, while images of paralysis and ineffectuality are associated with men (13–24). To this one would connect Nina Auerbach's argument that the portrayal of women in nineteenth-century literature, though it is distortingly polarized into the demonic and the angelic, is in fact an acknowledgement of the mythic centrality of female energy and life.[13]

Such a judgment does not exonerate Dickens from the charge of distortion and bias in his presentation of female nature, but it does allow for Dickens' acknowledgement of female activity and self-possession. This acknowledgement has been obscured by the evident satire in Dickens's portrait of active women such as Mrs. Pardiggle and Mrs. Jellyby. To this Moers responds well: "But there is more than mockery to Dickens's response to feminist agitation: there is in *Bleak House* a sense of anxiety that approaches respect, and an imaginative concern with the movement of women" (21). From this perspective, Lady Dedlock's swoon is not a lapse into passive victimization, however much the plot may seem structured that way. It is a stirring into motion, analogous in many ways to Margaret Hale's effort to recover her strength. That the swoon itself is not directly seen by the reader implicates, as we have seen, Tulkinghorn's reaction as one of the central concerns of the scene. He, no less than Dickens, imposes on the events a narrative of male manipulation of a passive female victim, yet his pursuit of this narrative is strangely unconsummated and unsatisfying for him. His surprised acknowledgement of her independence points partly to the unreliability of the swoon as a sign of female nature. Sir Leicester's reaction— "I never knew my Lady swoon before"—is nearer the mark, not only as an assessment of his wife's nature, but also as an oblique judgement on the increasingly anomalous sight of the fainting woman in nineteenth-century literature.

NOTES

This article has benefited from the attention of several readers. I want especially to acknowledge the help of Patrick Kelly, Raymond Stephanson, Catherine Harland, Kristin Brady, and Lilian Thorpe.

1. Kate Flint's recent book *Dickens* (Brighton: Harvester, 1986) tries to re-orient the study of Dickens' women in this way. Acknowledging that the depictions of female nature in Dickens come as much from tradition as from personal experience, Flint goes on to find examples in Dickens of characters who, if anything, destabilize the norm, or force us to leave the notion of coherent character behind.

A similar case is argued in relation to Esther in particular by Suzanne Graver, in "Writing in a 'Womanly' Way and the Double Vision of *Bleak House*," *Dickens Quarterly* 4 (1987): 3–15.

2. In a recent article, Paul Pickrel does point out the centrality of Lady Dedlock to the structure of the plot, but argues for other sources of pattern in the novel, sources that tend to marginalize her. See Paul Pickrel, "*Bleak House*: The Emergence of Theme," *Nineteenth-Century Literature* 42 (1987): 73–96.

3. A similar tone is struck by George Eliot in her essay "Silly Novels by Lady Novelists," where she describes how the silly novel heroine's "fainting form reclines on the very best upholstery . . ." *Essays of George Eliot*, ed. Thomas Pinney (London: Routledge & Kegan Paul, 1963) 303.

4. A compelling reading of this scene can be found in Jean H. Hagstrum, *Sex and Sensibility: Ideal and Erotic Love from Milton to Mozart* (Chicago: U of Chicago P, 1980) 191ff.

5. Another model for a simple use of the device that suggests the situation in *Bleak House* is in Chapter 48 of Scott's *The Heart of Mid-Lothian*, where Effie Deans finds herself sharing a theatre box with the Duke of Argyle, who promptly tells the story of the woman accused of killing her illegitimate child, unaware that Effie is the very woman. As she relates the incident to her sister in a letter: "It was too much for me at last, Jeanie—I fainted; and my agony was imputed partly to the heat of the place, and partly to my extreme sensibility; and, hypocrite all over, I encouraged both opinions . . ." (London: Dent, 1956) 484.

6. According to the religious tradition invoked by Esther's aunt, a child conceived in sin is marked by that sin. Several critics have pointed out how Dickens' language and imagery assimilates both Lady Dedlock and Esther to a familiar pattern of sin, punishment, and redemption. See Barry Qualls, *The Secular Pilgrims of Victorian Fiction: The Novel as Book of Life* (Cambridge: Cambridge UP, 1982), esp. pp. 112–21, and Janet Larson, "The Battle of Biblical Books in Esther's Narrative," in *Nineteenth-Century Fiction* 38 (1983): 131–60. Michael Steig has demonstrated how this identification is reinforced by the novel's original illustrations. See his "The Iconography of the Hidden Face in *Bleak House*," *Dickens Studies* 4 (1968): 19–22, and his *Dickens and Phiz* (Bloomington: Indiana UP, 1978), 146ff.

7. For a discussion of the various ways in which the fallen woman is handled in the period, see George Watt, *The Fallen Woman in the Nineteenth-Century English Novel* (London: Croom Helm, 1984), and Sally Mitchell, *The Fallen Angel: Chastity, Class and Women's Reading, 1835–1880* (Bowling Green: Bowling Green U Popular P, 1981).

8. The most incisive commentary on these scenes can be found in Fred Kaplan's *Dickens and Mesmerism: The Hidden Springs of Fiction* (Princeton: Princeton UP, 1975), esp. Chapters 7 and 8.

9. Carey, 160. On the sexuality of Tulkinghorn, see Joseph I. Fradin, "Will and Society in *Bleak House*," *PMLA* 81 (1966): 95–109. Tulkinghorn and Bucket have a kind of parodic foil in Guppy, who is openly ambitious for sexual conquest, and hopes that the possession of secret knowledge will advance his cause with Esther. Though his sexual forays are ludicrously incompetent, he is nevertheless an important detective, in that his intervention brings mother and daughter together, and effectively gives Lady Dedlock time to rehearse her response to Tulkinghorn.

10. That the moral pilgrim aspect of the figure was uppermost in Gaskell's mind can be seen from a letter she wrote while composing this scene. In the letter she

describes the point she has reached in the story: "M H̀ has just told the lie, & is gathering herself up after her dead faint; very meek & stunned & humble." *The Letters of Mrs. Gaskell*, ed. J. A. V. Chapple & Arthur Pollard (Manchester: U of Manchester P, 1966) 310.

11. See also Laura Cloridge, "Tess: A Less than Pure Woman Ambivalently Presented", in *Texas Studies in Literature and Language,* 28 (Fall, 1986), pp. 324 – 38; and Penny Boumelha, *Thomas Hardy and Women: Sexual Ideology and Narrative form* (Madison: U of Wisconsin P) esp. pp. 117 – 134.

12. The earlier versions can be found in the notes at the bottom of pp. 100 – 101.

13. This is the sustaining argument throughout *Woman and the Demon.*See note 9 above.

WORKS CITED

Auerbach, Nina. *Woman and the Demon: the Life of a Victorian Myth.* Cambridge, MA: Harvard UP, 1982.

Austen, Jane. *The Works of Jane Austen.* London: Oxford University Press, 1954.

Austen, Jane. *Emma* in *The Novels of Jane Austen.* Oxford: Clarendon, 1926.

Brady, Kristin. "Tess and Alec: Rape or Seduction?" *Thomas Hardy Annual* 4 (1986): 127–47.

Carey, John. *The Violent Effigy: A Study of Dickens' Imagination.* London: Faber & Faber, 1973.

Dickens, Charles. *Dombey and Son.* Ed. Alan Horsman. Oxford: Clarendon, 1974.

———. *Bleak House.* Eds. George Ford and Sylvere Monod. New York: Norton, 1977.

———. *The Life and Adventures of Nicholas Nickleby.* Philadelphia: U of Pennsylvania P, 1982.

Eliot, George. *Essays of George Eliot.* Ed. Thomas Pinney. London: Routledge & Kegan Paul, 1963.

Flint, Kate. *Dickens.* Brighton: Harvester, 1986.

Fradin, Joseph I. "Will and Society in *Bleak House*" *PMLA* 81 (1966): 95–109.

Gaskell, Elizabeth, *North and South.* Oxford: Oxford UP, 1982.

———. *The Letters of Mrs. Gaskell.* Ed. J. A. V. Chapple and Arthur Pollard. Manchester: University of Manchester, 1966.

Graver, Suzanne. "Writing in a 'Womanly' Way and the Double Vision of *Bleak House*" *Dickens Quarterly* 4 (1987): 3–15.

Hagstrum, Jean H. *Sex and Sensibility: Ideal and Erotic Love from Milton to Mozart.* Chicago: U of Chicago P, 1980.

Hardy, Thomas. *Tess of the d'Urbervilles*. Ed. Juliet Grindle and Simon Gatrell. Oxford: Clarendon, 1983.

Moers, Ellen. *"Bleak House*: The Agitating Women." *Dickensian*, 69 (1973): 3–24.

Kaplan, Fred. *Dickens and Mesmerism: The Hidden Springs of Fiction*. Princeton: Princeton UP, 1975.

Larson, Janet. "The Battle of Biblical Books in Esther's Narrative." *Nineteenth-Century Fiction*, 38 (1983): 131–60.

Mitchell, Sally. *The Fallen Angel: Chastity Class and Women's Reading, 1835–1880*. Bowling Green: Bowling Green U Popular P, 1981.

Pickrel, Paul. "Bleak House: The Emergence of Theme," *Nineteenth-Century Literature*, 42 (1987): 73–96.

Qualls, Barry. *The Secular Pilgrims of Victorian Fiction: The Novel as Book of Life*. Cambridge: Cambridge UP, 1982.

Richardson, Samuel. *Pamela: or Virtue Rewarded*. New York: Norton, 1958.

Rose, Phyllis. *Parallel Lives: Five Victorian Marriages*. New York: Random House, 1983.

Rymer, James Malcolm. *Varney the Vampyre: or, The Feast of Blood*, Vol. 1. New York: Dover, 1972.

Scott, Sir Walter. *The Heart of Midlothian*. London: Dent, 1956.

Slater, Michael. *Dickens and Women*. London: Dent, 1983.

Steig, Michael. "The Iconography of the Hidden Face in *Bleak House"* *Dickens Studies Annual* 4 (1968): 19–22.

———. *Dickens and Phiz*. Bloomington: Indiana UP, 1978.

Stewart, Garret. *Death Sentences: Styles of Dying in British Fiction*. Cambridge, Ma: Harvard UP, 1984.

Swift, Jonathan. *Poetical Works*. Ed. Herbert Davis. London: Oxford UP, 1967.

Watt, George. *The Fallen Women in the Nineteenth-Century English Novel*. London: Croom Helm, 1984.

Wollstonecraft, Mary. *Vindication of the Rights of Women*. Harmondsworth: Penguin, 1975.

Social Criticism and Textual Subversion in *Little Dorrit*

Sylvia Manning

Little Dorrit proffers a deal of ideological discourse, some of it ironic explication in the service of the novel's satirical stance, such as the analysis of How Not To Do It, and some of it wholly solemn expostulation to the same moral purpose, such as the narrator's commentary on Little Dorrit's suggestion that, because her father has paid with his life, he should not also have to repay his debts in money. Apparently congruent with this discourse are the Christian ideology implicit in the tale and the ideology of the novel form itself, which is the epistemological ground for the moral implications.

The ideology implicit in the story is constituted of a collection of comforting, radical eventualities: that the good shall be rewarded, that the mighty shall be cast down, that the lame shall walk (Mrs. Clennam) and the blind see (Arthur Clennam), that the prodigal daughter shall return (Tattycoram). The more fundamental ideology of novelistic plot assumes or asserts that events mean and tend towards larger outcomes; that individual action and chance combine into narratable history; that there are beginnings and endings; that there come points at which it is possible to say, "This happened and it was good [or bad]."[1]

What I hope to show, however, is that the narrator's discourse is repeatedly undermined; the resulting contradictions constitute the ideology of the book, distinct from and less radical than the narrative stance. The ideology inherent in the conventions of narrative form, on the other hand, is also steadily undermined, but here the effect is to radicalize. These are the conventions that allow us to create meaning, believing that we are finding it, extracting it, not falsifying to reach it. As these are disrupted, the text presents the possibility of a world in which all we are really doing is circumlocuting. That prospect is truly frightening, and we can see its terror in the outrage of contemporary reviewers. The reviewers expressed two kinds of outrage: at the narrator's satire—one side of the book's constitutive ideological contradictions—and at the contraventions of form.

The narrator's comment on Little Dorrit's proposition occurs just at the end of Book 1, prior to the departure from the Marshalsea. Little Dorrit has asked Clennam if the debts must be paid from the newly inherited estate, he has said that they must, and she has responded that it seems unfair. The narrator comments:

> The prison, which could spoil so many things, had tainted Little Dorrit's mind no more than this. Engendered as the confusion was, in compassion for the poor prisoner, her father, it was the first speck Clennam had ever seen, it was the last speck Clennam ever saw, of the prison atmosphere upon her.
>
> (Book 1, chapter 35)

The narrative voice of that paragraph and the voice of Mrs. Merdle's parrot, which doesn't parrot but counterpoints its keeper, seem hardly a continuous sensibility, yet they are presented as on the same side of the novel's social critique. To overstate it somewhat, the problem is that the narrator, like the parrot, is supposed to be right. He is the moral center that calibrates the satiric universe represented: he exposes, excoriates, mocks, derides folly when it is pernicious, and laughs more kindly at it when it is harmless. Moreover, by this point in the novel he has established certain specific values and valuations. These include: that the system of imprisonment for debt is foolish; that wealth is hollow, self-serving, and greedy; and that the building of human relations on a cash nexus is abhorrent. Little Dorrit's notion that perhaps an extent of suffering might annul a cash bond may strike us as consistent with these values. If they do, the narrator's comment—the paragraph I just cited—comes like a slap. It tells us that cash relations are not to be confused or re-shaped by human suffering.

Worse yet, the notion of the prison's taint on Little Dorrit that the narrator introduces here will be picked up, and carried as something of a motif, by three not very admirable characters, most notably Fanny, but Mr. Dorrit and Tip as well. It is the taint of the prison that accounts in their minds for such failures as Amy's attempt to assist the fainting Pet Gowan directly rather than sending her maid. And Amy herself accepts the idea that it is her prison-taint that prevents her from enjoying the sights of Venice and Rome and the daily social round.

This association of the narrator with the targets of his own satire may suggest that the ideological position of the novel is not where the satirist-narrator would have us believe. For a more extended instance of the same problem, we may consider Arthur's bankrupting of Doyce by his investment in Merdle's enterprises. The moral tone that surrounds this episode is established by the elaborated (one might argue, belabored) metaphor of illness and contagion leading to this crux and conveys a narrative valuation that finds it right for Arthur to suffer imprisonment in consequence. By the time Arthur arrives as a prisoner at the Marshalsea, in fact, the essential stupidity of the system seems to have been forgotten. Within hours, Arthur begins to sink into moral lassitude:

> In the unnatural peace of having gone through the dreaded arrest, and got there,—the first change of feeling which the prison most commonly induced, and from which dangerous resting-place so many men had slipped to the depths of degradation and disgrace by so many ways— . . .   (Book 2, chapter 27)

"So many men" fall to degradation because they are weak and weary. The brief views we have of the inmates remind us that at the beginning of the story too, except for Amy and Plornish they were no better than they should be; they may not have deserved the prison, but they suit it. Arthur, we are told in Chapter 28 (Book 2), remains throughout his stay aloof from his fellow-prisoners; to be saved for a better end, he must be different. The note of stupidity is struck only further on, at the end of Chapter 32, when Mr. Casby pronounces, "Let him pay his debts and come out, come out; pay his debts, and come out."

Not only is there no protest against Arthur's incarceration, but something hallowing has begun to hover around this particular prison. When Rugg urges Arthur to take his opportunity to go to the King's Bench instead, Arthur declines (Book 2, Chapter 26). From the moment he reaches the Marshalsea, the aura of Little Dorrit supervenes. When she herself returns, the place becomes virtually sanctified. The scene is worth looking at. Arthur has fallen into a feverish state of dozing and dreaming, has become aware of a bouquet of flowers without being able to focus on how it got there, has attempted some movements but given up:

> When the first faintness consequent on having moved about had left him, he subsided into his former state. One of the night-tunes was playing in the wind, when the door of the room seemed to open to a light touch, and, after a moment's pause, a quiet figure seemed to stand there, with a black mantle on it. It seemed to draw the mantle off and drop it on the ground, and then it

seemed to be his Little Dorrit in her old, worn dress. It seemed to tremble, and
to clasp its hands, and to smile, and to burst into tears. (Book 2, chapter 29)

The string of *seemed*'s marks the ghostly benign, the mistiness of vague
religious feeling, something so much too good to be true that we and Arthur
alike must be brought to it through the mediating possibility that it is only a
dream. The passage continues in this vein. Within a paragraph Little Dorrit
is in Arthur's arms and he is exclaiming upon her and the beloved old dress.
The dress is important because it marks the restoration of a prior, somehow
more desirable, state. Lest we miss the point, Dickens provides a second
marker as Little Dorrit continues:

> "I hoped you would like me better in this dress than any other. I have always
> kept it by me, to remind me: though I wanted no reminding. I am not alone,
> you see. I have brought an old friend with me."
>   Looking round, he saw Maggy in her big cap which had been long abandoned,
> with a basket on her arm as in the bygone days, chuckling rapturously.

(Probability is utterly abandoned. If Amy kept the dress, we have to assume
a secret closet and a secret trunk, or what did her maid make of it? And she
kept it to remind herself, though she needed no reminding.) Like Amy, Maggy
has gotten herself up for the occasion—has as improbably retrieved the old
cap as Amy retrieved the old dress. Maggy has no role in this scene, unless
one can imagine Little Dorrit in need of a chaperone. Her function is to
emphasize the note of restoration.

Restoration of what? Of the days of innocence, in which a love like Amy's
and Arthur's could grow. Of the days before the Dorrits' fall to wealth and
Arthur's sins of speculation. For Little Dorrit and Arthur, the Marshalsea has
become a purgatory, a vale of suffering that will purify them for each other.
That is why Arthur holds to the notion, grotesque if viewed rationally, of
staying in the prison right up to the moment of his marriage. They must go
directly from the prison to the church, from purgatory to heaven. That Amy
was better off without her wealth fits the novel's satiric program, but that by
imprisonment Arthur is purged of his economic error and his soul brought to
recognize its mate, does not. It sits awkwardly with how the prison appears
to stand in the first part of the novel, as well as with the rest of the prison
metaphor as it is generally understood.

Yet the scene gets more complex. After Little Dorrit has hung the old
bonnet in the old place, after her modest head has bowed to sew a curtain for
his room, after they have sat hand in hand and one bright star has risen in

the sky, Little Dorrit offers Arthur her money to obtain his release. He responds with one of the most convoluted lover's speeches on record:

> "If, in the bygone days when this was your home and when this was your dress, I had understood myself (I speak only of myself) better, and had read the secrets of my own breast more distinctly; if, through my reserve and self-mistrust, I had discerned a light that I see brightly now when it has passed far away, and my weak footsteps can never overtake it; if I had then known, and told you that I loved and honoured you, not as the poor child I used to call you, but as a woman whose true hand would raise me high above myself and make me a far happier and better man; if I had so used the opportunity there is no recalling—as I wish I had. O I wish I had!—and if something had kept us apart then, when I was moderately thriving, and when you were poor; I might have met your noble offer of your fortune, dearest girl, with other words than these, and still have blushed to touch it. But, as it is, I must never touch it, never!"

He does not stop here, but it gets no more lucid. Though others might not, as I do, have difficulty sorting out the respectable arrangement between declaring love and accepting money, the precise nature of that arrangement is less important than the fact that there is one. The implication is that the banker's scales and scoop take human relationships and coin together, and that that is as it should be. The marriage of Arthur's and Little Dorrit's true minds is as subject to the impediments (and impulses) of cash as are the marriages of Gowan and Pet or Fanny and Edmund Sparkler. And just as with Gowan's and Pet's marriage, the enabling banker is Mr. Meagles, retired but still able to straighten out such affairs.

Compare Arthur's speech to another on the subject of love that can no longer be:

> "Ask me not . . . if I love him still or if he still loves me or what the end is to be or when, we are surrounded by watchful eyes and it may be that we are destined to pine asunder it may be never more to be reunited not a word not a breath not a look to betray us all must be secret as the tomb wonder not therefore that even if I should seem comparatively cold to Arthur or Arthur should seem comparatively cold to me we have fatal reasons it is enough if we understand them hush!"   (Book 1, chapter 24)

Flora may fail a test of syntax, but there is a level at which her values are closer to those the novel touts than what the narrative gives, with tacit admiration, to Arthur. The novel claims the moral ground that holds love and charity superior to the ledgers of cash transactions, but the truest exemplar of these values is Flora, fat and prolix in a world where the best are thin and laconic, her sentences running over as her flesh runs over, an object of laughter more harsh than affectionate. There is no contradiction here: Flora is a pariah because the narrative subscribes to love and charity but bows to proper relations and proper-ty. (Flora is incapable of taking proper tea: she eats too much and prefers the nip of the wrong beverage.)

Another derided female worth considering in this regard is Fanny. The following dialogue takes place on a tired afternoon in Venice. Fanny is speaking first:

> ". . . Come! Has it never struck you, Amy, that Pa is monstrously polite to Mrs. General."
>
> Amy, murmuring "No," looked quite confounded.
>
> "No; I dare say not. But he is," said Fanny. "He is, Amy. And remember my words. Mrs. General has designs on Pa!"
>
> "Dear Fanny, do you think it possible that Mrs. General has designs on any one?"
>
> "Do I think it possible?" retorted Fanny. "My love, I know it. I tell you she has designs on Pa. And more than that, I tell you Pa considers her such a wonder, such a paragon of accomplishment, and such an acquisition to our family, that he is ready to get himself into a state of perfect infatuation with her at any moment. And that opens a pretty picture of things, I hope? Think of me with Mrs. General for a Mama!"
>
> Little Dorrit did not reply, "Think of me with Mrs. General for a Mama;" but she looked anxious, and seriously inquired what had led Fanny to these conclusions.
>
> "Lord, my darling," said Fanny, tartly. "You might as well ask me how I know when a man is struck with myself! But of course I do know. It happens pretty often: but I always know it. I know this in much the same way, I suppose. At all events, I know it."   (Book 2, chapter 7)

Amy continues with a series of doubting questions: "You never heard Papa say anything?" "And you never heard Mrs. General say anything?" "At least, you may be mistaken, Fanny. Now, may you not?" Fanny treats these questions with increasing contempt, but we may note that the contempt is not merely characteristic but, in this instance, perhaps called for. Though the text directs our sympathy as usual away from Fanny and toward Amy, as with the notation of the retort Amy did *not* make ("Think of me with Mrs. General for a Mama"), the fact is that Fanny is right and Amy is obtuse.

The narrative takes Fanny's part in so far as it accepts the notion that it is wrong for Mrs. General to marry Mr. Dorrit. One might ask why. Does he deserve better? No. Would he be unhappy with her? No. What is wrong is that she aspires. She is absurd as Young John Chivery is absurd in his aspiration for Little Dorrit's hand. In both instances the laughter or disapproval is based upon notions of appropriate matches that are essentially the same as those that chafe the dowager Mrs. Gowan and reconcile Mr. Meagles in their children's marriage. The disjunction between the tone that continues to disparage Fanny as she discusses Mrs. General's aspirations and the narrative's sharing of her perspective upon them signals a moment of tension in the ideological strands of the novel. Although every moment at which we feel dissonance may not indicate such a point of tension, the points of tension all seem to carry some such surface sign.

This sort of ideological crux also attends Little Dorrit's reappearance in the Marshalsea wearing the old plain dress and the old bonnet. The moment was prepared at the close of Book 1, when Amy is carried out to the departing family coach in the arms of Clennam. The perspective is not the narrator's, but Fanny's:

> ''I do say,'' she repeated, ''this is perfectly infamous! Really almost enough, even at such a time as this, to make one wish one was dead! Here is that child Amy, in her ugly old shabby dress, which she was so obstinate about, Pa, which I over and over again begged and prayed her to change, and which she over and over again objected to, and promised to change today, saying she wished to wear it as long as ever she remained in there with you—which was absolutely romantic nonsense of the lowest kind—here is that child Amy disgracing us to the last moment and at the last moment, by being carried out in that dress after all.''

Amy's steadfastness to the dress, of course, is intended to display her rejection of the material values of the rest of her family and her steadfastness to—to what? To her love for her father, perhaps, to a life in which duty is harsh but clear, but could it be also to her own centrality, to stasis, to the familiar? Again the text directs our sympathy wholly to Little Dorrit, and again there remains some unacknowledged validity to Fanny's critique of ''romantic nonsense of the lowest kind.''

If we set aside that sense of Amy deserving criticism as too perverse a claim, we remain with the dress as a revered icon. The true and the good cling to the shabby dress, the superficial and vain glory in bright new clothes. Consistent with this iconography, Young John is presented setting out upon his ill-fated courtship:

> He was neatly attired in a plum-coloured coat, with as large a collar of black velvet as his figure could carry; a silken waistcoat, bedecked with golden sprigs; a chaste neckerchief much in vogue at that day, representing a preserve of lilac pheasants on a buff ground; pantaloons so highly decorated with side-stripes that each leg was a three-stringed lute; and a hat of state very high and hard. When the prudent Mrs. Chivery perceived that in addition to these adornments

her John carried a pair of white kid gloves, and a cane like a little finger-post, surmounted by an ivory hand marshalling him the way he should go; and when she saw him, in this heavy marching order, turn the corner to the right; she remarked to Mr. Chivery, who was at home at the time, that she thought she knew which way the wind blew.   (Book 1, chapter 18)

So far, so consistent. It turns out, however, that pretension is not the only unacceptable mode. Here are the people who offer services to the inhabitants of the Marshalsea:

The shabbiness of these attendants upon shabbiness, the poverty of these insolvent waiters upon insolvency, was a sight to see. Such threadbare coats and trousers, such fusty gowns and shawls, such squashed hats and bonnets, such boots and shoes, such umbrellas and walking-sticks, never were seen in Rag Fair. All of them wore the cast-off clothes of other men and women, were made up of patches and pieces of other people's individuality, and had no sartorial existence of their own proper. Their walk was the walk of a race apart.
                                                                (Book 1, chapter 9)

There is a curious problem in the clause ''were made up of patches and pieces of other people's individuality.'' The syntax of the sentence suggests that the three clauses are re-statements of one another: ''[1] All of them wore the cast-off clothes of other men and women, [2] were made up of patches and pieces of other people's individuality, and [3] had no sartorial existence of their own proper.'' The middle clause thus confirms brutally the synecdoche of the clothes for the person: if you wear other people's clothes you are made up of other people's individuality. Does the narrator—Dickens—anyone—really mean to imply that one's individuality resides in one's clothing? By the logic of this description, Fanny's plunge into a sea of fine clothing, first at the family's liberation, but again, more assertively still, upon her marriage, is the expression of her individuality, her sartorial existence to reflect her selfhood. Now we can patch at this fault. For one thing, we know from our sojourns in the Dickens world that what is probably wrong with the attendants' clothes is not that they are old and threadbare and second-hand, but that they are not neat. Were they neat, these would be a better class of people. (Amy's ''shabby dress . . . being so neat'' virtually enhances her ''delicately bent head, . . . tiny form, [and] . . . quick little pair of busy hands'' [Book I, Chapter 5]). But I think that for all our patching the fault will remain, and the telltale failure of tone is in the passage describing the shabby attendants. Beneath the fault is the tension between a simple moral philosophy of clothes and something that shares the dandyism of Young John. Perhaps after all what is wrong about his finery is not that it is finery but that he does not know how to do it right: the difference between a fop and a pretentious fop, not foppery itself.

The narrative commentary is marked by ideological bits that seem regularly to cross purpose with other explicit or implicit ideological stances in the text. Similar contradictions appear around ideological bits carried implicitly by the action. For example: as a moment of high drama, as a reprieve from punishment achieved through a sudden impulse of regard for her stepson or perhaps through the release of long-pent guilt, Mrs. Clennam rises from her chair and walks through the streets of London. The action carries, implicitly, a Christian note of renovation in the motif of the lame walking. In the upsweep of events rapidly moving to a close that must be triumphant for Arthur and Amy, we are likely to succumb to the sentimental gratification afforded by this miracle. Rigaud must be defeated and, since Mrs. Clennam has repented (albeit rather suddenly), and since Arthur so much wants her to love him, perhaps, too, she may be redeemed—and perhaps the walking is the sign of that redemption. Her meeting with Little Dorrit is so powerful an image that we are likely to forget, soon after the book is closed, that this redemption is short-lived. Mrs. Clennam gets to walk from her house to the Marshalsea, and back, but not further. What she has willed, the narrative puts aside: the trauma of the collapsing house sends her into a paralytic stroke. This novel is of sterner stuff than the sentimentality that inclines toward redemption. In a novel in which the last farthing of debt must be repaid, in which human suffering has no place in the ledgers of cash transactions, and in which strict properties govern the mingling of cash and love, Mrs. Clennam cannot go unpunished. The lame shall walk only if they deserve to.

Repeatedly, conflicting ideological bits undermine satiric or radical stances assumed by the narrative, revealing a text paradoxically enmeshed in the system it is trying to criticize. The novel's maneuvers within the ideology of plot may seem at first surprisingly different. The story presents two initial strands: the Dorrits in the Marshalsea and the somewhat amorphous mystery Arthur is trying to solve—or perhaps trying to find in order to solve. One might expect that the solution to Arthur's mystery would somehow be entwined with the liberation of Mr. Dorrit, especially since Little Dorrit's employment at Mrs. Clennam's tells us that she has something to do with Arthur's dilemma. One might expect so because this is a novel and the more because Dickens assures us that things will indeed be fully linked:

> And thus ever, by day and night, under the sun and under the stars, climbing
> the dusty hills and toiling along the weary plains, journeying by land and

journeying by sea, coming and going so strangely, to meet and to act and react on one another, move all we restless travellers through the pilgrimage of life.

—at the end of Chapter 2, and again in Chapter 15, at Mrs. Clennam's:

Strange, if the little sick-room fire were in effect a beacon fire, summoning some one, and that the most unlikely some one in the world, to the spot that *must* be come to. Strange, if the little sick-room light were in effect a watch-light, burning in that place every night until an appointed event should be watched out! Which of the vast multitude of travellers, under the sun and the stars, climbing the dusty hills, and toiling along the weary plains, journeying by land and journeying by sea, coming and going so strangely, to meet and to act and react on one another; which of the host may, with no suspicion of the journey's end, be travelling surely hither?

And more:

Time shall show us. The post of honour and the post of shame, the general's station and the drummer's, a peer's statue in Westminster Abbey and a seaman's hammock in the bosom of the deep, the mitre and the workhouse, the woolsack and the gallows, the throne and the guillotine—the travellers to all are on the great high road, but it has wonderful divergencies, and only Time shall show us whither each traveller is bound.

But it does not come out that way. Mr. Dorrit is freed by the solution of a very different mystery, which is of no broader interest at all. And the mystery surrounding Arthur is entirely moot as to any effect it might have or any action anyone might take, except perhaps that Mrs. Clennam owes Little Dorrit 1,000 guineas. The confusion of the denouement enforces an impression that all the threads are being pulled together, but if we pause to unravel the detail we see that the convergence is not there. The conventions of plot, that we very much expect Dickens to uphold and that are expressed in the passages I just quoted, require signification in the juxtaposition of events. At the end of *Little Dorrit* the story breaks loose from this ideology.

The divergence of the two plot strands—Arthur's mystery and Little Dorrit's story—may be further masked, or confused, by the forced joining of their two iconic figures, Amy and Mrs. Clennam. Rigaud is a savvy operator who has laid his last trap with great care. Yet, almost spontaneously, Mrs. Clennam fools him. She gets away, gets out, and foils his fail-safe stratagem by confronting Little Dorrit, while he sits smugly in the window-seat awaiting her return. Why does she succeed? Perhaps because it is so irrational a move that Rigaud cannot anticipate it. What she achieves is that she gets the box of papers back from Little Dorrit, who otherwise would have followed Rigaud's instructions and handed them over to Arthur, thus betraying his step-mother's perfidy to him. But for one thing, as Mr. Meagles figures out right away, there remain the originals of the papers, hidden somewhere but still liable to cause mischief (especially without Rigaud's death, a happy event Mrs. Clennam could not have expected). For another, her sudden passion for saving her living image before Arthur is dramatically out of character. She also intends to bring Amy back to the house to display to Rigaud that Amy is not an alternate customer for his blackmail, but this would serve only a purpose of driving down Rigaud's price, not of suppressing the story, which he would be quite capable of revealing out of sheer spite were his plans for profit spoiled.

What I suggest is happening here is that iconographic representation is deforming plot and character to its purposes, and that these purposes turn out to be the representation of the novel's—though not the narrator's—ideology. Here is the narrator's, a doctrine of right and wrong, of a figure of light and a figure in shade:

> In the softened light of the window, looking from the scene of her early trials to the shining sky, she [Little Dorrit] was not in stronger opposition to the black figure in the shade than the life and doctrine on which she rested were to that figure's history. It bent its head low again, and said not a word. It remained thus, until the first warning bell began to ring.

The warning bell stirs Mrs. Clennam to action, and she and Little Dorrit set off to the house. Dickens shifts to a language of reconciliation:

> It was one of those summer evenings when there is not greater darkness than a long twilight. The vista of street and bridge was plain to see, and the sky was serene and beautiful. People stood and sat at their doors, playing with children, and enjoying the evening; numbers were walking for air; the worry of the day had almost worried itself out, and few but themselves were hurried. As they crossed the bridge, the clear steeples of the many churches looked as if they had advanced out of the murk that usually enshrouded them, and come much nearer. The smoke that rose into the sky had lost its dingy hue and taken a brightness upon it. The beauties of the sunset had not faded from the long light films of cloud that lay at peace in the horizon. From a radiant centre, over the whole length and breadth of the tranquil firmament, great shoots of light streamed among the early stars, like signs of the blessed later covenant of peace and hope that changed the crown of thorns into a glory. (Book 2, Chapter 31)

Not a sentence of this paragraph fails to underline the point: peace returns as the lion and the lamb hasten through the streets together. It is not simply peace, however: the novel acknowledges the values of only one, only the figure of light, but it participates in both. Little Dorrit's life and doctrine have been woven of devotion, loyalty, generosity; so have the novel's. Mrs. Clennam's history has been one of strictly told ledgers, long-nurtured vengeance, smug self-righteousness; so has the novel's. The two come together not in the triumph of one but in an impure mixture, the inconsistent, contradictory compromises wrought of the constitutive tensions of a popular art.

Despite the discomfort of some early reviewers, notably Fitzjames Stephen,[2] the novel is not seditious because it attacks the Circumlocution Office. If it is seditious at all, it is because it refuses to develop properly. The background plot is close to chaos (prompting such aids to the reader as the Penguin edition's summary in Appendix A), the hints about roads of life converging do not pan out, and the ending does not reach closure. The description I just read of the streets as Little Dorrit and Mrs. Clennam return to the house has the sense of ending we recognize—but there are two chapters yet to go. Mrs. Clennam, Amy and Arthur alike seek rest, stability, resolution. Mrs. Clennam gets it in the punitive form of paralysis. What Amy and Arthur achieve finds no resonance in the world around them, natural or human. These are the last lines of the novel:

> They went quietly down into the roaring streets, inseparable and blessed; and as they passed along in sunshine and shade, the noisy and the eager, and the arrogant and the forward and the vain, fretted and chafed, and made their usual uproar.

The page goes blank, but it was not the falling note we expected. The story completes its break from the ideology of plot: having not quite brought action and chance into coherent history, it does not quite close. There are still lumps in the paste.

Within the two strands of the plot—Arthur's mystery and Little Dorrit's story—other strands are identified but not developed. Peter Brooks, following Benjamin, reminds us that "traditional storytelling [is] allied with travel, with the reports of those coming from afar, and with the marvellous" (155) because the narratable must be beyond the ordinary. Little Dorrit, however, presents the potential for plot in exotic places only to reject it. Flora, ever of literary sensibility, recognizes this locus for story as she urges Arthur to an account of his experience:

> "Oh good gracious me I hope you never kept yourself a bachelor so long on my account!" tittered Flora: "but of course you never did why should you, pray don't answer, I don't know where I'm running to, oh do tell me something about the Chinese ladies whether their eyes are really so long and narrow always putting me in mind of mother-of-pearl fish at cards and do they really wear tails

down their back and plaited too or is it only the men, and when they pull their
hair so very tight off their foreheads don't they hurt themselves, and why do
they stick little bells all over their bridges and temples and hats and things or
don't they really do it?'' Flora gave him another of her old glances. Instantly
she went on again, as if he had spoken in reply for some time.
   ''Then it's all true and they really do! good gracious Arthur!—pray excuse
me—old habit—Mr. Clennam far more proper—what a country to live in for
so long a time, and wet the climate ought to be and no doubt actually is, and
the sums of money that must be made by those two trades where everybody
carries them and hangs them everywhere, the little shoes too and the feet
screwed back in infancy is quite surprising, what a traveller you are!''

                                                          (Book 1, Chapter 13)

Arthur is no more capable of responding than he was the first time she paused
for breath, but the problem is not merely the impossibility of talking to Flora.
Whatever Arthur's exploits in China were, they are not narratable. They
seem, indeed, not to have had any bearing on him. The twenty years are a
blank, a void that closes when Arthur returns to London, to take up the
unchanged relationship with his mother in the unchanged house of his
childhood.

   Similarly, Daniel Doyce's experience abroad is not narratable. It offers one
paragraph of contrived contrast to the dominion of the Barnacles, and beyond
that only a place to get Doyce off to so Arthur can fail and back from so that
Arthur can be revived.

   One might argue, however, that the motif of travel is centered on neither
of these two but on the Dorrit family in Book 2. But what turns out to be
narratable in their experience is only the continuation of the internal family
dynamics that form the subject of Book 1. The purpose of their journey is to
tell a false tale, to efface the narrative of Book 1. The effect of their journey
is to return them unchanged to its starting-point: the futility is etched in the
pathos of Mr. Dorrit's reversion to the Marshalsea in his last conscious hours.
For the Dorrits, travel is just what Mr. Meagles, the inveterate traveller with
nothing to tell, who never learns a language and stares at all he meets (Book
I, Chapter 14), calls it: just ''trotting about the world,'' a deal of motion that
may serve purposes of various sorts, but not narration.

   The promises of a tightly-knit plot were made in the metaphor of journey,
and broken. The travels themselves do not produce narrative. And the sense
of non-ending, the failure of closure, arises in part from this. Dickens' metaphor of journey at this point seems almost perverse:

   They all gave place when the signing was done, and Little Dorrit and her
   husband walked out of the church alone. They paused for a moment on the

steps of the portico, looking at the fresh perspective of the street in the autumn morning sun's bright rays, and then went down.

The phrase "went down" is a bit odd, certainly neither obvious nor necessary. Dickens makes it the structural basis of his next, and final, paragraph:

> Went down into a modest life of usefulness and happiness. Went down to give a mother's care, in the fullness of time, to Fanny's neglected children no less than to their own, and to leave that lady going into Society for ever and a day. Went down to give a tender nurse and friend to Tip for some few years, who was never vexed by the great exactions he made of her in return for the riches he might have given her if he had ever had them, and who lovingly closed his eyes upon the Marshalsea and all its blighted fruits. They went quietly down into the roaring streets, inseparable and blessed; and as they passed along in sunshine and shade, the noisy and the eager, and the arrogant and the forward and the vain, fretted and chafed, and made their usual uproar.

At the beginning of the paragraph the "went down" is made figurative—"went down into a . . . life"—but at the end it is re-literalized—"went down into the roaring streets"—so that the novel concludes its length of unnarratable journeys with the start of another.

We realize now that the plot notion of significant journey has been parodied from the start. The same chapter (I,2) that concluded with the sentence I quoted earlier, of "journeying by land and journeying by sea, coming and going so strangely, to meet and to act and react on one another," offered first another version of this motif:

> "In our course through life we shall meet the people who are coming to meet us, from many strange places and by many strange roads, . . . and what it is set to us to do to them, and what it is set to them to do to us, will all be done."

This is the voice of Miss Wade, who, seeing Pet shrink at the ominous tone, pushes it further:

> ". . . you may be sure that there are men and women already on their road, who have their business to do with *you,* and who will do it. Of a certainty they will do it. They may be coming hundreds, thousands, of miles over the sea there; they may be close at hand now; they may be coming, for anything you know or anything you can do to prevent it, from the vilest sweepings of this very town."

There is a promise here—or threat—of a tightly knit narrative converging on Pet or her parents, and later some foreboding of its fulfillment when Rigaud attaches himself to Gowan, but nothing happens, except for the death of Gowan's dog.

In place of the journey as the source of narrative, the novel appears to offer the plot of knowing, the mystery plot with the pusillanimous Arthur at its center. To Clarence Barnacle, he is the man who "wants to know," and the tag fits even better Arthur's relation to his mother and their past than it does his efforts on behalf of Amy. What the two efforts share is ineffectuality: Arthur never gets anywhere against the Circumlocution Office and he also never gets to learn the secret of his past. The reader finds out at the end, and Little Dorrit comes to know some of it, but Arthur remains wholly ignorant. And when, at Little Dorrit's nuptial request, he burns the codicil, he does not know that he is destroying his last chance of knowing. His father's name is withheld even from the reader, resulting in the awkwardness of Jeremiah Flintwinch's repeated reference to him only as "Arthur's father" even in private conversation with Mrs. Clennam (Book I, Chapter 14). All this diminution of the hero for the sake of saving Mrs. Clennam's memory (a grace she hardly merits) and emphasizing Little Dorrit's selflessness (a virtue that hardly needs repetition). Arthur sees, at last but not too late, his love for Little Dorrit, but he never learns his own story. The blind shall see, but only partially. Yet, unlike Mrs. Clennam's walking, Arthur's sight is a gift he would seem to deserve. His frustration appears to be something that, like the disappearance of Cavalletto at the end, the novel does not recognize. It is not just a matter of Arthur's not knowing something; it is a matter of his being denied knowledge he was specifically seeking, including the fact that this turned out to be the knowledge of his own birth. The novel is eliding its derailment of a mystery plot it has trailed through eighteen numbers by substituting a chaotic, unrememberable, and altogether creaky tale of double Flintwinches, double mothers, and double wills.

What we are left with is one mystery—the origins of the Dorrits that connect them to the unclaimed estate—solved by Pancks but not worth knowing (and not told to us), and another mostly known to us but not to the would-be detective hero. The novel has foiled our expectations for mystery as for adventure, expectations derived from our indoctrination in the ideology of nineteenth-century novelistic plot, from our belief in beginnings and endings. But it has done so so subtly, and surrounded its reversals with so much distraction, that we may not notice. We may be conscious not of a novel that subverts the conventions of its own form, but of the structures and statements that indicate continuity with those conventions: yet if we are true believers, we feel somehow uncomfortable, a sense of something amiss.

Dickens' contemporaries, undisturbed by the antics of the twentieth-century novel, were very much true believers, and to boot were equally agnostic of Dickens' infallibility. Listen, then, to the howl of pain from one reviewer, E. B. Hanley, writing for *Blackwood's* for April, 1857, with only sixteen numbers of *Little Dorrit* published (as though he could not wait):

> Even if, in the few remaining numbers, the joints of the story should be tightened up, and the different parts of the machinery made to work in something like harmony, yet that would not now retrieve the character of so aimless a work. A most cumbrous array of characters and scenes has been set in motion, and all for what?
>
> Absolutely, the only event yet described which can be called a leading incident, is the deliverance of old Dorrit from the Marshalsea. And how is this brought about? Not by any cause with which any of the characters are even remotely connected, but by the extremely probable circumstance, accidentally discovered, that the old gentleman, after a captivity of twenty years or so, has been all the time the right heir of the great estates of the "Dorrits of Dorsetshire," of which distinguished family we then hear for the first time. We would pardon this violent wrench in the story if the dislocation produced any interesting results, but the contrary is the case; for, whereas old Dorrit was, in his character of Father of the Marshalsea, the best-drawn personage and the most interesting study (we might really say the only one of any value) in the book, he becomes, in his accession to wealth, a prosy old driveller, whose inanities are paraded and circumstantially described in a long succession of twaddle, till the favorable impression made in his former phase is quite effaced before his decease, which happily took place in the last number, and which, to all appearance, might just as well have occurred a long time ago. There is positively no dramatic result whatever from the marvellous convulsion in the fortunes of the Dorrit family up to the old gentleman's decease, except that one of his daughters is married to a Mr. Sparkler, one of the amateur idiots of the book, who is the stepson of the great speculator, Mr. Merdle, another of the amateur idiots of the book.
>
> The fortunes of the Clennam family, occupying as they do a space nearly as large as those of the Dorrits, would, by an artistic writer, have been so interwoven that the opposing or blending interests should have elicited character and sustained curiosity; yet four-fifths of the book have elapsed without any connection being even hinted at, except that Little Dorrit came to work as a seemstress for Mrs. Clennam, without any result whatsoever, except that young Clennam noticed her peculiarity of taking home some of her dinner instead of eating it, and Mrs. Clennam (a most unpleasant old image, that sits always bolt upright in a wheeled chair like some grim heathen deity, and habitually talks in the most unchristian manner) once relaxes from her stony sourness so far as to kiss her. There is some hint of some influence that some Clennam may have had formerly on the fate of old Dorrit, but so obscure and shadowy as to induce the reader to believe that the author had not made up his mind as to what it should turn out to be, and was, therefore, anxious not to commit himself—a blemish that might injure a much better work than this. Meantime the Clennam household have experienced no vicissitudes, and are exactlty where they were

in the first number. Then there is the Meagles family, whose fortunes, whatever they may be, are totally distinct, so far, from the Dorrits and the Clennams, and have experienced only one change—viz., that the daughter, whose courtship was in progress when the book began, is now married, and has an addition to her family. The Casbys are *in statu quo*. A murderer and a smuggler, who were introduced at the beginning, in prison together, in a scene well calculated to excite attention, have done nothing in any way worthy of their formidable antecedents.

Unhampered by notions of Dickens' necessary excellence, Hanley is free to find fault (and he finds much more than what I quoted); deeply and unself-consciously committed to the ideology of novelistic form, he is sensitive to and outraged by the novel's contraventions of it. He points them out more thoroughly and succinctly than I have done, albeit with a very different understanding of the phenomenon. It is significant that he was not alone. The *Saturday Review*, for example, attacked *Little Dorrit* repeatedly. Here is an excerpt from July, 1857, probably by Fitzjames Stephen:

As far as we can judge he wrote *Little Dorrit*, month by month, at haphazard, without ever having sketched out a plan, and failed in executing his conceptions. He invests his characters with mystery, which he quite fails in clearing up. He suggests complications which involve nothing, and secrets which all end in no meaning. He hints at difficulties which are never unravelled, and we flounder on to the six hundredth page expecting to find a discovery when there is nothing to discover. Either idleness or inability compels him to abandon his characters with the unsatisfactory conclusion that they had no story to tell. Mrs. Clennam's house is haunted by some ghostly mystery—the weird old woman has some impenetrable secret—horrid anticipations of coming doom are in the garrets above and in the cellars below. Will Mr. Dickens assure us that the fall of the house in Tottenham-court road was not a happy solution to a difficulty which he had not the skill to disentangle? Does he ask us to believe that, when he first introduced us to the old house in the City at p. 23, he foresaw the very prosaic catastrophe of its fall at p. 600? Are we to understand that all Affery's horrors were meant to be resolved into the every-day phenomena of dry rot?

Then take Miss Wade. It is plain that the author intended to connect her former history with the other characters. He throws out hints and suggestions of some such relation between her and old Casby; but it all comes to nothing. . . . So again with Tattycoram. It is impossible to believe that the parentage of a foundling was not intended to be developed and woven into the plot. . . . Blandois, too, and Mr. and Mrs. Gowan—was it not meant that the future of the latter and the antecedents of the first should be connected with the drama of the tale?

In other words, the artistic fault of *Little Dorrit* is that it is not a tale. It neither begins nor ends—it has no central interest, no legitimate catastrophe, and no modelling of the plot into a whole. (15–16)

No beginning, no ending, and false directions throughout the long middle.

While reviewers worried about the British body politic fumed at the novel's satiric agenda, reviewers who cared for the experience of the novel were beside themselves at this one's disruption of their expectations. (Sometimes these were the same person.)

One could respond to the argument I have just made by saying that all it tells us is what we have long known, that the novel is another loose, baggy monster. One could support such a response with an analysis of another plot strand that does not develop: the Clennam/Pet Meagles/Gowan triangle. Here we have the beloved, the lover, the rival, and the father inclined towards the lover. Something should happen. Nothing does. The beloved marries the rival and they live unhappily ever after. The lover's fixation on this beloved blocks for a while, perhaps, his recognition of another love, but it is neither the sole nor the central cause of the blocking. Nor is there any suggestion that the second love is truer, as for instance in *David Copperfield* Agnes is truer than Dora. In the end, the romantic triangle turns out not to have much to do with anything, except possibly for those of us who harbor the undoubtedly inappropriate thought that a marriage between Arthur and Pet (achieved, say, through Rigaud's murder of Gowan) would be a lot healthier than his marriage with Little Dorrit. Little Dorrit becomes for Arthur at once child and mother, both endearing relations but, for the conventional among us, not comfortably joined with marital consummation. At this point, the road of our argument branches, and we may choose. Down one path lies the simple explanation, loose baggy monster. Down the other, the recognition of the fit between the odd-course development of this strand of plot and Dickens' recurrent circling around themes of incest and adolescent female sexuality. On this path we find numerous images compatible with a conventional ideology of love and marriage—Flora (fat women do not marry, or, frustrated women grow fat); Mr. F's aunt (the irreducible hatefulness of spinsters, distilled to an essence); Miss Wade (the dangers of uncontained female friendship); Minnie Gowan (the penance of a society-marriage); the Plornishes and the Chiverys (the silliness of the lower class); Fanny Dorrit (the emptiness of a society-marriage); and more—numerous images compatible with a conventional ideology of love and marriage surrounding, one might say obfuscating, a plot line that supports the unspeakable.

The secret of Arthur's birth and his father's will is a secret of sexuality. It may be that Arthur could not solve this mystery—or even learn what it was—for the same reason that the narrative obscures the nature of his relationship with Little Dorrit. On the fateful night at his lodgings, Arthur suggests that he call her "Little Dorrit":

"Thank you, sir, I should like it better than any name."
"Little Dorrit."
"Little mother," Maggy (who had been falling asleep) put in, as a correction.
"It's all the same, Maggy," returned Little Dorrit, "all the same."
(Book I, chapter 14)

Amy, "my child," whose womanhood shocks a prostitute, Amy the "little mother" who slips into her old place beside her father, beside Arthur: to love Amy is another way to keep the secret of human sexuality, as is to make hers the highest form of marriage. For both Arthur and the narrative, Amy is at once the medium of sexual denial and the locus of forbidden sexual impulse.

At this point of tension more than others one can perhaps see why Dickens does not follow through. This is a novel full of stories that do not get told: mysteries unsolved or unexplained, journeys unnarrated, romances unprecipitated. The undeveloped romance may demonstrate most clearly the connection between these deflections of narrative and the ideological contradictions. The novel represents the contradictions but cannot explain them: hence not only deflections, but confusions, doublings, and disruptions.

The novel's subversions of plot are not visible enough to show as radical and probably are not conscious. In contrast, where the novel presents itself as radical, in its professed ideological stances, it cannot hold position: it slips back, here and there, into the system it condemns. The contrast, however, is specious. What happens with the ideological issues I have looked at—debt, love, imprisonment, clothing—is confluent with the novel's disruptions of form and the ideological tenor of that form. It may seem that with one set the orthodox is undermining the radical and with the other the radical is deflecting the orthodox, but aside from the fact that radical and orthodox are matters of perspective, what is upsetting what matters less than the continuous process of upset. The continuous process of upset raises the spectre of indeterminacy—not of the text, but of the world implied by the text. The world has too much meaning to allow coherent interpretation, single vision, moral certainty, or neat plotting.

In psychoanalytic terms, one might understand the indeterminacy as defense, an obfuscation designed to repress, or at any rate to deflect, what Dickens does not wish to confront directly. If one were to apply such a reading more broadly, in terms not of the author but of the culture, one might argue that what the novel reveals is a society caught between what it cannot face and what it projects in consequence of this denial. More simply, one might educe the threat of indeterminacy as it stalks the novel, within the novel's own tropes.

In the face of indeterminacy, the entire novel may be circumlocution. Thus the Circumlocution Office becomes an (unintended) figure of the novel itself. At the Circumlocution Office, as at the novel, you can ask and ask, but you cannot know. Like the novel, the Circumlocution Office is concerned to perpetuate itself, by stringing out its business as long as possible. In the Circumlocution Office secrets are buried, information is obscured, and in consequence an endless flow of language—most of it on paper—is generated. So, too, in the novel. The Circumlocution Office battens on disorder, the frustration of inquiry and the inconclusion of enterprise. The Circumlocution Office, the novel, and Flora all take their fecundity from their incoherence: their actions fail to culminate in shapely outcomes, they evade beginnings and endings.

It may be that all any of us can do is circumlocute. That threat arises not from the Circumlocution Office as a satire upon British government, but from its emblematic relation to the novel's plot and the plot's contraventions of novelistic expectation. These provoked the deepest cries of pain from contemporary reviewers, and may continue to trouble us even today, when we are probably as smug about our superiority to the satire as Fitzjames Stephen was about its targets.

NOTES

1. In *Resisting Novels: Ideology and Fiction* (1987), Leonard Davis spends a full chapter (12% of a text to which I am much indebted) explaining what he means by ideology. At the end, he concludes that he uses the word in three "general and overlapping ways":
   - "a system of beliefs of a particular group or class"
   - "false ideas or false consciousness"
   - "the general cultural system for the creation of signs and meanings" (p. 51)
   I will use the word here principally in Davis's first sense, somewhat in his third, and not at all in his second. That is, to some extent as "the general cultural system for the creation of signs and meanings," but mainly as "a system of beliefs of a particular group or class."
2. See "Mr. Dickens as Politician," *Saturday Review*, 3 (January, 1857), 8–9.

WORKS CITED

Anonymous. "Little Dorrit." *Saturday Review* 4 (July 1857): 15–16.

Brooks, Peter. *Reading for the Plot.*

Davis, Leonard. *Resisting Novels: Ideology and Fiction.*

Dickens, Charles. *Little Dorrit*. London: Penguin Classics, 1967.

Hanley, E. B. "Little Dorrit." *Blackwood's Magazine* 52 (April 1857).

Stephen, Fitzjames. "Mr. Dickens as Politician." *Saturday Review* 3 (January, 1857): 8–9.

Sentiment and Resentment in *Great Expectations*

Brian Cheadle

When Pip sheds tears on catching the coach for London without Joe to see him off, Dickens comments (for the author and the mature Pip are indistinguishable at such sententious moments), "Heaven knows we need never be ashamed of our tears, for they are rain upon the blinding dust of earth, overlaying our hard hearts" (186). The remark sums up a belief in the moral efficacy of demonstrative sentiment that was one of the central premises of Dickens' practice as a novelist.[1] But Pip's tears fail to issue in appropriate moral action: indeed the passage is tinged with the suggestion that, if anything, they are part of the self-swindling mechanism that helps to inhibit the young Pip from effecting "a better parting"—like the reflection he indulges in the early stages of the journey, "for [his] comfort," that it would still be "quite practical to get down and walk back." Thus it is hard not to find irony in the ensuing phrase "I was better after I had cried, than before," for all that "better" is quickly (too quickly) glossed in moral terms as "more sorry, more aware of my own ingratitude, more gentle."

Such reflections bear out Michael Bell's argument in *The Sentiment of Reality* that there is a "tension or instability at the heart of the whole ethical enterprise of sentimentalism." Bell locates the instability, however, not in the gap between feeling and action, but in the ambiguities of sentiment itself, recalling that feeling and principle have traditionally been thought of as at odds in the moral life. Fred Kaplan acknowledges a further aspect of the instability in *Sacred Tears* when he points out that "characters like Jingle, Monk, Ralph Nickleby, Quilp, Carker, Heep, Orlick and Silas Wegg have moral sentiments to such a negligible degree that they challenge the assumption that moral sentiment is an innate human quality" (63). Unstable mixes can be richly volatile, however, and this is particularly true of *Great Expectations*, a novel far from the moral optimism which produced the "ideal and incorruptible innocence" of Oliver Twist and the open-heartedness of Nicholas Nickleby (Marcos 80). For *Great Expectations*, shadowed as it is by the dark anatomies of society and its ills, *Bleak House* and *Little Dorrit*, is the book in which Dickens struggles to reconcile his belief in the morality of sentiment with his ever more despairing analysis of class society. But it is also the book in which his deepening sense of the complexities of human impulses leads him to explore most fully the relationship between the impulses of moral sentiment and feelings of resentment—seemingly antonymic propensities of the heart.

1

Unlike its predecessor *David Copperfield*, *Great Expectations* is virtually a novel without a villain. Compeyson, the "evil genius" whose machinations are the temporal origins of the plot, remains a shadowy figure, appropriately muffled up when he lurks in the coastguards' boat (419). Drummle, for all the murderous potential which Jaggers recognizes in him, goes no further than beating, and does that offstage; and Orlick has an intriguing yet seemingly peripheral role. Nevertheless Orlick would seem the quintessential example of resentful villainy. Not only is he presented as slouching locomotively "Like Cain, or the Wandering Jew," but when accosted he looks up "in a half resentful, half puzzled way" as though the interruption were "injurious" (140). It is as though he resents the intercourse which being human entails, much as Rogue Riderhood is seen to be in "an uncommonly sulky state" when recovered from drowning (508). Drummle seems *equally* resentful of life itself. He strikes Pip as "so sulky a figure that he even took up a book as if its author had done him an injury"—hardly a reaction which would endear anyone to Dickens (225); and at Jaggers's dinner, when Startop shines as a "lively bright young fellow," Drummle seems to resent him as a direct personal affront" (238).

The book's emotional economy sets these two figures in opposition to Pip as the unfavored rivals for Biddy and Estella.[2] At the same time, the quite explicit alignment of Drummle and Orlick indicates the full social spread of resentment.[3] Orlick is resentful because he has to have truck with a world in which all are above him, and his rancor issues as the destructive brutality of a nature almost too weak to be amenable to nurture; Drummle is resentful because, though he is the next heir but one to a baronetcy and in his own eyes "one of the elect," his social superiority does not automatically accord him personal superiority and universal deference (215).

But if these two characters represent the social extremes of resentful reactiveness, the intervening social ranges are a stamping ground equally favorable to it. Mrs. Joe is a striking enbodiment of a more strictly Nietszchean *ressentiment*. The crucial passages of *On the Genealogy of Morals* afford the sense of the systematic repression by the weak of feelings such as envy, rage, and revenge towards those who make them feel insignificant, and their negation of everything other in order to arrogate to themselves a dubious merit and strength.[4] Max Scheler in his phenomenological reduction of Nietzsche's ideas argues that it is not Christian values but bourgeois morality that is at the roots of the ethic of *ressentiment*, in that it is pre-eminently in societies where social mobility has become possible that individuals assiduously compare their lot with that of other members of their own and of higher strata; and Scheler suggests that *ressentiment* will flourish, in particular, among the lower middle classes (*Ressentiment* 56, 66). The termagant Mrs. Joe, who opens her parlour and unwraps her ornaments from their "cool haze of silver paper" only for Christmas dinner (54), vies with Mrs. Wilfer of *Our Mutual Friend* in epitomizing this phenomenon, and such characters embody Dickens' understanding that the snobbery of the shabby-genteel and their slavish pursuit of what respectability demands is really the mark of an aggrieved envy of anything in life that is more generous, more gifted, and less self-regarding than themselves. Mrs. Joe's frustrated social pretensions are all the more acute in that she has to suffer the additional affront of being married to a blacksmith. She bears her apron bravely, however, stuck full of pins like a domestic St. Sebastian; and her suppressed rage finds its outlet in bringing Pip up "by hand," a further infliction, which she parades as the ultimate mark of her goodness. Her self-abasement before Orlick is a cruelly grotesque pillorying of the pretension of the weak to find a virtue in submission,[5] with the beater becoming cringer; and her fear of true strength is most clearly seen in Joe's wary admission that "she a'nt over partial . . . to my being a scholar for fear I might rise. Like a sort of rebel, don't you see" (79). It is Pip, even more than Joe, who suffers from this lack of partiality. Moreover, the eagerness of Mrs. Joe and her set to castigate Pip as "naterally wicious" is an even sharper reflex of resentment, for it comes across as obscurely reactive to Pip's innate potential for moral good (57). In such ways Mrs. Joe is made to mirror and indeed to epitomize the strength of bourgeois *ressentiment* in Victorian society.

Orlick, Drummle, and Mrs. Joe, the characters set against Pip, thus encompass the full social range of resentment, and provide an insight into the ways in which it comes to pervade a class society which has grown self-consciously aware of its divisions.[6] By ranging this trio of resentful characters against Pip, the moral hero, Dickens makes it clear that Pip's true antagonist is Victorian class society itself. At the same time, there is nothing of a mechanical demonstration in this alignment, for the characters remain profoundly convincing at the psychological level. Indeed nothing is more characteristic of Dickens' genius than his uncanny ability to create relationships that are simultaneously social epitomes and conduits to psychic depths.

Much of the straightforward interest of the novel, however, is in the spectacle of Pip's heart becoming first hardened and then once again opened to moral sentiment, as he struggles to come to grips with the antagonistic world that surrounds him. The broad process of his decline hardly needs to be recounted: his falling under the sway of great expectations (a "secret dream"[7] endemic to this society and even at best only a step away from the resentful sense that life owes one something); and his accession to class-consciousness when Estella dazzles him and pours shame on his coarse and common life. But the specific mechanism of Pip's fall is worth dwelling on. His all too human talent for self-swindling is laid bare from the very first tellingly crafted parenthesis in which he initiates the habit of repressing everything that he does not want to know: "I thought I overheard Miss Havisham answer—only it seemed so unlikely— 'Well? You can break his heart' " (89). More pertinent, however, is the crucial role played by resentment in the process of self-swindling, for the start of Pip's moral decline is most clearly signalled (perhaps too clearly signalled) in the scene in which he transforms his guilty awareness of the inadequacy of his feelings towards Joe into resentment at the fact that Biddy upbraids him for his attitude. The scene in question and a prelusive earlier one with Biddy are among the most pointed in the novel. In the first, Pip slips into his "lunatic confession" to Biddy that he wants to be a gentleman on account of the "beautiful young lady at Miss Havisham's" (156), at which Biddy astutely draws attention to the mingling of infatuation and a resentful desire to "spite" Estella in Pip's new aspiration. What is most telling here, however, is the way that Pip's tears of frustration serve only to fuel a smart that relieves itself by generalizing the resentment, leaving him in an Orlick-like state of feeling "vaguely convinced that [he] was very much ill-used by somebody, or by everybody" (157). The second scene, after Pip's great expectations have been declared, is that in which he voices his embarrassment with Joe's "learning and his manners" (175). Indignantly, for it is now Joe and not herself who is being slighted, Biddy informs Pip that Joe would be too proud to want to change himself. Pip's only aggrieved recoursse is to project his own resentment into her reaction: "You are envious, Biddy, and grudging. You are dissatisfied on account of my rise in fortune, and you can't help showing it. . . . It's a—it's a bad side of human nature" (176). Pip finds this so satisfying a formula for evading criticism that he hides behind it again when Biddy once more confronts him after he has at last returned to the forge for Mrs. Joe's funeral. For Pip is an avid learner, and these reactions show that he is well on the way to acquiring what Lionel Trilling in his essay on *Little Dorrit* calls, without directly invoking Nietzsche, "the great modern strategy of being the insulted and injured," deployed by those for whom "the will to status" is the ruling faculty (Trilling 58).[8]

Though Pip might seem to be readily submissive to the dominant discourse of his society, he is also quick to blame himself for everything that occurs. It is tempting to ascribe *both* these propensities in Pip to the fact that his upbringing and his earliest experiences have left him crippled by guilt.[9] Having formulated it in that way it is easy to write off the book's concern with moral sentiment as the relic of an outworn essentialism in which individuals are still conceived of as free moral agents, without pausing to reflect that there is something equally essentialist and equally unprovable in the much more fashionable view that our lives are decisively determined by the discourses of power in which we are enmeshed. But such a view of Pip too glibly elides his eagerness to rise with his reservations about rising; and it can be sustained only by keeping at a convenient distance from much of the detail. For there is a clear *gap* between the "guilt" that Pip is made to feel in his youth and the social shame that undermines him in the period of his great expectations. The "guilty" Pip of the early chapters is not submissive, but innately adept at the resistance which the novel's discourse endorses and which is the means of constituting him as an individual: he is, for example, spurred into the moral judgment that his elders find the prospect of convict-hunting on the moors "a terrible good sauce for a dinner," and he finds solidarity with Joe's natural compassion for Magwitch (64).

Indeed the proper verdict on the young Pip is *not* that he is guilty (particularly as his guilty reactions are presented in comic terms), but on the contrary that his moral sentiments are far finer than those of all around him, save Joe. This fineness of feeling is epitomized in the initiating incident of the central action—his spontaneous kindness towards the convict after he has returned to him with the file and "wittles." The young Pip's compassion for the convict might seem inseparable from self pity, as the whole strategy of the opening sequence is to establish an identity between the young boy, reduced to a "small bundle of shivers growing afraid of it all and beginning to cry", and the shivering, fearful convict with a click in his throat (36). But it is no more a part of Dickens' intention to suggest that the capacity for moral sentiment is peculiarly related to self-regarding weakness than it is to suggest that Pip is crippled by guilt; for Pip does not think of his own plight when he sees the convict shivering and ravening down his food like a dog, but of the extremity of the convict's need which he is so avidly sating. For all that Pip's expression of kindness is facilitated by his own intense experience of desolation, it is to be seen as an imaginative projection into the experience of the other; and it is in this sense that the book presents moral feeling as innate. For Pip's "innate" goodness is not the result of a mysterious sanctification, as is the case with Oliver Twist, but a function of his essentially imaginative capacity to engage with the feelings of others. The unself-regarding quality of this imaginative reaction is best understood by recognizing that when Pip is moved to say "I am glad you enjoy it" (50), he is rising above the natural temptation to feel resentment and is in effect saying, "I want you to know that I bear you no grudge, neither for the terror you induced in me nor for the thieving you have involved me in."

But in addition to proving himself capable of generous impulse, the young Pip actively resents being treated as though he were "naterally wicious"; and Dickens shows this to be the other half of moral growth. It is one of the complexities of Dickens' treatment of resentment that he recognizes it as having a strongly positive aspect; and the one continuity that he insists on between the young Pip and the Pip shamed by Estella is not his guilt, but rather the resentful "smart" of injustice which wrings tears of frustration and anger from him when Estella feeds him like a dog. The import of Pip's delaying his reaction to Estella's treatment of him until she can no longer see him is not that guilt has made him "morally timid" but that his unjust upbringing has made him *both* "morally timid" and "very sensitive" to injustice (92). Herbert stresses precisely this feature of Pip's nature when he describes him as "a good fellow, with impetuosity and hesitation . . . curiously mixed" (269); and it is this mix that is the source of Pip's interminable, and redemptive, quarrel with himself.

Dickens suggests then that Pip's conscience is sharpened on an early resentment of injustice, as is Pip's later sense that his is an unjust society. On the other hand, throughout the novel, and not only in his insistence that resentment is a crucial psychological ingredient in Pip's process of self-swindling,

Dickens insists on the vulnerability of moral impulses to the workings of resentment. Thus Magwitch's reckless gratitude becomes tainted by his class resentment of Compeyson and by the desire for revenge on those who have spurned him; and Miss Havisham's generous compassion for the young Estella becomes almost wholly corrupted by her "wild resentment" in a similar way (411), until, like that of Mrs. Clennam, it becomes a will to power that desires to master the very capacities for growth and responsive feeling. It is tempting to feel that the ambivalences of resentment might be clarified by drawing a distinction between legitimate, overt resentment of injustice, and *ressentiment*; but the lines are not so clearly drawn, for though Magwitch's resentment of Compeyson is overt enough, and justifiable, it colors his actions in a most unfortunate way. This propensity is made most appallingly clear, one might add, in Madame Defarge; for when resentment of injustice becomes all-encompassing it turns into a fanatical hatred that can function only destructively.

Dickens' own experiences, it would seem, had indicated the contrary possibility of a creative transfiguration of resentment. The climax of the Blacking Warehouse fragment is an extraordinary sentence: "I do not write resentfully or angrily: for I know how all these things have worked together to make me what I am" (Forster I: 23–24). The first half of that claim chimes dubiously, for all that it takes its self-congratulatory stand very definitely in the present; yet who can doubt Dickens' insight into the sources of his art, including the implicit acknowledgment that resentment and anger were among the powerful impulses that had come together in fostering his creative self.

2

Pip's final moral triumph depends precisely on overcoming his resentment that the returned convict should be "strongly attached" to him (357). Pip's first reception of Magwitch at his London lodgings is characterized by a puzzled courtesy, and there is a tinge of finer sentiment when, on realizing that the man has tears in his eyes, he feels somewhat ashamed of trying to be rid of him so speedily: "I had remained standing, not to disguise that I wished him gone. But I was softened by the softened aspect of the man, and felt a touch of reproach" (335). Even in the very first moments though, when Magwitch stands with hands outstretched, it is significant that Pip should have "resented the sort of bright and gratified recognition that still shone in his face . . . resented it because it seemed to imply that he expected me to respond to it'' (332). The insight that there is a strong human tendency to resist being pushed towards an emotional response is apt enough, but the point to stress is that it is only *after* Magwitch's full revelation that Pip's emotional recoil takes the extreme form of ''abhorrence . . . dread . . . repugnance . . . as though from a terrible beast'' (337). Proper allowance for the unsavoriness of Magwitch's appearance, and for the greater offensiveness of his ''admiring proprietorship'' (340), should not obscure the fact that what ultimately appalls Pip is the momral demand now made on him. The point is rubbed home by a whole run of subsequent comments of which the most anguished is perhaps his shuddering admission to Herbert, ''Yet I am afraid the dreadful truth is, Herbert, that he is attached to me, strongly attached to me. Was there ever such a fate!'' (357). The dreadful thing that Pip resents is not that he should hae been deceived in his great expectations, not that his fortune will have to be forfeited, not that Estella is not destined for him, not even the anguished recognition that it was for this that he deserted Joe, but rather the insistent knowledge that Magwitch is making a binding emotional claim on him.

Beyond its personal fatefulness for Pip, the reappearance of the outcast Magwitch represents, in terms of the book's social scheme, the return of the repressed truths that bourgeois society tries to forget. The achievement of the transported convict in making a gentleman out of Pip has brought out the arbitrariness of the distinction between ''high'' and ''low'' on which class divisions depend; and his return is an unpleasant reminder that the idleness and prosperity of the privileged classes are wholly dependent on the labor of others. Magwitch, however, has presumed not only to create, but also to ''own,'' a gentleman; a presumption which throws an interesting light on the bourgeois annexation of the gentlemanly ideal. The often-glossed passage that concentrates the ''impious'' nature of the convict's return in the image of Frankenstein is no less remarkable for its image of the Exhibitor, which makes it grotesquely apparent just how freakish and marginalized the values and accomplishments of a gentleman have become in this commercialized society:

> He would ask me to read to him— ''Foreign language, dear boy!'' While I complied, he, not comprehending a single word, would stand before the fire surveying me with the air of an Exhibitor, and I would see him, between the fingers of the hand with which I shaded my face, appealing by dumb show to the furniture to take notice of my proficiency. The imaginary student pursued by the misshapen creature he had impiously made, was not more wretched than I, pursued by the creature who had made me. (353)

Magwitch's confounding of the categories of high and low takes an even more radical turn, however, when he abandons the use of these terms as merely social discriminants and uses "low" as a measure of moral sentiments. Before Pip understands the full claim that Magwitch is making on him, he follows his bourgeois instincts in trying to buy Magwitch off by offering him clean money as a repayment of the dirty notes that had been the first token of the convict's intentions. Magwitch, of course, is equally compromised in the first moments of their renewed relationship because he has compounded his gratitude with revenge. While toiling in Australia and suffering the social contempt of the colonials, he both appeased and fed his resentment by thinking, "Which of you owns a brought-up London gentleman?" (339); and the same spirit breathes through when he tells Pip, "I've come to the old country fur to see my gentleman spend his money *like* a gentleman. That'll be *my* pleasure. *My* pleasure 'ull be fur to see him do it. And blast you all!" (347). But the frenzy of fear and dislike that this resentful outburst produces in Pip is precisely what brings Magwitch to *his* moral *peripeteia*. At insistent length he proceeds to repudiate his "lowness." His subsequent actions show that his "air of admiring proprietorship" (348) is not so easily to be shaken off, but the incident is nevertheless decisive in preparing for his "softening," and in reinforcing the moral issues at the crucial moment.

The effect of Magwitch's repudiation of his lowness is, significantly, to fill Pip with "some sense of the grimly-ludicrous" (347) in Magwitch and in the whole situation, as though he were finding himself cast not as a victim but as the butt of a monstrous cosmic joke. This turn is one of the finest things in the novel and it indicates just how faithful Dickens. had remained in the germ of the whole—to what he described in a letter to Forster as "the grotesque tragicomic conception," (Forster II: 204). Terence Cave has argued in *Recognitions: A Study in Poetics* that there is always something double-edged and scandalous about scenes of recognition, and this is certainly the case here. What returns to Pip is no more than what he has pretended all along that he can evade—the recognition of the moral imperative always to act in terms of one's best instincts; but it takes the scandalous spectacle of Magwitch bumbling on grotesquely about "lowness" to make the imperative inescapable.

In terms of the book's broad (and hence somewhat simplified) moral scheme, when Magwitch returns it is as the bestower of affection and loyalty, resented by the young man who has reneged on his instinctive capacity for generous impulse and for loyal affection because he has been corrupted by the *ressentiment* inherent in class society. But it is the mark of the book's complexity that the individual instance is always more ambivalent than the overall scheme. When Magwitch fingers one of Pip's rings, Pip says, "I recoiled from his touch as if he had been a snake" (338). This repugnance is so powerful as to seem almost instinctive, rather than a function of class conditioning; and indeed the recoil does have, in this instance, something of an instinctive rightness—for a materialistic gloating rather than affection governs Magwitch's fondling of the ring at this moment.

Given this sort of complexity, there is no possibility that the novel's *perpeteia* will produce a spontaneous flow of moral sentiment in the hero, as a more simplistic notion of sentimental morality might seem to demand.[10] To characterize the slow and complex process of Pip's moral recovery it will be helpful to see it as involving a reversal of the mechanisms of *ressentiment*. Nietzsche's initial exposition of the notion separates what might be thought of as three psychological features:

> While every noble morality develops from a triumphant affirmation of itself, slave morality from the outset says No to what is "outside", what is "different", what is "not itself" . . . its action is fundamentally reaction. . . .
> The man of *ressentiment* is neither upright nor naive nor honest and straightforward with himself. His soul *squints*; his spirit loves hiding places, secret paths and back doors, everything covert entices him as *his* world, *his* security, *his* refreshment; he understands how to keep silent, how not to forget, how to wait, how to be provisionally self-depreciating and humble. . . .
> Picture "the enemy" as the man of *ressentiment* conceives him—and here precisely is his deed, his creation: he has conceived "the evil enemy", "the Evil One", and this in fact is his basic concept, from which he then evolves, as an afterthought and pendant, a "good one"—himself!
> (*On the Genealogy of Morals* I: 10, 367, 38, 39)

The significance of another person makes one feel insignificant and in reaction one repudiates the other. This repudiation involves an extended repression of feelings such as envy, rage, and revenge. The repression has two aspects: denying that the other *is* significant, and arrogating merit to one's own insignificance. Recovery would thus depend on accepting the significance of the other as the way of triumphantly affirming what is in fact essential to the self. Instead of denying Magwitch's significance, Pip will have to accept that the love he offers cannot be either denied or repressed; and he will have to repudiate his own sense of superiority and recognize that the significance which Magwitch represents is what he himself truly desires, indeed what he has truly desired all along.

At first, once the initial shock has passed, Pip becomes understandably obsessed with the need to get Magwitch out of England. This is a symbolic indication that he is still intent on getting Magwitch out of his life and repressing his significance; and it is also an act which allows him to reinforce his sense of personal merit in not being a "murderer" (358) who would relinquish the "enemy" to the ultimate processes of the law.

The first crucial aspect of Pip's recovery, the recognition that Magwitch's otherness cannot be denied, is crystallized in the sequence in which the convict proves himself totally unamenable to any disguise. Pip's attempts in this regard begin on the morning after the convict's return:

> As he was at present dressed in a seafaring slop suit, in which he looked as if he had some parrots and cigars to dispose of, I next discussed with him what dress he should wear. He cherished an extraordinary belief in the virtues of "shorts" as a disguise, and had in his own mind sketched a dress for himself that would have made him something between a dean and a dentist. It was with considerable difficulty that I won him over to the assumption of a dress more like a prosperous farmer's; and we arranged that he should cut his hair close, and wear a little powder. (349)

Dickens lends Pip his own irrepressible sense of the drollery that can irradiate even the most terrible experiences, and all the terror, frustration, and rage that the return has occasioned is momentarily put at nought by the imaginative warmth of the comic impulse. The extraordinary thing is that the humor does not come as an intrusion, but seems the very warrant of the characters' authenticity. It is Wordsworth and his leech-gatherer all over again, and Magwitch is made to seem as intransigently there as the figure who robbed that earlier egotist of all his pretensions of superiority. Only a man such as Magwitch, totally incapable of conceiving how the world sees him, could have imagined himself capable of creating a gentleman, or of transforming himself by the assumption of "shorts." Only a boy capable of transforming the italic angularities of an engraving on a tombstone into the sense that his mother must have been freckled and sickly could, at the pitch of his frustrations, imagine Magwitch in "shorts" as "something between a dean and a dentist." It is the imaginative vivacity of the passage that convinces us that Pip is still capable of recovering the generous impulses of his finer self, even as it begins to initiate that recovery. The process of seeing and valuing Magwitch for what he is, and not as Pip's fears and resentments have colored him, is hereafter irreversible; and this is signalled most clearly in the luminous but disturbing later passage in which even the expedient of the powder for Magwitch's hair is abandoned:

> It had been his own idea to wear that touch of powder and I had conceded the powder after overcoming the shorts. But I can compare the effect of it, when

on, to nothing but the probable effect of rouge upon the dead; so awful was the
manner in which everything in him that it was most desirable to repress, started
through that thin layer of pretence, and seemed to come blazing out at the crown
of his head.   (353)

What this passage makes clear is that far from simply engaging with Pip's
immediate social and personal resentments, Magwitch has the force of a
deathly effigy in Pip's eyes, invested with the "blazing" power to consume
all pretenses and to release his deepest repressions. Once again Wordsworth
provides an apt comparison, for the effect is akin to nothing so much as the
passage in *The Prelude* (1850 version: 12.255ff.) where the young boy's
encounter with the gibbet and the murderer's name cut in the grass leaves
him confronted with the experience of pure ontological terror. Comparably,
Magwitch's return releases in Pip "the terror of childhood," the fear unforget-
tably evoked in the second paragraph of the book of being absolutely alone
and unloved in an alien universe (252). It is this fear that energizes his
immediate awareness when the convict comes into his rooms that he "knew
him" (333); and it is the same fear that makes the countering significance of
the love that Magwitch offers absolute.

As Dickens' belief in the moral efficacy of sentiment would lead one to
anticipate, the breaking down of the barriers between Pip and Magwitch
depends in large part on Pip's coming to feel pity for the story of the outcast's
life and an overriding responsibility for his safety; and also on his growing
ever more responsive to the ameliorating effect of Magwitch's own affection
and trust.

These changes in Pip are handled with convincing slowness and subtlety;
but the complementary process of Pip's coming to recognize that what Magwitch figures is what he has always desired depends on a much more audacious
effacement of the difference between the "outsider" and the self. At the
height of his good fortune, after Wemmick has taken him to see Newgate
prison, Pip marvels that he should still be "encompassed by all this taint of
prison and crime," and as he waits for Estella to meet him in London he
thinks "with absolute abhorrence of the contrast between the jail and her"
(284). Thus it is no surprise that after the return of his convict he should
"pause to ask how much of [his] shrinking from Provis might be traced to
Estella" (367). By some strange compulsion, however, Pip divides his activities, after Magwitch's return, between the preparations for getting Magwitch
out of England and a search for the secrets of Estella's parentage. It is as
though he feels intuitively that these two fated relationships and centers of
value in his life must somehow be brought together. At the level of plot,

the discovery that Estella is Magwitch's daughter is a melodramatic way of reinforcing the lesson of Pip's great expectations, the realization that though bourgeois society struggles to disclaim the depths out of which it has anxiously raised itself it has its origins in and depends upon the low. But at a psychological level Dickens makes this discovery the ultimate source of Pip's softening towards Magwitch. Pip himself remarks that the knowledge that Magwitch is Estella's father allows him to transfer to his benefactor "some rays of the romantic interest that had so long surrounded her" (420). Pip's softening towards Magwitch is thus made easier because he can feel it to be, as it were, a reconciliation for Estella's sake; hence it is that when Pip faces death at the hands of Orlick at the limekiln, what concerns him most is not what Herbert, Biddy, and Joe will think of him, but the thought that *"Estella's father* would believe I had deserted him" (436; emphasis added). In coming to love Magwitch, Pip is not only, in symbolic terms, finding the caring father he has always desired; he is also eliding Magwitch's value with that of Estella who has throughout been the lodestar of *all* his deepest aspirations and desires. It is in this most comprehensive of all possible ways that he effaces the difference between the outsider and the self.

After the escape attempt has failed, Pip finally acknowledges his love by allowing the shackled man in the boat to hold his hand in his, and Pip's repugnance all melts away precisely at the point where Compeyson is drowned, as though the death of that incubus symbolically drains away any capacity for evil in Magwitch. Then, at the convict's trial, when Pip aligns himself with Magwitch against the society which has made him a victim, Pip holds Magwitch's hand *in his* through the grid of the dock, thereby subtly reversing the notion of dependency and affirming a new sense of moral identity and moral responsibility. These two scenes achieve, through their iconic simplicity and singleness of gesture, the full moving power of "monopathic" emotion (Heilman 85). Their simplicity derives in large part from that "sentimentalization of morality" which entails the identification of ethical action with the achievement of basic states of familial fellow-feeling—here the love between (adopted) father and son, affirmed by the public holding of hands.[11] Thus the achievement of the whole sequence from Magwitch's return until his trial is to make virtuous action seem eminently natural and desirable, and not something almost impossibly hard, as a stricter ethical tradition would have it (as is the case, say, in Milton's sonnet "On His Blindness," or Dorothea's determination to do her duty by Casaubon). Love for the outcast Magwitch is made to seem no more than the heart's proper instinct, and certainly what every reader would want Pip to achieve. The importance of

Dickens' capacity to win the reader's complicity with his moral intentions in this sort of way cannot be sufficiently insisted on.

But despite the fact that its simple moral forthrightness is one of its greatest strengths, the book resists reduction to a moral fable; and the striving for what Mark Spilka calls "*affective* innocence" is by no means its most distinctive quality (164). When Pip talks of tears as "rain upon the blinding dust of earth, overlaying our hard hearts" (186), what is most heartfelt in the comment is its assumption that the natural condition of our hearts is to be "hard." The case for the efficacy of moral sentiment in literature is precisely that it is often only tears that will release our natural but stifled moral impulses; and *Great Expectations*, in some of its most powerful scenes, remains loyal to that belief. But in feeling the need to insist that "we need never be ashamed of our tears" Dickens is, in line with what Philip Collins has called "the decline of pathos" from the late 1850s on, showing himself alive to the embarrassment that overt expression of sentiment might arouse ("Pathos" 635–37). This remark is thus one of many indications that the novel as a whole is firmly and consciously set in a new kind of dialogism, a further mark of which is its exploration of the intimate relationship between sentiment and resentment which we have been considering.

3

The awareness that in *Great Expectations* Dickens is not merely exploiting moral sentiment but *exploring* its full affective ramifications by intuitive dramatic means might help to move us some way beyond the mix of confusion, sentimentality, and embarrassment that often besets discussions of the effects of feeling and in particular of moral feeling in Dickens' work. Here the matching pair of Jaggers and Joe provides something of an object lesson, for there is as little critical consensus on whether Jaggers is a villain as on whether Joe represents the book's moral ideal. Clearly the two *are* a matching pair, for, to invoke Boffin's phraseology,[12] where Jaggers has taught himself that it is a safe bet to think ill of a man, Joe is convinced that it is always a good thing to think well of everyone. Good sense on the matter would seem to lie in recognizing first that Dickens uses Joe and Jaggers opportunistically and hence at times inconsistently as characters (as is often his practice); and secondly (as is equally often his later practice) that he enlists them in his thematic explorations—in this case using them to represent extreme stances in relation to moral sentiment, both of which are shown to be inadequate.

Jaggers totally repudiates moral sentiments along with any sense of moral responsibility and any other kind of sentiment: "I'll have no feelings here" (427), he announces, demonstrating by the very fierceness of his authority the power that his freedom from all such impediments provides. The fascination of his character lies in the fact that in claiming to have no illusions he believes that he has placed himself beyond resentment as well as sentiment. He recognizes, one might say, that law itself is no more than an archetypal form of *ressentiment*, the masking of social revenge under the name of justice; and he commits himself to white-anting the processes through which his society enacts its revengeful exclusions. He does this simply because the processes of the law are so beset by false pretensions, moral or otherwise, that they provide the perfect arena for demonstrating the power of his own autonomy. But his bad faith is registered by the very compulsiveness of his need to wash his hands with scented soap, as though, like the dyer's hands, they cannot avoid becoming subdued to the element they work in. Dickens's dramatic demonstration of the inadequacy of this cynical stance is achieved by having Jaggers soften at the crisis and reveal not only that he desired to save Estella, but also that he is capable of smiling and even perhaps of having harbored his own "poor dreams" (426) of love—reactions that make him, needless to say, totally inconsistent as a character.

    A just assessment of Joe's significance, on the other hand, depends first on acknowledging the warmth of the early comic scenes involving Pip and Joe—scenes which win the sort of loving sympathy for Joe that is the prerogative of those who have made us laugh in a kindly way. Sacred tears fall so heavily in Victorian fiction that there is a tendency for them to overweigh discussions of moral sentiment, to the neglect of happiness and humor as even more efficacious vehicles. For sacred tears can also be the expression of joy and pleasure. A mere glimpse of two happy sisters enjoying the normal life from which she has always been excluded is enough to afford Little Nell "the softened pleasure . . . which lives and dies in tears" (396) and to fill her with a salving sense of sympathy, which "dwelt in her memory like the kindnesses of years" (315); a reaction that recalls Wordsworth's gentle insistence in "Tintern Abbey" that it is the "little, unremembered acts of kindness and of love" that are the best portion of a good man's life. It was with such considerations in mind that George Santayana, in his wonderful essay on Dickens, argued that as long as people continue to read Dickens "the springs of kindness and folly in their lives would not be dried up" (58). In this sense then, Joe, with his brimming kindness and folly, is a perfect conduit for moral sentiment. And it is thus very understandable that Pip uses his ingratitude towards Joe as the measure of his own moral failings, just as Dickens uses Joe's unfailing loyalty as a means of underlining that ingratitude.

But in assessing Joe in his own right it is important to notice that soon after he is introduced he is categorized by Dickens, somewhat condescendingly, as "a sort of Hercules in strength, and also in weakness" (40), and this is consistent with the way that Joe figures in Dickens's early indication of the "exceedingly droll" quality of the new book which he offered to Forster in October 1860: "I have put a child and good-natured foolish man, in relations that seem to me very funny" (Forster 11: 204). Of course generosity often comes clothed in gruffness and gaucherie, and humor has never been an enemy of sentiment in the English tradition. At the same time, there is something evasive about the humor with which Joe is presented at key moments. The single instance in which Pip dissociates himself from Joe's judgment is when Joe insists, despite the plain facts of the case, that his brutal father was "good in his heart" (77). Dickens glides around this foolishness by making a joke of Joe's one foray into poetry, the epitaph, enshrining that putative goodness of heart, struck out like a horseshoe complete in a single blow. But it becomes apparent that Dickens is using this incident to elicit sympathy that will carry over into Joe's subsequent explanation of why he has put up with Mrs. Joe and failed to protect Pip against her—namely, that what they have had to endure is a lesser evil than the aggression which would have been necessary to bring her to heel. Pip's disconcerting response to this fine example of turning the other cheek is to find himself "looking up to Joe in [his] heart" (80) in a new way. The extended sequence smacks of an uncomfortable attempt to cover up for what Joe himself admits to being "shortcomings" (80), in a context where it would have been inopportune for Dickens to come out *against* Joe and explore the limitations of a simple and sentimental "goodheartedness"—in the way that he had proved himself more than willing to do with Micawber or Skimpole.

One must allow for the fact that the conception of Joe's character and role in the book developed as Dickens went along: it is in later scenes when he disconcerts Miss Havisham, discommodes Jaggers, and nurses Pip back to health that his moral strength is impressive. One must equally recognise though that Joe is a marginalized figure in the book in two senses: he belongs to a pre-urban and almost a pre-social world, and structurally he is totally excluded from the long and crucial central section from Chapter 36 to 56 which deals with Pip's moral recovery. Moreover, the evasiveness and the whole sense of condescension to a simpler mode of being which invests the humor of his early scenes make it clear that there is no way in which Joe can be taken as an unqualified model of moral behavior. What he lacks is a sense of the properness of resentment as an index of injustice.

Beyond that, he is at certain moments invested with an aura of sentimental sanctity that seems a throwback to an earlier mode of Dickens's development, as in the mature Pip's eulogy to him just before he recounts the departure from the forge: "O dear good faithful tender Joe, I feel the loving tremble of your hand upon my arm, as solemnly this day as if it had been the rustle of an angel's wing!" (168). Peter Brooks has said of melodrama that it is a mode of "excess", striving to enlarge moral meanings in "a world voided of its traditional Sacred" (*Melodramatic Imagination* 11). The same is of course true of the mode of sentiment, and at times it strives too hard, as the falseness of the word "tremble" in relation to the blacksmith's touch makes all too clear.

4

The archetypal sentimental heroes or heroines of Dickens' early work such as Little Nell or Paul Dombey are *victims,* creatures of pathos whose suffering provides the reader with a gratifying opportunity to exercise "finer feelings"; and they are children. The unwritten premise behind casting them with that marginalized status is the conviction that absolute moral purity is to be found only in a pre-erotic state. (The premise applies to Joe too, for it is impossible to imagine him in bed with Mrs. Joe, or wanting to be there.)[13]

The moral hero like Pip, however, who resents his calling, is clearly a far cry from the sentimental hero or heroine. He is a troubled and troubling individual whose experience mirrors the deepest repressions and compulsions of his society, and who is accordingly subject to insidious forms of displaced resentment. Pip is endowed with erotic as well as with moral impulses; and this complicates Dickens' exploration of moral sentiments. Throughout the novel Dickens handles Pip's desire for Estella in an ambivalent way; and it is only a minor part of the problem that she is associated with those great expectations that are endorsed by Victorian society, but which the moral scheme of the book requires Pip to repudiate. That scheme requires the reader to feel, when Pip shows resentment at Biddy's upbraiding him for his lack of feeling for Joe and herself, that Pip's reaction is the sign of his perverse resistance to what he knows instinctively to be morally good in a situation where selfishness and the ethic of social advancement are at odds with what his heart tells him is right. But what Pip's heart tells him most imperatively at this moment is that Estella has all the glamor and promise of broader horizons that Biddy lacks. Nor is it enough to say that this prompting is simply a failure of moral feeling in Pip, as though virtue lay in having almost no expectations at all. The scenes between Pip and Biddy seem too "pointed" not because we resent art that has too palpable a design on us, but because Biddy's submissive goodness and her insistence that Joe would be too proud to want to change himself beg the question of whether or not it is right for *Pip* to want to grow and to change, and to follow the plot of his desire. When Pip finally declares his hopeless love to Estella he says rightly and movingly that she has "been in every line [he has] ever read . . . been the embodiment of every graceful fancy that [his] mind has ever become acquainted with," and that she cannot choose but remain "part of the little good in [him], part of the evil" (378). What is as compelling as the ardor and candor of the judgment is the sharpness of the realization that she has been the inspiration of all his imaginative growth. Clearly a life full of larks at the forge with Biddy and Joe in a state of pre-urban and pre-erotic communality is an idyllic fancy, not a real option, for a person of Pip's capacities; and it is this recognition that makes one aware that the real issues are being fudged in the scenes with Biddy.

The more fundamental problem in Dickens' presentation of the relationship between Pip and Estella is that Dickens seems to feel that he can maintain the ultimate purity of Pip's moral nature only by shearing off the essential aggressiveness of his erotic desire and displacing it onto Pip's antagonists. Thus, as with the relationship between David Copperfield and Uriah Heep, or that between Eugene Wrayburn and Bradley Headstone, there is a peculiarly intimate and sexually charged relationship between Pip and those set against him. His sister castigates him with a hard "tickler"; and Orlick, who has battered that sister into submission, lusted openly after another sister figure, Biddy, and guarded the gate of the castle of romance, turns on Pip at the limekiln in a scene suffused with strange passions. As the two struggle in the dark "a strong man's breast was set against" Pip's mouth to deaden his cries (434); and once Pip has been bound Orlick draws his hand across his own lips "as if his mouth watered for" Pip (436). The repressed eroticism is bequeathed upon the villain only to be turned back upon the hero as resentful rivalry of a strangely intimate kind. In a comparable way Eugene Wrayburn's nocturnal hauntings with the rancorous schoolmaster have something of the form of an eerie courtship, building up to a deathly (or near deathly) consummation; as though only in this way could Eugene exorcise the passion which is driving him towards the seduction of Lizzie. Likewise in David Copperfield's nightmare after Peggoty's financial debacle, he is haunted by the sense that he now has nothing to offer Dora in exchange for marriage but "one of Uriah Heep's gloves" (566). Given that Uriah's sexual aggression in the scene in which he proposes to Agnes is figured by the obsessive effort of his hand to penetrate those gloves, David's dream image would seem to bring together his resentment of Uriah's desire for Agnes and an uneasy intuition that he is perhaps himself drawn to Dora largely by sexual desire. The problem is that in the world that Dickens creates, moral and erotic sentiments cohabit, but are seldom allowed to lie easily together; and thus the morally simple opposition of hero and villain tends to become obscurely complicated by their mutually resentful rivalry in love.

Pip's aggressiveness, for its part, is allowed a direct outlet only in his desire to kill Orlick if he gets free, and more continuously in his jealousy of Drummle—except for the scene in which he knocks down the ineptly pugilistic Herbert, significantly enough the one action which wins a spontaneous kiss from Estella. Not only then is there a controlled dialectic between sentiment and resentment within the moral plot, there are also odd displacements in Dickens' handling of erotic impulses.

Nevertheless, the limekiln encounter can be seen as bringing Pip home disconcertingly to his own, if not to the novel's, psychopathology. For though the sickness unto death which the limekiln encounter precipitates is held off by the exigencies of Pip's attempts to save Magwitch, it ultimately overwhelms him after Magwitch's death. Its significance is figured in the two feverish nightmares in which he has the hallucinatory sense:

> that [he] was a brick in the house wall, and yet entreating to be released from the giddy place where the builders had set [him]; that [he] was a steel beam of a vast engine, clashing and whirling over a gulf, and yet that [he] implored in [his] own person to have the engine stopped, and [his] part in it hammered off.
> 471–72).

The dreams, if that is what they are, evoke vividly enough the repetitive and seemingly absurd compulsions that are part of the vertiginous alienation and torturing pulsations of fever; but their significance extends beyond that. The first dream, with its images of unsettling height and yet also of constriction, relates, obviously enough, to Pip's desire to free himself from the society in which he has been "set" by his great expectations, and from the experience of having the contours of his life constructed by others. The second dream has similarly pertinent suggestions of constriction and of an elevated extension above a threatening emptiness. But it is possible to see the posture of entreaty and, in particular, the notion of a hammering beam from which it would be a relief to be hammered off as charged too with all the giddy resentments of Pip's frustrated erotic experience—particularly if one links the idea of hammering off to Jaggers's disconcerting advice to Pip that if he loves Estella, "he had better . . . chop off that bandaged left hand of [his] with [his] bandaged right hand, and then pass the chopper on to Wemmick there, to cut *that* off, too" (426).

One final point might be made in this regard. The most intensely realized physical detail in the whole novel is Pip's apprehension of the hands of Estella's mother, the murderess Molly. What he sees in them is not only the scarring that violence of feeling can produce, but the contours of Estella's own fine hands; and his conviction that Molly is Estella's mother rises from this recognition. The implicit erotic revelation would seem to be that though bourgeois society struggles to sentimentalize the experience of desire and to lay claim to finer feelings than those accessible to the unblushing rabble, "the low" is, inescapably, "a primary eroticized constituent of its fantasy life."[14]

It is perhaps not surprising that Dickens can neither sustain such intuitions nor bring them to conscious realization.[15] They are, in a sense, "unimaginable" in the context of the Victorian audience for which he wrote. In addition, Estella has all along figured in Pip's imagination as the ultimate reward that would crown his great expectations, and the logic of the moral plot makes it difficult for him to be allowed to repudiate the aspiration and yet take the reward. In consequence, the handling of the love-plot seems beset by prevarications. One such prevarication is sounded by the ote of falsity which mars the scene at Magwitch's deathbed, when Pip tells him that his daughter is "a lady and very beautiful," and adds, "And I love her!" (470). One understands that Pip is subordinating his desire for Estella, which is now explicitly taboo as she is committed to Drummle, to his love for Magwitch, and in a sense dedicating it to him; but there is still a lie in the misconception that is foisted onto Magwitch, and it is soon to be compounded by the further lie implicit in Pip's going, immediately after recovering from his illness, to propose to Biddy. That attempt suggests an attenuation of desire which is apparent even in the final paragraphs of the revised ending. Pip takes Estella's hand in his and it might seem as though, in the words of Donne's "The Ecstasy,"

> So to intergraft our hands, as yet
> Was all our means to make us one.

But there is such an atmosphere of solemn sanctification in the imagery of the evening mists and tranquil light that one can hardly avoid the sense that it is still the case that "a great prince in prison lies."

5

The problems of the novel's ending (or endings) have had much attention. As David Gervais rightly argues, there is something muted about the prose of the whole closing section, and the resilience of comedy is virtually foregone (85–114). Pip, Estella, and Magwitch are all softened into a mood of melancholy sadness and renunciation, though Magwitch resists this movement by springing at Compeyson in a frenzy of murderous resentment as he is about to be apprehended, and Pip is allowed one burst of irritation with Pumblechook after that worthy has momentarily livened things up by finding a perhaps too pertinent moral in Pip's "abstinence from watercresses" and in the fact that he is no longer "like the Bee . . . as plump as a Peach" (488).

The proper measure of this final mood of resignation might seem to be provided by the anger of Gridley in *Bleak House:*

> If I took my wrongs in any other way, I should be driven mad! It is only by resenting them, and by revenging them in my mind, and by angrily demanding the justice I never get, that I am able to keep my wits together. (266)

Skimpole subsequently characterizes Gridley as "intellectually speaking, a sort of inharmonious blacksmith" (269), which establishes an odd subterranean link between Gridley and Pip that might seem to justify the contrast. Certainly by the end of *Great Expectations* Pip is not raging but simply sinking; "not waving but drowning." He thus joins the company of a long line of late Dickensian hero-lovers (including most prominently Arthur Clennam and Eugene Wrayburn) who seem to believe that virtue lies only in being, in Estella's phrase "bent and broken . . . into a better shape" (493) by suffering. It is a far cry from Gridley's resentful anger at injustice to the harmonious blacksmith's words over the dead body of Magwitch, "O Lord, be merciful to him, a sinner" (470). What is disconcerting about the allusion to the parable of the publican and the Pharisee is not, as some critics have argued, any implications of hypocrisy in Pip, is clearly thinking of himself as the one who has exalted himself and who will be abased, but rather the very notion, which Dickens clearly endorses, of Magwitch as a "sinner."

For the book has encouraged the reader to think of him rather as a victim; and the only sinful act he is seen to perform is the resentful leap upon Compeyson that occasions the latter's death—an act which it is one's instinct to applaud. What is harder to condone than that act itself is the prim punctiliousness of Pip's response to Magwitch's explanation that in the event he did not actually commit murder: "*I never had any reason to doubt* the exact truth of what he thus told me" (456; emphasis added). And it is hard, too, to condone the element of condescending gratification in Pip's sense that his dying benefactor "pondered over the question of whether he might have been a better man under better circumstances" (465)—as though there were no argument but that Magwitch's fierce will was something to be deprecated.

A Foucauldian view makes a good deal of sense of the last phase of the novel by seeing Pip as internalizing and valorizing social oppression under the guise of a noble suppression of the self. But the problem with the ending is not just that Pip forgets his alignment at the trial and mutes his resistance and his resentment by falling back on the more conventional response dictated by the dominant social discourse. The final sense of renunciatory passivity in Pip seems to go deeper than that. Peter Brooks draws on Freud's *Beyond the Pleasure Principle* to explain the final chastened effect of the novel in relation to "the problematics of reading," arguing that it is the essential function of plot to accomplish a binding of deviant energies and to return us to quiescence ("Repetition" 524). This view is close to Roland Barthes's presentation of "Sarrasine" in *S/Z* as emblematic of the final emasculation of desire which is the end of reading. But Brooks goes one step further by historicizing this process in relation to the nineteenth-century disappearance of God, and "the absence or silence of divine master-plots." In this absence, says Brooks, "the search for that significant closure that would illuminate the sense of an existence, the meaning of life," will never be satisfied, and we are condemned to an endless repetition and re-reading—an endlessness figured in the "infinitely repeatable palindrome" of Pip's name (525, 524, 526).

Brooks does more than illuminate the tone and the final effect of *Great Expectations* in such comments. Leaving aside the question of Dickens' actual religious beliefs, one might accept Brooks's remarks as a pertinent context for the persistent and characteristically Victorian undertow in Dickens' novels, from its emergence in *David Copperfield* on, of an "old unhappy feeling . . . like a strain of sorrowful music faintly heard in the night" which tells of "loss or want of something never to be realized" (765, 890)—a feeling which is given definitive expression in Dickens's wry remarks to

Forster about a sense of "one happiness missed in life and one friend and companion never made (Forster 11: 141).

But Brooks's notion of endless circularity is a pertinent final context too for the dialogic relationship between the antonymic impulses of moral sentiment and resentment which we have been tracing. However much a benign view of things might which to stress the generous aspect of moral impulses, such impulses are inescapably self-denying. As I contemplate Pip's final phase in the novel I feel my resentment rising at the fact that he would seem, for all his lingering regrets, to have joined Jaggers in renouncing desire as a "poor dream," and to have foreclosed on the possibilities of life (490), and I am tempted to give Nietzsche the last word on Pip by recalling his scandalous repudiation in *On the Genealogy of Morals* of the ascetic impulse (and seemingly of the moral impulse itself) as the ultimate flourishing of *ressentiment*:

> An ascetic life is a self-contradiction: here rules a *ressentiment* without equal, that of an insatiable instinct and power-will that wants to become master not over something in life but over life itself, over its most profound, powerful, and basic conditions; here an attempt is made to employ force to block up the wells of force; here physiological well-being itself is viewed askance, and especially the outward expression of this well-being beauty and joy; while pleasure is felt and *sought* in ill constitutedness, decay, pain, mischance, ugliness, voluntary deprivation, self-motification, self-flagellation, self-sacrifice.
>
> (3: 11)

But I cannot read the passage without registering the deep resentment that lies behind its repudiation of *ressentiment*, or without recalling that Nietzsche, with fitting circularity, felt himself forced to say almost ungrudgingly near the end of *On the Genealogy of Morals*: "All honor to the ascetic ideal *insofar as it is honest!*" (3: 26).

NOTES

This is a revised version of a paper that was presented at the conference "Sentimentality, Dickens and Victorian Culture" held at the University of California, Santa Cruz in August 1989. My attendance at the conference was made possible by grants from the University of the Witwatersrand and from the Human Sciences Research Council.

1. Dickens's beliefs in the moral efficacy of sentiment in art have, for the most part, to be inferred from his practice. One of his most overt pronouncements relates to the death of Little Nell:
   When Death strikes down the innocent and young, for every fragile form from which he lets the panting spirit free, a hundred virtues rise, in shapes of mercy,

charity, and love, to walk the world, and bless it. Of every tear that sorrowing mortals shed on such green graves, some good is born, some gentler nature comes.   (659)
A letter written some fourteen years later than this, in 15 July 1856 to Emily Jolly advising her to alter the end of "A Wife's Story," (*Nonesuch Letters* 2: 680) uses the same image of softening and hardening as the passage in *Great Expectations*:

So will you soften the reader when you now as it were harden, and so you will bring tears from many eyes, which can only have their spring in affectionately and gently touched hearts.

    Something of the broader complexity of the whole issue is suggested, however, by the fact that the image recurs in a cynical comment by Henry Hallam of 1847 on Paul Dombey's death, quoted by Fred Kaplan in *Sacred Tears* (Princeton; Princeton UP, 1987), p. 47: "I am so hardened as to be unable to look on it in any light but pure business!" Kaplan probably provides the fullest discussion of this whole matter, but see also David Paroissien, "Literature's 'Eternal Values': Dickens' Professional Creed" in *The Changing World of Charles Dickens,* ed. Robert Giddings (London: Vision Press, 1983).
2. The reader is encouraged to see Drummle in this light despite the fact that Estella marries him, for she has, after all, told Pip that her intention is to deceive and entrap her lovers, "all of them but you" (330).
3. Pip confirms the essential connection in kind between Drummle and Orlick by remarking of the former that his "slouching shoulders and ragged hair" (372) reminded him of Orlick.
4. Friedrich Nietzsche, *On the Genealogy of Morals,* ed. Walter Kaufmann (New York: Vintage, 1969). The crucial passages are sections 1.10 and 1.14.
5. The clearest embodiment of this tendency in Dickens is Mr. Bounderby in *Hard Times* who invents a low social origin for himself so that a "braggart humility" (161) may allow him to exercise power as "the Bully of humility" (58).
6. It is one of the running arguments of Fredric Jameson's *The Political Unconscious: Narrative as a Socially Symbolic Act* (Ithaca, New York: Cornell UP, 1981) that *ressentiment* is a fundamental nineteenth-century "ideologeme," though Jameson is mainly concerned with it in two guises: as a bourgeois mechanism for justifying the marginalisation of the lower classes, and as the reflex of the alienated intellectual. It is in the voice of Carker, "the Manager," that Dickens most uncannily anticipates the social grounding of Nietzschean *ressentiment* in a capitalist system. Carker tells his brother:
There is not a man employed here, standing between myself and the lowest in place . . . who wouldn't be glad at heart to see his master humbled: who does not hate him, secretly: who does not wish him evil rather than good: and who would not turn upon him, if he had the power and the boldness.   (733)
7. In the received text   (Penguin edition, p. 65). Pip responds to Jaggers's announcement of his "great expectations" by the thought, "my dream was out." In one of the relatively few additions to the reading version of the novel Dickens changed the phrase to "my secret dream." See *Charles Dickens: The Public Readings,* ed. Philip Collins (Oxford: The Clarendon Press, 1975), p. 332.
8. Lionel Trilling, "Little Dorrit," *The Opposing Self* (London: Secker and Warburg, 1955), p. 58. Trilling shows this strategy to be pervasive in *Little Dorrit* (in characters such as Miss Wade and William Dorrit, for example) but finds it

epitomized in Blandois who glories in the pose of "the natural genius against whom the philistine word closes its ranks."

9. Perhaps the most telling contribution in this vein is Jeremy Tambling's "Prison-bound: Dickens and Foucault," *Essays in Criticism* 36 (1986), 11–31, which, among other things, refers glancingly to Orlick as an example of *ressentiment* and which also raises searching questions regarding Pip's final relation to the dominant discourses and institutionalized values of his society. Nietzsche's second essay in *On the Genealogy of Morals,* entitled " 'Guilt', 'Bad Conscience', and the Like", might seem to provide a warrant for seeing a quickness to blame oneself as "bad conscience," a phenomenon related to *ressentiment* in that it is also ultimately a way to "affirm oneself" (2.2.60) through a kind of submission. I would resist this notion, as I believe Nietzsche himself finally does; but I pick up these ideas again at the very end of this essay.

10. Indeed other than in Joe the only flush of totally unprompted generous impulse in the book is Pip's decision to do something for Herbert, a gesture which has the crucial effect of convincing the reader that Pip is still to be regarded as the moral hero of the book, even when he is behaving at his worst. Dickens gives great prominence to this decision in the memoranda notes for the novel, stressing the comment, which is directly incorporated in the novel, that it was the one good thing that came of Pip's great expectations.

11. This is the aspect of the slave revolt in morality that Nietzsche had in mind when he said that it tended to reduce man to a "domestic animal" (*On the Genealogy of Morals,* I.11); but see the interesting discussion of the phenomenon by Peter Brooks, *The Melodramatic Imagination: Balzac, Henry James, Melodrama, and the Mode of Excess* (New Haven: Yale UP, 1976), pp. 44ff.

12. Boffin rebukes Alfred Lammle in *Our Mutual Friend* by insisting that "It's a very good thing to think well of another person" (716). Kaplan, in *Sacred Tears,* takes this as an epitome of Dickens' morality of sentiment.

13. The background to this veneration of the pre-erotic is the fact that by the end of the eighteenth century, as Ian Watt has pointed out in *The Rise of the Novel* (London: Chatto and Windus, 1957), p. 163, the ethical scale had come to be redefined "in primarily sexual terms." The key element in this development was the massive self-distrust of the "respectable" middle classes and their need to distinguish themselves from the lower classes.

14. Peter Stallybrass and Allon White make this comment in a general context in *The Politics and Poetics of Transgression* (London: Methuen, 1986), p. 5.

15. One might recall here as well A. L. French's comment that Dickens fails to follow through his dismaying insights into the psychology of beating and cringing because he so desperately wants to retain a more sanguine sense of the possibilities of human nature. See his "Beating and Cringing: *Great Expectations*", *Essays in Criticism* 24 (1974), 147–68.

WORKS CITED

Bell, Michael. *The Sentiment of Reality.* London: Allen and Unwin, 1983.

Brooks, Peter. *The Melodramatic Imagination: Balzac, Henry James, Melodrama and the Mode of Excess.* New Haven: Yale UP, 1976.

————. "Repetition, Repression and Return: *Great Expectations* and the Study of the Plot." *New Literary History*, 11 (1979–80) 503–26.

Cave, Terence. *Recognitions: A Study in Poetics*, Oxford: Clarendon, 1988.

Collins, Philip. "The Decline of Pathos." *The Listener* (8 May 1969): 635–37.

Dickens, Charles. *Great Expectations*. Ed. Angus Calder. Harmondworth: Penguin, 1965.

Forster, John. *The Life of Charles Dickens*. London: Chapman and Hall, n.d.

French, A. L. "Beating and Cringing: *Great Expectations*" *Essays in Criticism*, 24 (1974): 147–68.

Gervais, David. "The Prose and Poetry of *Great Expectations*." *Dickens Studies Annual* 13 (1984) 85–114.

Heilman, Robert. *Tragedy and Melodrama: Versions of Experience*. Seattle: U Washington P, 1968.

Jameson, Fredric. *The Political Unconscious: Narrative as a Socially Symbolic Act*. Ithaca: Cornell UP, 1981.

Kaplan, Fred. *Sacred Tears: Sentimentality in Victorian Literature*. Princeton: Princeton UP, 1987.

Marcus, Stephen. *Dickens from Pickwick to Dombey*. New York: Simon & Schuster, 1968.

Nietzsche, Friedrich. *On the Genealogy of Morals*. Ed. Walter Kaufmann. New York: Vintage Books, 1969.

Paroissien, David. "Literature's 'Eternal Values': Dickens' Professional Creed" in *The Changing World of Charles Dickens* Ed. Robert Giddings. London: Vision Press, 1983.

Santayana, George. "Dickens" *Soliloquies in England*. London: Constable, 1922.

Scheler, Max. *Ressentiment*. New York: Free Press, 1961.

Spilka, Mark. "On the Enrichment of Poor Monkeys by Myth and Dream; or, How Dickens Rousseauisticized and Pre-Freudianized Victorian Views of Childhood" in *Tennesee Studies in Literature* Vol. 27 published as *Sexuality and Victorian Literature*. Ed. Don Richard Cox. Knoxville: U of Tennessee P, 1984.

Stallybrass, Peter and Allen White. *The Politics and Poetics of Transgression*. London: Methuen, 1986.

Tambling, Jeremy. "Prison-bound: Dickens and Foucault." *Essays in Criticism*. 36 (1986) 11–31.

Trilling, Lionel. *The Opposing Self*. London: Secker and Warburg, 1955.

Watt, Ian. *The Rise of the Novel*. London: Chatto & Windus, 1957.

BAKHTINIAN POLYPHONY IN *MARY BARTON;* CLASS, GENDER, AND THE TEXTUAL VOICE

Marjorie Stone

> There's a grim one-horse hearse in a jolly round trot;
> To the churchyard a pauper is going, I wot:
> The road it is rough, and the hearse has no springs,
> And hark to the dirge that the sad driver sings:
>   "Rattle his bones over the stones;
>   He's only a pauper, whom nobody owns!"

"The Pauper's Drive" with its grimly humorous, jolting refrain of "Rattle his bones over the stones . . . " was published as an anonymous poem that "nobody owns" in the Chartist newspaper *The Northern Star* in 1842 (Kovalev 39).[1] The sardonic voice of "Rattle his bones" is one among multiple working-class voices and texts that Gaskell weaves into the agony" convulsing the "dumb people" of cities like Manchester in England's "Hungary" Eighteen-Forties (*Mary Barton* 37–38). Death is an absolute dumbness, but ironically the impoverished classes often speak through death in literary discourse before Gaskell's. Carlyle's Irish widow in *Past and Present* is a notable example, influencing the depiction of Ben Davenport's death in *Mary Barton*. Gaskell echoes the "The Pauper's Drive" in describing Davenport's funeral, noting that in his case, thanks to the charity of the poor to the poor, "there was no 'rattling the bones over the stones' of the pauper's funeral" (112). Yet characteristically, in this double-voiced utterance Gaskell simultaneously calls on a working-class text to articulate the opposing norm. Rather than imitating Carlyle in *Past and Present* by graphically preaching the agony of the "dumb people," Gaskell showed her middle-class readers that the "other half'' had other ways of speaking its suffering than death. Through her creation of a novelistic discourse that Bakhtin was later to find exemplified by Dostoevsky, in a work that may indeed have influenced *Crime and Punishment,* as C. A. Johnson notes,[2] she reveals the power and variegation of working-class utterances themselves. More radically, through her rhetorical and narrative strategies, she subverts the hegemony of middle-class discourse that empowers her to speak.

Mary Barton has customarily been viewed as a technically clumsy ''split novel.'' In Rosemarie Bodenheimer's view, Gaskell's focus on the domestic sphere fails to resolve the issues raised in the public world of politics; in John Lucas's, she retreats from the ''abyss'' created by the gulf between her ideological prescriptions and her powerful evocation of the plight of the poor (142). Like Bodenheimer, Stephen Gill objects to the ''bewildering shifts'' in the narrative voice (*Mary Barton* 3), while others criticize the split between the ''social-problem plot'' centering on John Barton and the ''romance plot'' centering on his daughter Mary.[3] More recently, in a refreshing shift of focus, Catherine Gallagher has shown how the contradictions in industrial narratives like ''Mary Barton'' grow out of the ''ruptures'' within the early nineteenth-century critique of industrialism, rather than out of their authors' personal limitations. These divisions reflect ''the contradictory structures of the social criticism the novelists tried to embody,'' Gallagher observes; and in Gaskell's case, they lead to ''formal inconsistencies,'' but also to a ''high degree of formal self-consciousness'' (33–34). This essay will argue more unreservedly for Gaskell's formal self-consciousness, from the viewpoint of Bakhtinian and reader-response theory rather than in the context of the critique of industrialism.

When Bakhtin's model of novelistic discourse is assumed, many of the apparent formal inconsistencies in *Mary Barton* can be seen as the outcome of Gaskell's innovative artistry and her exceptional ability to incorporate conflicting perspectives and the languages that embody them in the textual voice of her first novel. An operative concept of ''textual voice,'' incorporating all of the voices that sound in the text, seems called for in *Mary Barton* because a univocal and static idea of narrative voice or character voice cannot accomodate the effect of polyphony and debate that Gaskell's first novel creates.[4] ''Voice'' is itself a keyword in this work, where the reader is immersed in a constant, dynamic interplay of voices, not only in the dialogue of the working-class characters interacting with each other and with the propertied classes, and in the inner mental debate of the characters, but also in the multiple voices of the novel's authorial discourse, which debate with each other, with the character's voices, and with the inscribed readers who also proliferate in the novel. Added to these are the voices that speak in the novel's inset stories, and in its many mottoes and allusions, some derived from working-class or female discourse, others from the canonical texts of a male literary tradition. In Bakhtin's terms, Gaskell actively dialogizes the discourse of *Mary Barton* by incorporating in it the heteroglossia of multiple languages—languages understood in Bakhtin's stipulative sense, not as linguistically separate dialects, but as "ideologically saturated" embodiments of "socio-linguistic points of view" (271–73). Bringing the heteroglossia of working-class and women's discourse into collision with the official languages of male middle-class culture, Gaskell initiates what Bakhtin terms a "critical interanimation of languages" (296), designed to produce a "relativizing of linguistic consciousness" (323). The result is that middle-class male discourse—principally socio-economic and literacy discourse—is radically deprivileged. At the same time, varieties of middle-class, working-class, and women's discourse in *Mary Barton* are internally dialogized, as Gaskell reveals the multiplicity of languages and perspectives constituting each. This internal dialogization extends to the narrative voice, so much so that it is more accurate to speak of narrative voices, some female, some male, in this novel which, more boldly than George Eliot's early works, both exploits and disrupts the strategy of male impersonation.

In "Discourse in the Novel," Bakhtin identifies several "compositional forms for appropriating and organizing heteroglossia in the novel" (301). These include dialogue representative of the "social dialogue" of languages (285, 365); hybridizations, or the combining of two social languages or speech manners in a single double-voiced discourse (304,358); the creation of "character zones" or fields of action defined by the distinctive features of a character's language (316); "parodic stylizations of generic, professional and other languages" (302); the incorporation and stylization of other genres (308); the incorporation of maxims and aphorisms (322); and, more generally, any activation of the "internal dialogism" or words (279). All of these stylistic features are markedly present in *Mary Barton*, the last most conspicuously in Gaskell's play with multiple interpretations of keywords such as "duty" and "improvidence," both in her characters' discourse and in her own authorial discourse. The mixing of regional and occupational dialects, and of fictive and historical voices, and the proliferation of chapter mottoes, quotations and footnotes also contribute to the dialogization of discourse in *Mary Barton*. Most notably, however, Gaskell further dialogizes the discourse of *Mary Barton* through combining gender-inscribed languages and plots, a possibility that Bakhtin curiously ignores, as Wayne Booth has pointed out. Those who divide the world of *Mary Barton* into an implicitly or explicitly male political sphere and a female private sphere, or who split the "social-problem" or "tragic" from the "romance" or "domestic" plot of the novel, endorse gender-inflected paradigms that Gaskell's own novelistic practice repeatedly subverts. As Patsy Stoneman suggests in her critique of the conventional view of Gaskell as a "split" novelist, women and the working classes were alike muted groups in Victorian society, enjoined to "suffer and be still" (13, 63). In *Mary Barton,* members of both assume the power of speaking subjects, but Gaskell also shows how these two groups, themselves internally divided, act to silence their own warring members and each other.

    The most straightforward of the dialogic strategies apparent in *Mary Barton* is dialogue embodying the social dialogue of classes. In contrast to a novelist such as Jane Austen who, as Tony Tanner observes, excludes "not only the unassimilable roughness and dissonance of working-class speech but also any of the potential discordance of colloquial or vernacular discourse" (38), Gaskell portrays the voices of the poor with the loving and intimate detail that made her such an important follower of Scott and precursor of George Eliot. Her achievement in depicting Lancashire dialect has long been recognized. But less attention has been given to the cumulative effect of her calculated focus on working-class voices that are at once individualized and representative, and to the manner in which these voices interact with those woven into Gaskell's authorial discourse.[5] Middle-class literary discourse typically frames the polyglot world or working-class discourse in nineteenth-century industrial novels, but in *Mary Barton* the framed interpenetrates the frame. As for bourgeois socio-economic discourse in *Mary Barton,* it seems swallowed up in the working-class discourse it is accustomed to suppress. This effect results partly from Gaskell's portrayal of a relatively narrow spectrum of the propertied classes, a feature of her first novel that was strongly criticized and that she sought to redress in *North and South.* In *Mary Barton,* only the members of the Carson family are individualized among the propertied classes. Moreover, although Gaskell presents a "medley" of the masters' conflicting voices in Chapter 16, where they meet to deal with the strike, she chooses to do so on an occasion when they do not appear in a particularly positive light. Thus the most humane master weakly suggests that the employers must "'try and do more'" than make two "'cow's heads into soup'" every week to feed the starving for several miles around, while the most brutal denounces the strikers as "'more like wild beasts than human beings'" (232).

Representing the working classes, on the contrary, we encounter a broad spectrum of fully individualized characters, embodying conflicting cultural backgrounds and ideological perspectives, ranging from the Chartist radicalism of the Manchester-born John Barton, to the political passivity of George Wilson, a laborer still shaped by his rural roots, to the Christian pacifism of the aptly named Job Legh. Moreover, John Barton and Job Legh speak with an eloquence that finds no counterpart in the speech of the masters. John's speech is most moving in Chapter 16 in his spontaneous address to the striking workers, when they discover that one of the masters addressed by their delegation has crudely caricatured their tattered appearance in a cartoon:

> John Barton began to speak; they turned to him with deep attention. "it makes me more than sad, it makes my heart burn within me, to see that folk can make a jest of earnest men; of chaps, who come to ask for a bit o' fire for th' old granny, as shivers in the cold; for a bit o'bedding, and some warn clothing to the poor wife as lies in labour on th' damp flags; and for victuals for the children, whose little voices are getting too faint and weak to cry aloud wi' hunger. For, brothers, is not them the things we ask for when we ask for more wages? . . . We do not want their grand houses, we want a roof to cover us from the rain, and the snow, and the storm; ay, and not alone to cover us, but helpless ones that cling to us in the keen wind, and ask us with their eyes why we brought 'em into th' world to suffer?" He lowered his deep voice almost to a whisper.
>
> "I've seen a father who had killed his child rather than let it clem before his eyes; and he were a tender-hearted man." (238–239)

By this point in the novel we have already heard the story of John Barton's son dying of disease because his father could not obtain the food he needed. And we have already heard the narrator present the debate between strikers and masters in "technical" economic terms. Critics have often faulted the narrator's remark in Chapter 15 of *Mary Barton*, "I am not sure if I can express myself in the technical terms of either masters, or workmen" (220), as an example of Gaskell's feminine diffidence and ignorance of economic theory. But such criticisms overlook Gaskell's evident knowledge of Adam Smith, her unconventional and undisguised intervention as a modest female voice in the "masculine" realm of political economy–sometimes with the additional force of an abrupt interruption–and the subversive equality she grants to the workers in acknowledging that they, like the masters, have their own "technical" economic terms.[6] Clearly, however, she puts less stock in this abstract discourse than in the concrete and moving language that John

Barton later speaks, which makes his listeners see and hear what is being
described, as Gaskell sought to do through her own art (Sharps 8–9). Indeed,
the masters and workers do not themselves think or speak principally in
rational "technical" terms, as she reveals through her skillful use of free
indirect speech and hybridizations to depict the economic debate. The masters
insist that they will not be "bullied" by the workers, while the workers cry
"Shame on them!" in response to the masters' low wages (221–22).

The social dialogue of classes is far from the most original element in *Mary
Barton*. Joseph Kestner has shown that such dialogues were a common feature
of English social narratives written by women like Hannah More and Harriet
Martineau long before Disraeli presented the "two nations" of rich and of
poor in *Sybil* (23–25), 41). Gaskell's greater accomplishment, according to
Kestner, is her ability to locate "the expression of social conditions within
the consciousness of her characters" (121). This achievement results chiefly
from Gaskell's depiction of her working-class characters in dialogue among
themselves and, in John and Mary Barton's case, within themselves. Most
notably, John Barton's radical language and views are clearly opposed to Job
Legh's Christian submission, although Gaskell by no means sets up a simple,
one-dimensional opposition between Chartism and Christianity in which her
characters becomes walking mouthpieces for social ideologies. Accordingly,
she initially depicts Barton engaged in dialogue not with the articulate Job,
but with George Wilson, whose ideological position is not clearly formulated.
More important, she gives to the Chartist Barton some of the most Biblically
resonant language in the novel, a feature that is not out of character since, as
Angus Easson notes, the Chartists frequently adapted Christian discourse to
their own purposes (57).[7]

Thus it is John who invokes the parable of Dives and Lazarus in the novel's
opening chapter, and John who caustically observes that he would rather see
his daughter "'earning her bread by the sweat of her brow as the Bible tells
her,'" instead of living like "'a do-nothing lady, worrying shopmen all
morning, and screeching at her pianny all afternoon, and going to bed without
having done a good turn to any one of God's creatures but herself'" (44–45).
In mixing Chartist radicalism and popular idioms with Christian doctrine
and imagery, Gaskell activates the "critical interanimation" of languages in
Barton's discourse. A reverse dialogization subsequently occurs when she
depicts the delirious Methodist, Ben Davenport, who habitually speaks "'as
good as Bible-words'" about "'God being our father, and that we mun bear
patiently whate'er he sends,'" cursing and swearing in his final illness like
the popular middle-class conception of a raving Chartist (103–104).

The central debate between John Barton's radical activism and Job Legh's pacifism gradually emerges as the novel develops, but before Job is introduced Gaskell has embodied this conflict in various ways, most strikingly in the text of the Lancashire song, "The Oldham Weaver," that she "copies" for her readers in Chapter 4. In this song, the speaker is a poor cotton weaver who laments:

Owd Dicky o'Billy's kept telling me lung,
Wee s'd ha better toimes if I'd but howd my tung,
Oi've howden my tung, till oi've near stopped my breath,
Oi think i' my heart oi'se soon clem to death, . . .   (72)

The message that he should "howd his tung" is, in effect, Job's answer to John's Chartist criticisms. (Significantly, we learn in the next chapter that Job's hobby of collecting insects keeps him "'silent'" [79].) Parliament also in effect tells the Chartist delegates to "howd" their tongues when they appeal to it with the 1842 Petition and "all the force of their rough, untutored words," only to be ignored (141).

"The Oldham Weaver" is not only woven into the debate of working-class submission versus activism in *Mary Barton,* but is also dialogized through Gaskell's mode of presenting it. Evidently, she deliberately chose not to modify the diction and pronunciation of the Lancashire dialect to make the song more comprehensible to her middle-class readers, as she customarily does even in presenting John Barton's speech.[8] The result is that the language seems almost grotesquely deformed and the song's pathos is lost in the reader's bewilderment before the alien idioms and the unfamiliar orthography. Indeed, as the narrator observes, though "it is a powerfully pathetic song," "to read it . . . may, perhaps, seem humorous" (73). To counteract this effect, Gaskell emphasizes the cultural context of the song and the suffering it reflects. More subtly, she presents Margaret Legh singing it with a "superb and flexible voice," then going on to "burst forth with all the power of her magnificent voice . . . in the grand supplication, 'Lord remember David'" (74). This is a characteristically complex instance of dialogization in *Mary Barton* because Gaskell's combining of voices mixes social classes, genders, low and high genres—a Lancashire folk "ditty" with a grand Hebrew psalm—and history and fiction, the last through the comparison of Margaret to the historical Deborah Travers, an Oldham factory girl whose singing made her the "darling of fashionable crowds" (74).

The mixing of genders evident in Margaret's singing "The Oldham Weaver"—a song in which the male speaker in turn speaks for his silent wife—pervades Gaskell's depiction of working-class discourse in *Mary Barton*. Thus, in describing the fire at Carson's mill, the narrator observes that the crowd utters "a sob, as if of excited women," in watching the dramatic rescue of the entrapped men (90). And in Chapter 9, old Jennings, who accompanied Job Legh to London when his son and Job's daughter fell sick, "'screeched out as if he'd been a woman'" when he saw the corpses of the unhappy couple (146). This dialogization of speech occurs in a narrative that calls attention to the crossing of gender lines by presenting the spectacle of two old men in their fumbling attempts to nurse a hungry female baby, which gropes around with its mouth and insists on "'crying for its pobbies'" (148). Old bearded Jennings even puts on a woman's nightcap in an attempt to trick the crying baby into thinking that he is female. In this delightfully comic touch, Gaskell indicates how much the feminine is a social construction, based on gender-inflected meanings attached to arbitrary signifiers.

Job's homely, conventionally female story of nursing baby Margaret is further dialogized by the narrative structure of *Mary Barton* because it appears in the same chapter as John Barton's historic, conventionally male story of the journey to London with the Chartist petition. Gallagher overlooks the complex interactions between these two stories when she divides the novel into two mutually exclusive plots—a domestic tale focusing on Mary and a tragedy focusing on John—and argues that Job's domestic tale acts to suppress John's tragic story of the fate of the Chartist petition (82; see Bodenheimer, 203, for a similar argument). On the contrary, Gaskell consistently employs the hungry child metaphor to link the two stories, the first of which articulates a desperate cry of hunger on the part of an entire class whose members were often viewed as refractory children or infants by the middle classes. In Chapter 8, for instance, the narrator describes the petition to Parliament as the "darling child" of the Chartists' hopes because they believe that the country's legislators must be unaware of their suffering—much as parents might "make domestic rules for the pretty behaviour of children, without caring to know that those children had been kept for days without food" (127). The rejection of the petition thus symbolically entails a double rejection of children: both of the Chartists themselves, and of the "darling child" of their hopes. In Chapter 9, the child metaphor continues as John Barton recalls being "'like a child'" lost in wonder at the spectacles of London (143). Then, as Job's story of the rescue of his infant granddaughter closes, John's daughter Mary falls asleep on her father's knee, "sleeping as soundly as an infant" (153). Both stories are much concerned with the cost and difficulty of obtaining food, for working class adults and for children. "'We were wanting our breakfasts, and so were it too, motherless baby!''' Job says at one point in his tale (151). Job's focus on private hunger reinforces the point of John's story, and brings it home to the reader in personal terms. As the chapter ends, the public and private spheres of the two stories are fused in Samuel Bamford's poem "God Help the Poor," which again brings together the hunger of forlorn adults and children among the poor.

Both dialogue and narrative structure enter into another notable instance of dialogization at this point in *Mary Barton*, as Gaskell shows Barton shifting from weeping to cursing, much as she had earlier described the suffering factory workers collectively: "the sufferers wept first, and then they cursed" (126). After telling of the rejection of the Chartists, Barton says to Mary, "'man will not hearken: no, not now, when we weep tears of blood''' (141); and subsequently he declares, "'as long as I live I shall curse them as so cruelly refused to hear us''' (145). This transition from a conventionally female response to a conventionally male one is then epitomized in one of the mottoes to the following chapter, which foreshadows Barton's act of cursing Esther, his fallen sister-in-law, in the private as opposed to the political sphere: "'My heart, once soft as woman's tear, is gnarled hair / With gloating on the ills I cannot cure''' (157).

If Gaskell's working-class men often speak or act in conventionally female ways, so too her working-class women speak in ways that undermine conventional alignments of gender and sphere. Thus in Chapter 8, when John Barton is described in a double-voiced construction as holding " a levée" before he sets off for London with the Chartist Petition, we hear a female as well as male neighbors besieging him with conflicting political messages—most notably, Mrs. Davenport, who urges him to speak out against the laws keeping children from factory work (128).[9] In Chapter 10 we again hear women, this time unaccompanied by men, promoting factory legislation to prevent married women from working, in contradiction to Mrs. Davenport's earlier stance regarding children. Mrs. Wilson remarks that Prince Albert "'ought to be asked how he'd like his missis to be from home when he comes in, tired and worn,''' and insists that Prince Albert is the one to approach because, although the Queen makes the laws, "'isn't she bound to obey Prince Albert?''' (166). This is another interesting example of Gaskell's quietly subversive irony and crossing of gender and class lines, particularly if it is viewed in the context of the popular controversy in 1839 and after concerning gender reversal implicit in Victoria and Albert's courtship and royal relationship. One lithograph, for instance, comically presents Victoria proposing to Albert as royal etiquette required (Marshall 71).

Although P. J. Keating includes no women at all in his catalogue of representative working-class characters in Victorian fiction (26–27), Gaskell portrays a broad spectrum of working-class women in *Mary Barton* and her other works, as Stoneman notes (46). Like their male counterparts, the working-class women in *Mary Barton* represent different ideological perspectives and speak different languages in Bakhtin's sense of the term. At one extreme, we encounter the vulgar unchecked "utterance" of Sally Leadbitter (132), whose discourse is chiefly shaped by the popular theater (427) and the "romances" of fashionable life read by Miss Simmonds's seamstresses (121). Sally's "witty boldness" gave her "what her betters would have called piquancy," the narrator slyly observes, crossing class lines in another double-voiced construction (132). At the other extreme, we meet the pious old Alice Wilson, Job's female counterpart, who preaches and lives by a doctrine of passive submission to God's will, and speaks a biblical idiom—"'Let the Lord send what he sees fit'" (69). Many around Alice assume as Sally does that her religious discourse is "'Methodee,'" but Alice is in fact Church of England as Mary points out (134). Thus Gaskell mixes the discourse of denominations, perhaps in an attempt to promote a common Christian spirit of belief. Alice is flanked by Margaret, who emphasizes womanly submission more than Christian submission. Both of these women have been viewed as Mary's better angels opposing Sally the tempter (Bodenheimer 29). But Margaret conspicuously fails Mary when the question of Jem Wilson's guilt is at stake, and Alice quietly dies in the second half of the novel when Mary, who initially plays the role of a passively waiting Mariana in her relation to Jem, decides that it is her duty not to wait and to submit like Alice, but to act and to speak out in Jem's defense.

Mary's inner conflict between submission and action is presented in the context of a running debate about what constitutes "duty" in *Mary Barton*, a debate that connects class to class, and women to men. The focus on this keyword is clearest in Chapter 14, where Gaskell echoes Carlyle's injunction in *Sartor Resartus* to "do the duty that lies nearest" as she presents Jem Wilson's successful struggle to subdue his vindictive rage against Harry Carson (216). In Chapter 33, Jem experiences conflict again as he first accepts Job's advice that it is his "duty" to stay with his distraught mother instead of with Mary after the trial (404), and then rejects Margaret's rebuke for going to see Mary on the day of his Aunt Alice's death. You remember the dead "'without striving after it, and without thinking it's your duty to keep recalling them,'" he points out to Margaret (411). However, Jem's interpretation of his duty is far less problematic than either John Barton's or Mary's of theirs. In depicting these characters and the complexity of their ethical choices, Gaskells plays out Carlyle's authoritarian precept in what Carol Gilligan calls "a different voice," as she adapts his characteristic strategy of multiplying and interrogating meanings for her own purposes (Holloway 41–47).

When Job reminds Jem of his duty in standing by his mother, he at the same time criticizes John Barton for neglect of his daughter: "'To my mind John Barton would be more in the way of his duty, looking after his daughter, than delegating it up and down the country'" (404). At this point, Job is still unaware of the assassination John has undertaken in fulfilling a very different conception of duty. In murdering Harry Carson, John Barton speaks on the behalf of the workers, not in an act of private revenge such as Jem considers and rejects, but because "perverted reasoning" had made "the performance of an undoubted sin appear a duty" (436). But although he repents his means of carrying out his "duty," and the narrator describes it as the result of perverted reasoning, the message of the novel about John's duty is altogether more multivoiced and mixed—particularly if we consider that his desperate attempt to make death speak, middle-class death this time, is the catalyst that brings about old Mr. Carson's conversion and recognition of his "duty" to those less fortunate than himself (457).

Gaskell's dialogization of the Victorian keyword "duty" interacts with her exploration of the meanings of "justice" and "revenge" in the innovative adaptation of the traditional revenge tragedy plot she undertakes in *Mary Barton*. Old Mr. Carson believes that his desire to avenge his son's death reflects his "duty" (439) and his desire for simple justice, but the narrator asks, "True, his vengeance was sanctioned by the law, but was it the less revenge?" (266); and she later emphasizes his fury when he believes that "the slayer of his unburied boy would slip through the fangs of justice" (398). In fact, John Barton's action in assassinating Carson's son, later correctly interpreted as an act of class revenge by Mr. Carson and Job (455), is less tainted by vindictive motives than Carson's cry for "justice," since Gaskell pointedly refuses to provide Barton with a direct personal motive for revenge on Harry Carson. The assassination is a dreadful duty that falls to him by lot, not, as it easily might have been in a melodrama or a traditional revenge tragedy, his response to Harry Carson's attempt to seduce his daughter.[10] Bodenheimer argues that the splitting of the stories of Mary's sexual harassment and the economic exploitation of the workers softens the "systemic analysis of industrial oppression" in *Mary Barton* (208; see Lucas, 173, for a similar view). Yet Gaskell's focus on John Barton's political rather than personal motives foregrounds the unconventional class revenge the novel depicts, and at the same time generates sympathy for her working-class avenger and the sense of "duty" that governs him.

In dramatizing the contradictory interpretations of "duty" embraced by John, Job, and Mr. Carson, Gaskell activates the internal dialogism of words as Bakhtin conceives them. "The word, directed towards its object, enters a dialogically agitated and tension-filled environment of alien words, value judgments and accents," he observes; "and an artistic representation" may "activate and organize" this "dialogic play of verbal intentions" (276–77). The question of what "duty" means or should mean for John's daughter Mary is brought into this complex field of "dialogic play." Gallagher, interpreting Mary as the sentimental heroine of a domestic take, suggests that "duty is clear" for women in Gaskell's tales off this sort (79); while Kestner sees Mary's function as merely "focusing the men's interests" in the novel (119). But Mary's "duty" of acting and speaking out on Jem's behalf, so contradictory to the womanly submission enjoined upon her, is dialogized both through her mental debate depicted in Chapter 22, and through her later debate with Job, when she refuses to depute what she sees as "her duty, her right" to a man (340). The parallel between the father's duty and the daughter's—John's taking a life in the name of duty and Mary's saving a life—emerges if one considers how John is driven by the desire to save working-class lives, and how Mary risks ending her father's life by trying to save Jem.

In Gaskell's "interanimation" of diverging definitions of "duty," Mr. Carson's concluding recognition of his duty to the less fortunate brings a middle-class perspective into the conflicting social and ideological interpretations of this keyword. However, it is Job who points out this duty to him, and who speaks to it most eloquently. Consequently, working-class interpretations of duty, situated in the intricate intersections of private and public responsibility, dominate the novel. This dominance is not surprising since, as I implied in the introduction, everywhere we turn in *Mary Barton*—in the textual voice of the novel's narrative and commentary as well as in the dialogue of the charachers—we encounter working-class languages, texts, and perspectives. Gaskell weaves into her text at every opportunity not only passages from Chartist poems like "The Pauper's Drive" and Lancashire "ditties" like "The Oldham Weaver," but also proverbs and maxims, nursery rhymes like "Polly put the kettle on" (the motto to Chapter 2), and quotations from ballads, from poets pointedly identified as "Anonymous," as in the mottoes to Chapters 17 and 24, and from working-class poets like Robert Burns, Ebenezer Elliot, and Samuel Bamford. Subsequent novels by Gaskell do not exhibit this plenitude of working-class discourse to nearly the same degree, and there is much to suggest that it results from deliberate narrative and rhetorical strategies in *Mary Barton*.[11]

In Chapter 10 the narrator notes the soothing effect "in times of suffering or fierce endurance" of "the mere repetition off old proverbs" such as "it's a long lane that has no turning" (157), a proverb which Job Legh in fact speaks in the preceding chapter (151). Gaskell also draws freely on working-class idioms that she acknowledges may sound like "trivial, everyday expres-sion[s]" (186), as in depicting Mrs. Wilson's love for her helpless, silly twins: "want had never yet come in at the door to make love for these innocents fly out at the window" (115). In another instance, Margaret reacts to a goodnatured kiss from Jem by asking "'What would May say?'", Jem replies, "'She'd nobbut say, practice makes perfect,'" and in between the narrator observes, "Lightly said, lightly answered" (81). Such hybridizations create a double-voiced effect as the narrative voice fuses with the voices of the working-class characters. *Mary Barton* is thus typical of the dialogized novel as Bakhtin describes it, in that the heteroglossia entering through dia-logue is also diffused through authorial discourse (316).

In addition, Gaskell's chapter mottoes, many off them drawn either from working-class texts like Ebenezer Elliot's, or from the texts of authors associ-ated with working-class causes like Tom Hood and Caroline Norton, do much to establish a matrix of working-class discourse in a novel that is insistently intertextual, although in a different way than more conventional literary works. Stoneman suggests that *Mary Barton* is a text haunted by literary "fathers" (85), but she does not address the unconventional working-class identity of many of these "fathers," or the extent to which Gaskell also echoes literary "mothers" such as Norton, Charlotte Elizabeth Tonna, and Elizabeth Stone (see Kestner; also Wheeler, "The Writer as Reader"). Ten out of the first eleven chapters begin with mottoes derived either from popular, anonymous discourse, or from authors associated with working-class causes. Often Gaskell employs these mottoes dialogically, as when she prefaces Chap-ter 9 with a quotation from Norton's "Child of the Islands" which presents one half of a debate between the rich and the poor. In the motto, the rich ask the poor of what they "complain"—and the chapter itself, incorporating John Barton's narrative of the rejection of the Chartist petition, provides the an-swer. A similar question and answer relation is set up between the motto and the chapter's contents in Chapter 33, but this time it is the poor who ask if "brothers" would treat them as the rich do (451), a question which both the dying John Barton and Job Legh reiterate in the ensuring chapter, and which Mr. Carson and the reader are left to answer. Elsewhere, as in Chapter 10 discussed below, Gaskell anticipates George Eliot in combining two mottoes to set up a dialogue of opposing voices played out in the ensuing chapter.

Gaskell's principal rhetorical strategy in creating a dialogue of voices, both in the characters' speech and in her authorial discourse, seems to be juxtaposing differing modes of discourse in order to emphasize the common humanity of differing classes and genders, or to foreground conflicting ideologies and cultural perspectives. An example of both effects combined occurs in Chapter 15, where she presents young Harry Carson's contrast of his own dandified appearance to Jem Wilson's grimy appearance in his mechanic's clothes. Recalling his own reflection in his bedroom glass, Harry thinks: "It was Hyperion to a Satyr. That quotation came aptly; he forgot 'The man's a man for a' that'" (227). Gaskell's focus here on the literacy and ideological intertext shaping Carson's aristocratic prejudices indicates that her own repeated quotations from writers of the people such as Burns—a writer frequently lauded by the Chartists— are a deliberate strategy.[12] Moreover, her opposition of Harry's field of allusion to Jem's is a clear example of dialogization involving what Bakhtin terms "character zones"—that is, textual territories surrounding particular characters that are penetrated by their distinctive discourse. Typically too, the mixing of allusions here is quietly ironic, as we watch the conceited young Harry applying to himself the praise Hamlet applies to his dead father.

The allusion to *Hamlet* belongs to the other main group of allusions and mottoes in *Mary Barton*, derived from traditional literary texts rather than working-class discourse: in particular, from Greek and English revenge tragedies, and from Romantic poetry. Michael Wheeler ("The Writer as Reader") and Graham Handley have shown how intricately patterned some of these allusions are, contrary to Henry James's view of Gaskell as naively unintellectual (Ganz 29), and to Johnson's impression that Gaskell's Biblical and literary allusions are "scattered" while Dostoevsky's are carefully patterned (48). In fact, Gaskell seems to make calculated dialogic use of quotations from the traditional "high" genres of poetry and drama in order to invest her humble characters' actions with heroic or epic significance—much as she uses her footnotes on dialect to connect the humble idioms of her Lancashire working-class characters to writers such as Chaucer, that "well of English undefiled," Wycliffe and Ben Johnson.[13] Quotations from such genres are particularly frequent in the second half of *Mary Barton*, where Gaskell uses them to relate her working-class tragic hero and the middle-class Mr. Carson to the aristocratic protogonists of classical and English revenge tragedy. It is Mr. Carson to the aristocratic protogonists of classical and English revenge tragedy. It is Mr. Carson, however, who emerges as the more bloodthirsty revenger—the "Orestes" who passes as a Christian in the nineteenth century (266). The motto of Chapter 18 from Dryden's *Duke of Guise*—"'My brain runs this way and that way; 'twill fix hair / On aught but vengeance'" (254)—applies most directly to Mr. Carson's fury at the close of the chapter, as he confronts the corpse of his beloved son.

Mary is associated even more insistently than her father with epic and tragic figures, a feature often overlooked by those who see her simply as a domestic heroine. Indeed, Maria Edgeworth said that Gaskell's heroine was placed in a "situation fit for the highest Greek Tragedy" (Sharp 67). Mary's divided feelings about her father and her participation in his guilt are intimated in the trial scene through a comparison linking her with Beatrice Cenci (389), while Mr. Carson erroneously sees her as the "fatal Helen, the cause of all" (388). More intriguingly, she is linked with Saturn's wife in Keats' *Hyperion* through the motto to Chapter 22. This last motto seems intended to add epic stature to Mary at a point when her "innate power" of "judgement and discretion" is called upon in the attempt to free Jem (302). At the same point, Mary is also compared to Spenser's Una in *The Faerie Queen*. In the next chapter, a gender reversal figures her as the archetypal romance hero: "She was like one who discovers the silken clue which guides to some bower of bliss,and secure of the power within his grasp, has to wait for a time before he may tread the labyrinth" (311).

One other persistent set of textual allusions relates both Mary and her Aunt Esther to Coleridge's Ancient Mariner, and to Christabel and her stepmother Geraldine respectively (Handley 134–36). The connection of Esther, the fallen woman, to the Ancient Mariner is a daring and effective dialogization of the prostitute's forbidden discourse. "To whom shall the outcast prostitute tell her tale!" the narrator asks (207). Gaskell does not let us forget that the "leper's" discourse of the fallen women is suppressed even by those members of the working classes who might be expected to understand the economic deprivation leading to prostitution. The combination of mottoes prefacing Chapter 10 highlights the irony involved in John Barton's refusal to listen to Esther's warning about Mary, immediately after the chapter in which he has described his anger at the legislators' refusal to listen to the Chartists' appeal. Later the reader, like Coleridge's hapless wedding guest, must listen to the "outcast prostitute's" tale along with Jem as Esther insists, "'I will have the relief of telling it'" (210). Another literary precedent from a high Romantic genre subsequently appears for the telling of this inset story, as Esther is linked through the motto to Chapter 21 to the seduced Margaret in Goethe's *Faust*.

Gaskell's mixing of genres and genders through her use off allusions and mottoes dialogizes literary discourse internally, at the same time as it democratizes it through collision with the languages of the illiterate and the nonliterary. Further dialogization occurs through Gaskell's opposition of the languages of different regions and professions. In a reversal designed to relativize the linguistic consciousness of her London readers, she presents John Barton commenting on the alien sound of "'tongue-tied'" Londoners who "'can't say their a's and i's properly'" (144). Sailor Will's nautical "way of speaking" (203), evident in his inset comic story of the scorpion, finds its regional counterpart in the Liverpool ship slang that Mary finds "unintelligible" at times— slang that the narrator says she cannot "repeat correctly" because she is "too much of a landlubber" (352). Young Charley, Mary's waterside guide, says that "'women know nought about'" such language (349), but ironically even Job is perplexed by the "confused use of the feminine pronoun" that Charley's reference to Will's ship as "she" entails (367).

Much as different regional and professional languages, marked by internal gender differences, are juxtaposed in *Mary Barton*, so fictional and historical voices intermingle. Indeed, a startling effect of "faction" rather than fiction is frequently created when Gaskell feigns to report the comments of actual witnesses to her fictitious events. Thus, after Margaret is depicted singing the song "What a single word can do," the narrator says, "As a factory worker, listening outside, observed, 'She spun it reet fine!'" (139). Presenting Mary at the trial, the narrator comments, "I was not there myself; but one who was, told me . . . that her countenance haunted him, like the remembrance of some wild, sad melody, heard in childhood" (389). And the discovery of the caricature of the strikers drawn by Harry Carson, one of the most crucial incidents in the plot, is presented in a similar way as a "by-play" at the meeting of the masters and men "not recorded in the Manchester newspapers" (235). These reportorial remarks seem calculated rather than accidental, since Gaskell plays differing versions of the Carson murder off against each other, among them a newspaper version which reduces it to "some dispute about a factory girl" (344) and the opposing legal versions at the trial, in effect forensic fictions streaked with melodrama.

Gaskell's parodic stylization of professional languages thus interacts with the parodic stylization of genres in *Mary Barton* to reveal how much the apparently factual accounts of Harry Carson's murder produced by the newspapers, the law courts, and the police rely on the conventions of genres such as farce, melodrama, and the detective novel. Gallagher, who observes that "*Mary Barton* is partly about the ways in which narrative conventions mask and distory reality," notes how Faskell parodies the conventions of farce and melodrama even as she employs the latter herself to play upon the reader's expectations (67–68). Much the same can be said of Gaskell's use of the conventions of the Newgate or detective novel noted by Wright (237). When the police are hot on Jem Wilson's trail, the narrator observes how "they enjoy the collecting and collating evidence, and the life of adventure they lead; a continual unwinding of Jack Sheppard romances, always interesting to the vulgar and uneducated mind" (273). The version of the murder the police piece together is not very different from the cruder version told by the "halfpenny broadsides" hawked in the streets, with their "raw-head-and-bloody-bones picture of the suspected murderer" (283). Similarly reductive is the police interpretation of Esther's situation after she is cursed and thrown aside by John Barton when she tries to warn him about Mary. Seeing "the close of these occurrences," a policeman arrests Esther, and the next day she is charged and committed to the New Bailey. "It was a clear case of disorderly vagrancy," the narrator says (170). In this ironic hybridization, Gaskell "does the police in different voices" with the virtuosity of Dickens.

Gaskell's sustained and complex "critical interanimation" of voices and discourses—working-class and middle-class, female and male, oral and written, vernacular and literary, historical and fictional, regional and professional—provides a context in which to view the inconsistencies of the narrator in *Mary Barton*. Existing criticism has typically privileged one or two of the multiple narrative voices in the novel, and objected to contradictions between these, or between the teller and the tale. Bodenheimer, for example, sees Gaskell as shifting awkwardly between the roles of a sympathetic and accurate "domestic observer" of the poor and a stilted middle-class "social historian" (198).[14] However, dichotomizing labels do not capture the flux and diversity of the narrative voicing in the novel. Sometimes the voice is that of a neighborly gossip. "Do you know 'The Oldham Weaver?' Not unless you are Lancashire born and bred. . . . I will copy it for you" (71). At other times, it is an intimate voice urgent as Esther's, as when we hear of Mary's dark suspicion that her father is Harry Carson's murderer: "I must tell you; I must put into words the dreadful secret" (299). Sometimes this intimate voice is oddly intrusive and personal. Most notably, the account of Mrs. Wilson's distressed dreams after her son's arrest is interrupted to reveal the narrator's grief and solace in the land of "dreams—(that land into which no sympathy nor love can penetrate with another . . . where alone I may see, while yet I tarry here, the sweet looks of my dead child)" (327).

These particular voices seem overtly female, in ways that George Eliot's narrative voice never is in *Adam Bede* and *The Mill on the Floss*, two works that show the influence of *Mary Barton*.[15] Yet, when Gaskell's first novel was published anonymously, there was some controversy about the gender of the author: Carlyle and W. R. Greg detected a feminine hand, while reviewers in the *Athenaeum* and the *Independent* assumed the writer was male (Hopkins 17; Stoneman 3). The controversy seems understandable if one considers that some of the narrative voices assumed in *Mary Barton* have the masculine tone of a Carlylean prophet or preacher. Chapter 10, for example, begins with a sermon-like exhortation to middle-class readers to "remember" the suffering of the poor, and then invokes the Old Testament story of Rehoboam in 1 Kings 12. The people had found the "yoke" of poverty hard to bear in preceding years, the narrator observes, "but this year added sorely to its weight. Former times had chastised them with whips, but this chastised them with scorpions" (157). Since in the Biblical story, it is not the "times" that chastised the people, but the "yoke" of oppression imposed by Rehoboam, this allusion sharpens Gaskell's social satire, at the same time as it prophesies the downfall of rulers as oppressive as Rehoboam, subsequently replaced by the people's advocate Jeroboam. Having spoken in the conventionally male voice of the preacher, Gaskell then typically shifts in the next paragraph to a colloquial, conventionally female voice, as she describes how John Barton and Mary tried to subsist on her salary—"But the rent! It was half a crown a week—nearly all of Mary's earnings" (158).

The abstract, univocal concept of the "implied author" cannot accomodate this multiplication of narrative voices in *Mary Barton*. Nor can the diverse readers posited or actively engaged by Gaskell's multiple narrative voices be accomodated by the concept of "the implied reader," which many reader response critics now reject as too abstract and reductive (Suleiman 14, 25–26). In *Mary Barton*, many of these readers are actually inscribed in the text, as opposed to implied, and they shift in identity as the narrative voice shifts. Sometimes addressed as "you," sometimes as "we," the inscribed reader is at times individual, at times collective. Sometimes the "you" evokes the careless, anonymous man—or is it woman?—in the streets, who cannot "read the lot of those who daily pass you by. . . . How do you know the wild romances of their lives . . .?" (101). Sometimes the "you" evokes a womanly neighbor or friend: "Can you fancy the bustle of Alice to make tea . . .?" (67). At other points, the "you" might be the educated clubman in an armchair whom Thackeray often addresses in *Vanity Fair*—or it might just possibly be an educated woman or self-educated working man. "If you will refer to the preface to Sir J. E. Smith's Life (I have it not by me, or I would copy you the exact passate), you will find that he names a little circumstance corroborative of what I have said," the narrator observes in describing the self-educated working men of Manchester like Job (76). Such an address has the potential to cross both class and gender lines, given its context and its juxtaposition with narrative comments conventionally coded as female.

The shifting narrative voices in *Mary Barton* and the multiplication of inscribed readers further contribute to the actively dialogic nature of the novel's discourse because both narrator and reader participate in the internal and external debates the characters experience. Christine Brooke-Rose describes the dialogical novel as one in which "the author has a constant metatextual dialogue with his characters" (Suleiman 145); while Bakhtin observes that even in Turgenev's works, "substantial masses" of the novelist's apparently monologic language are "drawn into the battle between points of view, value judgments and emphases" embodied by the characters (315–16). This effect occurs in *Mary Barton* when both narrator and reader are drawn into the debate Mary experiences concerning "duty." Should Mary submit and wait as Alice and Margaret advise? Or should she act? The narrator asks the reader a propos of Mary's dilemma, "Do you think if I could help it, I would sit still with folded hands to mourn?" (301).

At other points, what seem to be irritating middle-class platitudes on the part of the narrator emerge, when viewed contextually, as components in extended debates pervading the narrative commentary and the dramatic presentation of the characters' thoughts and actions. One notable example of apparently platitudinous commentary in *Mary Barton* appears in Chapter 3, when the narrator comments on John Barton's anger at the rich who, in his eyes, do not suffer during bad times:

> I know that this is not really the case; and I know what is the truth in such matters: but what I wish to impress is what the workman feels and thinks. True, that with child-like improvidence, good times will often dissipate his grumbling,

and make him forget all prudence and insight.   (60)

This interruption has seemed jarring to many readers (Bodenheimer 199–200 and Gill, *Mary Barton* 3–24 are representative). But, rather than being seen as epitomizing Gaskell's subscription to middle-class ideology, this patronizing commentary can be viewed as playing an integral part in a sustained debate in which she elicits the stock opinions of her middle-class readers (and no doubt of one part of her own mind) in order to destabilize those opinions. Precisely this effect occurs as Gaskell progressively complicates and interrogates the assumption that the working classes are "improvident" in the first half of *Mary Barton*.

The motif of improvidence first appears in Chapter 1, when John Barton's appearance is described as "stunted," giving the impression that he had "suffered" from the scanty living consequent upon bad times, and improvident habits" (41). Here the opinion that the working classes are improvident seems something that the narrator is not even conscious of, yet one notes how "improvident habits" hangs in potential conflict with "bad times" as an explanation of the suffering of the poor. The motif next appears indirectly in the narrator's description of the Bartons' domestic belongings in Chapter 2. Here there is a curious insistence on household articles that are "really for use," like a table, in contrast to more ornamental articles like the "bright green japanned tea-tray" and "crimson tea-caddy," and the "triangular pieces of glass to save carving knives and forks from dirtying table-cloths," for which one would have fancied their possessors could find no use" (49–50). It's as if Gaskell were embodying the first impressions of a working-class home in the mind of a typical middle-class visitor representing the Manchester and Salford District Provident Society, to which she herself belonged. A similar voice seems to be speaking in the disruptive narrative commentary of Chapter 3, cited above. After the description of the Bartons' home, the "improvidence" motif is intermingled with the focus on distinguishing between objects of use and objects of ornamentation. The motif recurs in the description of Alice's meagre domestic possessions, which include an "unlackered, ancient, third-hand tea-tray" (66); and it takes on an ironic note when Mr. Carson's home is described as "furnished with disregard for expense"—"many articles chosen for their beauty and elegance adorned his rooms" (105). This description appears in Chapter 6, where we first vividly see, smell, and feel the dark, foetid, clammy Davenport cellar, stripped even of the plainest articles of use (101). Finally in Chapter 10, in a passage remarkable for its quiet but caustic ironies, the narrator describes the stripping of the Barton house itself, as the family of father and daughter sink into penury, not because of improvidence but because of "bad times" aggravated by the blacklisting of John as a Chartist:

"By degrees the house was stripped of its little ornaments. . . . And by-and-by Mary began to part with other superfluities at the pawn-shop. The smart tea-tray, and tea-caddy, long and carefully kept, went for bread for her father. He did not ask for it, or complain, but she saw hunger in his shrunk, fierce, animal look. Then the blankets went, for it was summer time, and they could spare them; and their sale made a fund, which Mary fancied would last until better times came. But it was soon all gone; and then she looks around the room to crib it of its few remaining ornaments." (159)

When blankets become classified with "superfluities" and "ornaments"—when objects of use are so barely defined—life is cheap as beasts', and the assumptions that expect such a life of the poor are shown to be cheap and mean-spirited themselves.

The narrator's apparent platitude about the workers' "child-like improvidence" can thus be seen to exist, like the concept of "duty," in a "dialogically agitated" environment that destabilizes and subverts it. This dialogical agitation is further intensified because the conjunction of "childlike" with "improvidence" implicates the latter term in Gaskell's complex development of the child metaphor noted above, a development that generates sympathy, not criticism, for the starving workers. Bakhtin emphasizes the potential reductiveness of abstracting "direct authorial speech" from its context in a text and viewing it in isolation as epitomizing the author's "style" or authorial identity (265–66). Unfortunately, this critical practice has led to the under-appreciation of Gaskell's artistry, and to monologic conceptions of a narrative voice that is persistently dialogical.

Of course, not all of the shifts and contradictions in the narrative voicing of *Mary Barton* can be explained in terms of Gaskell's innovative dialogization of authorial discourse. For instance, the often noted contradictory use of the Frankenstein metaphor in Chapter 15, in which Gaskell seems first to deny, then to affirm, that the uneducated like John Barton have a "soul," is best explained by Gallagher's analysis of the conflict between social determinism and free will in nineteenth-century narratives (74–75). Other inconsistencies can be interpreted psychologically as unconscious manifestations of what Gaskell, in a striking phrase, referred to as her many "Mes": "One of my mes is, I do believe a true Christian—(only people call her socialist and communist), another of my mes is a wife and mother. . . . Now that's my 'social' self I suppose. Then again I've another self with a full taste for beauty

and convenience. . . . How am I to reconcile all these warring members?''
(*Letters* 108). However, the point where psychology ends and artistry begins
is difficult to determine. Gaskell's conceptualization of her identity as made
up of "warring members" is itself notable for its self-reflexive dialogization
of consciousness, a feature that casts some light on her remarkable ability—one might say her "negative capability"—to accomodate conflicting
discourses and perspectives.

It is not surprising that this ability should have been highly developed in a
woman with Gaskell's personal history and experience. Her struggle as a
Southerner like Margaret Hale with alien Manchester idioms and viewpoints,
her encounter as a middle-class social worker with working-class perspectives, her parallel literary encounter with the working-class poets she studied
with her husband, and her struggle as a woman with discourses like political
economy conventionally viewed as masculine—all no doubt contributed to
the relativizing of her linguistic consciousness. Her tendency to incorporate
the heteroglossia of female and working-class discourses in double-voiced
constructions can furthermore be seen as the predictable consequence of her
status as a member of a "muted" group within a dominant masculine culture.[16] More remarkable is the intricacy and daring with which she challenges
the dominant discourses of her culture by opposing these to suppressed discourses, instead of simply translating the latter into some form of dominant
discourse.

The success of *Mary Barton* has traditionally been assessed in light of its
formal consistency. A more appropriate measure might be Hans-Robert
Jauss's criterion for evaluating the artistry of a work: the "distance between
the horizon of expectations and the work, between the familiarity of previous
aesthetic experiences and the 'horizon change' demanded by the response to
new works'' (Suleiman 36). Because it is such an intensely dialogical novel,
Mary Barton provoked a horizon change in its middle-class readers.[17] It did
so not by overt iconoclasm, which might have alienated much of its reading
public, but by engaging its readers, like its characters and its author, in a
complex series of interlocking debates and encounters with conflicting languages and ideologies. In the process, even the more conspicuously middle-
class voices among the narrator's "many mes" play their part because a
horizon of expectations can only be changed when that horizon is acknowledged from the inside, as the viewers see it, and simultaneously penetrated
by what is outside. This is what Gaskell achieves through the polyphony of
voices she orchestrates in *Mary Barton*.

NOTES

1. A poem of six stanzas, "The Pauper's Drive" deftly combines black humour, caustic social satire and pathos. Kovalev does not identify the author. He notes that poems like "The Pauper's Drive" were conventional in working-class writings before the Chartists (371). For a translation of Kovalev's Russian introduction see Chaloner.
2. *Mary Barton* was the first foreign novel published in translation by the Dostoevsky brothers in their magazine *Vremya*. Johnson notes that Dostoevsky may have been influenced in *Crime and Punishment* by Gaskell's "Dantesque scenes" of urban suffering, her Christian ideology, and her depiction of an ideological murderer like Raskolnikov, whose character deteriorates in the course of the novel.
3. See also Michael Wheeler, *English Fiction of the Victorian Period* (36). Bodenheimer and Lucas offer the most thought-provoking discussions of the divisions within *Mary Barton*. Margaret Ganz relates these to the split in Gaskell herself between the Knutsford world of *Cranford*, and the Manchester world of *Mary Barton* and *North and South* (31–32).
4. On the complexity of "voicing" in Victorian fiction, though not in *Mary Barton*, see Mark Kinkead-Weekes.
5. Bodenheimer notes in passing that Gaskell's "society of the poor is so full of its own dictions and traditions, so various in its own right, that the middle-class voices we hear at the Carsons' or before the Liverpool Assizes seem genuine intrusions from another linguistic universe" (214). And Coral Lansbury similarly suggests that, surrounded by these voices, the narrator's own voice begins to sound like a fiction (*Elizabeth Gaskell: The Novel of Social Crisis* (25). The most useful treatment of dialect in *Mary Barton* remains Sanders's "A Note on Mrs. Gaskell's Use of Dialect."
6. Gaskell proposed several readings in political economy to her daughter Marianne: "first I think we should read together Adam Smith on the Wealth of Nations. Not confining ourselves as we read to the limited meaning he attaches to the word 'wealth'" ([7 April 1851], *Letters* 148). For one of Gaskell's bolder interruptions of male discourse, see Chapter 16 in *Mary Barton* where the narrator interrupts the masters' comments on the beast-like workers: "(Well! Who might have made them different?)" (233).
7. Some Chartist poems are entitled "hymns" (see Kovalev, 118, 164). Like the Owenites described by Barbara Taylor in *Eve and the New Jerusalem* (158), with their *Social Hymn Book* and millenarianism, the Chartists adapted Christian rhetoric to their revolutionary purposes.
8. Edgar Wright (260–62) and Kathleen Tillotson (213–24) have suggested that Gaskell's depiction of working class dialect is limited, particularly in the depiction of Mary, who often speaks in standard English. But Gaskell's variations in "editing" dialect indicate that she was highly conscious of her own novelistic modifications. She depicts Mary using more dialect terms in speaking to members of her own class than to the middle-class Harry Carson.
9. These political messages from women find an analogue in "The Oldham Weaver," where the male speaker says that his wife Marget has declared "Hoo'd goo up to Lunnon an' talk to the' greet mon" if only she had "cloo' as to put on" (73). Taylor notes that women weavers were particularly active in labor agitation, in Oldham and elsewhere. "In the desperate years following the Napoleonic Wars," women weavers had "often served as violent shock-troops," and

"so it was again among power-loom weavers in the early 1830s, when women led the way in riotous confrontations with the military in Oldham and other textile centres" (91).

10. Taylor notes that the "torrid tales of innocent daughters of the people seduced and ruined by dastardly blue-bloods or lascivious employers filled the radical press" in the 1830s and 40s (201).

11. In *North and South*, the novel where one might most expect to encounter the pervasive presence of working-class discourse again, the principal working-class characters, Nicholas and Bessy Higgins, play marginal roles. Occasional chapters make use of epigraphs from poets such as Elliott (Chapters 21 & 43) and Hood (Ch. 37) or from the *Corn Law Rhymes* (Ch. 22); several other epigraphs are anonymous (Chapters 5, 11, 17, 34, 48). On the whole, however, the textual voice is much less polyglot, in part because of the use of Margaret Hale as a center of consciousness.

12. Passages from Burns also appear as mottoes for Chapters 11 and 33 in *Mary Barton*. See Kovalev, 298 & 305, for indications of the popularity of Burns among the Chartists. Kovalev points out that to compare a writer with Burns was "the highest honour Chartist critics could confer" (Chaloner translation, 128).

13. Stephen Gill notes this function of Gaskell's footnotes on etymology (*Mary Barton* 474), as does Norman Page (52). Gustav Klaus overlooks the complexity of Gaskell's rhetorical strategies when he infers that she "felt obliged to defer to her readers' sensibilities by adding footnotes to, or translating into standard English, the colloquial utterances of her working-class characters" (52).

14. Gill similarly distinguishes between Gaskell as "imaginative artist" and as middleclass "mediator between the classes" (*Mary Barton* 24); and Lucas opposes the novel's "sensitive exploration" of John Barton's experience to "Mrs Gaskell's prim interpolations" '162–63). Coral Lansbury points to the "disjunctions between the narrative mediator and the action of the plot," and comments that the "major difficulty" with *Mary Barton* is "a concilatory narrator who is often so mealy-mouthed and platitudinous that the reader's teeth are set on edge" (*Elizabeth Gaskell* 10 & 14). Responding to another of the narrative voices in the novel, Gary Messinger observes that "the persona of the authoress is that of a nurse who sees no final remedy for the sorrow she witnesses daily" (Welch 92).

15. In a letter to Gaskell dated November 11th, 1859, Eliot acknowledged the influence of the "earlier chapters of *Mary Barton*" on her art (*The George Eliot Letters* III 98). But the entire plot structure of *Mary Barton* seems to have influenced *The Mill on the Floss*: both begin with the tragedy of a humble man, and in each the man's daughter replaces the father as the center of interest in the second half of the novel. The depiction of the relationship between Gaskell's depiction of Jem Wilson's relationship with his mother while Esther's moral development in *Felix Holt* resembles Mary's in some respects. Both begin as rather flippant young women, who grow in stature and who choose working-class lovers in the end.

16. The tendency of "muted" groups to produce "double-voiced" discourse is discussed by Elaine Showalter (31) and by Sandra Gilbert and Susan Gubar. Stoneman notes Gaskell's use of such discourse (12–14).

17. See the "resisting" reviewers, perceptively analysed by Lucas (164–69).

WORKS CITED

Bakhtin, Mikhail. *The Dialogic Imagination: Four Essays*. Ed. Michael Holquist; trans. Carlyl Emerson & Michael Holquist. Austin & London: U of Texas P, 1981.

Bodenheimer, Rosemarie. "Private Griefs and Public Acts in *Mary Barton.*" *Dickens Studies Annual* 9 (1981): 195–215.

Booth, Wayne C. "Freedom of Interpretation: Bakhtin and the Challenge of Feminists Criticism," *The politics of Interpretation.* Ed. W. J. T. Mitchell. Chicago & London: U of Chicago P, 1983. 51–82.

Chaloner, W. D. "Y.V. Kovalev: The Literature of Chartism," *Victorian Studies* (1959): 117–138

Easson, Angus. *Elizabeth Gaskell.* London: Routledge & Kegan Paul, 1979.

Eliot, George. *The George Eliot Letters.* Ed. Gordon S. Haight. New Haven: Yale UP, 1954. Vol. 3.

Gallagher, Catherine. *The Industrial Reformation of English Fiction: Social Discourse and Narrative Form 1832-1867.* Chicago & London: U of Chicago P, 1985.

Ganz, Margaret. *Elizabeth Gaskell: The Artist in Conflict.* New York: Twayne, 1969.

Gaskell, Elizabeth. *Mary Barton.* Ed. Stephen Gill. Harmondsworth, Middlesex: Penguin, 1970.

——— *The Letters of Mrs. Gaskell.* Ed. J.A. V. Chapple & Arthur Pollard. Cambridge, Mass.: Harvard UP, 1967.

——— *North and South.* Ed. Martin Dodsworth. Middlesex: Penguin, 1970.

Gilbert, Sandra & Gubar, Susan. "Sexual Linguistics: Gender, Language, Sexuality." *New Literacy History* 16 (1985): 515–43.

Gilligan, Carol. *In A Different Voice: Psychological Theory and Women's Development.* Cambridge, Mass. & London: Harvard UP, 1982.

Handley, Michael. "Mrs. Gaskell's Reading: Some Notes on Echoes and Epigraphs in *Mary Barton,*" *Durham University Journal* 59 n.s. 28 (1967): 131–38.

Holloway, John. *The Victorian Sage: Studies in Argument.* 1953; New York: Norton, 1965.

Hopkins, Annette B. "*Mary Barton*: A Victorian Best Seller," *Nineteenth-Century Fiction* 3 (1948): 1–18.

Johnson, C.A. "Russian Gaskelliana," *Review of English Literature* 7 (1966): 39–51.

Keating, P.J. *The Working Classes in Victorian Fiction.* London: Routledge & Kegan Paul, 1971.

Kestner, Joseph. *Protest and Reform: The British Social Narrative By Women 1827–1867.* Madison: U of Wisconsin P, 1985.

Kincead-Weekes, Mark. "The Voicing of Fictions." *Reading the Victorian Novel: Detail Into Form.* Ed. Ian Gregor. New York: Barnes & Noble, 1980. 168–192.

Klaus, Gustav. *The Literature of Labour: Two Hundred Years of Working-Class Writing*. New York: St. Martin's Press, 1985.

Kovalev, Y.V., ed. *An Anthology of Chartist Literature*. Moscow: Foreign Languages Publishing House, 1956.

Lansbury, Coral. *Elizabeth Gaskell*. New York: Twayne Publishers, 1984.

———— *Elizabeth Gaskell: The Novel of Social Crisis*. London: Elek, 1975.

Lucas, John. "Mrs. Gaskell and Brotherhood." *Tradition and Tolerance in Nineteenth-Century Fiction*. Ed. David Howard *et al*. London: Routledge & Kegan Paul, 1966. 141–205.

Marshall, Dorothy. *The Life and Times of Victoria*. London: Book Club Associates, 1972.

Page, Norman. *Speech in the English Novel*. London: Longman, 1973.

Wheeler, Michael. *English Fiction of the Victorian Period*. London & New York: Longman, 1985.

———— "The Writer as Reader in *Mary Barton*." *Durham University Journal* 67 n.s. 36 (1974): 92–102.

Sanders, Gerald Dewitt. *Elizabeth Gaskell*. New York: Russell & Russell, 1929.

Sharps, John G. *Mrs. Gaskell's Observation and Intervention: A Study of Her Non-Biographic Works*. London: Linden Press, 1970.

Showalter, Elaine. "Feminist Criticism in the Wilderness." *Writing and Sexual Difference*. Ed. Elizabeth Abel. Chicago: U off Chicago P, 1982. 9–35.

Stoneman, Patsy. *Elizabeth Gaskell*. Bloomington and Indianapolis: Indiana UP, Key Women Writers Series, 1987.

Suleiman, Susan R. & Crosman, Inge, eds. *The Reader in the Text: Essays on Audience and Interpretation*. Princeton UP, 1980.

Tanner, Tony. *Jane Austen*. Cambridge, Mass.: Harvard U P, 1986.

Taylor, Barbara. *Eve and the New Jerusalem: Socialism and Feminism in the Nineteenth Century*. New York: Pantheon Books, 1983.

Tillotson, Kathleen. *Novels of the Eighteen-Forties*. 1954; 2nd ed. London: Oxford UP, 1956.

Welch, Jeffrey. *Elizabeth Gaskell: An Annotated Bibliography*. New York & London: Garland Publishing, 1977, p. 92.

George Eliot and the Power
of Evil-Speaking

Rosemarie Bodenheimer

> Who shall tell what may be the effect of writing? If it
> happens to have been cut in stone, though it lie face down-
> most for ages on a forsaken beach, or "rest quietly under
> the drums and tramplings of many conquests," it may end
> by letting us into the secret of usurpations and other scandals
> gossiped about long empires ago: —this world being appar-
> ently a huge whispering-gallery.
>
> —*Middlemarch*

"The best history of a writer is contained in his writings—these are his chief actions . . . Biographies generally are a disease of English literature" (Eliot *Letters* 7:230). So George Eliot wrote at the end of 1879 to a friend who had innocently inquired whether there was to be a biography of the late George Henry Lewes. Her venom was only a footnote in a campaign against biography that she conducted in her letters during the 1870s; she consistently attacked "that idle curiosity which, caring little for the study of an author's work, is pleased with low gossip about his private life and personal appearance" (6:163), and refused to answer most requests for biographical information even when the facts circulated by others were incorrect. So marked a resistance to biography-as-gossip is hardly surprising in a writer who had conducted an immensely private life against the pressure of public disapproval, but George Eliot's strong desire to separate the work from the life had its specific history as well. That history begins with her life-long personal resistance to gossip, and centers in an episode that foregrounded its activities in several different lights: the Liggins imposture that flourished after the publication of *Adam Bede* in 1859, when a Warwickshire clergyman was credited with the authorship of her fiction.

George Eliot's letters during and after the Liggins affair set the tone of scorn for "idle gossip" and "hard curiosity" (3.376) that was to be revived during the last decade of her life, when the stunning sales successes of *Middlemarch* stimulated increasing numbers of requests for biographical information from the unwilling author. Her hatred of personal gossip is most readily explained by her sensitivity to rejection on the grounds of her famous non-marriage to George Henry Lewes; her pseudonymic writing had functioned from the first as antithesis and expiation for her violation of Victorian sexual convention. The roots of the resistance lay in her early life, however: in her young Evangelical ban on "evil speaking," and in the experience of living down the gossip she had activated by her flamboyant rejection of religious practice at the age of twenty-two.[1] Yet George Eliot's strenuous personal resistance to gossip must also be read in relation to other facts: she was a novelist who made her living by retailing and commenting on the private destinies of fictional characters; her career as a realist began when she told a true story about a curate she had known, related by a narrator who establishes his credentials by depicting and overriding gossip; she was the creator of some of the greatest representations of gossip in English fiction. George Eliot may have suffered from gossip in her life, but she profited from it in her art.

George Eliot's fictional representations of gossip are most often discussed in relation to her idea of community, or as the "medium" in which individual characters must work out their lives. Some critics—like Steven Marcus and, more recently, Alexander Welsh—emphasize the more benign aspects of community talk as the medium of opinion within and against which the identities of major characters are defined; others, like D. A. Miller and Patricia Spacks, describe gossip in *Middlemarch* as a leveller which threatens and excludes individual ambition and desire.[2] Each emphasis reflects one side of an ongoing history of tension in George Eliot's relationship with gossip, but both represent gossip as a background against which individual careers are silhouetted. I propose in this essay to shift the terms, foregrounding the difficult history of George Eliot's relationship with gossip as it is recorded both in her fictions and in her letters, particularly in those written during the period of the Liggins imposture.

George Eliot's first story, "The Sad Fortunes of the Rev. Amos Barton," makes gossip its plot, and demonstrates the tension between the writer's intense interest and skill in depicting the dynamics of social talk, and her wish to erase or condemn it. In this story gossip plays the role of the fiction against which "realism" is first defined; the truths of domestic life are almost fully separated from the line of gossip and slander. As George Eliot negotiated and absorbed the crisis of the Liggins affair, the split between others' talk and internal truth was both maintained and complicated to the point of transformation: *The Mill on the Floss* records the shock and anger of the crisis; in *Middlemarch* gossip becomes a more or less distorted mirror of the truths the subject represses. The gradual alignment of gossip with psychological realism marks a crucial, if characteristically subtle, move in George Eliot's fictional penetration of her own biographical defenses. It is a move that was finally and wittily celebrated in *The Impressions of Theophrastus Such*, and especially in its opening sketch, "Looking Inward."

1

Throughout her life George Eliot wrote elaborate notes of remorseful apology to persons with whom she had allowed herself talk of a kind her conscience disapproved. A remarkable sample of this genre, sent by the twenty-nine-year-old Mary Ann Evans to her step-sister Fanny Houghton, is an act of sackcloth-and-ashes penitence which illustrates the power of her struggle with the satirical bent of her intellect. Mary Ann writes in an elevated religious style, and cannot bring herself to name her offense except as "the sins of my tongue—my animadversions on the faults of others, as if I thought myself to be something when I am nothing." She moves quickly to sermon-like abstraction: "though my 'evil speaking' issues from the intellectual point of view rather than the moral,—though there may be gall in the thought while there is honey in the feeling, yet the evil-speaking is wrong. We may satirize character and qualities in the abstract without injury to our moral nature, but persons hardly ever" (1:276). It is not difficult to see what fiction-writing offered to a mind that so carefully preserves its distinction between intellectual gall and moral honey; novels are opportunities to exercise both voices "without injury to our moral nature."

"The Sad Fortunes of the Rev. Amos Barton," enacts just such a victory over the power of evil-speaking. "Amos Barton" is all about gossip; its plot is simply the transformation of gossip into slander and then into pity. The story is also an indirect recreation of the situation of its writing: the curate Barton appears as he struggles unsuccessfully to find an audience in his congregation, becoming instead the victim of gossip. Meanwhile his creator,

in male garb, offers herself to her new audience as his antithesis, and dramatizes gossip in order to triumph over it with narrative understanding and
sympathy.[3] Ensconced in the double invisibility of anonymity and male impersonation, George Eliot addressed her presumed audience of town-dwellers
without a twinge of fear that she was repeating the life story of a recognizable
living soul.

Early in the narrative a gossip scene is followed by these reflections:

> It was happy for the Rev. Amos Barton that he did not, like us, overhear the
> conversation recorded in the last chapter. Indeed, what mortal is there of us,
> who would find his satisfaction enhanced by an opportunity of comparing the
> picture he presents to himself of his own doings, with the picture they make on
> the mental retina of his neighbors? We are poor plants buoyed up by the air-
> vessels of our own conceit: alas for us, if we get a few pinches that empty us
> of that windy self-subsistence! The very capacity for good would go out of us.
>
> (51–52)

George Eliot's first pronouncement about the relation between gossip and the
self emphasizes their disconnection: it is better for Barton that he remain
ignorant of his parishioners' gossip, just as it is better that the author disreputa-
bly attached to George Henry Lewes pursue her work with her ears closed to
the scandals about her. Precisely this disconnection turns out to be the point
of the tale: the privileged reading audience understands that Barton's
story—much like the Lewes's at this time—is about poverty, while the gossiping characters turn it into one about sexual scandal, only to be disabused by
the sad death of Milly Barton. The stories gossip tells are crude melodramas
imposed on very specific clusters of fact; thus Eliot's first claims for realism
are energized not only by her calls to attend to the ordinary, but also by the
narrative activity of portraying and overriding gossip.

Amos Barton's shaky position in Shepperton comes about because he does
not have the talent to speak to his flock persuasively; he cannot imagine their
concerns or adapt his language to his audience. George Eliot dramatises
only one encounter with a live audience: the workhouse scene in which she
enumerates in painful detail ''the faces on which his eye had to rest, watching
whether there was any stirring under the stagnant surface'' (61). Barton's
complete inability to ''bring his geographical, chronological, exegetical mind
pretty nearly to the pauper point of view, or, of no view'' (63) renders the
exercise a failure in every respect. In other circles of Shepperton society,
Barton's mediocre preaching and his insensitivity to the community tradition
of anthem- rather than hymn-singing has equivalent effects: his parishioners
talk about him but they do not listen to him.

Barton's failure to create an audience is contrasted with the popularity of Mr. Cleves and Mr. Gilfil, who is mentioned in "Amos Barton" and described in the frame of "Mr. Gilfil's Love Story." Their success grows from their ability to adapt their language to their audiences. "Mr. Cleves has the wonderful art of preaching sermons which the wheelwright and the blacksmith can understand; not because he talks condescending twaddle, but because he can call a spade a spade, and knows how to disencumber ideas of their wordy frippery" (93). Gilfil's habit is "to approximate his accent and mode of speech to theirs, doubtless because he thought it a mere frustration of the purposes of language to talk of 'sharrags' and 'yowes'" (125). In sentences like these the narrator simultaneously makes his own claim to connection with his audience: he too can move easily between one level of language and another; he too has the power to speak the colloquial dialect, and to mix abstractions with concrete instances. When he pauses to exhort his reader on the wonders of farmhouse cream, he knows both how the cream is made and how the town reader probably drinks it (45); when he pauses for a narrative apostrophe on calumny, he rather ostentatiously eschews quoting Virgil in favor of a homely comparison of gossip to the unstoppable flow of black ink over "fair manuscript or fairer table-cover" (88). The narrator's frequent and direct demands on his reader's attention suggest his determination to avoid Barton's fate by reaching out to touch his invisible audience in a whole range of different languages.

Cleves and Gilfil are not gossiped about but revered by their parishioners, as though they were proof positive of their author's wishful belief that successful communication holds gossip at bay. Barton's case represents the corresponding fear: his real story of domestic poverty is misread as a sexual scandal when two forms of gossip, about him and about the Countess, converge to damage his reputation. The two kinds of gossip embody George Eliot's simultaneous wish to acknowledge the humorous truth in gossip and to condemn gossip as slander. And the kinds are gendered: malicious love of sexual scandal is attributed in the first instance to women, marking George Eliot's participation in the defensive gendering and denigration of gossip that has been fully described by Patricia Spacks.[4]

Taken by himself, Barton's unpopularity stems mostly from his tactlessness, which includes his refusal to countenance others' gossip about the Countess. (The refusal might be in his favor if it were a principled objection, but Barton supports the Countess because she offers the approbation and flattery he fails to get from his parishioners.) The townspeople's criticisms of him are not incorrect, though they are motivated by selfish concerns; when the narrator seeks to give us an alternative picture of Barton he only deepens the criticisms with inside looks at Barton's self-delusions. The only real difference he offers is a perspective that would make us look sympathetically at sincere failure: had Barton only followed his father as cabinetmaker and deacon of an Independent church, he would have been a "shining light" in his circle; as a Churchman of strong opinions, he is like a tallow candle stuck in a silver candlestick and brought into the drawing-room (60–61). The narrator would have us believe that Barton is a victim of gossip for the same reason he ought to be an object of sympathy: because his ambition exceeds his talent, he is mis-matched with his social circumstances.

The gossip about the Countess Czerlaski is another matter. The Countess comes to Milby because she thinks it safer to seek a husband in "a neighborhood where people were extremely well acquainted with each other's affairs" (78), and ironically becomes its central figure of gossip and mis-representation. The talk about her is summarized and attributed to a set of envious women we never meet as characters, "the gossips of Milby, who made up their minds to something much more exciting" than the truth about the Countess (78). Their unfounded assumption that the Countess is living with a lover and looking for another provokes a strong censure from the narrator.

> Indeed, the severest ladies in Milby would have been perfectly aware that these characteristics [the faults and vanities of the Countess] would have created no wide distinction between the Countess Czerlaski and themselves; and since it was clear there *was* a wide distinction—why, it must lie in the possession of some vices from which they were undeniably free.   (79)

When the Countess throws herself upon the poverty-stricken Barton household, the male and the female streams of gossip merge to "blacken the reputation" of Amos Barton (88). The Countess *is* behaving scandously; she fails to notice the immense burden that her presence places on the ailing Milly Barton and on the family finances. The villagers turn this situation into a series of sexual innuendos linking Barton with the Countess, and withdraw their previous charities to the household. The most horrible twist in the gossipers' accounts occurs when Milly, the wronged wife in gossip's tale, is blamed for allowing it to occur; again Eliot presses the point that women's gossip is irrationally relentless to women. Milly indeed becomes a sacrificial victim, but of the Bartons' fecund poverty: shortly after the Countess finally departs, she dies after the birth of her seventh child.[5] Only her death releases the Barton household from the spell of the scandal: the villagers quickly learn to cherish their curate in pity, and the flow of charity begins again.

The turning point of "Amos Barton" is simply the separation of the true story from the false one. Gossip makes little happen, though it does increase the Bartons' poverty and isolation during the Countess's stay, and helps to spur on her eventual departure.[6] The Bartons are too busy surviving to pay much attention to the scandal, although they know of it; Milly cares for Amos's sake, and Amos reacts with a mixture of innocence and indignation that includes some defiance. Their resistance to gossip is established early in the story, when Amos refuses to be converted to Mrs. Farquhar's view of the Countess and Milly deplores the pains people take "to find out evil about others" (56). The status of this self-insulation from "electric communication with the world beyond" (100) is not clearly defined by the narrator: Amos is stubborn, but on the other hand his refusal to succumb to the power of scandal is one of the few dignities the story allows him. The organization of the narrative does emphasize, however, that Barton life and the life of scandal flow along different and incommensurate tracks. It is the difference between the two stories that is shocking; that is why Milly's death quells the gossipers and transforms them into sympathizers.

The track of gossip itself is plotted through the series of dialogues in which Barton's situation is discussed by his neighbors and colleagues. In these scenes gossip has an ebb and flow of its own that is determined largely by the characters and relationships of the participants; and the question of audience is transferred to the gossip-speakers and hearers themselves. In such scenes men and women are equally portrayed: male voices carry much of the burden of gossip in this story, and the doctor Mr. Pilgrim is portrayed as the most inveterate carrier of gossip in the community. For when George Eliot imagines gossip concretely, she turns it into the satiric comedy of language and motive that marks her dialogue writing at its best; it is transformed from an invisible, feminized threat into an opportunity for delineating the dynamics of talk as a social activity.

Speech defects are foregrounded in the gossiping world, suggesting that every character has—if not a physical speech oddity like Pilgrim's splutter or Farquhar's Sleary-like lisp—some special relation to language that shapes his or her role in the common talk. Pilgrim finds his authority by quoting others, the rector Mr. Fellowes got a living by his mellifluous tongue and the "fluency with which he interpreted the opinions of an obese and stammering baronet" (92), the sympathetic Mr. Hackit, ready to speak and sing *extempore*, delivers a speech on Barton's lack of talent in that department, Mr. Ely insinuates his resistance to gossip but actually perpetuates it, Mrs. Hackit has her odd comparisons and her love of dissent, and so on. Once it turns scandalous the gossip itself consists in trying out innuendo in which the sexual and economic situations in the Barton household are hopelessly conflated; in the absence of either fact or genuine allegation, the social game is to enhance one's position as a knowing partner.

Thus it happens that Mr. Cleves emerges as an examplary figure simply because he understands how gossip works and tries to unmask it. To a point, he shares the honors with Mrs. Hackit, who also keeps her eye on the real story, the facts of poverty and childbirth in the Barton household. Mrs. Hackit makes her special place in the community by maintaining strong dissenting opinions and real charitable relationships—although her defense of the Bartons carries with it some advertisement of her own generosity. But the aura of sexual irregularity goes beyond the limits of Mrs. Hackit's ability to dissent, and she defends her desertion of Milly by blaming her for the Countess's presence. Her dissent is in effect her form of the self-definition that gossip provides; Mr. Cleves, in the company of his fellow-clerics, dissents from the language of gossip itself. He begins humorously, by correcting the "corrupt text" that represents Barton dining alone with the Countess while Milly stays in the kitchen: "The original text is, that they all dined together *with* six—meaning six children—and that Mrs. Barton is an excellent cook." Failing to end the conversation with wit, he turns serious: "There is some simple explanation of the whole affair, if we only happened to know it." Finally he deconstructs Mr. Duke's hypocritical sympathy—"there are greater signs of poverty about them than ever"—in a direct attack which suggests that Barton's honesty is superior to Duke's: "that's something in Barton's favour at all events. He might be poor *without* showing signs of poverty" (95–96). Cleves explicitly makes the move on which the dialogues are implicitly built: the finger points back at the gossiping self.

In these ways "Amos Barton's" exhortations to literary realism through attention to the ordinary and mediocre are dramatized through the difference between the ordinary sad story of the Bartons and the melodramatic gossip about them. Part of its definition of realism is that the two stories remain separate: gossip occurs; then death occurs, and shuts up the lips of gossip. Quite a different sequence was to attend the story's fate in the world, which generated a good deal of gossip by reconnecting Amos and other characters in *Scenes from Clerical Life* with their Warwickshire models. When George Eliot returned to portrayals of community opinion in *The Mill on the Floss* and *Middlemarch*, she had negotiated directly with ''gossip,'' and its fictional guises cut increasingly close to the bone.

2

On 13 June 1859, just as the publication of *Adam Bede* was making ''George Eliot'' famous, the original Amos Barton declared himself to Eliot's publisher John Blackwood. The Rev. John Gwyther of Yorkshire was responding to the newspaper publication of assertions that a Nuneaton man named Joseph Liggins had written *Adam Bede*, and anonymous denials, constructed by the Leweses, that he had done so. Unaware of course that the denials were muzzled by the need to maintain the incognito of a woman writer whose real identity might shock her audiences, Gwyther innocently contributed to the proliferation of gossip that the anonymous denials in fact stimulated: he wrote to suggest yet another candidate for the author of what he frankly admitted to be ''an episode in my own life'' (3:83–84). Like the perpetrators of the Liggins rumor, Gwyther based his case on the notion that only a longstanding local resident could possibly know the personal facts from which the stories in *Scenes of Clerical Life* and *Adam Bede* had been made. He admitted that he had been hurt by reading his own story two years earlier in *Blackwood's Magazine*, but ''Time passed away, and my pained feelings at the making public my private history abated''; he now asked that his ''kind remembrances'' be conveyed to his candidate for the authorship, former curate of Nuneaton Rev. W. H. King, ''although I thought it unkind and taking a great liberty with a living Character.'' Gwyther's letter, received just as the Liggins imposture was heating up, provided a voice of ingenuous truth in the midst of blatantly false rumor, but it only deepened the implication of George Eliot's stories with the Warwickshire gossip from which she was trying to disconnect them.[7]

Eliot's (again anonymous) response to the letter tries hard to deny Gwyther the validity of his hurt feelings. She admits that she had imagined him dead, but goes on to say that the story's incidents, ''must have been so varied from the actual facts, that any one who discerned the core of truth must also recognize the large amount of arbitrary, imaginative addition.'' Her conclusion mixes a twinge of remorse with her own growing annoyance at the public pressure the Liggins matter was putting on *her* private existence: ''But for any annoyance, even though it may have been brief and not well-founded, which the appearance of the story may have caused Mr. Gwyther, the writer is sincerely sorry'' (3:86). The argument that imaginative addition far outran the core of truth was one she had already used, and was to use many times again before the Liggins affair had run its course.[8] It is of course the appropriate argument, the one any fiction writer would make. But the defensive vehemence with which George Eliot made it takes on a special charge in the light of her fictional rendering of gossip in ''Amos Barton''; in fact her eagerness to disavow the allegation that she was retailing other people's lives in her fiction could be read as a covert admission that fiction is gossip, in which bits of fact are imaginatively altered and recirculated.

Her whole effort was, however, to deny this possibility. The Liggins matter is especially interesting for her strenuous resistance to the notion that she was writing ''portraits''; even after Liggins was largely discredited as author the chief perpetrator of the rumor, Charles Holte Bracebridge, continued to link Eliot characters with their supposed originals, and to insist that she had gotten her information from Liggins or from the originals themselves. In September and October 1859 Lewes, George Eliot, and her old Coventry friend Charles Bray conducted a rather embarrassing triangular correspondence with Bracebridge, finally forcing him to a written retraction (3:145–79). During this period Eliot's angry desire to vindicate herself from Bracebridge's claims that the characters in *Adam Bede* were portraits of her aunt and uncle the Samuel Evanses, and that she had copied Dinahs Morris's sermon and speeches from her aunt's papers, did not abate; even after the retraction she continued to wax indignant to Blackwood about the insult to her emotional and imaginative powers. (3:184–85).

At the end of June she had admitted to the Brays and Sara Hennell that ''There *are* two portraits in the Clerical Scenes; but that was my first bit of art, and my hand was not well in.'' The retrospective admission was made in the service of another denial, that *Bede* contained a ''portrait'' of her father (3:99). On 7 October she wrote a long letter to Sara in which she spelled out for posterity the exact nature of her relationship with her aunt, specifying the differences between Mrs. Samuel Evans and the character Dinah Morris. (Sara dutifully published the letter in the *Pall Mall Budget* after her death). ''It is not surprising,'' the letter concludes, ''that simple men and women without pretension to enlightened discrimination should think a generic resemblance constitutes a portrait, when we see the great public so accustomed to be delighted with *mis*-representation of life and character, which they accept as representations, that they are scandalized when art makes a nearer approach to truth'' (3:176–77). It is difficult to follow the precise logic of this sentence, although it clearly wishes—like ''Amos Barton'''—to defend her good art against silly fiction, and to scorn the way that good art turns into scandal in the public mind. But the notion that the urban reading public, inured to gossipy fiction, is therefore "scandalized" by "a nearer approach to truth" almost gives away its game by suggesting that the scandal is generated by the very connection with life which she was denying. All of these angry and defensive protests clearly show how deeply the Liggins episode had troubled George Eliot's carefully maintained distinction between gossip and art; the incident was like a ludicrous nightmare in which the historicized gossiping characters in her books rose up and began to circulate false rumors about their creator.

The decision to relax the secret of the pseudonym also altered George Eliot's relationship with gossip, for it was made in direct response to the literary talk, probably circulated by John Chapman and Herbert Spencer, which had already connected George Eliot to the woman living with Lewes.[9] On 25 June 1859 Eliot had drafted a third angry letter to the *Times* accusing Liggins of being an imposter and a swindler (3:92–93); but, while Blackwood was persuading her to tone it down, her friend Barbara Bodichon retailed to her the London gossip: "They assured me all the literary men were certain it was Marian Lewes: . . . that they did not much like saying so because it would do so much harm . . . " (3:103). This letter brought into the open the fear the Leweses had prevented themselves from expressing as they angrily battled Liggins: that the reputation of the novels would be damaged if it was known that Marian Lewes had written them. Exactly because it was now expressed as an opinion in other minds, a decision could be taken. The next day Marian withdrew her *Times* letter; two days later Lewes wrote to Barbara: ". . . we have come to the conclusion of no longer concealing the authorship. It makes me angry to think that people should say that the secret has been kept because there was any *fear* of the effect of the author's name" (3:106). The repeated gossip had served a crucial purpose: by externalizing their fears, it had allowed the Leweses to take up a stance of defiance against them. Moreover, they now entrusted their secret to gossip's circulatory system, making "no categorical statement" (3:99), but allowing the talk about the authorship to go on as it might.

These affairs might have enlightened George Eliot about the practical uses of gossip, but their immediate effect was to increase her already acute sensitivity to its damaging power. During this period her remorseful notes castigating herself for evil-speaking include an elaborate apology even for "having listened with apparent aquiescence to statements about poor Agnes which a little quiet reflection has convinced me are mingled with falsehood" (3:91). After revealing her authorship to her Coventry friends, the Brays and Sara Hennell, she discovered that talking about her books to friends was also dangerous to her mental health; as she wrote them a week after telling the secret, "Talking about my books, I find, has much the same malign effect on me as talking of one's religion, or one's feelings or duties toward one's father, mother, or husband" (8:251–52n.). The "effect" she means is related to the betrayals of gossip; it is apparently one of disloyalty to a private or sacred relationship. In her horrified reaction to having been seen through the anonymity of her narratives, her books became personal secrets not to be violated, even in the sanctuary of home.

The Mill on the Floss, the last novel in which George Eliot drew directly upon her Warwickshire childhood, was written during the year of Liggins, between April and December 1859. At the end of the novel Eliot drowns not only her childhood but the whole world of her early fiction; there were to be no more allegations of portrait-painting. She did not, however, end the book without leaving in it a record of the anger generated by that turbulent year of uncontrollable talk.

3

Gossip bursts into the text of *The Mill on the Floss* like a flood of violence that only flood can overcome. Until the final three chapters the story of Maggie has been told as a series of intimate relationships of conflict: her audiences are her family and lovers. Once she returns to St. Ogg's from the aborted elopement with Stephen Guest, the narrative turns to its attack on "the world's wife" with a vengeance that is matched only by the unstoppable power it attributes to the talk of the town (428). Maggie virtually disappears in this section; gossip is scapegoated as the murderer of her social existence. By the time of the flood scene, she is socially dead; the final "rescue" fantasy takes place in asocial, ahistorical time.

In its focus on the elaborated detail of sexual scandal, this representation of gossip feels like an emanation from a mind well-practiced in the projection of nightmarish voices. These voices are rendered neither in imagined dialogue nor in narrative summary, but in a collective free indirect discourse that evokes the qualities of fearful fantasy. The speakers are nameless and faceless, but the sound of their—ostentatiously female—voices and the insane logic of their judgment is perfectly audible. Although the narrative irony makes it perfectly clear that "the world's wife" is vicious and self-serving, ready to pander to female success and happy to kick a fellow-woman when she's down, George Eliot's invention of two hypothetical gossip stories instead of one has the eerie side-effect of linking gossip more closely with the inner life of its subject. For the two stories invented by the narrator on behalf of the "world's wife" are crass distortions of the two sides of Maggie that are in mortal struggle.

The first story—the one that would have been told had Maggie returned to St. Ogg's as a well-dressed married woman—is a pot-boiler romance in which the handsome hero, overcome by passion for the young girl, sweeps her away against her will and continues to worship her in marriage. In this version the losers are pitied and dismissed from the main plot: Lucy, a passive victim, is sent to the seaside to recover; Philip is consigned to the continent where such deformed persons belong. The romantic and ambitious Maggie wishes for this story; her own passion has sketched it out for her. Yet the gossips' success story is exactly the one her conscience disallows, and much painful irony lies in the fact that she has gallantly squelched the one fantasy that gossip would label morally acceptable.

The story that is told turns Maggie into a fallen woman "actuated by mere unwomanly boldness and unbridled passion" (428). In this version Stephen is at the mercy of a "designing bold girl," the connection with Philip is a sign of something disgusting in Maggie, and Lucy does not figure except as part of "the Deanes," whose kindness Maggie has betrayed. The actual evidence of Stephen's letter exonerating Maggie is simply woven into the story as a gentlemanly fabrication. Yet this story too is a translation into melodrama of the guilt, remorse, and resignation to a life of penitence that Maggie feels; she has in effect generated the story out of herself. As George Eliot shows the scandal deepening and widening to include and finally vanquish the best counter-effects of the clergyman Dr. Kenn, it begins to seem that her own floodgates are opened by an imaginary situation in which gossip is so grotesquely allied with self-accusation.

Of course the scandal section has its more controlled narrative uses. In an almost ritualistic way it isolates Maggie and prepares her and the reader for a death more gracious than life in society. And it provides a field against which the novel makes as its definition of heroism the ability to resist and transcend what other people say. Maggie's own resistance is part of the obliviousness to gossip that got her into her fix to begin with, but it brings back a bit of her "old proud fire" when she refuses to leave St. Ogg's because of what people are saying about her (434). Her pride, like Amos Barton's, is dangerous but good: the alternative would be slavishness to what others think.

Final accolades of heroism are given out successively to Mrs. Tulliver, Aunt Glegg, Philip, and Lucy, each of whom sticks by Maggie in the face of social pressure. Dr. Kenn complicates the rather simple moral sequence by finally succumbing to his parishioners' wish that he fire Maggie lest he lose his influence over his flock; he makes a compromised decision because he sees gossip as an unbeatable power and chooses to retain his audience. Like Farebrother in *Middlemarch*, Kenn raises the question of survival by accomodation from which Eliot exempts her major characters.

The vilification of gossip thus serves its turn in a novel which ends by washing away the limited world in which Eliot grew up. But the force of the attack should not be absorbed by its narrative purposes. Maggie herself hears nothing in gossip that is hers; her head is full of her own voices of self-reproach. It is the narrator who hears and reproduces voices that are despicable exactly to the extent that they intersect with Maggie's inner struggle. In "Amos Barton" the sexual scandal is foregrounded so as to be declared beside the point; here it is relevant, despite Maggie's technical innocence and loyal virtue. Like the revealing reconciliation fantasy of the flood itself, the gossip fantasy gives us a glimpse of George Eliot at a moment when gossip's threat to the idealizations of the highly wrought moral life is most angrily resisted.

By the time she wrote *Middlemarch*, George Eliot had come to a new understanding of the relationship between gossip and the self-comforting fictions of its subjects. *Middlemarch* dramatizes what George Eliot learned in retrospective meditation upon the Liggins affair: in that extraordinary book, what others say is repeatedly depicted as the mirror of what the subject represses.[10]

4

Middlemarch is a virtual anatomy of all the different ways people can talk about each other. To read the novel with "gossip" as a protagonist is to recognize how difficult it is to distinguish gossip from other kinds of dialogue, how fully George Eliot had become interested in an objective depiction of the processes through which information about people is circulated, blocked, or distorted. Gillian Beer has shown how the metaphor of circulatory systems organizes the novel, connecting gossip with financial status (47–62). Yet the pervasiveness of gossip eludes any single characterization: George Eliot creates several precisely distinguished and separate circles of gossip, and defines every character through a particularized relationship with the talk of others. By the end of the novel every talking circle discusses the Bulstrode-Lydgate affair, now become a genuine scandal; but had Raffles not picked up a stray bit of paper from Rigg-Featherstone's hearth the normal whirlpools of gossip would not–the narrator suggests–have combined into "catastrophe" (302).

While the broad movement from gossip to scandal repeats the pattern set by George Eliot's earlier stories, the representations of gossip itself open a more complex terrain, in which the talk of others is not only inevitable but often essential to the circulation of information needed by members of the community. Moreover, both gossip and scandal tell the truth in *Middlemarch*—not the truth their subjects acknowledge, but a kind of truth they have fearfully or scornfully repressed. Because of this penetrating dialogue between gossip and individual repression, the novel persistently resists one of its most popular readings, as a story of desiring subjects blocked, broken or excluded by community opinion.[11]

In *Middlemarch* the sheer range of dialogue about absent others challenges the reader to define the activity of gossip. Is Mrs. Cadwallader a gossip when she brings James Chettam the news that Dorothea is engaged to Casaubon? When she insinuates that Celia is interested in him? When Fred asks Rosamund what Mary said is he gossiping? What is Naumann doing when he rhapsodizes on Dorothea at Rome? Is James Chettam a gossip when he tries to persuade Mr. Cadwallader to interfere in Dorothea's engagement to Casaubon? What about the hospital board when it meets to discuss the candidacy for the post of hospital chaplain? Is the attack on Brooke's estate management in the *Trumpet* gossip or politics? When Farebrother is asked to discuss Fred with Mary, or when he brings news about Fred's doings to the Garth household, is he gossiping?

Such activities have to be set against more outright forms of gossip: the spread of rumor and speculation clustering around Lydgate—his medical practice, his association with Bulstrode, and his engagement to Rosamond— and to a lesser extent around Ladislaw. Eliot devotes a long chapter (45) to rumor about Lydgate in which she concentrates fully on the misinterpretations of Lydgate that prepare his fall: the uneducated fear he wants the hospital as a source of corpses to cut up, the surgeons resent his refusal to make his fees dependent on dispensing drugs. In such analyses, and briefer ones about Ladislaw, it is clear that true gossip might be defined as talk laden with titillating fantasy or innuendo that draws conclusions from a lack of evidence, and arises from distrust, jealousy, or hostility. Nevertheless such talk is part of a continuum that includes almost all the talk in the novel, and all the shades of meaning and feeling that distinguish gossip from something else.

There is, for example, a fine line between gossip and getting information to people who need to know it. Mrs. Cadwallader performs a service when she tells James Chettam of Dorothea's engagement; she spares him considerable humiliation. Celia twice breaks through the hush-up atmosphere created by gossip to give her sister vital information, about Sir James's intentions and about Casaubon's will. The whole of Chapter 59 is devoted to the chain of gossip that finally and belatedly ends with Rosamond telling Will about his role in that will; the news is exactly suited to the banalities of Rosamond's romantic imagination, yet her breaking of confidence comes as a great relief in the conspiracy of silence that constitutes the courtship of Will and Dorothea. When Eliot returns to the "world's wife" theme in Chapter 74, she satirizes the gossiping women less for the quality of their dialogue than for the obstruction they pose to Mrs. Bulstrode's need for information about her husband.

This theme illuminates Sir James Chettam's role in the novel: he is the gossip-fearer, always vigilant about the reputation of his family, always trying haplessly to get someone else to prevent actions that threaten to stir up gossip. He wants others to undo the Dorothea-Casaubon marriage, keep Mr. Brooke out of politics, keep Dorothea from knowing the contents of Casaubon's will, get Ladislaw out of town, and then, ironically, prevent Dorothea from "meddling" in the Lydgate scandal, all to maintain—without his overt interference—the dignity of his position. When he wants Dorothea to know the gossip about Will and Rosamond he delegates the dirty work to Mrs. Cadwallader. Failing to halt any of the gossip-worthy courses of action he deplores, Chettam is a comic reminder that the effort to prevent gossip is equivalent to putting a ban on life.

The tactful Mr. Farebrother is his corrective, for Farebrother takes on the complex responsibility of mediating between individuals and the gossip about them. Speaking out against ill-founded rumor is only the easiest task for this fully-articulated successor to Mr. Cleves; Farebrother's story is all about the sensitive application of rules for when to say what to whom. He knows gossip about Lydgate before the new doctor comes to town, but he tells no-one except Lydgate himself that he has heard of him. He mounts a campaign to sensitize Lydgate to the opinions of his colleagues, and another to defend Lydgate in the town's professional circles; unlike the masterpiece of tact and honesty that is his mediation of the Fred-Mary courtship, these honorable efforts fail. In the end it is tact itself that is finally found wanting: after

Farebrother has heard gossip about Lydgate's debts, offered help, and been rebuffed, he is unwilling to repeat the intrusion on Lydgate's pride in the bribery scandal. Dorothea's leap of faith in Lydgate shows up Farebrother as a coward, yet his fear that what gossip says may be true is only a special extrapolation from the pattern set by the novel itself.

For gossip in *Middlemarch* is always the externalization of a repressed truth. Bulstrode's case lies at the center of this pattern, not only because what Raffles knows of him is true, but because Bulstrode himself can only see the story when he is faced with its appearance in others' eyes: his repression of his step-daughter's existence and his hush money to Raffles "was the bare fact which Bulstrode was now forced to see in the rigid outline with which acts present themselves to onlookers" (452). For other characters to gossip provides the disturbing shock of the true. Casaubon's sexual unfitness for marriage is apparent to everyone but himself and Dorothea. The random gossip about Ladislaw's "shady" background is corroborated by the news Raffles brings. Celia's relay of gossip forces Dorothea to see James Chettam's friendship as the courting she has high-mindedly been repressing; Casaubon's will, his final act of gossip, propels her into love with Will under "the effect of the sudden revelation that another had thought of him in that light" (360). Lydgate is told by town talkers two facts that he strenuously denies: that he has linked his professional ambitions to Bulstrode's money, and that he is courting Rosamund Vincy. Even the bribery scandal contains its uncomfortable seed of truth, as Lydgate recognizes when he wonders if he would have left Raffle's death uninvestigated had he not accepted Bulstrode's check. Only the gossip generated by professional competition or provincial ignorance is presented as seriously false; it is undeniable that Lydgate is victimized by medical scare stories and professional jealousy.

Because resistance to the "petty medium" of gossip is resistance to a truth about the self, the linkage of moral heroism with the power to defy gossip is a complicated matter in *Middlemarch*. Mary and Caleb Garth's refusals to have anything to do with their employers' scandalous doings—last-minute will-burnings, mysterious blackmailers—only make them firmer links in the chain of catastrophe. Lydgate carries around a fantasy of heroic resistance in which all gossip is defined as "silly conclusions which nobody can foresee" (333); yet even the heroic stance carries with it the seeds of defeatism: "it was as useless to fight against the interpretations of ignorance as to whip the fog" (329). And Lydgate's visible actions—his vote for the hospital chaplaincy, his engagement to Rosamund, his financial dependence on Bulstrode—are ones in which the posture of defiance blurs only his own vision of the fact that he has at least partially become what the talkers say he is.[12]

Against this tragic limitation we should presumably place the transcendant innocence of Dorothea, and perhaps the successful resistance to opinion that John Kucich finds in the love story of Dorothea and Will.[13] Yet the obliviousness to gossip celebrated in this marriage is won only through a process of exquisite sensitivity to gossip's power. Dorothea's generous faith in Lydgate—"I believe that people are almost better than their neighbours think they are""—is fueled by a derailed wish to defend Ladislaw from the gossip that separates them: "Some of her intensest experience in the last two years had set her mind strongly in opposition to any unfavourable construction of others" (537). That "intensest experience" is primarily her inner cherishing of a belief in Ladislaw's goodness against the Chettam-Cadwallader version of Ladislaw as a "low" philanderer. Dorothea's susceptibility to gossip emerges during Will's second farewell scene, when she suddenly suspects him of leaving to escape Rosamond rather than herself; when his final outburst makes it clear that he loves her, her joy includes the relief of vindication: "He had acted so as to defy reproach, and make wonder respectful" (465). When she goes to clear Lydgate in Rosamond's eyes only to find Ladislaw in the midst of an apparent love-scene, the psychological entanglement of the two situations is represented by the plot: suddenly Dorothea becomes Rosamond, a woman who instantly believes that the gossip about her lover is true. In her anger Will becomes "a detected illusion," one "among the crowd" (576); her noble mission to "save" Rosamond's marriage has as its premise the idea that Ladislaw is what her friends have been calling him. Thus she is as dependent on Rosamond's vindication of Ladislaw as Rosamond is on her belief in Lydgate; and when Will comes for the final interview she goes to meet him with a renewed sense of love as vindication, "a sense that she was doing something daringly defiant for his sake" (591). This is not a love that turns away from gossip, but one that is nourished by resistance to it.

Ladislaw's side of the story is even more entirely shaped by his resistance to what he imagines others will think of him. In his sensitivity he pre-empts the terms of Casaubon's will before he knows of it; when Brooke tries half-heartedly to keep him away from the Grange, Will thinks "Her friends, then, regarded him with some suspicion? Their fears were quite superfluous: they were very much mistaken if they imagined that he would put himself forward as a needy adventurer trying to win the favour of a rich women" (365). His determination "to give the lie beforehand" (399) to that suspicion makes it impossible for him to say anything coherent to Dorothea, and begins the muffled comedy of courtship conducted as a joint effort of vindication in which the partners lack necessary information about each other. Will is then subjected to a series of unpleasant revelations—Rosamund tells him about the will, Raffles tells him about his parents, and Bulstrode offers him repentance money—which only increase his desire to defy the stories that he knows Chettam gossip will make of these matters. "However, let them suspect what they pleased, they would find themselves in the wrong. They would find that the blood in his veins was as free from the taint of meanness as theirs" (447). He refuses Bulstrode's money in large part because he knows he could not bear to tell Dorothea that he had accepted it, and begins his last talk with Dorothea by telling her that he has done so. All of this adds up to a portrait of a man talented in anticipating what he looks like to others, whose defiance of conventional stories proves a salutary—even a disciplinary—influence on his character. If Will escapes being what gossip calls him, it is because he outwits it at its own game.

Or would, were not his author open to every conceivable twist of the game. When Eliot, in a chapter that must surely have amused her, follows the chain of gossip that ends with Rosamond telling Will about the will, she puts in Rosamond's mouth the story of romantic love that is in fact the story of Dorothea and Will. "It is really the most charming romance: Mr. Casaubon jealous, and foreseeing that there was no one else whom Mrs. Casaubon would so much like to marry, and no one who would so much like to marry her as a certain gentleman; and then laying a plan to spoil all by making her forfeit her property if she did marry that gentleman—and then—and then—and then—oh, I have no doubt the end will be thoroughly romantic." And she adds "I dare say she likes you better than the property" (438–39). Like every other light-minded gossip Rosamond fails to comprehend the rage of peculiar feeling this news arouses in Will as he storms out saying "Never! You will never hear of the marriage!" Yet she is right, as all the Middlemarch gossips are right in their ways; it is really the most charming romance.

If gossip in *Middlemarch* functions as a mirror of what the subject represses, the stories of Bulstrode and Casaubon reveal that George Eliot knew what she was up to: it is not gossip but paranoia that kills in this novel. In these two characters Eliot explores the pain of audience-consciousness in extreme forms, saving her utmost horror for those to whom the world is nothing but a "whispering-gallery." Casaubon's existence is determined by his fear of being seen by others; like his cousin Ladislaw he has keen suspicions about what others suspect, but unlike him he has no talent, energy, youth, or passion to oppose his fears. "To let any one suppose that he was jealous would be to admit their (suspected) view of his disadvantages: to let them know that he did not find marriage particularly blissful would imply his conversion to their (probably) earlier disapproval. It would be as bad as letting Carp, and Brasenose generally, know how backward he was in organizing the material for his 'Key to all Mythologies''' (276–77). Casaubon suspects others–notably Dorothea, who comes to embody his hostile imaginary audiences—"without confessing" his failures to himself (307); he has thoroughly projected his fears upon others, who loom over him and paralyse his every endeavor. Casaubon—like a part of George Eliot's creativity—seems to die of being seen; his forced intimacy with Dorothea is the beginning of his end.

The question the narrator asks of Bulstrode might equally apply to Casaubon: "Who can know how much of his most inward life is made up of the thoughts he believes other men to have about him, until that fabric of opinion is threatened with ruin?" (504). In Bulstrode's case the answer seems to be "all of it"; the horror of his story lies less in the evil of his past crime than in the psychological machinations through which Bulstrode constructs a personality that will do anything rather than risk the disgrace of exposure. Bulstrode's imagination is coarser than Casaubon's; he does not seem to intuit that everyone except his wife hates him already, that the "fabric of opinion" is his own fabrication. Yet his fantasy of an approving world is no less a projection than Casaubon's repressed choruses of disapproval; and it is equally fragile. Like his scholarly counterpart, his life shrivels into nothing in the face of exposure.

In both stories the narrator is most effectively sympathetic at the moments when the dread of exposure is most intensely imagined. Nevertheless the slaves to how things look—including Rosamond—are the villains of the novel; self-consciousness is a greater threat than gossip if only because it creates a dangerous vulnerability to the talking world that no one can escape.[14] In the universe of *Middlemarch* it is necessary for sanity and survival to admit the talk of others into an open—if openly resistant—dialectic with the self.

All of this takes us a long way from George Eliot's first representation of gossip in "Amos Barton." In *Middlemarch* it is not better not to know what your neighbours are saying; not hearing is a symptom of a deceptive relationship with the self. Gossip and truth do not move on separate tracks; they are different perceptions of the same one. And gossip can make things happen: in a fiction built on the activities of self-deception and exposure, the plot is no more or less than the action—and in Eliot it is an action—of being seen. In this novel George Eliot took command of the whole register of her self-consciousness, externalized it in the intense relation of character and gossip, and made it sane.

5

Middlemarch brought George Eliot to the height of her fame, but it did not alter her wish to remain visible only in the public privacy of her texts. Her resistance to biography, and her desire to regulate what others saw and thought of her continued after Lewes's death, through the final "scandal" of her marriage to John Cross, and even beyond her death, in the carefully edited version of *George Eliot's Life* that Cross produced. The recognitions of *Middlemarch* did, however, have a sequel: in the strangely intimate essay "Looking Inward," the male narrator Theophrastus Such entrusts his audience with a directly autobiographical image of the writer's self in hiding. In this last work, Eliot's fear of being seen and discussed by her audiences was turned into confessional comedy and rehearsed for their benefit.

Impressions of Theophrastus Such (1879) is concerned with exposure: several of the sketches in this heterogeneous text are portraits of writers in the critical marketplace, others satirize the self-delusions that certain character types impose upon their acquaintances. The opening essay, "Looking Inward," purports to be an autobiographical confession in which "Such"—the English surname suggests a particularly placed and comic version of the generic figure— offers an apology for the satires that follow by asserting his inward complicity with the follies of others. "Dear blunderers, I am one of you," he claims; and the essay ends with a reiteration of this point, now made with the full Eliot rhetorical regalia: "But there is a loving laughter in which the only recognized superiority is that of the ideal self, the God within, holding the mirror and the scourge for our own pettiness as well as our neighbours'" (5-6, 19). The hyper-self-consciousness of Such's narrative as a whole may, however, suggest George Eliot's special need to apologize in fictional self-deprecation for her indulgence in the outright satire—the "evil-speaking"—she had licensed herself to practice when she adapted the convention of the Theophrastan "character" essay.[15] The intense and circular introspection of Such certainly goes far beyond anything that would have been necessary to make the official point of fellowship in folly. In fact, his self-underminings undermine the official point as well, for they consistently emphasize the psychological gap between him and his audiences.

"Looking Inward" is about the possibility, or the impossibility, of writing autobiography to be read by others. The essay opens with this question: "It is my habit to give an account to myself of the characters I meet with: can I give any true account of my own?" (3). Such is immediately overtaken by his consciousness that others—while not knowing what he knows of himself—are all too likely to know things he does not know about himself; that is, he is instantly threatened by the critical potential of his audience. "Is it then possible to describe oneself at once faithfully and fully?" he asks again; and again his imagination leaps to his audience: it is possible to reveal the truth about oneself unintentionally, as Rousseau does, "from what he unconsciously enables us to discern" (6-7). Such, whose main problem lies in his belief that no one is interested in hearing what he has to say, is simultaneously freighted with the fear that others will see too well what he prefers to conceal.

"Looking Inward" dramatizes the fear of constructing a "false view of the self in relation to others" that Eliot had observed when she read the autobiography of Harriet Martineau (Letters 6:371); it also includes pious strictures against the autobiographical revelation of material that gossips about living others, or show human nature in "its lowest fatalities, its invincible remnants of the brute" (6). But its most autobiographical moments—moments when the narrative sounds suddenly neither like the semi-comic Such nor the like the pietistic Eliot narrator—are the ones in which the imagination of a responding audience is most fully present. This voice breaks through when Such is confessing that he would simply rather not hear the critical things others say about him: "In brief, after a close intimacy with myself for a longer period than I choose to mention, I find within me a permanent longing for approbation, sympathy, and love" (8). It returns when he describes turning to the act of writing to escape the sense of invisibility that accompanies his talent for sympathetic listening to others. As a friendly listener he is nothing but an audience (a strategy he has developed in order not to feel like a disappointed outcast from the human condition), but writing "brings with it the vague, delightful illusion of an audience nearer to my idiom than the Cherokees, and more numerous than the visionary One for whom many authors have declared themselves willing to go through the pleasing punishment of publication." This fantasy audience is "a far-off, hazy, multitudinous assemblage," a projection of the self which makes "approving chorus to the sentences and paragraphs of which I myself particularly enjoy the writing." It is necessarily hazy, for if any face becomes distinct, it "is sure to be one bent on discountenancing my innocent intentions; it is pale-eyed, incapable of being amused when I am amused or indignant at what makes me indignant"

(17). Such is more cowardly—or less ambitious—than his creator, for he will only submit his work posthumously, but he shares with her a knowledge of the necessary illusions that make writing possible in the first place.[16]

Theophrastus Such never answers his own questions about whether it is possible to give a faithful account of the self; the self and its audiences reach a draw in their competition for true knowledge of character. He remains stuck between his wish not to know anything about his audience that is not a projection of himself, and his recognition that an audience may see more about him than he wants them to know. George Eliot's rather good-natured portrayal of his dilemma includes, for the first time, a sentence that grants her audiences the right to gossip: "I am not indeed writing an autobiography, or pretending to give an unreserved description of myself, but only offering some slight confessions in an apologetic light, to indicate that if in my absence you dealt as freely with my unconscious weaknesses as I have dealt with the unconscious weaknesses of others, I should not feel myself warranted by common-sense in regarding your freedom of observation as an exceptional case of evil-speaking. . ." (7). The creation of a first-person narrator who says, however grudgingly, "I talk about you, you talk about me" makes a last little rent in the veil of privacy with which George Eliot had obscured her active participation in the arts of gossip and satire. Perhaps she knew, as she publically embraced the role of satirist, that her career in fiction had run its necessary course.

NOTES

1. I have commented on this episode in detail in "Mary Ann Evans's Holy War: An Essay in Letter-Reading," *Nineteenth-Century Literature* 44 (December, 1989): 335–63.
2. See Marcus, "Literature and Social Theory: Starting in with George Eliot" in *Representations: Essays on Literature and Social Theory* (New York: Random House, 1954), p. 196. Other critics who emphasize the community of gossip include Elizabeth Ermarth, *Realism and Consensus in the English Novel* (Princeton: Princeton UP, 1983), pp. 222–56. Her idea of consensus owes something to Quentin Anderson's essay "George Eliot in *Middlemarch*" (1958), in Boris Ford, ed. *From Dickens to Hardy: The Pelican Guide to English Literature* (Penguin, 1963–67), 6:274–93). For discussions of gossip as a levelling force in *Middlemarch* see especially D. A. Miller, *Narrative and Its Discontents: Problems of Closure in the Traditional Novel* (Princeton: Princeton, 1981), pp. 110–29, and Patricia Meyer Spacks, *Gossip* (New York: Knopf, 1985), pp. 195–202. Alexander Welsh takes the more pastoral view of gossip in contrast to blackmail; see *George Eliot and Blackmail* (Cambridge, MA.: Harvard UP, 1985), pp 135–37.

3 The substitution of the clergyman for the novelist was a repeated move in George Eliot's writing. In her *Westminster Review* essay, "Evangelical Teaching: Dr. Cumming" (1855), she had explicitly compared the preacher to all other public speakers and writers, showing how he is the least open to audience criticism and correction by virtue of his position. In this context, critics, the press, and skeptical listeners play the role of safeguards against irresponsible teaching. See Thomas Pinney, ed., *Essays of George Eliot* (London: Routledge and Kegan Paul, 1963), p. 161. As late as 1874 Eliot continued to use the analogy; in a letter to Blackwood she compares a writer whose work has deteriorated to "an eminent clergyman's spoiling his reputation by lapses and neutralizing all the good he did before" (6:75–76).

4. For a history of gossip's ill repute, see Spacks, *Gossip*, chapter 2, which includes a discussion of its traditional association with loose-tongued women. George Eliot's attacks on female gossips may stem from a personal distrust of women that Edith Simcox records in her autobiography: "when she was young, girls and women seemed to look on her as somehow 'uncanny,' while men were always kind." See *Letters*, 7:299.

5. Steven Marcus reads "Amos Barton" as a story that represses its true topic: Milly's death from a passionately sexual marriage. He (probably correctly) identifies the illness in the middle of the story as a miscarriage that makes it unsafe for Milly to bear yet another (seventh) child; and concludes that there is some indirect truth in the sexual scandal about the Bartons. To read the story this way fulfills his plan to initiate more provocative and questioning readings of George Eliot's pieties, but it seems another version of the gossipers' need to discover something more exciting than poverty and overwork beneath the surface of the tale. See *Representations*, pp. 205–213.

6. Elizabeth Ermarth implicates the community in Milly's death (see *George Eliot* [Boston: Twayne, 1985], p.61); but there is no real indication that more sacks of coal or community baby-sitting would have prevented it. Eliot disconnects the two events so as to silence gossip through the force of mortality.

7. For full accounts of the Liggins episode see Gordon S. Haight, *George Eliot: A Biography* (Oxford: Oxford, 1968), pp. 280–94; Ruby V. Redinger, *George Eliot: The Emergent Self* (New York: Knopf, 1975), pp. 392–400, and Alexander Welsh, *George Eliot and Blackmail* (Cambridge, MA: Harvard UP, 1985), pp. 128–31.

8. See *Letters* 2:459–60, and 3:155–160.

9. The actual connection between the literary gossip and the Liggins rumor remains a matter for speculation. Redinger wonders whether the rumor was started by London literary men who hoped to "smoke out" the Leweses (*George Eliot: The Emergent Self*, p. 393); Welsh sees the Liggins affair as a distraction that allowed Eliot to feel less guilt about her liason with Lewes (*George Eliot and Blackmail*, p.131).

10. As Alexander Welsh says, the novels after *Romola* "are much more efforts of representation than of projection." *George Eliot and Blackmail*, p. 199.

11. The most brilliant of such readings is D.A. Miller's; see *Narrative and Its Discontents* (Princeton: Princeton UP, 1981), pp. 111–29. Since Miller identifies "the" community as the drive toward the "non-narratable," he has to make of it a monolithic force, yet many of his insights complicate this view by suggesting how the desiring subjects are implicated in community opinion.

12. D.A. Miller sees this problem as an instance of "the uncanny" working to make internal choices correspond with external necessity. See *Narrative and Its Discontents*, pp. 117–19.

13. See John Kucich, *Repression in Victorian Fiction* (Berkeley: U of California P, 1987), for the argument that this love affair is fed by the internal dialectic between renunciation and desire: "In love, for both characters, the power of external influence is deliberately minimized" (p. 146). This is part of Kucich's larger point, that Eliot's "favored characters . . . are all made to seem impervious to the judgments of others about them" (pp. 182–83). D.A. Miller represents the opposite pole: "Dorothea and Will are kept apart for so long precisely by their overwhelming consciousness of what people might say" (p. 164). My argument places Eliot's dialectic between these two positions.

14. See Kucich for a related argument that George Eliot defines egotism as an excessive reliance on the opinions of others. *Repression in Victorian Fiction*, pp. 183–200.

15. For an informative discussion of Eliot's adoption of this genre, see G. Robert Stange, "The Voices of the Essayist," *Nineteenth-Century Fiction* 35 (1980): 312–30. Stange sees in the work a desire to recover earlier narrative voices, after the impersonal vision of *Daniel Deronda*.

16. Redinger reads "Looking Inward" as straight autobiography, an analysis of Eliot's "futile attempts to free herself from the cruelly indifferent auditor within her" (*George Eliot: The Emergent Self*, p. 372). In her account only the efforts of G. H. Lewes stand between Eliot and the publication failures of Such. Redinger fails to see the comic self-knowledge in the piece.

WORKS CITED

Anderson, Quentin. "George Eliot in *Middlemarch*" in *From Dickens to Hardy: The Pelican Guide to English Literature*, New York: Penguin, 1963–1967.

Beer, Gillian. "Circulatory Systems: Money and Gossip in *Middlemarch*" *Cahiers Victoriens & Edoaurdiens* 26 (October 1987): 47–62.

Bodenheimer, Rosemarie. "Mary Ann Evans's Holy War: An Essay in Letter-Reading." *Nineteenth-Century Literature* 44 (December 1989): 335–63.

Cross, J.W. *George Eliot's Life as Related in Her Letters and Journals*. New York: Harper and Brothers, 1885.

Eliot, George. *The George Eliot Letters*. Ed. Gordon S. Haight. Volumes I–IX. New Haven: Yale UP, 1954–1974.

———. *Essays of George Eliot*. Ed. Thomas Pinney. London: Routledge and Kegan Paul, 1963.

———. "Impressions of Theophrastus Such": *The Works of George Eliot*. Standard Edition Edinburgh and London: William Blackwood and Sons, n.d.

———. *Middlemarch*. Ed. Gordon S. Haight. Boston: Riverside, 1961.

———. *The Mill on the Floss*. Ed. Gordon S. Haight. Boston: Riverside, 1961.

———. "The Sad Fortunes of the Rev. Amos Barton." *Scenes of Clerical Life.* Harmondsworth: Penguin, 1973.

Ermarth, Elizabeth. *George Eliot.* Boston: Twayne, 1985.

———. *Realism and Consensus in the English Novel.* Princeton: Princeton UP, 1983.

Haight, Gordon S. *George Eliot: A Biography.* Oxford: Oxford UP, 1968.

Kucich, John. *Repression in Victorian Fiction.* Berkeley: U California P, 1987.

Marcus, Stephen. "Literature and Social Theory: Starting in with George Eliot." in *Representations: Essays on Literature and Social Theory.* New York: Random House, 1954.

Miller, D. A. *Narrative and Its Discontents: Problems of Closure in the Traditional Novel.* Princeton: Princeton UP, 1981.

Redinger, Ruby V. *George Eliot: The Emergent Self.* New York: Knopf, 1975.

Spacks, Patricia Meyer.*Gossip.* New York. Knoph, 1985.

Stange, G. Robert. "The Voices of the Essayist" *Nineteenth-Century Fiction* 35 (1980) 312–30.

Welsh, Alexander. *George Eliot and Blackmail*: Cambridge, MA: Harvard UP, 1985.

Gyp's Tale: On Sympathy, Silence, and Realism in *Adam Bede*

James Eli Adams

In Chapter 21 of *Adam Bede*, the narrator remarks upon the quiet "drama" of three laborers learning to read: "It was almost as if three rough animals were making humble efforts to learn how they might become human" (281). Commentators on Eliot's novel frequently single out this evocation of an obscure struggle against mystery and dispossession: it has "unmistakably the quality of an allegorical panel," as one critic remarks.[1] But a tribute to the humanizing power of literacy is curiously discordant in a work which so strenuously insists on the inadequacies of formal education. Adam, after all, is not made any more human by his literacy: that hopeful view is gently parodied in Bartle Massey's lament that the catastrophe "might never have happened," if Adam, "poor fellow," had "gone into the higher branches" of mathematics (463). Moral education–that which makes one truly human—rests instead on the "lesson" of sympathy, which is transacted in a very different language, under the silent, often inchoate tutelage of suffering. "That is a long and hard lesson," the narrator remarks after Thias Bede's funeral, "and Adam had at present only learned the alphabet of it in his father's sudden death"(255). Formal literacy is thus subordinated to a language whose "alphabet" has no phonic counterpart, nor any established script.

In an earlier epoch, such language was the province of religious doctrine and ceremony. But for Eliot, it is the novelist who must take up the burden of representing the ineffable—of rendering in words the experience of suffering and moral redemption. Eliot's moral design in *Adam Bede* thus offers peculiar challenges to the novelist. If, as the novel eloquently insists, what is most precious in human experience is that which cannot be articulated—"something unspeakably great and beautiful"—then the largest significance of formal education and eloquence, whether spoken or written, will be ironic. Eloquence, like literacy, calls attention to the complexity and significance of that which it cannot adequately articulate. Although it represents a uniquely human power, literacy thus confirms in addition a pronounced bond between man and "rough animals." Indeed, what might seem one of the novel's more hackneyed motifs, the uncannily precocious dog population of Hayslope, is but one facet of Eliot's sustained meditation upon the powers and limits of human expression. In the dogs, Eliot portrays creatures who seem to possess a rudimentary inner life, but who, since they lack speech, must struggle to find an outlet for that life in other forms of expression. Whatever their sentimental value, "the dumb creatures," as Mrs. Poyser calls them, thus assume the role of mute choric figures offering oblique commentary on the eminently *human* struggle to find an adequate language for feeling. That human predicament is most obviously embodied in the form of Adam's dog Gyp, the devoted companion who lacks a tail, and is thus "destitute of that vehicle for his emotions."

In stressing the limits of human expression, however, Eliot also engages in a Carlylean celebration of the ineffable that tends to render eloquence inherently suspect. If what is most truly and richly "human" are those states of mind that resist articulation, then those who trust to eloquence or "notions" to represent their experience are not only doomed to frustration; they are destined to seem emotionally impoverished, insufficiently responsive to the integrity of human feeling, which ultimately can be respected only by silence. Conversely, utterance which is inarticulate and incoherent may confirm the authority of the feeling it cannot directly express. Gyp's missing tail, after all, makes its own eloquence felt in the consequent pathos of Gyp's struggle to express his emotions, a struggle whose intensity humanizes him beyond any other dog in the novel. *With* a tail, Gyp would be less emphatically the object of "fellow-feeling." The inability to articulate one's most profound feelings and thoughts may be an obstacle to heightened consciousness—as Eliot would obviously have it in the case of Hetty Sorrel; yet the same failure may also be evidence of the depth of one's feelings, and thus of one's capacity for sympathy.

Such a stance obviously places peculiar and strenuous burdens on the novelist. More precisely, the mistrust of eloquence lends extraordinary pressure to the problematics of realistic representation. Eliot's rejection of religious doctrine, which impels her appeal to the authority of experience, also renders morally (not merely ontologically) suspect the reliance on language to conjure up "experience" as a realm of immediate, external presence. This tension informs a feature of *Adam Bede* often explained away as an awkward device of the inexperienced novelist: the reliance on historical present, which is frequently conjoined with exhortations that the reader "see" the scenes being described. Eliot's predicament as a narrator, along with the moral problematic informing it, is thus projected with particular complexity in the figure of Dinah Morris. Celebrated as the vehicle of a profound sympathetic understanding, Dinah is effectively silenced after her marriage to Adam, when she must renounce her preaching. The ending is frequently criticized as a failure of nerve, a capitulation to the pressures of novelistic convention and male sentiment.[2] But however one accounts for the outcome, Dinah's silencing articulates the novel's equivocal view of eloquence. As an evangelical preacher, Dinah is of all the characters the most vulnerable to the suspicion of eloquence; she is also the most obvious surrogate of a novelist notorious for her moral commentary on the action she narrates. The logic which silences Dinah is central to a novel which, in its effort to faithfully represent the complexities of moral experience, is in effect constantly trying to write itself into silence.

Jane Welsh Carlyle, writing to the as-yet-unknown author of *Adam Bede* in 1859, praised the novel in these words:

> In truth, it is a beautiful most *human* Book! Every Dog in it, not to say every man woman and child in it, is brought home to one's "business and bosom," an individual fellow-creature! (Eliot *Letters* III: 18)

The canine population of Hayslope may recall the devoted hounds that are a sentimental fixture of Victorian genre painting. But Mrs. Carlyle—no mere sentimentalist—here seizes upon a central concern of the novel. The peculiar emotional sensibility of Hayslope dogs (notable even by mid-Victorian standards) places them within Eliot's sustained exploration of what it *means* to be a "fellow-creature." Their choric role is established in the novel's opening chapter, where Adam's dog Gyp alerts us to the distinctive features of his master's voice. Lest we miss the connection, Seth Bede is there to call it to our attention. "Thee'st like thy dog Gyp," he tells Adam, "thee bark'st at me sometimes, but thee allays lic'st my hand after." Gyp's subsequent entrance offers the narrator occasion to elaborate the analogy:

. . . no sooner did Adam put his ruler in his pocket, and begin to twist his
apron round his waist, then Gyp ran forward and looked up in his master's face
with patient expectation. If Gyp had had a tail he would doubtless have wagged
it, but being destitute of that vehicle for his emotions, he was like many other
worldly personages, destined to appear more phlegmatic than nature had made
him.

"What! Art ready for the basket, eh, Gyp?" said Adam, with the same gentle
modulation of voice as when he spoke to Seth.

Gyp jumped and made a short bark, as much as to say, "Of course." Poor
fellow, he had not a great range of expression.   (54)

The narrator's commiseration offers a coy but nonetheless suggestive gloss
on the distinct limits to Adam's own "range of expression." Adam conveys
his rigid sense of duty with a ready eloquence, both in his impatient attack
on wiry Ben's mockery, and in his lengthy, impromptu *credo*—"sarmunt,"
Ben calls it—extolling a religion of hard work. The forthright vehemence of
Adam's speech is faithful to his Carlylean creed, but, as Gyp's presence
emphasizes, it allows little outlet for an awkward tenderness in his character
that is suggested by his words to Seth and Gyp. Adam's subsequent ordeal
softens his "iron will" and nurtures his tenderness into a richer and more
comprehensive sympathy. That moral development is charted in a struggle to
find a more adequate vehicle for his more complex emotions. Ultimately, he
arrives at a new form of eloquence that can acknowledge the claims not only
of personal duty but of human frailty.

Adam's growth is paradigmatic of the novel's moral action, in which the
central characters undergo a kind of Feuerbachian baptism: through suffering,
they are led to "a regeneration, the initiation into a new state," which Eliot
summarizes as the experience of sympathy, "the one poor word that contains
all our best insight and our best love" (531).[3] This "lesson," as the narrator
describes it, involves the mastery of a new form of language, and in each of
the central characters the new understanding is confirmed by a shift in patterns
of speech. This transformation is most starkly presented in the figure of Hetty,
whose persistent silence through most of the novel reflects her utter incapacity
for sympathetic participation in the world around her. Adam's range of expression may be limited, but Hetty's mute egoism is a powerful emblem of
her isolation from other human beings. During her bewildered flight from the
exposure of her pregnancy, the narrator's imagery reduces her being almost
to the level of a frightened animal; after her arrest, she can only reconfirm
her humanity by being brought to speak, to confess her responsibility in a
human moral order.

Hetty's ordeal confirms the narrator's tribute to Bartle Massey's students: the mastery of language signifies a new level of humanity. Elsewhere, however, enlarged moral awareness is confirmed by the faltering of a former eloquence. Arthur Donnithorne is Hetty's partner in egoism and vanity, but by virtue of his sex and social position he embodies in more complex fashion the relation between insight and eloquence. Arthur is rarely at a loss for words, but his speech, even in his patronizing tenderness towards Hetty, is a tissue of superficial and evasive pleasantries, the language of a gentleman eager to maintain the regard of himself and others. Of his private thoughts, his vague moral qualms and self-mistrust, he cannot bring himself to speak, even with Mr. Irwine. Arthur's eventual acknowledgment of responsibility obviously parallels Hetty's confession, but since his disgrace has destroyed the foundations of his public rhetoric, he can only convey his new insight through a faltering of his former eloquence, as he struggles to master a vocabulary of sincerity he has never before called upon.

Adam's forthright speech—"I speak plain, sir, but I can't speak any other way"(207)—jars the decorum sustained in Arthur's urbane evasions. But Adam's frankness is the expression of an unyielding sense of duty that similarly limits the capacity to acknowledge the complexities of moral experience. His eloquence, after all, draws its conception of human experience from arithmetic: "Life's a reckoning we can't make twice over; there's no real making amends in this world, any more nor you can mend a wrong subtraction by doing your addition right" (247). This trope chimes with Eliot's insistence on the irrevocability of action, but it also represents a stance that cannot easily adapt to unexpected complexity in human experience.[4] As suffering calls into question the adequacy of Adam's moral arithmetic, his eloquence, like Arthur's, begins to falter. With the discovery that Hetty has murdered her infant, his rigid, "hard" speech finally gives way to broken sobs, and he vows to Bartle Massey, "I'll never be hard again." Finally, "with hesitating gentleness," he even manages to forgive Arthur (455,475,516).

Dinah at first glance stands outside this pattern: her immense fund of ready sympathy seems to require no correction or expansion. Yet she, too, ultimately enacts the pattern of faltering eloquence. Throughout most of the novel the conviction and support she derives from her sense of vocation are registered in the unwavering calm of her voice. Her appearance at Stoniton jail is typical: "There was no agitation visible in her, but a deep concentrated calmness, as if, even when she was speaking, her soul was in prayer reposing on an unseen support" (492). Even in response to Seth's declaration of love Dinah retains her composure, as the narrator quietly emphasizes: she replies "in her tender but calm treble notes" (79). Adam's presence alone disturbs this self-possession. Initially she greets him as she does Seth, "in her calm treble," but under the scrutiny of Adam's "dark, penetrating glance" she abruptly experiences "for the first time in her life . . . a painful self-consciousness" (163). As the novel approaches its close, this self-consciousness infuses her voice. When Dinah visits Adam after her night in the prison with Hetty, she recalls their first meeting, and speaks with "a trembling in her clear voice" (501). Later at the farm, when the conversation turns to her future, she speaks, "trying to be quite calm"; with Adam in the cottage, she is "trembling, but trying to be calm;" when he finally proposes, even her tears are "trembling" in response (501,523,536).

Dinah's peculiar susceptibility to Adam may seem the stuff of those "silly novels by lady novelists" that Eliot attacked. Still, the motif answers to a more strenuous moral design: Eliot clearly wants to enrich Dinah's character by complicating the forces that govern her single-minded existence. Yet this complication is prepared from the very outset as a resistance to Dinah's vocation, which is made to seem—like Adam's very different sense of vocation—"hard" and peremptory in its demands. So receptive to the divine Word that she strives to convey to her listeners, Dinah is less responsive to the claims of more mundane human needs. Mrs. Poyser seizes upon this theme in exasperation at her inability to persuade Dinah to remain with her relatives in Loamshire: "I might as well talk to the running brook and tell it to stand still" (123). Shortly afterwards, Irwine's conversation with Dinah prompts a similar analogy: "he must be a miserable prig who would act the pedagogue here," Irwine thinks, "one might as well go and lecture the trees for growing in their own shape" (136). While they pay tribute to the integrity of Dinah's vocation, both judgments also align that vocation with the profoundly equivocal character of nature itself. The bounties of Dinah's sympathy, they suggest, are bound up with a spiritual allegiance that, like natural forces, may be utterly indifferent to human needs.[5]

The faltering of Dinah's eloquence thus comes to mark a resistance to the specific character of Dinah's vocation. Such resistance is hardly surprising, inasmuch as she is, after all, a Methodist preacher in a novel permeated by Eliot's own rejection of doctrinal religion. That rejection is most obviously embodied in Irwine, who is largely the mouthpiece of a remarkably secular sympathy. "If he had been in the habit of speaking plainly," the narrator informs us,

> he would perhaps have said that the only healthy form religion could take in such minds was that of certain dim but strong emotions, suffusing themselves

as a hallowing influence over the family affections and neighbourly duties. He thought the custom of baptism more important than its doctrine, and that the religious benefits the peasant drew from the church where his fathers worshipped and the sacred piece of ground where they lay buried were but slightly dependent on a clear understanding of the Liturgy or the sermon. Clearly, the rector was not what is called in these days an "earnest" man. (112)

No, but he sounds remarkably like the novel's narrator— even to the gently patronizing note in "such minds."[6] Not surprisingly, Irwine's assessment is borne out by Lisbeth Bede's comic quibbles over interpretation of "the tex"—"thee allays makes a peck o' thy own words out o' a pint o' the Bible's," she tells Seth, Dinah's fellow Methodist (90). The same "healthy" independence of theology is exemplified in the community's church services, at which elderly worshippers who cannot read nonetheless sit contented, "following the service without any very clear comprehension indeed, but with a simple faith in its efficacy to ward off harm and bring blessing" (242).

Most importantly, however, this aversion to religious doctrine is seconded by Adam. His endorsement was evidently of some importance to Eliot: in the famous Chapter 17, the narrator offers it through the fiction of an encounter with Adam in old age—a cumbersome device, but one which exempts Adam's judgment from qualification by the novel's subsequent action:

I've seen pretty clear, ever since I was a young un', as religion's something else beside notions. It isn't notions sets people doing the right thing—it's feelings. . . . There's things go on in the soul, and times when feelings come into you like a rushing mighty wind, as the scripture says, and part your life in two almost, so as you look back on yourself as if you was somebody else. Those are things as you can't bottle up in a "do this" and "do that;" and I'll go so far with the strongest Methodist ever you'll find. That shows me there's deep, speritial things in religion. You can't make much out wi' talking about it, but you feel it. (226–27)

Adam thus identifies Dinah's predicament: "talking about it" is precisely her vocation. In presenting her Eliot must confront the problem of separating Dinah's sympathetic power from her doctrinal language, and, more generally, of rendering her an authoritative moral presence *in spite of* the vocation by which she defines her very identity.

Throughout the novel Eliot strives to soften the force of Dinah's Methodism by obscuring its particulars—much in the way Irwine blurs Anglican theology. In every instance, moreover, the resistance to theology entails a check upon her preaching. Thus the narrator dwells on, for example, Dinah's respect for the "mystery" of feeling, which informs her instinctive understanding of when to remain silent, and the sympathetic power she conveys even in that silence. But the most subtle means to this avoidance of doctrine is the description of Dinah's speech as a form of music—most arrestingly, in the account of her sermon on the Hayslope common:

> Hitherto the traveller had been chained to the spot against his will by the charm of Dinah's mellow treble tones, which had a variety of modulation like that of a fine instrument touched with the unconscious skill of musical instinct. The simple things she said seemed like novelties, as a melody strikes us when we hear it sung by the pure voice of a boyish chorister, the quiet depth of conviction; with which she spoke seemed in itself evidence for the truth of her message.
>
> (71)

This passage tellingly interrupts—and displaces—that portion of Dinah's sermon exhorting her audience to fear damnation. The musical analogy, along with the subsequent shift into oblique oration, directs the reader's attention away from Dinah's sermon to its effect on her listeners, and refers that effect not to the specific content of her words but to the very sound of her voice. Indeed, "the traveller"—"chained to the spot, against his will"—seems to be introduced here, as elsewhere in the novel, to further register the visceral, sensory impact of the scene before him.[7]

Music in this passage has a particular tactical value rarely noted in all the attention given to music in Eliot's novels.[8] In the account of Dinah's preaching, music incarnates a critical norm much like that ratified in Pater's dictum that all art constantly aspires towards the condition of music (*The Renaissance* 106). Of course Eliot does not share Pater's formalism, but here she clearly does wish to minimize, in Pater's terms, "the mere matter" of Dinah's sermon. Dinah's preaching, the figure urges, resembles music in its expression of exquisite feeling unalloyed by discursive content. The force of Dinah's sympathetic "music" is subsequently borne out when she visits Lisbeth Bede in Chapter 10. Lisbeth's response to Dinah's "nice way o' talkin'"—"it puts me i' mind o' the swallows" (157)—is exemplary in being scrupulously divorced from any clear comprehension of Dinah's "earnest prayer":

> Lisbeth, without grasping any distinct idea, without going through any course of religious emotions, felt a vague sense of goodness and love, and of something right lying underneath and beyond all this sorrowing life. She couldn't understand the sorrow; but, for these moments, under the subduing influence of Dinah's spirit, she felt she must be patient and still.   (159)

Dinah's presence thus comes to nourish a "simple faith" of rustic parishioners like Lisbeth, a faith that Eliot celebrates as a vital, enduring emotional sustenance abstracted from any distinctly religious conception. That celebration is a consummately Victorian tribute to continuity in the face of social and spiritual upheaval. It also exemplifies the submergence of theology in psychology that Eliot's critics typically refer to the influence of Feuerbach. On this point, however, *Adam Bede* seems equally responsive to Carlyle, whose example T. H. Huxley memorably summed up: *"Sartor Resartus* led me to know that a deep sense of religion was compatible with the entire absence of theology.''[9] The congruence is suggestive, because Eliot's tributes to such a "deep sense of religion" in *Adam Bede* articulate a dynamic strikingly akin to Carlyle's mistrust of self-consciousness. In the novel, a Carlylean aversion to "notions," as Adam puts it, readily passes into an exaltation of precisely those states of mind that cannot be articulated, or even comprehended. Sympathy, that is, can only be understood as one of those intricate complexes of thought and emotion that must remain, in Eliot's resonant adjective, "unspeakable." We're once again recalled to Gyp's predicament, which embodies a similar gap between feeling and language. But rather than standing as a mark of human inadequacy, Gyp's missing tail begins to seem a sign of moral depth. Hence the unexpected complexity of a passage, for example, that describes Adam "waiting for [Hetty's] kind looks as a patient trembling dog waits for his master's eye to be turned upon him" (399). What purports merely to give words to the reader's disdain for Adam's blind devotion manages at the same time to pay tribute to the depth of his emotional being and to the pathos of a seemingly universal inability to find adequate language for one's feelings. As Kenny Marotta has remarked, "Precisely in Adam's inarticulateness is his closeness to the truth of feeling" (59). The opening chapter's juxtaposition of man and "the dumb creatures" in this sense establishes a kinship that is confirmed, rather than transcended, through moral education.

Early in the novel, Mrs. Poyser broaches this topic comically: "Oh, sir," she tells Arthur, "the men are so tongue-tied—you're forced partly to guess what they mean, as you do wi' the dumb creaturs" (315). A few pages later her barb takes on a more somber resonance when Irwine defends the villagers from his mother's genteel contempt:

> The common people are not quite so stupid as you imagine. The commonest man, who has his ounce of sense and feeling, is conscious of the difference between a lovely, delicate woman and a coarse one. Even a dog feels a difference in their presence. The man may be no better able than a beast to explain the influence the more refined beauty has on him, but he feels it.   (320)

Dinah, however, most eloquently seizes upon the affinity; characteristically, she describes it not in condescension but as the recognition of a common bond. When Adam points out Gyp's friendly response to her presence—"he's very slow to welcome strangers"—Dinah's own response confirms the emblematic moral resemblance between Adam and Gyp established in the opening chapter. "Poor dog," she says, patting Gyp,

> I've a strange feeling about the dumb things as if they wanted to speak, and it was a trouble to 'em because they couldn't. I can't help being sorry for the dogs always, though perhaps there's no need. But they may well have more in them than they know how to make us understand, for we can't say half what we feel, with all our words.   (163)

Illuminated by Dinah's sympathy, "the dumb things" become emblems of a fundamental human predicament. In acknowledging the inadequacy of human speech, Dinah calls attention to the richness and complexity of the feelings it cannot articulate—to those experiences which, as she tells Irwine, "I could give no account of, for I could neither make a beginning nor ending of them in words" (135).

Yet this same insistence on the richness of the ineffable also redounds upon the authority of Dinah's vocation. Even more than the specific doctrinal content of her preaching, a suspicion of eloquence *per se* ultimately compromises Dinah's authority as an agent of moral redemption. If, as the novel continually suggests, the most profound moments of human experience are those that elude speech, then *any* verbal eloquence claiming moral authority becomes vaguely suspect. Adam's musings in Chapter 17 make this transition more explicitly. Initially Adam questions only the adequacy of "notions" as a source of motivation; after repeating his objection, however, he goes on to suggest that notions reflect a fundamental poverty of experience:

> I've seen pretty clear, ever since I was a young un, as religion's something else besides doctrines and notions. I look at it as if the doctrines was like finding names for your feelings, so as you can talk of 'em when you've never known 'em, just as a man may talk 'o tools when he knows their names, though he's never so much as seen 'em, still less handled 'em.   (226–27)

Dinah's preaching may aspire to the condition of music, but her words stubbornly continue to denote, to operate as the"names" Adam mistrusts. Under the pressure of Adam's sentiment, Dinah's preaching not only reinforces her status as an alien in Hayslope; it subtly undermines her claim to moral authority within the novel. The novel's epilogue, in which Dinah marries Adam and gives up her preaching, may ratify popular convention, but it also confirms the logic inherent in the novel's celebration of sympathy.

In her essay, "The Natural History of German Life," Eliot emphasizes the significance of a rural community's dialect as a vehicle of continuity with the past. "This provincial style of the peasant is again, like his *physique*, a remnant of the history to which he clings with the utmost tenacity" (*Essays* 275). This essay is often cited as a rehearsal of the concerns that govern *Adam Bede*, and certainly the novel bears witness to Eliot's care in depicting this "historical language." (Mr. Casson, for example, seems almost wholly designed to underscore Hayslope's linguistic integrity: "I'm not this country-man, you may tell by my tongue sir" [59].) In the novel, however, the history embodied in particular lives and a particular language is ultimately subordinated to the universal language of sympathy, "binding together your whole being past and present in one unspeakable vibration . . . blending your present joy with past sorrow and your present sorrow with all your past joy" (399). It is the inchoate, "unspeakable" experience of sympathy that links the unity of an individual life with the fundamental continuity of human existence itself. When Adam responds to the "language" of Hetty's face, or Dinah acknowledges the claims of Adam's love, a character submits to a knowledge beyond what words, or "notions," can convey.[10] And the novel seems to aim at a precisely congruent transformation in the reader, who would submit to the authority of a sympathy derived from participation in the experience of suffering represented in the novel. In this sense, the entire novel aspires constantly towards the condition of music—music, that is, conceived as the emblematic language of sympathy. If Eliot turned to the life and language of a rural community to affirm moral and spiritual continuity in the face of change, the novel discovers that assurance in a language beyond words.

In its celebration of the ineffable, *Adam Bede* complicates received views of Eliot's intellectual allegiance, and does so by locating in Dinah's vocation an image of the novelist's. "He who cannot express himself is a slave," writes Feuerbach, in a comment that, Robert Kiely argues, characterizes Eliot's attitude to the significance of language (103–123). Certainly the claim elucidates the narrator's comment on Bartle Massey's students, as well as the emblematic significance of Hetty's silence. But the rhetoric of silence in *Adam Bede* responds to a very different view of language, a view modeled less on Feuerbach than on the *Logos* of St. John. To be sure, Eliot's later novels increasingly abandon this divided allegiance, subordinating the theological paradigm to a view of language as, in Kiely's words, "the regulated product of civilization" (Kiely's essay, significantly, deals almost entirely with *Middlemarch*.) But *Adam Bede* helps to explain this trajectory by suggesting at once the attraction and the costs of the older view. Most obviously, to exalt a language beyond words imposes an enormous burden on the novelist: like Gyp, she lacks an adequate vehicle of expression. Indeed, in the effort to convey moral authority in writing, Eliot is exposed to the very suspicion that implicates Dinah's eloquence. Moreover, the novelist must likewise reconcile her evocation of sympathy with a peculiarly "hard," unsympathetic doctrine of her own—Eliot's central tenet that "consequences are unpitying." [11]

But the affiliation of preacher and novelist, along with the peculiar challenges both confront, is most suggestively conveyed in the various passages where the narrator pauses to call attention to the challenges of representation. Much as Dinah in her preaching attempts, through words, to bring an unseen reality before her listeners' eyes—exhorting her audience to "see" an image of the Lord shining through the visible landscape—so the narrator of *Adam Bede* exhorts readers to "see" a world beyond the printed page: "Let me take you into that dining-room. . . ." "See there in the bright sunshine. . . what do you see?" "See, he has something in his hand" (98,507). The novelist's technique thus mimes the Methodist style so closely reproduced in Dinah's sermon. [12] Much as this device has exasperated some of Eliot's critics, it is not a mere gesture of sympathetic participation in local color. Rather such exhortation crystallizes a central impulse of the novel's moral design, and indeed of Eliot's aesthetic: it appeals to readers to respond to the words on the page as to experience itself, that language whose "alphabet" is human feeling, and whose "lesson" is the experience of sympathy. [13]

Of course, this appeal is at odds with the strenuous distancing of the subject matter that Eliot cultivates through historical setting and pastoral tradition. [14] So formulated, moreover, the appeal to the reader may seem crudely naive. Indeed, in the novel's opening sentences Eliot wryly acknowledges the leap of faith it embodies. "With a single drop of ink for a mirror, the Egyptian sorcerer undertakes to reveal to any chance-comers far-reaching visions of the past. This is what I undertake to do for you, reader" (49). In a sense, Eliot thus preempts all grammatological critics by conceding that the moral authority of her text is a "sorcery" founded on absence, that the "alphabet" of experience has no existence apart from writing. But what the narrator thus demystifies is more than the awkward yearning of the first novelist, or even the particular moral project undertaken in *Adam Bede*. The appeal to experience so plangently made in Eliot's use of the authorial present is, after all, an appeal made with varying degrees of urgency and explicitness in all realistic novels. Gyp's missing tail might thus stand for the problematics of representation that attend the project of "realism" in the broadest sense. The novelist *always* lacks an adequate vehicle for representing a realm located outside of language.

But Gyp's tail—like the tale it so curiously animates—has a more precise historical significance. In "the first major exercise in programmatic literary realism in English literature," as John Goode has called *Adam Bede*, a familiar Victorian crisis of moral and religious authority assumes a form more far-reaching in its significance than conventional literary history has recognized.[15] The urgency of the moral dilemma informing *Adam Bede*, and the explicitness with which Eliot dwells upon it, allows the novel to encapsulate in unusually suggestive form a historically momentous logic, which leads from a mistrust of specifically religious "notions" to a far more comprehensive and radical skepticism concerning the authority of language. Through a skeptical dynamic central to the realistic novel at large, the authority of the general claim or maxim is subordinated to the more particularized forms of an extra-linguistic "experience," which—as *Adam Bede* so powerfully illustrates—in turn urges the novelist towards a still greater restriction of linguistic authority. The particular, immediate apprehension of particular, concrete fact becomes the only truth to which the novelist can appeal. Of course the specifically religious concern recedes in Eliot's subsequent novels, along with the bald appeals to the reader's sympathetic participation. But the raw urgency of the moral burden in *Adam Bede* issues in a rhetoric that marks a powerful bridge between Eliot's writings and the work of novelists we are accustomed to consider far more "modern" in outlook and technique. The yearning of Eliot's narrator to make us "see" the reality of the novel's action will be echoed, for example, in James's elaborate insistence on presentation and "solidity of specification," and in Conrad, in his more emphatic claim in the Preface to *The Nigger of the "Narcissus"*: "My task which I am trying to achieve is, by the power of the written word to make you hear, to make you feel—it is, before all, to make you *see*" (XIV). The fictional worlds of Conrad and James may seem remote from that of *Adam Bede*. But the novelist's struggle to convey a reality beyond words testifies to the persistent eloquence of Gyp's missing tail.

NOTES

1. Herbert 422. The panel, Herbert adds, "makes a powerful comment on the large question of man's relation to Nature." Other critics who comment on Massey's students include: John Goode, "Adam Bede," in Barbara Hardy (ed.) *Critical Essays on George Eliot* (London: RKP, 1970), p. 22; Dorothy Van Ghent, *The English Novel: Form and Function* (New York: Holt, Rinehart, Winston, 1953), 177; Daniel Cottom, *Social Figures: George Eliot, Social History, and Literary Representation* (Minneapolis: U of Minnesota, P, 1987), 12.

2. The ending was G.H. Lewes's suggestion, and has been roundly condemned as inconsistent with what precedes it; an exception is Barnard Paris, *Experiments in Life: George Eliot's Quest for Values* (Detroit: Wayne State UP, 1965).

3. U.C. Knoepflmacher analyzes the Feuerbachian structures of the novel in *Religious Humanism and the Victorian Novel* (Princeton: Princeton UP, 1965), 52–59.

4. On Adam's arithmetic, see Barbara Hardy, *The Novels of George Eliot: A Study in Form* (London: Athlone, 1985), 41–45, and Sally Shuttleworth, *George Eliot and Nineteenth-Century Science: The Make-Believe of a Beginning* (Cambridge: Cambridge UP, 1984), 37–38.

5. This seeming intractability links Dinah to Adam, who is similarly characterized by Seth: "You may's well try to turn a wagon in a narrow lane" (51). On the crucial significance of "nature" in the novel, see Knoepflmacher, *George Eliot's Early Novels*, 117–18; Herbert, "Preachers and the Schemes of Nature," 419–427, and Philip Fisher, *Making Up Society: The Novels of George Eliot* (Pittsburgh: U of Pittsburgh P, 1981), 43-45.

6. "The very slackness of Irwine's doctrine is the sign in him of an almost saintly moral excellence," remarks Herbert, "Preachers and the Schemes of Nature," 417—an overstatement, but salutary in stressing the inverse relation between doctrine and moral authority.

7. Eliot's crucial appeal to the reader on this point is overlooked by critics who see Dinah's sermon as a departure from her normal patterns of speech. See, for example, Herbert, "Preachers and the Schemes of Nature," 415–16, and Goode, "Adam Bede," 38–39.

8. A recent book on the subject by Beryl Gray, *George Eliot and Music* (New York: St. Martin's Press, 1989), makes no reference to this tactic.

9. Cited in William Irvine, *Apes, Angels, and Victorians: Darwin, Huxley, and Evolution* (New York: McGraw Hill, 1972), 131. Eliot sent a copy of *Adam Bede* to Jane Welsh Carlyle, expressing her hope that "the philosopher" would receive from it a pleasure like that which she had received from *Sartor Resartus* (*The George Eliot Letters*, III, 23); Mrs. Carlyle responded in the letter quoted above.

10. Of course, the "natural" language embodied in beauty is not always readily legible, and can be deceptive; see Dianne Sadoff, "Nature's Language: Metaphor in the Text of *Adam Bede*," *Genre* 11 (1978), 411–426.

11. As Jay Clayton has suggestively argued, in "Visionary Power and Narrative Form: Wordsworth and *Adam Bede*," *ELH* 46 (1979), 645–72, the ending of the novel seems an effort to soften and humanise this doctrine, by in effect breaking the rigorous chain of "unpitying" consequences, passing from narrative to the evocation of sympathetic vision. Clayton's fine reading identifies what might be seen as a narratological counterpart of the repeated faltering of eloquence I have been discussing. But the formalistic bent of Clayton's argument impoverishes the significance of Dinah, who becomes "the representation of an absence . . . an

attempt to place within the hard bonds of the narrative the author's choice to disrupt that narrative'' (660). Dinah seems more richly viewed as Eliot's representation of the equivocality of moral (as well as narrative) authority in mid-Victorian discourse.

12. Valentine Cunningham, *Everywhere Spoken Against: Dissent in the Victorian Novel* (Oxford: Clarendon Press, 1975), 151–61, studies Eliot's reliance on the Methodist idiom. Knoepflmacher, *George Eliot's Early Novels*, 105, notes in this appeal Dinah's resemblance to the novelist, but sees it as an appeal to an audience's ''relation to universals'' outside of sensuous perception—an explanation which obscures the link between Dinah's appeals and those of the novelist attempting to conjure up an emphatically visible image.

13. W.J. Harvey, who finds the technique ''all the more infuriating because it is unnecessary,'' nonetheless gestures towards this rationale in noting that Eliot ''generally juggles her tenses in this way to introduce us to a new aspect of her subject'' (more precisely, to impress upon us a new scene) ''or to give greater force to a moment of crisis or climax'' (*The Art of George Eliot*, 78). The gentleman spectator—which may seem a similarly extraneous device— is likewise designed to register the palpable sensuousness of a particular moment.

14. On such distancing, see Steven Marcus, ''Literature and Social Theory: Starting In With George Eliot,'' in *Representations: Essays on Literature and Society* (New York: Random House, 1975), 183–213.

15. John Goode, ''Adam Bede,'' 37. ''The final interest of Adam Bede is that it casts its shadow before it,'' Ian Gregor has urged, although he locates that historical significance (as do most commentators) in the image of the narrating consciousness conveyed in the famous ''pier-glass'' passage in Chapter 17. (*The Moral and the Story* [*London: Faber, 1962*], 30–32.

WORKS CITED

Clayton, Jay. ''Visionary Power and Narrative Form: Wordsworth and *Adam Bede*.'' *ELH* 46 (1979) 645–72.

Conrad, Joseph. *The Nigger of the Narcissus* in *Complete Works* vol. 23. Garden City: Doubleday, 1925.

Cottom, Daniel. *Social Figures: George Eliot, Social History and Literary Representation*. Minneapolis: U of Minnesota P, 1987.

Cunningham, Valentine. *Everywhere Spoken Against: Dissent in the Victorian Novel*. Oxford: Oxford UP, 1975.

Eliot, George. *Adam Bede*. Ed. Stephen Gill. Harmondsworth: Penguin, 1980.

———. *The George Eliot Letters*. Ed. Gordon S. Haight, New Haven: Yale UP.

———. *The Essays of George Eliot*. Ed. Thomas Pinney. New York: Columbia UP, 1963.

Fisher, Philip. *Making Up Society: The Novels of George Eliot*. Pittsburgh: U of Pittsburgh P, 1981.

Goode, John. "Adam Bede" in Hardy (ed.) *Critical Essays*.

Gray, Beryl. *George Eliot and Music*. New York: St. Martins, 1989.

Hardy, Barbara. Ed. *Critical Essays on George Eliot*. London: RKP, 1970.

──────. *The Novels of George Eliot: A Study in Form*. London: Athlone, 1985.

Herbert, Christopher. "Preachers and the Schemes of Nature in *Adam Bede*." *Nineteenth-Century Fiction* 29 (1975): 412—27.

Irvine, William. *Apes, Angels and Victorians: Darwin, Huxley and Evolution*. New York: McGraw, 1972.

Kiely, Robert. "The Limits of Dialogue in *Middlemarch*." In J. H. Buckley Ed. *The Worlds of Victorian Fiction*. *Harvard English Studies* 6. Cambridge: Harvard, 1975, 103–123.

Knoepflmacher, U.C. *George Eliot's Early Novels*: The Limits of Realism. Berkely: U of Calif. Press, 1968.

──────. *Religious Humanism and the Victorian Novel*. Princeton: Princeton UP, 1965.

Marcus, Steven. "Literature and Social Theory: Starting in with George Eliot." In *Representations: Essays on Literature and Society*. New York: Random House, 1975.

Marotta, Kenny. "*Adam Bede* as a Pastoral." *Genre* 9 (1976): 59–72.

Paris, Bernard. *Experiments in Life: George Eliot's Quest for Values*. Detroit: Wayne State UP, 1965.

Pater, Walter. "The School of Giorgione," *The Renaissance: Studies in Art and Poetry* Ed. Donald L. Hill Berkeley: U of California P, 1980.

Sadoff, Dianne. "Nature's Language: Metaphor in the Text of *Adam Bede*." *Genre* 11 (1978): 411–26.

Shuttleworth, Sally. *George Eliot and Nineteenth-Century Science: The Make-Believe of a Beginning*. Cambridge: Cambridge UP, 1984.

Van Ghent, Dorothy. *The English Novel: Form and Function*. New York: Holt, 1953.

Wilkie Collins and the Origins
of the Sensation Novel

John Sutherland

The generally accepted historical starting point for sensational fiction is 1859 and the serial publication of Wilkie Collins's *The Woman in White* in *All the Year Round* (26 November 1859–25 August 1860). *The Woman in White* was received by its first readers as a distinctly novel kind of novel. Specifically it was the originality of device that excited Collins's contemporaries and kept readers like Thackeray—someone who yawned over most popular fiction—turning pages "from morning till sunset" (Page 13). The same originality made other contemporaries—writers such as Braddon, Reade, and possibly even Dickens—aspire to imitate Collins's new tricks. All witnesses testify to the contemporary impact of *The Woman in White*, its "shock" effect, as a not entirely approving Mrs. Oliphant labelled it (Page 118). The newness of *The Woman in White* inheres, I suggest, in two cardinal features. First, the detective feats of the heroic trio against their criminal rivals; second, the high-impact narrative. Disdaining conventional chapter structure, *The Woman in White* unfolds as a series of testimonies, or evidence given by involved parties, none of whom has the traditional fictional prerogative of omniscience. Collins's narrative has a pseudo-documentary surface and a real-time chronology which teasingly negate the work's inner identity as fiction. Victorian readers were not used to this and they liked it.

My paper is primarily concerned with Collins's innovations, but I shall digress briefly on *The Woman in White* and the science of criminal detection in mid-Victorian England. The idea that crime constituted an intellectual problem to be "solved" (as opposed to an offence to be punished) was not something that originated in the imagination of writers of fiction—although it was quickly and profitably exploited by them. To mobilise detective intelligence against criminal cunning was a main motive in the Police Act of 1856. The strictly forensic procedures of law were no longer felt to be sufficient for the uncovering of serious felony, any more than hue and cry or the assistance of bribed street informants were now sufficient to capture the cleverer class of thief. Significantly, the first *OED*-recorded use of the word "detective" in its modern sense of ingenious policeman dates from 1856[1]. Underlying the 1856 Police Bill was a profound scepticism that crime would invariably uncover itself; that it never paid; that murders would out though all the world overwhelmed them to men's eyes. These proverbial truths—truths very dear to the traditional novel with its canons of poetic justice—no longer held. A child of the time, Fosco waxes eloquently on the subject at Blackwater Park: "It is truly wonderful," the fat archcriminal observes,

> how easily Society can console itself for the worst of its short-comings with a little bit of claptrap. The machinery it has set up for the detection of crime is miserably ineffective [he is talking in 1850]—and yet only invent a moral epigram, saying that it works well, and you blind everybody to its blunders, from that moment. Crimes cause their own detection, do they? And murder will out (another moral epigram), will it? Ask Coroners who sit at inquests in large towns if that is true. . . . Ask secretaries of life-assurance companies.
>
> (202)

Fosco concludes: "there are foolish criminals who are discovered, and wise criminals who escape. The hiding of a crime, or the detection of crime what is it? A *trial of skill* between the police on one side, and the individual on the other"(210–11; my italics). Criminals, it was felt in the 1850s, were becoming cleverer—geniuses in some cases. In fiction that founded a line of anti-heroes, which begins with Fosco—who discourses with scientists on equal terms—and leads to that strange contradiction, the academically distinguished arch-criminal like "Professor" Moriarty and "Doctor" Nikola. Before 1850 the liaison between erudition and low crime would have seemed freakish.[2]

Two varieties of clever crime particularly obsessed mid-Victorians—secret poisoning and forgery. At their most skilful, these felonies involved long premeditation, duplicity, and superior intellect. They, and crimes like them, called for enhanced police skills in detection. The 1856 police act was, of course, only concerned to set up a corps of professional detectives—sworn officers of the law.[3] A year later, in 1857, the Matrimonial Causes Act—Britain's new and relaxed divorce legislation—mobilised a whole new army of amateur and unofficial detectives; namely, the suspicious spouse and his or her agent. What the 1857 act decreed was that divorce should be a legal option if adultery could be proved against the erring wife; and if adultery—aggravated by such additional things as incest, violence, outrageous cruelty, bigamy, desertion, or sodomy—could be proved against the erring husband. Adultery is notoriously an offence which has many participants but very few eyewitnesses. It may be, as the Latin phrase has it, delightful, but it is rarely flagrant. Typically, the adulterous act must be reconstructed from circumstantial evidence—such things as hotel registers, private letters, travel movements, suspicious absences. Typically, adulterers go to great lengths and use enormous ingenuity, to cover their tracks. One thinks, for instance, of the lengths Dickens went to in concealing his connection with Ternan, and Wilkie Collins his cohabitation with Martha Rudd. A demonstration of adultery which will stand up in court often requires formidable detective resources. The first use of the term ''private detective'' recorded in the *OED* relates to Samuel Bozzle in Trollope's *He Knew He Was Right* (1869). Bozzle is the agent employed by Louis Trevelyan to spy on his wife and discover her (nonexistent) adulteries. The 1857 act gave a huge boost to the detective profession, more particularly the private investigator or ''eye.'' Philip Marlowe, Sam Spade, and Magnum PI may all find a main line of their ancestry in the Victorian keyhole peeper like Bozzle.

The 1857 act insured that the relationship of wife to husband was subtly altered. Prudent partners realised that in their own interest they should keep a file on their other half. Spouses became spies. This suspiciousness is not, of course, flattering to the holy state of matrimony. Victorian wives—angels in the house—cut a particularly poor figure steaming open their husband's letters or rifling pocket books. Wilkie Collins sanitizes his saintly Laura by having the resourceful Marian, her half-sister, do the actual snooping; snooping which includes listening at keyholes, intercepting mail and —in one heroic act of domestic espionage—perching on a window sill during a rainstorm in order to eavesdrop on Percival, the errant husband. The novel persuades us that such low acts are necessary, if a Victorian wife is to protect her rights.

In one of its main aspects, then, *The Woman in White* can be read as a study in divorce Victorian-style. And one of the many narrative problems facing Collins as he galloped through the serialization of the novel, improvising desparately as he went,[4] was how decently to cast asunder man and wife, Laura and Percival Glyde, so that she might eventually be free to marry Walter. The novelist eventually solved his problem by full-blooded melodramatic device. Glyde is finally burned to death in a church—whose sacraments he has defiled—attempting to destroy evidence of his illegitimacy. (This, rather disappointingly, is the great "secret" about which eager readers of the serial were casting bets among themselves.) Glyde's immolation is poetic but unlikely. The more realistic outcome in 1860 would have been for Sir Percival's private detectives to discover Laura and Walter cohabiting in the East End of London. This would constitute *prima facie* proof of adultery in the hands of any competent counsel, who would make hay of the defence that the couple were living as brother and sister.[5]

I have suggested that 1856 and 1857 are significant dates if we want to reconstruct the idea of *The Woman in White*, as it formed in Wilkie Collins's mind in 1859. There is another significant date—1855. In this year the last of the so-called "taxes on knowledge" (i.e., the newspaper stamp) was removed. The result was what histories of British journalism record as a "stupendous" growth in popular one penny newspapers—of which the best known and most enduring was the *Daily Telegraph* (Fox Bourne ii. 232). These cheaper prints contained many more crime stories than their four and five pence rivals, like *The Times*. More to the point here, the one penny press with its larger circulation and more competitive tone fostered what we now call investigative reporting. The investigative reporter has close affinity with the detective (whether private or on the force) and in the modern thriller the two types are interchangeable as heroes. The *Telegraph's* most famous investigative reporter was George Augustus Sala—who had learned his craft on *Household Words* writing for Charles Dickens. Sala was an exact contemporary of Wilkie Collins, a comrade on the *Household Words* team, and like Collins he went on to become a pioneer sensation novelist (if a less successful one). Among everything else, *Household Words* can be seen as a nursery of investigative journalism and a cradle of sensation fiction—stories with the immediacy of the day's newspaper headlines.

2

I want now to turn to Collins's idiosyncratic or "high impact" mode of narration in *The Woman in White*. Collins expounds his technique to the reader in the "Preamble" to the novel, using Hartright's voice:

As the Judge might once have heard it, so the Reader shall hear it now. No circumstance of importance, from the beginning to the end of the disclosure, shall be related on hearsay evidence. When the writer of these introductory lines (Walter Hartright by name) happens to be more closely connected than others with the incidents to be recorded, he will describe them in his own person. When his experience fails, he will retire from the position of narrator, and his task will be continued, from the point at which he has left it off, by other persons who can speak to the circumstances under notice from their own knowledge, just as clearly and positively as he has spoken before them. Thus the story here presented will be told by more than one pen, as the story of an offence against the laws is told in Court by more than one witness—with the same object, in both cases, to present the truth always in its most direct and most intelligible aspect; and to trace the course of one complete series of events, by making the persons who have been most closely connected with them, at each successive stage, relate their own experience, word for word.   (1)

The novel is as good as Hartright's word. A succession of witnesses lines up to address the reader, from principals like Hartright, Marian, Fairlie, and Fosco, to friends of the principals like the lawyers Gilmore and Kyrle and even humble bystanders like Hester Pinhorn the illiterate chambermaid or the gullible Eliza Michelson, housekeeper (dismissed) of Blackwater Park. Each offers his or her piece of circumstantial evidence to the great jigsaw puzzle.

Wilkie Collins complacently claimed in his 1860 preface to *The Woman in White* that his evidentiary technique was entirely original: ''an experiment is attempted in this novel which has not (so far as I know) been hitherto tried in fiction'' p. (xxxv). This is an overstatement and several commentators have contradicted or modified Collins's claim to uniqueness. What about *Wuthering Heights* they ask; or the final sections of Hogg's *Confessions of a Justified Sinner* and Bulwer's *Eugene Aram*, where the narratives dissolve into facsimile documents and reportage? As a number of reviewers pointed out, the eighteenth-century epistolary novel—or novel in letters—anticipated main aspects of Collins's technique. Henry James—who disliked the ''ponderosity'' of *The Woman in White*—called it dismissively ''a kind of nineteenth century version of *Clarissa Harlowe*'' (Page 122).

There were also two more direct inspirations for *The Woman in White*'s method, one at least of which was cited in reviews. In 1856, *Household Words* offered in its extra Christmas number a tale ''by several hands'' (principally those of Dickens and Collins) called *The Wreck of the Golden Mary*. This tale took the form of linked testimonies to a disaster at sea, given in the form of ''The Captain's Account,''''The Mate's Account,''''The Old Sailor's Story,'' and so on. The other commented-on forerunner of *The Woman in White* was Dinah Mulock Craik's *A Life for a Life*. This narrative takes the form of two intertwining diaries whose entries cumulatively tell the story of a doomed love. Craik's novel came out in late July 1859, while Collins was at Broadstairs, racking his brains how to begin *The Woman in White* (Clarke 99).

The unoriginality of *The Woman in White* was pointed out, more or less small-mindedly, by Collins's contemporaries in a spirit of nothing new under the sun. But arguably they all missed the point. What Collins primarily stresses in his opening remarks is the analogy of *The Woman in White*'s narrative to the process of *law*, as it is ritually played out in the English criminal court. The novel's technique is forensic, not historical. We know that Collins is not always to be trusted when he talks about his working methods, his inspirations and the sources for his stories. But that the central plot of *The Woman in White* was substantially drawn from an actual law case is established.[6] The conspiracy against the heiress Laura Glyde, her being drugged and incarcerated in a lunatic asylum, are known to be taken from Maurice Méjan's *Recueil des causes célèbres* and its account of the Madame de Douhault case, which occurred in the late eighteenth century.

Collins's copy of Méjan's *Recueil* was published in 1808. Kenneth Robinson tells us that the novelist picked it up from a Paris bouquiniste in March 1856 while visiting the French capital with Dickens (Robinson 98). If true, this date—1856—is very interesting. Interesting, that is, in the light of something else that Collins said about the genesis of *The Woman in White*, late in life:

> One day about 1856 he had found himself at a criminal trial in London. He was struck by the way each witness rose in turn to contribute a personal fragment to the chain of evidence. "It came to me then . . . that a series of events in a novel would lend themselves well to an exposition like this . . . one could impart to the reader that acceptance, that sense of belief, which was produced here by the succession of testimonies. . . . The more I thought of it, the more an effort of this kind struck me as bound to succeed. Consequently when the case was over I went home determined to make the effort."[7]   (Davis 211)

Collins does not identify the 1856 trial that he attended. But it is not hard to work out what it must have been. The trial of William Palmer, the Rugeley poisoner, was not just the crime sensation of 1856, but of the whole decade. It was, as the *Annual Register* (387) observed, discussed at every fireside in the land over the summer of 1856. The Rugeley poisoning was England's mania that year. An Act of Parliament was passed, so that a show trial could be mounted in London. Public interest was at fever pitch. There was a cut-throat competition for courtroom tickets. Accounts of the trial dominated the newspapers for the twelve days it ran in May 1856, and it inspired books, pictures, doggerel verse and a huge amount of rumor, some of it crediting Palmer with the poisoning of scores of victims. The trial also inspired the still-current salutation between drinkers—"What's your poison?."

Dickens was obsessed with William Palmer over the summer of 1856 (a period in which he was at his most intimate with Collins) and wrote an essay on the poisoner's infuriatingly inscrutable demeanour for *Household Words* in June 1856. Why would not "The Poisoner" *look* like the criminal he manifestly was? Palmer was "the greatest villain that ever stood in the Old Bailey dock,"[8] yet he had the gall to appear as respectable as the lawyers who questioned him. It was maddening. Collins too, we may assume, was as fascinated by the monster of Rugeley as his friend and editor.

The details of the Palmer case were indeed fascinating. But the main importance of it to *The Woman in White* was in the legal precedent which the trial set. It was, above all, a triumphant vindication of the power of circumstantial evidence in the hands of a skilful prosecution. There was absolutely no material evidence against William Palmer. He was tried for one murder only, although rumor credited him with many more. And his victim's corpse could be found to contain no lethal amount of poison whatsoever. The alleged motive for the murder was flimsy and to the thoughtful observer virtually nonexistent. There was no witness to the alleged crime. Palmer—who showed no remorse or anxiety at all—steadfastly denied his guilt, and went to the gallows protesting that he was in fact the murdered man. The case was won, as everyone conceded, by the skilful accumulation of circumstantial evidence alone, which was brilliantly expounded to the jury by one of the most powerful prosecuting teams ever gathered for a murder trial in the nineteenth century.

The main events in the Rugeley poisoning can be summarized from four sources: reports in *The Times,* the *Annual Register* for 1856, the *DNB* entry on William Palmer, and Robert Graves's 1957 book *They Hanged My Saintly Billy*.[9] William Palmer was born in 1824 in Rugeley—a small town in Staffordshire. His background was comfortably moneyed. His father had been a timber merchant. His mother was left a young widow in William's early childhood and was estimated to be worth some £70,000. William inherited £7,000 of this fortune on coming to man's estate in 1846. His childhood was easy and as a boy he was "spoiled" by his fond parent. On leaving Rugeley grammar school, William was apprenticed to an apothecary, or druggist, in Liverpool. There he misconducted himself with a local girl, embezzled his master's money, and was dismissed. He was subsequently apprenticed to a surgeon in the Rugeley area, and again disgraced himself. Eventually, Palmer qualified at St. Bartholomew's Hospital, London. He was admitted a member of the Royal College of Surgeons in August 1846 and set up as a general practitioner in his home town later that year.

Palmer was by all accounts a skilled surgeon. But he took to the turf and wasted his fortune and all his professional prospects gambling and setting up a stable for brood mares. By 1853 William Palmer had transferred most of his business to a Rugeley druggist called Benjamin Thirlby—and was in desperate financial straits, borrowing money at 60 percent interest to stave off bankruptcy. He had married in October 1847 and had a family of his own. But, as was commented on later, four of his five children died within a month of their birth. Palmer, as it was recalled, frequently complained of the expense of raising offspring (although he was happy enough to raise foals). It was also noted that Palmer's mother-in-law, a wealthy woman whom he was treating, died prematurely of what was loosely called apoplexy.

By 1854 Palmer was forging bill acceptances using his mother's signature. In the summer of that year he took out a large insurance on his wife's life with the Prince of Wales company. He paid only one premium, of 700-odd pounds, before she died in September 1854 of what was termed "English cholera" on the death certificate. Her husband had been dosing her with his own medicines. William Palmer duly came into £13,000 insurance benefit with his wife's death. But his debts and compulsive gambling soon ate up this second fortune. Later in that same eventful year, 1854, he again forged his mother's acceptance to yet another £2,000 bill. And—using his London moneylender as an intermediary—he took out another life insurance policy on his brother Walter for £13,000 (an oddly recurrent figure in this story) with the same insurance company, who did not at first realize that the beneficiary was the William Palmer who had just cost them so dear. Neither, apparently, did the Prince of Wales company know that Walter Palmer was a chronic alcoholic with advanced delirium tremens which he treated with the homely remedy of a quart of gin a day. A corn factor, Walter had also squandered his £7,000 patrimony, and was now bankrupt. William Palmer—although evidently acutely short of money—undertook to pay the £1,000 a year premium for his brother.

By August 1855, William Palmer's debts, in the form of forged bills, were again threatening to overwhelm him. At this crisis, Walter conveniently died of "apoplexy" after taking some pills made up by his brother. The insurers were informed. But, when they understood who was the beneficiary, they consulted the redoubtable Inspector Charles Field (Dickens' Inspector Bucket) and refused to pay up, defying Palmer to take them to court—which he declined to do. By now William's affairs were entangled with those of John Parsons Cook, a 28-year-old Leicestershire man. Cook was something of a dandy and like Palmer had run through his fortune (of around £13,000) on the race track where, it was reported, "he did not bear a high reputation." He too owned horses and gambled unluckily. Cook had also been unlucky in love and contracted syphilis, now in an advanced condition. It seems that William Palmer was treating his young friend confidentially for his complaint. The two sporting men also had had some complicated financial arrangements which were never unravelled, even at the subsequent trials.

Palmer's problems boiled over in the middle of November 1855. He now owed London moneylenders £12,500, and renewals were becoming very difficult. Forgery of his mother's name would no longer serve. He needed £400 in cash immediately for interest payments, and at some not too distant point, the principal would have to be repaid. He had other obligations. He had consoled himself since his wife's death with a local girl of the lower classes and procured an abortion for her. She was now blackmailing him for £100, for the return of thirty-five "lascivious letters" that she would otherwise show to her father. Palmer was utterly destitute, and had no way of meeting any of these demands. He had even to borrow £25 from a Rugeley butcher in order to attend the Shrewsbury races on 13 November. At the races, however, fortune at last smiled on him. Cook's mare, Polestar, was suited by the heavy going and won the main handicap event. This meant winnings of £800 and the horse became a valuable property for the purposes of breeding.

Cook celebrated his success at the ominously named Raven Hotel in Shrewsbury. There he was taken suddenly and violently ill after drinking what he called some "strange tasting grog," prepared by Palmer. In great distress, he was removed to the Talbot Arms Hotel in Rugeley where, after swallowing morphine pills and drinking some broth (both prepared for him by Palmer), he died of a series of horrifically violent tetanic spasms. This occurred on 20 November 1855, a week after the race meeting. Cook's winnings were not to be found in his belongings at the Talbot Arms. Palmer meanwhile was settling various long-standing local debts in cash.

There was a universal prejudice that William Palmer was a mass murderer. Cook's stepfather, a man called William Stevens, vowed to bring his boy's killer to justice. Inquests were made on the deaths of Cook, Annie Palmer (William's wife), and Walter Palmer. On the basis of post-mortem examinations and other evidence the coroner found in December 1855 that all three had been murdered by William Palmer. He was duly arrested and imprisoned, but the charges relating to his wife and brother were later dropped for insufficient evidence. More specifically, the exhumed corpses of the two dead Palmers revealed no trace of poison. (The examinations had not been easy for the pathologists; Walter Palmer's corpse virtually exploded when his lead-lined coffin was opened.)

The scantiness of their evidence—and the fact that two charges had melted away—alarmed the authorities. The case that Palmer had murdered Cook, their last chance to convict him, was at best flimsy. Certainly it was flimsier in regard to motive than the other two alleged victims. No one doubted that William Palmer was a murderer—possibly of as many as sixteen people. But it looked as if he might be too skilful a murderer for the English legal system. This could not be allowed. A decision was made in high places to nail Palmer; and if necessary to bend the law to do so. An act of Parliament was passed in April 1856 allowing the case to be tried outside the original area of jurisdiction (Leeds), in the Central Criminal Court, London, where state resources and public opinion could be more effectively mobilised against the accused. The case was scheduled for two weeks in May 1856. Lord Chief Justice Campbell presided. Other big guns were recruited for the prosecution team. The Attorney General Alexander Cockburn—the most brilliant barrister in England—and Mr. Edwin James made the case for the Crown. No expense was spared. The prosecutors had the assistance of the best expert witnesses in the land, including such authorities in their field as Sir Benjamin Brodie, professor of chemistry at Oxford and one of the country's foremost scientists.

Nonetheless, for all its official backing, the prosecution had an uphill road. His family had decided to stand by Palmer, and his mother was wealthy enough to retain a very able lawyer, Mr. Serjeant Shee. The main evidence against Palmer was that he was alleged to have bought several grains of strychnine on 19 November (two days before Cook's death) and to have persuaded the chemist's apprentice he bought it from not to enter the transaction in the poison book. Palmer did not deny the purchase. His explanation was that he intended to poison some stray dogs that were worrying his brood mares. But he disputed the date, claiming he was in London on 19 November. There was a strong suspicion that the witness might have been bribed or coerced by Stevens.

There remained other intractable weaknesses in the prosecution case. Palmer was desperately short of money in November 1855. But Cook's £800 (or what was left of it) would not have gone far towards the £12,500 he owed. And by Cook's death he was liable to further debts, incurred by them jointly. Very simply, William Palmer did not stand to gain much by murdering his friend. The post-mortem (which Palmer attended) and the organ samples which were sent to Guy's hospital for analysis were of no help whatsoever to the prosecution. Tiny quantities of antimony were detected, but not enough to hurt a baby. No trace of strychnia was found. The prosecution's allegation—far-fetched enough—was that Palmer had administered antimony (in the form of tartar emetic) sufficient to weaken Cook at Shrewsbury, then delivered the *coup de grâce* with strychnine (disguised as morphia pills) at Rugeley, judging the dose so accurately that all the poison was absorbed in the body during the death throes, leaving no residue whatsoever. Pharmacologically this was unconvincing.

Great harm was done to Palmer's defence by the evidence of two maids at the Talbot Arms Hotel. One of them, Elizabeth Mills, claimed to have tasted some broth Palmer sent Cook, and then to have been taken violently ill. This was confirmed by another maid. But it was alleged by the defence, quite plausibly, that these two women had been bribed to give false evidence by Cook's vindicative stepfather, Stevens. If nothing else, it was extremely unlikely that Palmer would have tried to kill Cook two different ways—with poisoned pills and poisoned soup. Palmer had other strong points in his defence. Cook's death bore all the signs of epilepsy, or of tetanus, both of which are known complications of the syphilis from which he was suffering. The medical evidence on this matter was most persuasive.

On the evidence, Palmer should have been acquitted, but had he got off scot-free, English criminal justice would have been thoroughly humiliated. The prosecution, aided by the judge, ruthlessly biased the proceedings against any such outcome. Whenever the defence brought forward some evidence favorable to their client, the prosecuting lawyers would throw their arms in the air, and go through a pantomime of disbelief. They kept the most helpful defence witnesses out of court, by threatening to divulge in cross-examination damaging information which the police had turned up. All in all, the trial was, as Shee complained, "an organized conspiracy to hang our client." But what clinched the case against Palmer was a superb summing up by the prosecuting counsel, Alexander Cockburn. Without notes, he dazzled the jury with his inductions from the purely circumstantial evidence. After the guilty verdict was delivered by the jury, Palmer scrawled a note to his counsel: "It was the riding that did it." His racing slang meant that Cockburn's rhetorical and narrative skill—not the quality of his evidence—had won the event for the prosecution. Palmer was sentenced to hang at Stafford gaol. He did not confess his guilt even in the death cell. He maintained to the end his sober demeanour and only complained that he could not get the racing news in prison. He went to the gallows with the enigmatic remark that Cook "was never poisoned by strychnine." (By what, then?)

3

William Palmer had a manifestly unfair trial, but one can see why it was necessary. Everyone *knew* that he was a killer, and quite probably a mass murderer. For him to have escaped justice because he was cleverer than the forces of law would have been intolerable. By hook or by crook (crook as it turned out) Palmer had to swing. I have suggested that this trial—with its display of prosecutorial brilliance—was the one that Wilkie Collins credits with inspiring him to write *The Woman in White*, and I want now to look at the novel, and various points of connection between it and the Rugeley murder(s). There is no need to summarize all of *The Woman in White* (something that is not easily done), but it will help to go over the details of the novel's poison plot.

The complications of the plot unfold when the obnoxious Percival Glyde holds Laura to the engagement arranged by her dead father. Glyde's motives are purely mercenary. Laura has a fortune of £20,000 at her own disposition and £3,000 a year when her Uncle Fairlie dies—a remote eventuality, as it happens. It is evidently Glyde's expectation that he can soon coerce his enervated wife into signing over her fortune to him. After a six-month honeymoon in Italy the Glydes return to Hampshire, in company of the Foscos. Improbably, Fosco also has an interest in Laura's fortune. On Lady Glyde's death, Fosco's wife (Laura's aunt) will inherit £10,000. On their return, Glyde and Fosco are financially embarrassed, to the amount of thousands and hundreds respectively. One assumes that while abroad they have been gambling at the tables or the bourse. They try to bully Laura into signing, unseen, a deed making over her fortune to her husband. Her resolve stiffened by Marian, Laura refuses—unless she is shown what she is signing. Baffled, Fosco and Glyde resort to money-lenders, which gives them three months' reprieve until the bills fall due.

Glyde meanwhile tells Fosco about Anne Catherick, the mysterious lunatic with the uncanny physical resemblance to Laura. The Italian virtuoso of crime sees a scheme—but one which is extraordinarily complicated. As has been established early in the narrative, Fosco is a "chemist" of genius. Anne, as he plans, will be substituted for Laura and then subtly poisoned (Collins 570). Meanwhile Laura will be packed off to Anne's private lunatic asylum, where her protestations that she is in fact Lady Glyde will be taken as the ravings of a madwoman. (In passing, it may be noted that this unidentified asylum must be one of the most inefficient institutions in the history of medicine. Not only can inmates apparently walk out whenever the whim takes them, but the staff will not observe the fact that one of their patients has overnight been transformed from a near-illiterate peasant to a highly-cultivated woman capable of playing the piano, painting watercolors, and speaking French.) It is a bizarre plan. Why not just poison Laura? She is chronically delicate. When Walter first encounters her, she is resting in her room with a sick headache; the marital embraces of Glyde have evidently exhausted her even further. She could die at any time, without raising too much suspicion. The not very convincing reason for the complex shuffling of victims and the murder of just one of them is that it will kill two birds with one stone. Anne (improbably enough) knows of Glyde's illegitimacy, and the knowledge will die with her. But if the keepers at the asylum will not believe Laura's protestations that she is Lady Glyde, why should they believe Anne's protestations that Sir Percival's parentage is not what he claims? The sensible course of action for any unscrupulous gang would be to poison Laura during one of her many indispositions and to do away with Anne Catherick during one of her frequent leaves of absence from the asylum.

Anyway, Fosco and Glyde go ahead with their cumbersome scheme. It involves hiring two henchwomen in Hampshire (Mme. Rubelle and Margaret Porcher) and any number of accessories before and after the fact in London. All these represent a huge risk of detection and/or blackmail. Nor does Fosco seem inclined to minimize his risks, even when opportunities drop, heaven-sent, into his lap. Marian, for instance, falls ill after her drenching night outside the window. Her fever develops into English typhus—a perfect cover under which Fosco could slip her out of the world with a little friendly strychnine. Instead of which, with incredible perversity, he saves her life by overruling the doltish quack who is treating her. Meanwhile, Laura is drugged (again, with Dawson in attendance, this would seem the perfect time to kill her and blame typhus). There ensues some jiggery pokery with rooms. Laura is made to think that Marian has gone on ahead, and is bundled up to London without any friend to protect her. In St. John's Wood, she is drugged again, and secreted in the asylum. As it was planned, Anne would have been poisoned immediately after the switch. But she had a weak heart and unluckily dies before Laura arrives in the metropolis on 25 July. This then is the fiendishly cunning plot devised by Count Fosco, the Napoleon of crime. It is, to put it charitably, no masterpiece of criminal art, nor would it have been even if Anne Catherick had survived long enough to be poisoned. But such is the brio of Collins's narrative technique, with all its pseudo legalism, that we don't notice; or do not care to notice how half-cocked Fosco's machinations are.

My argument has depended on four theses:

1. That *The Woman in White* is peculiarly a product of the 1850s.
2. That *The Woman in White* is the formative text in the evolution of the sensation novel as a genre.
3. That a main element of The Woman in White's sensationalism is its use of the courtroom, or forensic narrative technique.
4. That Collins was influenced in the invention of this technique by the Rugeley poisoning sensation.

The fourth thesis is the weakest. It relies on Collins's recollection that an unnamed 1856 trial inspired *The Woman in White* and that Palmer's trial was the *cause célèbre* of 1856. But it seems plausible, at least to me. Collins's interest in poisoning (something not found before *The Woman in White*) seems something more than coincidence. But even I would not maintain that *The Woman in White* is a close transcript or a *roman à clef* version of Palmer's story—as Bulwer-Lytton's *Lucretia*, for instance, transcribes Thomas Wainewright's ''arsenical'' crimes, or the Merdle subplot of *Little Dorrit* transcribes the forger John Sadleir's crimes. *The Woman in White* is more in the nature of a meditation on the Palmer affair and the issues it raised in the mind of the thoughtful observer of the 1850s. Principal among these issues is the status of circumstantial evidence. The Palmer case depended, above all, on being skilfully *narrated* by Cockburn, so as to gloss over the inadequacy of his material evidence. (This was the ''riding'' to which Palmer paid tribute.) In marshalling his circumstantial evidence to best effect, the lawyer in effect became a kind of novelist. So might Collins's novel become a kind of legal transcript.

The question of material versus circumstantial evidence is given prominence by one of the most enigmatic aspects of *The Woman in White*'s plot. The detective trio hunt unavailingly for documentary proof that Laura's trip to London post-dated Anne Catherick's death. Were they to find this key piece of evidence, they would be home and dry. The reader waits expectantly for proof of the mismatched dates to turn up. It never does. In the end, the trio have to resort to extra-legal means to foil Fosco—namely, the threat of betrayal to Pesca's Mafia-like secret society. This results in Fosco fleeing the country, only to end up on a slab in the Paris morgue—executed, albeit indirectly, by Walter Hartright. Baffled in their attempt to proceed lawfully, the novel's heroes fight crime with crime. And what after all is Fosco's crime? He does not, for all his grandiose Napoleonizing, actually *poison* anyone in *The Woman in White*. In fact he saves Marian's life. The worst that can be charged against him is that he is a party to (unsuccessful) fraud—not a capital offence in 1852.

I believe Collins was reflecting, ruefully, on the Palmer case in all this. He knew as well as anyone that Palmer probably was not guilty of poisoning Cook—or at least, that there was no proof. The clinching evidence (traces of toxin in the body) and the necessary motive simply were not there, however hard they were sought. As with Fosco, it was necessary to go beyond the law in order to enforce the law. Among other inventions, then, Collins can plausibly claim paternity of the vigilante novel, a line which leads from *The Woman in White* to *Death Wish 4*.

NOTES

1. Significantly, the example is taken from the *Annual Register* account of the trial of William Palmer, of which more later.
2. Freakish or obscene. When Bulwer made the murderer-hero of *Eugene Aram* (1831) a scholar, there was a furious outcry, and the novelist was obliged to alter his novel. See Michael Sadleir, *Bulwer and his Wife* (276–77).
3. For a useful account of the emergence of the modern police detective force, and the effect of the 1856 Act, see chapter 9 ("The Police") of Philip Collins's *Dickens and Crime* (196–219). One of the main provisions of the 1856 Police Act was to oblige local authorities to establish their own forces.
4. For Collins's improvising see my "Two Emergencies in the Writing of *The Woman in White*," *The Yearbook of English Studies* 7 (1977) 153–56.
5. This is very hypothetical, since, for his own reasons, Collins chose to conclude *The Woman in White* in 1851, six years before the liberations of the new divorce law.
6. See Harvey Sucksmith's Appendix E (The Main Source of *The Woman in White*) to his edition of the novel pp. 599–600.
7. According to Davis, Collins's statement "is re-Englished from a direct quotation in Louis Dépret's *Chez les Anglais* (Paris, 1879), p. 250."
8. "The Demeanour of Murderers," *Household Words*, 14 June 1856, pp. 594–98.
9. Graves's book, published a hundred years after Palmer's execution, is written as a vindication of a wrongly-hanged man.

WORKS CITED

The Annual Register, 1856. London: Rivington, 1857.

Clarke, William M. *The Secret Life of Wilkie Collins*. London: Allison and Busby, 1988.

Collins, Philip. *Dickens and Crime*. London: Macmillan, 1962, repr. 1964.

Collins, William Wilkie. *The Woman in White*. Ed. Harvey Peter Sucksmith. London: Oxford University Press, 1975.

Davis, Nuel P. *The Life of Wilkie Collins*. Urbana: U of Illinois P, 1956.

Fox Bourne, H. R. *English Newspapers*. 2 vols. London: Chatto and Windus, 1887.

Graves, Robert. *They Hanged My Saintly Billy*. London: Cassell, 1957.

Norman Page, Ed. *Wilkie Collins, the Critical Heritage*. London: Routledge and Kegan Paul, 1977.

Robinson, Kenneth. *Wilkie Collins, a Biography*. New York: Macmillan, 1952.

Sadleir, Michael. *Bulwer and his Wife*. London: Constable, 1931, repr. 1933.

Probability, Reality and Sensation in the Novels of Wilkie Collins

Christopher Kent

It is always salutary for the historian and the literary critic alike to be reminded that Victorian novelists and their critics assumed that the novels of their day would be read by posterity as social history. This assumption raised certain difficulties for the sensation novel, as Geraldine Jewsbury remarked: "If in after times the manners and customs of English life in 1864 were to be judged from the novels of the day, it would naturally be assumed that people were committing bigamy en masse" (qtd. in Fahnestock 57). Although Jewsbury may seem to us to be projecting a rather naive reader, we should not be too condescending. How we read novels as and for history remains problematic and is indeed returning to favor as a topic of scholarship and debate, though more among students of literature than history. It was a central tenet of Victorian literary realism that the novel should maintain a high level of representational probability. Its incidents and events should not depart too far from the way things usually are and usually happen in the real world. Such is roughly what we and they mean by everyday reality. The sensation novel affronted this reality by intentionally focusing on the aberrant.

Our temptation is to be too much like Jewsbury's sophisticated future reader, and to dismiss the sensation novel as unreal. Such seems to be Walter Kendrick's approach in remarking of *The Woman in White*: "The reader of a sensation novel engages in the discovery of an artificial pattern, and the enterprise need not teach him anything, even anything false, about the real world" (21). Such a non-referential Collins may be satisfying to a certain kind of critic, but I don't think it is the right Collins. I would suggest that his novels do teach readers something true, and something new, about the real world. Collins did so by emphasizing to an unusual degree among Victorian novelists the extent to which reality was a construct undergoing significant change in their own time, a change which entailed a redefinition of the boundaries of probability and possibility.

Hitherto, probability had been largely a metaphysical concern, a means of coming to terms with our inadequate understanding of a providential or mechanistic universe. In the nineteenth century, thinking about probability underwent a significant reorientation. Instead of concerning itself with the consequences of scarcity of information, it was increasingly concerned with the consequences of abundant information—what Ian Hacking has called the "avalanche of numbers." For the first time huge quantities of statistical information became available on matters of life and death through the information-gathering agencies of governments. They also provided some striking illustrations of the so-called law of large numbers, as regularities now began to appear in events which had long been regarded as quintessentially accidental and random. In the post office it was discovered that the number of misaddressed letters received each year was a constant. More alarming was the statistical demonstration of constancy of the annual suicide rate. Did such regularities in actions assumed to be freely willed indicate that society was somehow determined by mysterious laws of social mechanics? Many thought so, since certainty was assumed to inhere in the real world. The even more disturbing alternative seemed to be that the very regularities that held together reality itself were nothing but the random movements of blind chance.[1]

Wilkie Collins began his career as a novelist at a time when the question of probability was entering a particularly vexed state. In 1857 Henry Thomas Buckle published his controversial *History of Civilization* in which he drew attention to the law-like regularity of the suicide rate and proclaimed the advent of a truly scientific history, to be based on statistics and comprehending society as a whole, not just an arbitrarily chosen string of individuals and events (Buckle 15, 3). Inspired by the Belgian statistician Quetelet, Buckle was an ardent apostle of the "average man," that statistically perfect, if unreal figure who could represent the mass of statistically imperfect but real human beings. His writings were greeted with strong disapproval by the Victorian intellectual establishment, which was particularly alarmed to note that his ideas entailed the denial of free will in history. Charles Dickens, non-member of that establishment, was among the many who were impressed by Buckle's scientism. Percy Fitzgerald noted that Dickens would "often dwell on the dreadfully tyrannical power of the law of average, which must be carried out." Talking of deaths in London's streets he quotes Dickens as remarking "Now here we are in November and the number of accidents is much below what it should be. So, is it not dreadful to think that before the last day of the year some forty or fifty persons *must* be killed--and killed they will be ." (I, 207) This is an exemplary statement of statistical determinism, a notion that had a fascinating, if brief, vogue in the mid-nineteenth century (Hacking, "Cracks" 467). Another of Buckle's readers at this time was the brilliant young physicist James Clerk Maxwell, whose mind leapt analogically from the behavior of the average man to that of the average molecule, and proceeded to formulate the kinetic gas theory.

The great stumbling block in probability theory at this time was the problem of chance. Complete randomness, blind chance, was and still is a disturbing notion. But the speculations of scientists like Clerk Maxwell, devout Calvinist though he was, were already moving towards indeterminism. And even Darwin, who did not wish to believe that evolution was a product of chance, that the continued variations which were essential to the process of natural selection were random, could not find a satisfactory alternative explanation. Consequently Darwin's theory was criticized for its hints of an un-law-like indeterminism. Even his "bulldog," Thomas Huxley, complained that since "no law had been made out, Darwin is obliged to speak of variation as if it were spontaneous or a matter of chance" (qtd. in Gigerenzer 67).

We now know that the "taming of chance," to use another of Hacking's vivid phrases, was imminent with the advances in statistical theory that were just below the horizon around 1860. But what had such matters to do with Wilkie Collins? If he is not generally thought of as an "intellectual" novelist, in the sense that George Eliot or George Meredith are, he was surely better read and informed than is often recognized. (He may have cultivated his unintellectual image deliberately in the interests of popularity.) We can safely assume he read Buckle in 1857, because "everybody" did. He certainly read Balzac at a time when that author was hardly known in England. Like Buckle, Balzac had a vision of society as the object of scientific study. He saw himself as the physiologist and natural historian of modern life. Balzac also once stated rather neatly the dilemma that intrigued Collins:

> The historian of manners obeys harsher laws than those·that bind the historian of facts. He must make everything seem plausible, even the truth, whereas in the domain of history properly so called, the impossible is justified by the fact that it occurred. (quoted in Watson 180)

For Collins, too, the problem of probability was subjective, a matter of perception and belief. While he was certainly no Clerk Maxwell or Darwin, his novels demonstrate a quite sophisticated awareness of the ambiguities and implications of popular consciousness of probability in his own time.

At the level of everyday life the common perception of improbability was altered by communications. As the sphere of vicarious experience widened, the improbable was being made more probable, particularly by the press. Journalism has a natural bias towards the improbable, mass journalism particularly so. News values are strongly determined by improbability. As the old journalist's adage goes: "'Dog bites man,' isn't news: 'Man bites dog,' is." The Victorian press was thorough in its coverage of interesting bankruptcies and major crimes and trials, dwelling especially on the most unusual, such as the trials of William Palmer and Constance Kent, and the Northumberland Street mystery. Establishment of the divorce court in 1857 provided a rich new seam of sensation for the press to mine, and the invention of the telegraph almost the whole world to draw on for disasters and other improbabilities. They can be sampled in scrapbooks compiled by such connoisseurs of the bizarre as Henry Wills, Dickens's *Household Words* editor whose collection of strange police court cases came into Charles Reade's hands, or the Laird of Rammerscales, recently treated in Thomas Boyle's book. Such were the riches of improbability from which the real world of sensation was constructed.

Before Collins established his close friendship and collaboration with Charles Dickens, he was writing for the avant-garde *Leader*, an unjustly neglected weekly with perhaps the most talented corps of contributors of its time, including G. H. Lewes, Herbert Spencer, George Eliot, James Anthony Froude, Harriet Martineau, Edward Whitty, W. J. Linton, Thorton Hunt, and G. J. Holyoake. His association with it began when his boyhood friend Edward Pigott took it over in 1851. The *Leader* was militantly radical, socialist, and free thought. Its writers were determinedly unconventional, particularly when it came to their marital arrangements. As intellectuals, they were especially interested in exploring and defining the outer limits of reality. One of Collins's first contributions was a series of letters on Animal Magnetism, sympathetically describing the telepathic demonstrations of a Russian count and his pretty young French accomplice. The letters were addressed to G. H. Lewes, the *Leader*'s resident man of modern science and scoffer at spiritualism. Collins's last letter was titled "The Incredible not Impossible," and attempted to rebut some of Lewes' sceptical observations. A year later Lewes would turn his guns on the mysterious spontaneous combustion of Krook in *Bleak House*, pointing out in the *Leader* that such a phenomenon was neither unusual nor improbable, but quite simply impossible; the testimony Dickens assembled to justify it, adopting the classic procedure of appealing to authority on matters of probability, was irrelevant to the laws of chemistry which prohibited it. Dickens responded with his unrepentant preface to *Bleak House*, in which he reaffirmed his faith in spontaneous combustion, ending with his famous commitment to '' the romantic side of familiar things,'' a commitment which Collins had already demonstrated.

The *Leader* devoted considerable attention to the boundaries between fact and fiction. When Pigott took it over, Collins, who had recently been called to the bar, urged him to devote more space to crime and the courts (Lawrence 400). Pigott obliged and the paper started to carry extensive coverage of murder, fraud, and wife and child abuse cases, with frequent reflections on the sensational nature of such crimes. The *Leader*'s extensive coverage of the coroner's inquest on the Rugeley poisonings, which resulted in the trial of William Palmer, is particularly striking. It may even have been the work of Collins himself who was deeply involved in the running of the paper at this time (Beetz 25). The reporter is described editorially as "that true novelist" (19 Jan. 1856, 61), and no other known contributor seems so likely a candidate though another has been proposed (Boyle 95). For further discussion on the Palmer case see John Sutherland's essay on p. 30.

Two weeks later the *Leader* recounted at length another alarming item from the courts, beginning thus: "Truth is stranger than fiction, not only by deceiving ordinary expectation and thus departing more from verisimilitude than fiction rightly can, but by producing events which, save for their occurrence, we might declare to be impossible." There follows the story of an Irish gentleman who, on coming into a considerable estate entailed on male descent, and having no son, decides to get rid of his wife by conspiring with his servants to accuse her of adultery with a groom. He terrorizes her into signing a false confession and then has her committed to an asylum. The court obligingly grants him a divorce. "It looks like fiction," concluded the *Leader*,

> yet it is not simply invented upon paper but is done in fact, and worked out upon flesh and blood. It looks like an experiment in the mode of obtaining a divorce under which an innocent lady is driven wild with terror and left in a state of settled insanity. If a writer of fiction were to represent such a state of things in the United Kingdom at this day, his readers would laugh at the extravagancy; yet here it is asserted on the strong testimony of real life."
>
> (9 Feb. 1856, 133-34)

The *Leader* was at this time packed with appalling court cases involving violence and cruelty, particularly against women and children, frequently printing them under the sardonic standing headline ''Our Civilization.'' Another interesting department of the paper was titled ''The Romance of *The Times*,'' and contained a selection from the so-called agony column, one of the most widely read parts of that august journal (and appropriately printed on its front page). Here were advertisements for lost heirs, pleas for missing husbands, coded forbidden communications, and cryptic plans for secret trysts—hints of innumerable true sensation plots to set the reader's imagination aflame. The bohemian staff of the *Leader* was always ready to call attention to the gulf that frequently separated social convention and public perception from actual practice in marriage, business and politics. Some of the yeastiness of this milieu comes out in E. M. Whitty's novel *Friends of Bohemia* which satirizes the *Leader* as the *Teaser* and portrays its bohemian contributors as the true realists, ready to see and portray the world in its nakedness (147–49).

By this time Collins had already published *Basil*, his first novel of contemporary life. It's Dedication might be called a sensationalist manifesto. After assuring the reader that the novel's main event is ''founded on fact within my own knowledge''—love at first sight on a London omnibus—Collins assures his readers that he would not

> stoop so low as to assure myself of the reader's belief in the probability of my story, by never once calling on him for the exercise of his faith. Those extraordinary accidents and events which happen to few men seemed to me as legitimate materials for fiction to work with . . . as the ordinary events which may and do happen to us all.   (v)

Collins is self-evidently talking here about probability as subjective belief in the mind of the ordinary reader who calls upon personal experience to assess the likelihood of everyday matters, but whose personal experience does not extend to the extraordinary and must therefore take such matters on authority or ''faith,'' as Collins puts it. Collins's management of the reader's faith, and of his own authority, deserves some attention, involving as it does a carefully calculated economy of probability about which he is quite open. Indeed Collins's novels are unusual in that they are not so much about the probability of representation—that is, the likelihood of their likeness to everyday reality. Rather, they are about the representation of probability. Collins makes probability one of the main themes of his novel by showing it, subjective probability particularly, at work in the minds of his characters. He does so with a minimum of explicit authorial intervention by having his characters deal with the problem of probability in confused and confusing ways which are recognizable to us still.

Collins was fond of love at first sight. It recurs in his novels, perhaps because it is a sort of coincidence, a sort of randomly occurring mystery which combines the subjective and the objective. To the external manifestation of the right person at the right time and place, is added the subjectivity of susceptibility. Perhaps only a certain kind of person believes in love at first sight, or is capable of it, someone who is open to chance, who gives space to contingency. Someone like Collins, or Basil, a young gentleman about town and would-be novelist who ventures on to that vulgar conveyance, an omnibus, and becomes infatuated with a pretty young woman who turns out to be the silly daughter of an unpleasant shopkeeper. "Could this be love? pure first love for a shopkeeper's daughter whom I had seen for a quarter of an hour on an omnibus. . . ? The thing was impossible," Basil reflects (36; pt.1, ch. 7). But he pursues his infatuation, which he attributes, with its resultant catastrophe, to "fatality" and "destiny" (81, 87; Pt. 1, Ch. 11, 12). By contrast, Mr. Sherwin, when asked by his future son-in-law whether he has "ever heard of such a thing as love at first sight," replies sarcastically, "In books, Sir" (64; Pt. 1, Ch. 10). Recognizing a promising speculation on social advancement, he consents to the match. But his approach to probability is business-like: he imposes a year's secrecy and non-consummation in order to improve the chances that Basil's blood-proud father will recognize the marriage. He also requires of Basil "a little insurance on your life," a basic form of bourgeois risk management (83; Bk. 1, Ch. 11). Despite the marriage, Margaret Sherwin is seduced by her father's clerk Mannion, another thwarted novelist who is the self-appointed "instrument of fatality" against Basil's family (252; Bk. 3, Ch. 5). Basil is rescued from the consequences of his fatalistic resignation by his black sheep elder brother, the bohemian Ralph, who takes charge of the situation with an aggressively sporting attitude towards probability. "500-1 we get our divorce," he declares, confronting Sherwin. Shortly afterwards he will "lay another wager" against Mannion's ever bothering them again (272, 283; Bk. 3, Ch. 6, 7).

Collins reverted regularly in subsequent novels to the technique of contrasting characters in terms of their attitudes towards probability—their differing ways of accounting to themselves for the uncertainties of reality. By deploying multiple narrators speaking for themselves he is able to offer a rich phenomenology of the various ways in which people perceive and deal with the problem of chance in everyday life. This is an important if neglected aspect of the way in which reality is perceived, constructed, and lived. In

The Woman in White Walter Hartright, another victim of love at first sight, also adopts the passive language of destiny and fatality. But after returning from the wilds of Central America, where he finds his manhood, he becomes much more calculating and assertive, frequently using the phrase "in all probability" as he takes up the pursuit of Glyde and Count Fosco. In finally defeating Fosco he outwits a formidable opponent in probabilistic calculation, a man of science who regularly uses the activist language of chance and risk. In *No Name* we witness a striking duel of wits between Captain Wragge and Mme. Lecount, two shrewd worldlings who are constantly calculating the probabilities of each other's actions. Wragge, as a professional confidence man, makes his living by judging subjective probabilities, the conventional probability judgements of others which he manipulates and uses to his own advantage. However, he is a prudent, small-time risk taker, carefully avoiding major gambles on his judgement until he is caught up in Magdalen Vanstone's daring deception, a challenge to which he rises brilliantly. There is a fine passage where Mme. Lecount, who has uncovered the Wragge/Vanstone deception but is still unable to prove it to her employer, attempts to flush Wragge out with the heavily ironic observation "strange coincidence," to which Wragge, knowing her dilemma, retorts with brazen equanimity, "Very strange" (330; Sc. 4, Ch. 6). When Magdalen, despairing of the success of Wragge's scheme, decides to gamble at even odds on committing suicide in the famous suspense scene where she counts the ships that appear on the horizon, Collins enriches the motivation by lending probability to her very act of fatalistic probabilism in the form of external authority. Magdalen gets the idea of her gamble by recalling a newspaper story about the trial of a farm worker who decided whether to kill his girl friend, whom he suspected of unfaithfulness, by tossing his ploughshare (413; Sc. 4, Ch. 13).

It has been remarked, by Simone de Beauvoir among others, that the circumstances, biological and conventional, of women's existence have inclined them to construct a more fatalistic reality to account for their lives (563). Thus women are believed to be more likely than men to turn to the horoscope page in the newspaper. Collins, however, frequently chose to portray women taking a more active approach to the problem of probability, often in contrast to male characters who are more fatalistic or less inclined to attempt a rational calculation of probabilities. The adventuress Lydia Gwilt, by contrast with both the Armadales, is a bold risk taker and calculator of the odds, who takes advantage of circumstance and accident to shape the perceptions of probability of men to meet her own requirements. In *Poor*

Miss Finch it is Mme. Pratolungo who, despite her idealistic political pronouncements—which we are invited to consider unrealistic, and probably the
residual legacy of her husband, a failed revolutionary—is the most accurate
judge of probabilities and realities as against the fatalistic Oscar Dubourg. In
Collins's last completed novel, *The Legacy of Cain*, we meet Miss Chance,
at first a rather sinister figure, who later as Mrs. Terbruggen emerges as
another of Collins's strong women, physically and intellectually. She becomes
a masseuse and succeeds in legally separating herself from her parasitical
husband. "If I believed in luck, which I don't, I should call you a fortunate
man," she says at one point (217; ch. 47). By contrast the defrauded spinster
Miss Jillgall, her great admirer, does believe in luck, though the refrain of
her favorite song is "My heart is light / My will is free" (82, 117; Ch. 18,
27). Of the two young women brought up as sisters whose contrasting characters provide the test of heredity which is a central theme of the novel, Helena,
the nasty one, writes in her diary of her "fatal passion" for Philip, her sister's
weak-willed lover: "There is a fate in these things. If I am destined to rob
Eunice of the one dear object of her love and hope—how can I resist?" (107;
Ch. 25). But this invocation of fate is a hypocritical cover for active jealousy
and malice. Helena is no passive believer in fate: thwarted, she later tries to
poison Philip. After serving two years for attempted murder she goes to
America where she quickly makes her fortune, founding a religious cult as
"Priestess of the Worship of Pure Reason" (301; ch. 64). Her last name,
that of her kind but weak clergyman father, is significant: Gracedieu.

Collins's religious views are a matter of some debate. In an early letter to
Pigott protesting the *Leader*'s disrespectful attitude towards Christianity, he
declared: "I believe Jesus Christ to be the son of God" (Lawrence, 396).
However his religious views were certainly not conventional. Though brought
up in the orthodox high Anglicanism of his father, who regarded the first
Reform Act as divine punishment for the follies and political sins of the
English people, his attitude towards providence was not his father's, nor that
of many Victorian novelists, including Dickens. In a well-known passage of
a letter written to Collins just after the publication of *A Tale of Two Cities*,
Dickens compares his method of plotting to "the ways of Providence, of
which ways all art is but a little imitation" (95). Whatever the implications
of this statement for Dickens, it can be said that Collins's interest in providence lay in the extent to which others believed in it, and found in it an
adequate explanation of events. His characters use it in varying ways: Count
Fosco mockingly: "Light, sir, is the grand decree of Providence" (*Woman
in White*, 323; 2nd epoch, Frederick Fairlie); Michael Vanstone selfishly,

when he declares his brother's death providential in restoring to him his rightful fortune (*No Name*, 134; Sc. 1, Ch. 15); the Reverend Mr. Finch irresponsibly, as he constantly invokes "inscrutible Providence" when alluding to his financial difficulties or his daughter's blindness (*Poor Miss Finch*, 69, Ch. 12; 103, Ch. 18).

In the eighteenth century probability theory had been used to support providentialism. The very improbability of an event or phenomenon, such as the incredible combination of chances necessary to sustain the notion of the accidental creation of the world, argued for divine intent. Behind all the probabilism of *Robinson Crusoe* lies an argument in support of divine providence, the true reason for Crusoe's rescue and salvation. There is resonant irony, therefore, in Gabriel Betteredge's use of *Robinson Crusoe* in *The Moonstone*. The old servant makes it his secular bible to the extent of practicing sortilege with it, opening it at random to find a text to guide him in moments of uncertainty. The word "providence" was being used with increasing looseness in the nineteenth century, being drained of much of its theological content and becoming assimilated to the non-Christian cluster of probabilistic terms such as luck, chance, fortune or fate. "Fate or providence, call it what we may. . . ," says the sympathetically presented prison governor in *The Legacy of Cain*, whose agnostic uncertainty is honest (157; Ch. 35). Not so is Helena Gracedieu's disclaimer: "We are not responsible for an accident . . . we are not responsible for the feelings implanted in our natures by an all-wise Providence" (169; Ch. 37). This recalls Samuel Butler's caustic *mot*: "As chance would have it, Providence favoured me" (qtd. in Auclair 77).

Although one of Collins's acquaintances labelled his religious position as "Materialist," he was interested in spiritual phenomena, and was at least reluctant to rule out their existence in our world. From his "Magnetic Evenings at Home" to his last novels he regarded them as at least within the realm of possibility. *Heart and Science* takes a hostile attitude towards science in its strongly materialist form, embodied particularly in the monomaniacal vivisectionist Dr. Benjulia, a man devoid of human feelings, who pursues his researches into the workings of the brain and nerves through experiments on live animals. He cynically asks "Who knows what love is?" assuming his question to be unanswerable. "God," is the heroine's innocently crushing retort (232, Ch. 44). When Mrs. Gallilee, the atheistic society woman who dabbles in amateur science, finds her careful scheme to foil her son's planned marriage (yet another case of love at first sight) unravelling, she wonders: "When some people talked of Fatality, were they quite such fools as she had hitherto supposed them to be?'' Lowering herself to the intellectual level of an ignorant servant, "The modern Muse of Science unconsciously opened her mind to the vulgar belief in luck'' (155; Ch. 29). In this novel Collins railed authorially against the arrogant, self-important "parasites that infest Science,'' contrasting them with true scientists like the great Michael Faraday whose words he reverentially quotes: "The first and last step in the education of the judgement is—humility'' (285; Ch. 54). Interestingly, since one of Mrs. Gallilee's areas of ''expertise'' was atomic theory, J. J. Thomson, Lord Rayley, Sir Oliver Lodge, and William Crookes, four of the most eminent late-nineteenth-century English physicists, shared an active interest in spiritualism and psychical research. The latter two became presidents of the Society for Psychical Research, a body which claimed the membership of some of the country's most distinguished intellectuals (Oppenheim 330). The subatomic universe, the mysteries of x-rays, and the improbable energy levels and behavior of improbably small particles encouraged a new readiness to consider the supernatural, once dismissed by scientists as mere superstition. The open-mindedness about the probable and the possible called for by Collins was indeed necessary to come to terms with such new phenomena.

Just as the indeterminate implications of sub-atomic physics were barely discernable to the leading minds when Collins was writing *Heart and Science* in the 1880s, so it was with Darwinism, which also pointed ultimately towards a random universe that would have alarmed Darwin and even Huxley. In *The Legacy of Cain* Darwin is not mentioned, but the novel thematizes the implications of heredity through the concerned eyes of the prison governor. Hereditary criminality was one of the growth points of social scientific theorizing in the late nineteenth century, criminal statistics, and prison populations being a prime area for probabilistic research, though the thrust was in a largely deterministic direction. Hereditary determinism had its literary votaries among naturalist writers like Zola, Dreiser, and Moore, but in Collins's novels hereditary determinism was usually defeated, though not without a literal struggle between nature and nurture, such as that between Eunice's secret ''hereditary maternal taint''—her birth mother was a convicted murderess—'' and the counterbalancing influence for good'' produced by her upbringing in a minister's household (186; Ch. 40). Eunice successfully fights back the impulse to murder her malicious sister. Struggle against heredity is also part of the complex thematic web of *Armadale*, though in the case of Ozias Midwinter it can hardly be said that a benign upbringing counters a hereditary taint. He is twice damned by heredity and environment. In both cases the deciding factor in the outcome is left unclear in such a way as to justify referring it to chance. This is a distinctly "modern" way of settling the dilemma of free will versus determinism that vexed discussions of probability in Collins's time.

It may seem paradoxical to talk of Collins's novels as thematizing probability with a particular emphasis on chance when they are themselves so elaborately and tightly plotted. He was supremely the novelist who left nothing to chance in the writing, as Walter Besant found when he completed Collins's unfinished last novel *Blind Love* (1890), a task made easy by the extensive notes and careful plot outline left by the dead writer (preface). How different from Trollope, Thackeray, and even Dickens, whose novels were much more contingent in the sense that their authors "made it up as they went along" in a spirit of openness to whatever might turn up. Trollope in particular emphasized this point in contrasting his work with Collins's and making the distinction between the novel of plot and the novel of character that was such a popular theme in criticism in Collins's own time (qtd. in Page 223). In these more contingent novels one can imagine things turning out differently, and a different story being the result. With Collins one cannot. If things had happened differently, there would be no story; this one is the only one. The oppressive tightness, the relentless significance of detail may seem unrealistic as against the more relaxed looseness of Trollopian realism, but is it?

The absence of the authorial presence as narrator is certainly an important factor in this loss of contingency. There is no sense of a presiding creator who could tell it differently. The participant narrators who have lived through it can only tell us what they knew and what happened to them. The documentary narrative technique conveys a particularly strong sense of the story being already over and having a specific ending, but for which the documents would not be assembled, or even called into existence. Moreover, the story can be assumed at the outset to be a fairly unusual one, otherwise it would not have generated such documentation (illustrating the historical commonplace that ordinary people do not break into history unless extraordinary things happen to them). Adopting the protective mantle of history in the form of documentation might be expected to confer exemption from charges of improbablity, particularly of excessively large and frequent coincidences, but it did not. Collins was regularly convicted by the reviewers on these charges, though interestingly the reviewers did not always agree on what constituted an improbability, and the novelists among them, such as George Meredith, Mrs. Oliphant, and Henry James tended to support Collins (Page 15, 79, 112, 123). The most magisterial indictments were handed down by the *Saturday*

Review whose anonymous contributors were among the most confident arbiters of Victorian reality:

> The weak part of his plots, perhaps, is that he relies too much upon startling and improbable coincidences. *Le vrai n'est pas toujours vraisemblable.* The most remarkable coincidences may be found in real life; but when coincidences happen in shoals, one's faith in the novelist's conceptions becomes somewhat weakened. There is such a thing as economy in the free use of improbabilities, and though odd things do occur in the world, they do not keep on occurring to the same people every other day. But the story of *Armadale* hinges almost entirely on miraculous combinations, the arithmetical chances against which are simply infinite.   (16 June 1866, 727; quoted on Page 153)

Coincidence was of course a common feature of the Victorian novel. George Eliot remarks defensively of the coincidence which leads to the discovery of Bulstrode's letter in *Middlemarch*: "To Uriel watching the progress of planetary history from the Sun, the one result would be just as much a coincidence as the other" (302; Bk. 4, Ch. 41). Collins avoided sententious intellectualism, but one occasion when he does intervene in his own voice is at the beginning of *Heart and Science*. He offers a characteristic defence of coincidence which, if it might not fully satisfy a Saturday Reviewer, is not without point:

> When two friends happen to meet in the street do they look back along the procession of small circumstances which had led them both, from the starting point of their own houses, to the same spot at the same time? Not one man in ten thousand has probably ever thought of making such a fantastic inquiry as this. And consequently not one man in ten thousand, living in the midst of reality, has discovered that he is also living in the midst of romance."   (2)

If a coincidence is an intersection of two or more causally unrelated sequences of events, such things are not rare in life, though most go unremarked since little of human concern issues from the intersection. One's sense of coincidence depends on the improbability of the coincidence, which depends in turn on the initial distance between the sequences, and the magnitude of the consequences. If the former is a more or less objective matter—an intersection in a large area of space and time is obviously more coincidental than one in a small area; an unplanned meeting in a large distant city is more coincidental than one in a departmental corridor—the other is more subjective, since consequences depend on future human actions. Collins's novels do not contain as many coincidences in the strict sense as is often thought because of the tightness of the plotting and the fact that so many of the characters are themselves plotting, which means that the causal sequences are rarely fully independent. A good example of a chance coincidence of extremely high improbability is Captain Kirke's discovery of Magdalen Vanstone at the brink of death in a London slum (*No Name*, 473; last scene, Ch. 1). But then the captain of the *Deliverance* is a *deus ex machina* to a degree unusual in Collins. An incident that has been cited for excess by Michael Irwin is Lydia Gwilt's encountering her former lover in the chorus of Bellini's *Norma* at the Naples opera (31). Yet she had tried to keep out of sight in her box, aware that "it was impossible to be sure that some of my old friends of former days might not be in the theatre" (*Armadale*, 492, Bk. 5, Ch. 2). The reader's impulse to take affront at a coincidence is also blunted when characters call attention to it themselves. Lydia Gwilt declares herself "completely staggered by this extraordinary coincidence" when she learns her actions have coincided with Armadale's dreams (499; Bk. 5, Ch. 1).

Collins's novels are about people plotting and counterplotting, forcing reality in a way that often makes them aware of the ambiguous relationship between life and literature. Documentary realism requires documentary probability. When an omniscient author decides to tell us a story we don't expect to be told why he is doing so. When we encounter a first-person narrator who has created his document, we expect some explanation of why he has done so. In *Basil* the narrator is a frustrated novelist telling his story in "now it can be told" circumstances following his father's death. Concern for documentary probability becomes somewhat clumsy at the end, in Basil's letter accompanying his manuscript to the friend who ultimately published it:

> How are the pages I am about to send you to be concluded? In the novel-reading sense of the word, my story has no real conclusion. . . . Is it fit that I should set myself, for the sake of effect, to *make* a conclusion, and terminate by fiction what has begun and thus far, has proceeded in truth? In the interests of Art, as well as the interests of Reality, surely not!   (339, Letters in Conclusion, 3)

Documentary provenance and justification is provided in other novels. The narrative depositions in *The Woman in White* are presented as testimony towards a legal action, though in fact no such action takes place, nor could it since the potential defendants are dead at the end. Collins frequently employed letters written by various characters which have an intrinsic documentary probability. Lydia Gwilt's diary is an important part of her life. Bored and alone, she writes, "I think I shall look back through these pages and live my life over again when I was plotting and planning and finding a new excitement to occupy me in every new hour of the day'' (483; Bk. 5, Ch. 1). Later she answers a question which may have crossed the reader's mind:

> Why do I keep a diary at all? Why did the clever thief the other day (in the English newspapers) keep the very thing to convict him in the shape of a record of everything he stole? Why are we not perfectly reasonable in all that we do? Why am I not always on my guard, and never inconsistent with myself like a wicked character in a novel? Why? Why? Why? (495; Bk. 5, Ch. 1)

Several contemporary reviewers of *Armadale* in fact questioned the Gwilt diary, one calling it "unnatural" (Page 148, 149). Yet the evidence of a number of Victorian trials of women for murder and adultery indicates that some real women did keep artful, highly "literary" diaries which in many cases contained elaborately developed fictions (Hartman 257, Boyle 115). The fictional Lydia Gwilt, by contrast, kept a true diary. Reviewers might at least have given her credit for that—unless that was what was meant by "unnatural"! Where her diary does contain "lies," it is the "miserable made-up story" she tells Midwinter about herself, "the commonplace rubbish of the circulating libraries," which she records while it is fresh in her mind so that she can refer to it on subsequent occasions (436; Bk. 4, Ch. 14). Captain Wragge in *No Name* takes similar precautions. As a prudent con man, he keeps business-like records of his "moral agriculture" so as not to be caught out by inconsistencies (183; Sc. 2, Ch. 2). He keeps a book, *Skins to Jump Into*, with full biographical details of dead persons whom he can impersonate when he needs a new identity (269; Between the Scenes, 3 and 4, Pt. 12). On one occasion he boasts of being "the architect of [Magdalen Vanstone's] fortunes, the publisher, so to speak, of her books" (209; Between the Scenes, 2 and 3, Pt. 8). Such ingenious variations on the theme of life imitating art imitating life recur in Collins's novels.

Collins also plays upon the privileged status of the newspaper as a touchstone of reality. "Reading the morning paper is the morning prayer of modern man," Hegel once remarked (Rosenkranz, 543). The newspaper puts us in touch with the "real world out there," assuring us of its existence. But what sort of real world? For the journalist, a prime touchstone of newsworthiness is the unusual and improbable. Mrs. Oldershaw the cosmetician, suggesting an improvement in Lydia Gwilt's plot, writes, "Don't suppose I am at all overboastful about my own ingenuity. Cleverer tricks than this trick of mine are played off on the public by swindlers, and are recorded in the newspapers every week" (191; Bk. 3, Ch. 5). Mrs. Oldershaw's words have particular contemporary resonance in that she was probably based on a Mrs. Rachel

Leverson, a viciously fraudulent cosmetician who preyed upon numerous gullible women during the 1860s and whose exploits, beside which Oldershaw's do look somewhat pale, did indeed end up in the newspapers (Ellis 37; Jenkins 1–30). Miss Garth, the governess in *No Name*, responds to Mrs. Vanstone's surprise at Magdalen's throwing herself on the unworthy Frank Clare, with

> " . . . it happens every day! . . . I know a great many excellent people who reason against plain experience in the same way -- who read the newspapers in the morning, and deny in the evening that there is any romance for writers or painters to work upon in modern life."   (69; Sc. 1, Ch. 8)

Variations on the phrase "romance of modern life" appear a number of times in Collins's novels (e.g., *Legacy of Cain* 243; Ch. 52; *Poor Miss Finch* 51; Ch. 9).

Newspapers also provide realistic mechanisms for forwarding Collins' plot in numerous ways, for example in *Armadale* the agony column appeal by lawyers seeking one Allan Armadale in connection with a legacy (43; 61; Bk. 2, Ch. 1). In *No Name*, Captain Wragge uses the agony column to anonymously sound out Noel Vanstone, fortuitous inheritor of Norah's and Magdalen's father (217; Between the Scenes 2 and 3, Pt. 9). The propensity of the press to report unusual deaths is vital to Lydia Gwilt's plotting (505, 513; Bk. 5, Ch. 2). In *The New Magdalen*, as a street-smart orphan child, Mercy Merrick takes advantage of its propensity to publicize "interesting cases" of young orphan girls, who get taken up by charitable sensation seekers (303; Ch. 27). Collins takes advantage of the growing symbiosis between the war and the press by making one of the important characters in *The New Magdalen* a war correspondent in the Franco-Prussian conflict, an occupation which had only come into existence some fifteen years earlier. War is one of the richest sources of improbabilities, and because of its increasing scale, an excellent example of the workings of the law of large numbers. Hardly any possibility goes unrealized in a major war. It was widely recognized at the time that the press played a large part in establishing the conditions of possibility of the sensation novel—Dean Mansel for instance, speaking of the "newspaper novel" (261). But this was arguably symptomatic of a deeper development: journalism's pushing forward the frontier of the probable in the popular phenomenology of reality. In so doing it opened up new territory for the novel.

Like most Victorian novelists, Collins was aware of the traditional objection that novels gave readers false notions of the real world, particularly

women readers whose circumscribed personal experience made them particularly prone to dangerously false assumptions about reality on the basis of
novel reading. There is a darkly comic episode in *Heart and Science* where
Benjulia's servant, who has been reading *Pamela, or, Virtue Rewarded*,
concludes that her master is about to propose marriage to her. But Benjulia
cruelly encourages her fantasy, before disabusing her of it (201; Ch. 37), and
the very grotesqueness of the scene mocks the supposed dangers of novels.
Collins evidently felt that, if anything, suspicion of the novel had embedded
itself too deeply in the public mind: ''How unnatural all this would be if it
was written in a book!'' Lydia Gwilt exclaims (*Armadale* 500; Bk. 5, Ch.
2). Basil uses almost identical words (*Basil* 43; Pt. 1, Ch. 8). ''It's like a
scene in a novel—it's like nothing in real life,'' muses Noel Vanstone (*No
Name* 452; Sc. 5, Ch. 1). Collins suggests that the response of the novelist
to this public suspicion, is to confine his reality within too narrow
bounds—such as those suggested by the cynical Dr. Le Doux (late Downward) for the English novelist who is allowed to enter his Sanatorium: ''All
we want of him is—occasionally to make us laugh; and invariably to make
us comfortable'' (*Armadale* 563; Bk. 6, Ch. 3). One serious consequence of
such constraints is that already indicated by Balzac: the threshold of probability must be set higher in the novel than in real life than in real life itself—establishing a double standard of probability.

This is perhaps one of the most important things that Collins, despite Walter
Kendrick's judgment, has to teach his readers about the real world. If Collins
never practiced law he was fascinated by, and had a considerable knowledge
of, matters pertaining to crime and criminal justice. Criminal trials are the
grand assizes of probabilistic judgment: a human life may hang in the balance.
In England, unlike the continent, the conviction or acquittal of those charged
with capital crimes depends not on the judgment of experts, but on the
judgment of common sense embodied in the twelve honest men of the jury
who must decide the probability of guilt or innocence, in the well-known
words, ''beyond reasonable doubt.'' This requires more than everyday probability, and should admit some degree of improbability: the crucial question
is how much? On this point juries were often given some guidance. A well-
known example cited by Welsh is that given in 1849 to jurors in the Manning
murder trial by Chief Baron Pollock, who required of them ''that degree of
certainty in the case that you would act upon it in your own grave and
important concerns'' (73). Collins, whose novels are particularly resonant
with echoes of famous mid-Victorian criminal trials, may well have felt that
the standard of probability implied here was unduly high.[2] He refers several

times to the dangers of applying the standard of probability appropriate to everyday life to those cases wherein a human life literally hangs in the balance.

In *Armadale* young Bashwood, the private detective, describes how Lydia Gwilt some years earlier was tried for the poisoning of her husband, a wife beater. All the legal evidence seemed to point irrefutably towards her guilt, and she was duly found guilty of murder. But she was saved from the gallows by "two or three of the young Buccaniers [sic] of Literature" (471; Bk. 4, Ch. 5), investigative journalists who found doctors to dispute the judgment of expert Crown witness and stirred up public opinion to such a degree that the Home Secretary was forced to grant her a pardon. There are numerous resonances with real life here: to the dubious testimony of the expert witness in the 1856 Palmer case; to the Road murder case of 1860 where the press generated sympathy for the main suspect, a young girl named Constance Kent who was not charged, but later "confessed"; and to the Madeleine Smith trial of 1857. This last involved a pretty young Glaswegian accused of poisoning her French lover. She got off, despite powerful evidence against her, with the verdict "not proven," a peculiarly Scottish form of verdict which could convey the message: "We think the accused is probably guilty but the Crown has not sufficiently made its case." Perhaps in the Madeleine Smith verdict the message was: "We prefer not to confront the probability that a pretty young woman of a respectable family could have been responsible for such an act." Collins later protested against the "not proven" verdict in *The Law and The Lady*, where this weak-kneed, unmanly verdict is overturned by the efforts of a woman. In *Armadale* Lydia Gwilt is the dubious beneficiary of the male chauvinism of public opinion that declares "Woman can't be like that!" It is at least possible to read Collins's account of the trial of Lydia Gwilt as a protest against the social construction of the inequality of women: the double standard of probability meets the double standard of sex.

Numerous examples can be cited of Collins showing his readers how the consensual version of probability can be contrary to reality and lead to miscarriages of justice—the murder trial of Oscar Dubourg in *Poor Miss Finch* (46-8; ch. 8) for instance. Or the two lawyers' judgments in *The Woman in White*: Mr. Gilmour's judgment that "the probabilities . . . were plainly with" Sir Percival Glyde's explanation of Anne Catherick's committal to an asylum (130; Vincent Gilmore, 1); or Mr. Kyrle's judgment that "in all probability" a jury would find against the claim Laura Glyde was still alive (406; 3rd epoch, Hartright 2, 4). The very organization of *The Moonstone* and *The Woman in White*, Collins's most popular novels, implicitly invites the reader to take a judicial position. Gabriel Betteredge, thinking of the future readers of his narrative is explicit: "What a compliment he will feel it . . . to be treated in all respects like a judge on the bench" (232; per. I, Ch.23). Most daunting of all is Collins's invitation to the reader at the end of *Armadale* to decide for himself whether to interpret the Dream according to "the natural or the supernatural theory" (Appendix).

The stern realist of the *Saturday Review* unkindly likened Collins's invitation to "Lord Dundreary's metaphysical problem—'If you had a brother, do you think he would like cheese?'" (Page 154). Why should real readers be implicated in the novelist's unreality? Yet the seriousness with which that journal took novels belied such levity. For instance, nobody read Dickens' novels with greater anxiety about their power over readers' perceptions of reality than did James Fitzjames Stephen, the *Saturday Review*'s most powerful pen (Stephen 8). But let the historian close by turning the tables on Wilkie Collins, and asking how well he calculated the probabilities in and of his own "real life." He was sufficiently his father's son to purchase life insurance with his illegitimate children as beneficiaries. His taste for dry champagne, paté de foie gras, snuff, and of course laudanum, made him a poor risk for the insurer. But there were also risks for the insured in choosing an insurer. Not all of them survived, and some were crooked. Collins died in the midst of a novel in which an actual recent insurance fraud was thinly fictionalized. Although Collins apparently chose a sound company, accidents occurred to his arrangements, and his dependents were left largely unprovided for (Clarke 99, 176).

NOTES

1. The study of probability has become particularly lively since the publication of Hacking's Foucault-inspired *Emergence of Probability*. Gigerenzer *et al.* provide an up-to-date overview. In the specifically literary sphere, Patey's work is comprehensive and scholarly. Newsome's stimulating study specifically avoids the thematization of probability, the concern of this essay. See also my study "The Average Victorian."

2. Altick, Boyle, Miller, and Trodd are among those who draw attention to specific mid-Victorian criminal cases, certain distinctive features of which are embedded in Collins's novels.

WORKS CITED

Altick, Richard D. *Evil Encounters: Two Victorian Sensations*. London: John Murray, 1987.

Auclair, Georges. *Le mana quotidien: structures et fonctions de la chronique des faits divers.* 2nd ed. Paris: Anthropos, 1982.

Beauvoir, Simone de. *The Second Sex.* New York: Bantam, 1961.

Beetz, Kirk H. "Wilkie Collins and *The Leader.*" *Victorian Periodicals Review* 15 (1982): 20–29.

Boyle, Thomas. *Black Swine in the Sewers of Hampstead: Beneath the Surface of Victorian Sensationalism.* New York: Viking, 1989.

Buckle, Henry Thomas. *Introduction to the History of Civilization in England.* New ed. London: George Routledge, n.d.

Clarke, William M. *The Secret Life of Wilkie Collins.* London: Allison & Busby, 1988.

Collins, Wilkie. *Armadale.* New York: Dover, 1977.

———. *Basil: A Story of Modern Life.* New York: Dover, 1982.

———. *Blind Love.* London: Chatto & Windus, 1890.

———. *Heart and Science: A Story of the Present Time.* London: Chatto & Windus, 1890.

———. *The Legacy of Cain.* New York: F.M. Lupton, n.d.

———. *Man and Wife.* London: Chatto & Windus, 1927.

———. *The Moonstone. A Romance.* London: Penguin, 1968.

———. *The New Magdalen.* New York: Scribner's, 1908.

———. *No Name.* New York: Dover, 1978.

———. *Poor Miss Finch: A Domestic Story.* London: Chatto & Windus, 1875.

———. *The Woman in White.* London: Collins, 1952.

Eliot, George. *Middlemarch.* Boston: Houghton Mifflin, 1956.

Ellis, Stuart M. *Wilkie Collins, Le Fanu and Others.* London: Constable, 1951.

Fahnestock, Jeanne. "Bigamy: The Rise and Fall of a Convention." *Nineteenth Century Fiction* 36 (1981): 47–71.

Fitzgerald, Percy. *The Life of Charles Dickens as Revealed in his Writings.* London: Chatto & Windus, 1905.

Gigerenzer, Gerd, et al. *The Empire of Chance: How Probability Changed Science and Everyday Life.* Cambridge: Cambridge University Press, 1989.

Hacking, Ian. "The Autonomy of Statistical Law." *Scientific Explanation and Understanding.* Ed. Nicholas Rescher. Lanham, Md.: U.P. of America, 1983.

————. "Biopower and the Avalanche of Numbers." *Humanities and Society* 5 (1983): 279–95.

————. *The Emergence of Probability: A Philosophical Study of Early Ideas about Probability, Induction and Statistical Inference*. Cambridge: Cambridge UP, 1975.

————. "Nineteenth Century Cracks in the Concept of Determinism." *Journal of the History of Ideas* 44 (1983): 456–75.

Hartman, Mary. *Victorian Murderesses: A True History of Thirteen Respectable French and English Women Accused of Unspeakable Crimes*. New York: Schocken, 1977.

Irwin, Michael. "Readings of Melodrama." Ian Gregor, ed. *Reading the Victorian Novel: Detail into Form*. New York: Barnes & Noble, 1980.

Jenkins, Elizabeth. *Six Criminal Women*. London: Sampson Low, 1949.

Kendrick, Walter M. "The Sensationalism of *The Woman in White*." *Nineteenth Century Fiction* 32 (1977): 18–35.

Kent, Christopher A. "The Average Victorian." *Browning Institute Studies* 17 (1989), 41–52.

Lawrence, Keith. "The Religion of Wilkie Collins: Three Unpublished Documents." *Huntington Library Quarterly* 52 (1989): 389–402.

Mansel, Henry L. "Sensation Novels." *Quarterly Review* 113 (1863): 251–68.

Miller, D.A. "From *roman policier* to *roman-police*: Wilkie Collins's *The Moonstone*." *Novel* 13 (1980): 153–70.

Newsome, Robert. *A Likely Story: Probability and Play in Fiction*. New Brunswick: Rutgers UP, 1988.

Oppenheim, Janet. *The Other World: Spiritualism and Psychical Research in England, 1850-1914*. Cambridge: Cambridge UP, 1985.

Ousby, Ian. *Bloodhounds of Heaven. The Detective in English Fiction from Godwin to Doyle*. Cambridge, Mass.: Harvard UP, 1976.

Page, Norman. *Wilkie Collins: The Critical Heritage*. London: Routledge & Kegan Paul, 1974.

Patey, Douglas. *Probability and Literary Form: Philosophic Theory and Literary Practice in the Augustan Age*. Cambridge: Cambridge UP, 1984.

Reed, John R. *Victorian Conventions*. Athens: Ohio UP, 1975.

Rosenkranz, Karl. *Georg Wilhelm Friedrich Hegels Leben*. Darmstadt: Wissenschaftliche Buchesgesellschaft, 1963.

Stephen, James Fitzjames. "Mr. Dickens as a Politician." *Saturday Review* 3 (1857): 8–9.

Trodd, Anthea. "The Policeman and the Lady: Significant Encounters in Mid-Victorian Fiction." *Victorian Studies* 27 (1984): 435–60.

Welsh, Alexander. "The Evidence of Things Not Seen: Justice Stephen and Bishop Butler." *Representations* no. 22 (1988): 60–88.

Watson, George. *The Study of Literature*. London: Penguin, 1969.

Whitty, Edward Michael. *Friends of Bohemia, or; Phases of London Life*. London: Smith, Elder, 1857.

Madgalen's Peril

Lewis Horne

1

In *No Name* (1862), Wilkie Collins chronicles the "progress" of Magdalen Vanstone in her pursuit of justice—and in doing so chronicles what the reader is intended to perceive as the moral decline of Magdalen herself. Robbed of name by the ill luck of her parents, denied recognition and inheritance by her father's brother, she sets out to regain the inheritance she feels belongs in fairness to her and her sister. A reader's reaction to the description of her efforts can be ambiguous. While Collins's narrator certainly wants us to feel that Magdalen chooses to carry out actions "evil" in nature, we can seldom help admiring her single-mindedness of plan and endeavor, her courage in confronting a world new to her, her persistence in daring the unknown. Yet however strong the reader's admiration, however weak the narrator's admonitions concerning moral choice, Magdalen is in peril. Single-mindedness can become mania, courage a ruthless goad, and persistence an obsession. Whether or not the reader takes seriously that peril in the light of the variety of episode and climax, the assembly of singular characters, the certainty that all will be resolved in the end is another matter. Collins's mode is that of melodrama. Extravagance of incident, hyperbole of gesture, sequences of action that assume polarized imperatives of good and evil—these are features a reader is likely to notice. Yet besides the trappings of melodrama, a reader might glimpse remnants, too, of the tragic.

If most agree that melodrama "represents a degenerate form of the tragic," a reader is not likely to be surprised by reminders of the tragic in a work by its nature so fully melodramatic.[1] A drawing of specific differences between the two modes need not concern us here, but the dangers in Magdalen's progress do. For the nature of the dangers places Magdalen within the more

281

loosely defined margins of tragedy. While Magdalen's physical perils throw us into the world of melodrama and are acted out in such encounters as those between Captain Wragge and Mrs. Lecount, the spiritual dangers place her in the lineage of such heroines as the title figure of Euripides' *Hecuba*, figures who in the fierceness of their endeavors come close to losing or, indeed, do lose their humanity. The way these two modes are interwoven in *No Name* is examined, here. This paper considers first the personal design that drives Magdalen throughout the novel, its origin in her life, and the similarity of Magdalen's situation to that of such a heroine in a recognized tragedy as Hecuba. Then this paper considers Collins's recounting of the way Magdalen carries out her design: it examines certain features that mingle qualities of the two modes and then those features that belong basically to melodrama. Such an examination should yield a fuller understanding of the nature of Magdalen's experience, clarifying in the process the mixed character of the reader's response to it.

2

At the beginning of the novel, Magdalen's is a nature sheltered and untried. Pampered and trusting, self-contradictory and pleasure-loving, she is unmethodical in habits, all of her actions based upon an "overflowing physical health which strengthened every muscle, braced every nerve, and set the warm young blood tingling through her veins, like the blood of a growing child" (17). A reader would think the eighteen-year-old girl scarcely equipped for the calamity she and her sister have to face. Her openness and trust could only make the betrayal of her lot more painful and more difficult to struggle against. But such openness in the face of betrayal is a feature of tragedy. Martha C. Nussbaum makes the point in *The Fragility of Goodness*: "Euripides, Aristotle, and Thucydides concur in the view that openness is an essential condition of good character and that a mistrustful suspiciousness, which can come to an agent through no moral failing, but only through experience of the bad things in life, can be a poison that corrodes all of the excellences, turning them to forms of vindictive defensiveness" (481). In Magdalen's case, the passage applies in both its first clause, pointing to Magdalen's guileless trust in existence at the beginning, and in its second, pointing to the threatened corrosion of her good qualities, her "excellences," that deepens with her mistrust as the novel develops.

Initially, to whatever extent Magdalen and Norah are betrayed, the betrayal is unwitting on the part of her parents who turn out to be, legally, something other than what she thought. In terms of their feelings, their conduct, their character, her parents are still the same people she has always known. But following their deaths, when Michael Vanstone rekindles the flames of his old hostility and acts in a manner neither compassionate nor uncle-like, the sense of betrayal Magdalen feels alters her view of human decency, something she had earlier had no reason to distrust. The structure of her world changes. Its values are altered. She is forced from the home she grew up in. Nussbaum writes of Hecuba: "[T]he person of noble character is, if anything, more open to this corrosion [of human excellence] than the base person, because it is the noble person, not the base, who has unsuspiciously staked a world on the faith and care of others" (417). In reference to Magdalen, a reader can question the aptness of the adjective "noble," but in other features the statement applies to Collins' heroine and her situation.

Once "the thunder-clouds of Affliction" burst (93), Magdalen's youthful qualities are quickly transformed. Collins has, in part, prepared the reader for the change. The narrator's choric comment on the young British girl's name is full of ironic portent: "Surely, the grand old Bible name—suggestive of a sad and sombre dignity; recalling, in its first association, mournful ideas of penitence and seclusion—had been here, as event had turned out, inappropriately bestowed? Surely, this self-contradictory girl had perversely accomplished one contradiction more, by developing into a character which was out of all harmony with her own Christian name!" (17). But the name harmonizes well, how well the reader begins to learn once news of Michael Vanstone's recalcitrance comes. "Something in her expression had altered, subtly and silently; something which made the familiar features suddenly look strange, even to her sister and Miss Garth; something, through all after years, never to be forgotten in connection with that day—and never to be described" (135). Mr. Pendril, the sympathetic family lawyer who has brought the news, notes that her courage begins from "the white hot," adding, "So much the worse for her, and for all belonging to her" (136). The plan Magdalen subsequently forms is less for revenge than for justice, though the deadly earnest with which she follows it through appears at times vengeful: all her aims "hung on her desparate purpose of recovering the lost inheritance, at any risk, from the man who had beggared and insulted his brother's children" (189).

Following the way Magdalen works out her plan, the reader traces the corrosion of those moral excellences that are hers. Collins lays out the "progress" in the novel's tidy structural arrangement. The work is divided into eight "Scenes," each set in a different place, each devoted to one chief activity. The scenes are separated by short sections, "Between the Scenes," in which the narration is continued mainly in the form of letters. In each of the central sections, the reader finds Magdalen in a different role or disguise. In "The First Scene," she is simply Magdalen Vanstone, the healthy eighteen-year-old girl with unquestioning trust in her destiny. In "The Second Scene," as she wanders about Skeldergate, York, hoping to see an acting agent, she becomes in effect "No Name," a fugitive, forced from her home, hiding from her sister, Norah, and Miss Garth, as she seeks means to further her plan. In "The Third Scene," at Vauxhall Walk, Lambeth, she disguises herself as Miss Garth and invades Noel Vanstone's house. So the novel continues. In "The Fourth Scene," she is Susan Bygrave and lives at Aldborough, intent on seducing Noel Vanstone into marriage. In "The Fifth Scene," she is Mrs. Noel Vanstone, living with her new husband in an isolated cottage in Dumfries. "The Sixth Scene" finds her in London following Noel's death, preparing to disguise herself as Louisa, her maid, in order to invade Admiral Bartram's home, St. Crux-in-the-Marsh. This act she carries out in "The Seventh Scene," hoping to find the Secret Trust at St. Crux-in-the-Marsh, betraying the Admiral's trust and kindness. "The Final Scene" takes place in London with Magdalen seriously ill, going under the name Gray, until she is rescued and prepared to become Mrs. Robert Kirke. Through noting the figure Magdalen becomes and the place in which she becomes it, the reader can trace her moral decline, witnessing it through what is, in a way, a series of transformations, akin to those metamorphoses of Greek deities, heroes, and heroines. In taking account of the division of the novel into units that Collins labels "Scenes" and "Between the Scenes," the reader also recognizes a simulation of the tendency in staged melodrama to move toward what Peter Brooks calls "a few thunderous and decisive scenes" (129).

In the novel, the line between the tragic and melodramatic is not easy to draw: scenes of tragic import are presented with the accoutrements of melodrama; devices associated with tragedy are used with the hyperbole and extravagance of melodrama. Even so, when a reader reads of the struggle in Magdalen of Good and Evil, notes situations of providential intervention, he can see in Magdalen's "progress"—scene by scene—the "risk of defilement" that was Hecuba's (Nussbaum 419). In one example, the risk is made apparent when Mrs. Lecount returns to Noel Vanstone at Balliol Cottage, Magdalen departed for the week, and discovers in the cupboard the laudanum Magdalen purchased. Mrs. Lecount leaps to the conclusion, fair enough in the circumstances, that Magdalen intended the poison for Noel. The reader knows that Magdalen purchased it for herself, tempted to suicide rather than marry Noel Vanstone. Now that the couple are husband and wife, a new will drawn up, Mrs. Lecount believes that Noel is the intended victim. Suicide or murder—both are perilous options. Whatever Magdalen's design, the public reading of the situation turns her into a potential murderer. Even the innocent Admiral Bartram believes the lurid accusation. So, too, his nephew George Bartram, now in love with Magdalen's older sister. Through her obsession, Magdalen comes to murder of the self—her degenerated health, the physical and spiritual toll of her activities, the debilitated state in which Captain Kirke found her. "Into the space of little more than a year," says the narrator, "she had crowded the wearing and wasting emotions of a life" (542). At the same time, murder—of someone other—is suspected. Public self, private self—both are defiled.

Though capable of being misread, Magdalen's debasement is nevertheless real. In recognizing her defilement, a reader might be reminded of Hecuba's debasement and the way it is finally marked. After she has blinded Polymestor and killed his sons, Hecuba explains to Agamemnon: "'Good words should get their goodness from our lives / and nowhere else; the evil we do should show, / a rottenness that festers in our speech / and what we say, incapable of being glozed / with a film of pretty words" (Euripides lines 1188–1192). Polymestor then foretells that when Hecuba dies, her tomb will be called *"Cynossema, the bitch's grave, a landmark / to sailors"*—an emblem of Hecuba's great defilement (Euripides lines 1271–1272).

Whatever the depth of her debasement, Magdalen's fate is nothing so severe, results in no emblem so strong to mark her. She left Combe-Raven with three items—banknotes; a lock of Frank's hair; "the extracts which she had copied from her father's will and her father's letter" (188). By the end of the novel, the banknotes are gone. She has thrown away Frank's lock. In her possession the longest are the extracts from the will and letter, one of the reminders that drives her to a near self-destructive and anonymous end, to a tomb not for a dog but for a woman without a name.

3

The way the treatment of Magdalen's progress mingles the tragic and the melodramatic probably lies behind some of the comments from early reviewers who read the novel more singlemindedly as melodrama. In the *Athenaeum*, for example, H. F. Chorley wrote that Magdalen's "persistence in her evil purposes can only be explained by admitting that there existed in the heroine's character hard and . . . coarse elements.'' He finds ''meanness'' and that same ''coarseness'' in her actions. Chorley's criticism suggests a view attuned to melodrama, expecting perhaps a heroine whose singleness of nature would belong more purely to the melodramatic mode. Mrs. Oliphant suggests something similar in her complaint in *Blackwood's Magazine* about the ending of the novel. There, she writes, Magdalen emerges ''at the cheap cost of a fever, as pure, as high-minded, and as spotless as the most dazzling white of heroines.[2] In one sense, such views are understandable. But if we consider some of the ways the two modes are combined, note how a few purer strands of the tragic are woven into the colorful cloth of the melodramatic, we find that meanness and coarseness have deeper echoes: Magdalen's nature is tarnished. ''Corroded''—Nussbaum's term—would be a better word. She is not, indeed, a tragic heroine. But echoes of the tragic sound in her nature and in her actions.

The narrator works hard to make us recognize the direction in which her activities are leading her. Again and again, he comments on the nature of the choice Magdalen makes, on the nature of her activities. Two examples will serve. When the two sisters learn their parents' secret and its consequences, the narrator comments on their reactions: ''Are there, infinitely varying with each individual, inbred forces of Good and Evil in all of us, deep down below the reach of mortal encouragement and mortal repression—hidden good and hidden Evil, both alike at the mercy of the liberating opportunity and the sufficient temptation?'' (127). In its generalized nature, the question resembles the responses of the chorus in a Greek tragedy. So, too, the following passage a few paragraphs later, which speculates on Miss Garth's thoughts:

> It might be, that under the [upper] surface [of their characters] so formed—a surface which there had been nothing, hitherto, in the happy, prosperous, uneventful lives of the sisters to disturb—forces of inborn and inbred disposition had remained concealed, which the shock of the first calamity in their lives had now thrown up into view. Was this so? . . . If the life of the elder sister was destined henceforth to be the ripening ground of the undeveloped Good that was in her—was the life of the younger doomed to be the battlefield of mortal conflict with the roused forces of Evil in herself? (127–28).

Such passages are given their choric nature through the references to Good and Evil in the abstract. But unlike the statements one is likely to encounter in choruses of Greek tragedy, the concepts of Good and Evil are applied simply, even though presented in the form of questions, and show little sense of the complex issues that adhere to the tragic. Paradoxically, they further derive their choric nature from the reader's very sense of their separation from the action of the novel. They are comments from an observer of events. But do they apply to Magdalen's situation? Only in part. For even though we can describe them as choric, the questions they ask assume a world divided into the camps of good and evil strongly inherent in melodrama, the same kind of world that early critics like H. F. Chorley and Mrs. Oliphant appear to anticipate.

This mixture is vividly demonstrated in "The Fourth Scene." The longest in the novel and skillfully plotted, this "Scene" centers on Magdalen's attempt to marry Noel Vanstone. Chapter I describes a choice to be made and the different ways both Captain Wragge and Magdalen go about deciding whether or not to follow the plan that Magdalen sketches out for the captain. The two ways illustrate the mode of fiction to which each belongs. True to the nature of a rogue, Captain Wragge reaches his decision easily, weighing out in a neat and orderly manner the advantages and disadvantages of Magdalen's proposition to him. Even weighing those, resentment at the niggardly way Noel Vanstone treated the captain's offer of information decides the man. For Captain Wragge, according to the narrator, "the motive of malice carried the day" (286). For Magdalen, the situation is more difficult. She has made her plan, has thought it through in such detail her intentions can be in little doubt. Yet her commitment is still to be finally made. Doing so causes her great anguish. Having, like Hecuba, "staked a world on the faith and care of others," Magdalen chooses to take a step that will defile her basic self. "The short way and the vile way lies before me," she says. "I take it, Captain Wragge, and marry him" (282).

Collins makes clear the difficulty of her choice, mainly by showing us what part of herself Magdalen surrenders in making her decision and how intense the moral seriousness involved. When she arrives in Aldborough where he has been waiting for her, Captain Wragge detects "a serious change," "a settled composure on her face" from when he last saw her. She is "interested in nothing" (273). She is, she says, "always weary now; weary at going to bed, weary at getting up" (275). Later, on the beach, she tells the captain, "I have lost all care for myself," ripping at the grass as she does so, a gesture reflective of her feelings, reflective as "she scatter[s] the grass to the winds" of the tattered old self she is getting rid of. But of still more than that. "I am nothing to myself," she continues; "I am no more interested in myself than I am in these handfuls of grass" (278). The way she throws the grass to the wind can be seen as reflective of the destiny—or chance or Providence—that has brought her to where she is. She is no more, she might say, than an agent of that destiny:

> "I suppose I have lost something. What is it? Heart? Conscience? I don't know. Do you? What nonsense I am talking! Who cares what I have lost? It has gone; and there's an end of it. I suppose my outside is the best side of me—and that's left, at any rate. I have not lost my good looks, have I? There! there! never mind answering; don't trouble yourself to pay me compliments. I have been admired enough today. . . . Have I any right to call myself a woman? Perhaps not; I am only a girl in my teens. Oh me, I feel as if I was forty!" (278–79).

In still other ways in the same scene, Collins demonstrates this casting off of the old self. As a part of the land, defenseless "against the encroachments of the sea" (272), Aldborough is an apt reflection of Magdalen's self. "The site of the old town . . . has almost entirely disappeared in the sea," the narrator writes. "The German Ocean has swallowed up streets, market-places, jetties, and public walks. . . " (272). The association of the sea, in this instance, with death or the destroyer gives added meaning to Magdalen's new name—Bygrave. Finally, at the moment of concluding choice, "she had taken the lock of Frank's hair . . . and [like the grass?] had cast it away from her to the sea and the night" (288). She does so out of sight of Captain Wragge, obscured by the darkness that has been gathering throughout her conversation with the captain, a darkness that elsewhere in the novel obscures observation at moments of moral choice or activity, and in this instance can only leave the pain of Magdalen's decision to the captain's—and to the reader's—imagination.

If the captain's decision is made quickly and neatly, Magdalen's has been surrounded with emblems and gestures indicative not only of emotional stress but of moral warning. Magdalen may have devised her plan before she reached Aldborough, but only during the conversation with Captain Wragge, only after she gets assurance of his assistance, can she commit herself to the endeavor. She does so out of reach of his eyes, out of reach of any light that reveals, does so in a darkness emblematic of a greater darkness, one without principle, to which she is surrendering. The drama of choice has the portent of tragedy, the colorings of its presentation the exclusivity of melodrama, a combination of opposites, ultimately unreconcilable. It attempts, like melo-drama, to tell all.[3] The mixture is a curious one.

It is further revealed in an illuminating passage describing the captain's rumination as he weighs Magdalen's offer. The passage helps define the natures of the two figures:

In the prospect *after* the marriage he dimly discerned, through the ominous darkness of the future, the lurking phantoms of Terror and Crime, and the black gulfs behind them of Ruin and Death. A man of boundless audacity and resource, within his own mean limits; beyond those limits the captain was as deferentially submissive to the majesty of the law as the most harmless man in existence; as cautious in looking after his own personal safety as the veriest coward that ever walked the earth. But one serious question now filled his mind. Could he, on the terms proposed to him, join the conspiracy against Noel Vanstone up to the point of the marriage, and then withdraw from it, without risk of involving himself in the consequences which his experience told him must certainly ensue?   (285–86)/

If the captain will always draw back, if in final analysis he will submit to the law, if he will operate upon the principles of the insider, however skillfully he can use and manipulate them, Magdalen will not. She braves "Terror and Crime." She comes close to "Ruin and Death." That daring, that moving on at all costs—to self and to others—is one of the features of the heroine of tragedy, one of the features that marks her difference from other human beings in the work. In this, Magdalen is alone among the figures of the novel.

With Captain Wragge, we are tipped into the world of melodrama. A figure more colorful and more vividly drawn than most, Captain Wragge belongs among those supernumeracy figures enlisted for or against the hero or heroine. The man is a rogue pure and simple, a reader might feel inclined to say, except that the captain is neither pure nor simple. Like the rogue figure or picaro, he is a vagabond by nature. Like the rogue, he lives "on his wits," of which he has a large supply (31): he is ready and quick of mind; he describes himself proudly as "a moral agriculturalist," a term describing his method of operation; he knows the ways of the world well. Yet the captain turns out to be a sensitive man, more so than a Becky Sharp or Barry Lyndon or other roguish figures of their like. The passage just quoted describes the limits to which the captain will go in his operations. Here, his concern is only for himself. But as the novel continues, as Magdalen moves closer and closer to the "phantoms of Terror and Crime,"bringing herself nearer to "the black gulfs behind . . . Ruin and Death," the captain begins to feel concern for Magdalen, a feeling not customary for him. By the end of the novel, when he returns with his wife to the barely conscious Magdalen, he has become almost a member of the community.[4]

But the captain's central role in the novel, and in "The Fourth Scene," in particular, is to wage a battle of wits and skill with Mrs. Lecount. The two share similar features. Both are clever and resourceful, the captain with more experience in the ways of the world, Mrs. Lecount with an ability for intuitive leaps of discernment. Both have a passion for neatness and order, for laying out plans with a logician's scrupulosity and care. Both have a weak person in their charge, a person over whom for whatever reason—Mrs. Wragge's simple-mindedness, Noel Vanstone's peevish overlordship—they can not finally have control. In the attempt to carry out Magdalen's plan to marry Noel Vanstone, though, the two lines are drawn up for what it is, in effect, a Game of skill.[5] The world in which they operate is a closed one with its own rules. The only people brought into it—Mr. Pendril, Miss Garth, Norah—are introduced as ploys of the Game. Noel and Magdalen are the pawns. Neither Captain Wragge nor Mrs. Lecount are enemies. To him, she is a "sharp practitioner in petticoats," something he has dealt with before (317). To her, he is an opponent because of his alliance with Magdalen. As they struggle to promote or hinder a marriage between Magdalen and Noel, both adhere to necessary laws or rules: Magdalen's identity and purpose must not be admitted to Mrs. Lecount, even though she knows who the girl is; Mrs. Lecount must prove that she knows who Magdalen is before anyone can be accused; the appearances of basic social manners must hold for a portion of the struggle. And so on. In none of this gamesmanship are we near anything like tragedy. The narrator is careful, even to the end, to maintain the neutrality of the two opponents, to keep them performing as players. At the point where Captain Wragge prepares the letter that will trick Mrs. Lecount into leaving Aldborough, the narrator deflects blame from the captain to Noel Vanstone. The captain can continue to exercise "the pleasure of playing" and is allowed to remain in the world "of mock passions, not real ones" (Auden 422). Because Noel takes responsibility for the duplicity of the maneuver, the captain remains, like a rogue, free of the tarnish of villiany. The narrator writes:

> Mean, selfish, and cowardly as he was, even Noel Vanstone might feel some compunction at practicing such a deception as was here suggested on a woman who stood toward him in the position of Mrs. Lecount. She had served him faithfully, however interested her motives might be—she had lived since he was a lad in the full possession of his father's confidence—she was living now under the protection of his own roof. Could he fail to remember this; and, remembering it, could he lend his aid without hesitation to the scheme which was now proposed?   (360)

He can—and does. Yet the Game is complicated in nature. For Captain Wragge, skill is at stake: "*The woman actually thinks she can take me in!!!*" he exclaims (318). But for Magdalen, nothing of what she is doing is a Game. Her interest provides the moral drive for the enterprise, an enterprise that takes her toward Terror, Crime, Ruin, Death.

and operates with the same ruthless indifference to motive as a typhoid germ''
(36). Melodrama asks for a choice between good and evil. The choice asked
for in tragedy is more likely to be between two ways of equal value, something
reflecting ''the same ruthless indifference to motive as a typhoid germ.''

In their own peculiar form, I believe, both conditions operate in *No Name*,
and help to account for the curious division in readers' reactions to the novel.
Both Norah and Magdalen inherit from the past the consequences of their
parents' guilt—as much as the descendants of the House of Atreus. Such a
comparison is extreme but illustrative. Both girls are stripped of name through
no fault of their own. Both are disinherited through no fault of their own.
Through no fault of their own, both are cast out of the home that has been
theirs. Nor can much blame be laid at the feet of their parents. Their misfortune is the result of bad luck, misfortune, chance, or—if Collins were writing
in an earlier time—destiny. Both lives have suffered pollution from family
indiscretion and family quarrels deriving from a past they knew nothing of.
Magdalen's determination to get back what she sees as hers is corrosive to
her nature—something Collins tries to demonstrate through her use of disguise, her alliance with Captain Wragge, her going on stage professionally,
her giving herself in marriage to a man as ill-favored as Noel Vanstone, her
intrusions on the privacy of others. These are activities unbefitting a daughter
of Michael and Norah Vanstone, the parents. They are carried out singlemindedly without regard for danger to herself—or, sometimes, to other people. She can be ruthless. Yet whenever the knowledge of the corrosive character of her activities is internalized, Magdalen's conscience begins to sting and
the sense of moral decline is emphasized. In the presentation are on the one
side the sober garments of tragedy, presented mainly through the consequences of external agency, and on the other the sometimes gaudy apparel of
melodrama, those things that reflect Magdalen's choice of the path of evil.
The features of tragedy that show in the corrosion of spirit are, for the reader,
generally more convincing than the features of melodrama, the side of the
narrative that speaks of sin, something that appears added on, mainly in
narrative commentary. A reader will acknowledge that Magdalen's character
is corroded but is less likely to agree to the accusation of guilt and sin.

The reader's view of Magdalen, then, is dual. So far as Magdalen can be
seen as moving through an experience of choice that will corrode her spirit,
the reader will acknowledge the threat involved in her choice, will recognize
the nature of her moral peril as he might recognize the peril to which Hecuba
submits herself—and so fear. But so far as the dramatization of that choice
draws on the paraphernalia and mannerisms of melodrama, so far as the

experience is seen as an adventure (Magdalen and Captain Wragge against Noel Vanstone and Mrs. Lecount, for example), the reader will tend to see an obsessed will as evidence of determination, self-destructive behavior as feminine pluck—and so admire. From the mingling of the two—fear and admiration—is some of the novel's complexity and power for the reader drawn.

NOTES

1. Leo B. Levy calls melodrama "mock tragedy" (*Versions of Melodrama: A Study of the Fiction and Drama of Henry James, 1865–1897* [Berkeley: U of California P, 1957] 2). Robert B. Hellman spells out differences between the two genres in *Tragedy and Melodrama: Versions of Experience* (Seattle: U of Washington P, 1968). Chapter Three, "The Structure of Melodrama," I have found particularly useful. So, too, Peter Brooks' *The Melodramatic Imagination: Balzac, Henry James, Melodrama, and the Mode of Excess* (New Haven: Yale UP, 1976). "[A + cb degenerate form of the tragic" is Brooks' phrase and appears in "The Melodramatic Imagination," *Partisan Review* 39 (1972): 206. I could not find the phrase in the section of his book developed from the article.

2. These reviews are reprinted in Norman Page ed., *Wilkie Collins: The Critical Heritage* (London: Routledge, 1974) 133, 143.
   A reader finds little treatment of *No Name* among recent critics. Robert Ashley does not mention the novel in either of his surveys of Collins criticism (Lionel Stevenson, ed., *Victorian Fiction: A Guide to Research* [Cambridge: Harvard UP, 1964], pp. 277–84; George H. Ford, *Victorian Fiction: A Second Guide to Research* [New York: MLA, 1978] 223–29). One of the few treatments appears in G. Robert Stange's review of the novel on the occasion of its reprinting by Dover (*Nineteenth-Century Fiction* 34 [June 1979]: 96–100). Stange suggests that the way Collins calls attention to his narrative method adumbrates the self-conscious narration of modernism: "[t]o find the key to Collins's moral vision we must look to his principal interest—complication of narrative" (99). In his discussion in *Wilkie Collins* (New York: Twayne, 1970), William H. Marshall takes a different approach, writing of the way Collins "assume[s] his role as social critic" (66) and exploring some of the larger implications of "the myth of Magdalen's moral journey" (67).

3. See Brooks, "Registers of the Sign," *The Melodramatic Imagination*, 44-49. In considering this scene, we might note, too, part of an earlier comment by Brooks: "Melodrama is similar to tragedy in asking us to endure the extremes of pain and anguish. It differs in constantly reaching toward the 'too much' . . . " (35).

4. For views concerning the rogue figure, I have relied on Robert B. Heilman, "Variations on Picaresque (*Felix Krull*)," *The Sewanee Review* 66 (1957): 547–77; reprinted in Henry Hatfield, ed., *Thomas Mann: A Collection of Critical Essays* (Englewood Cliffs, N. J.: Prentice, 1964) 133–54.

5. For comments on features of the Game, see W. H. Auden, *The Dyer's Hand and Other Essays* (New York: Vintage, 1968) 422.

WORKS CITED

Auden, W.H. *The Dyer's Hand*. New York: Vintage, 1968.

Brooks, Peter. *The Melodramatic Imagination: Balzac, Henry James, Melodrama, and the Mode of Excess*. New Haven: Yale UP, 1976.

Collins, Wilkie. *No Name*. 1873. New York: Dover, 1978.

Dodds, E. R. *The Greeks and the Irrational* (Berkeley: U of California P, 1958. Vol. III of *Euripides* in *The Complete Greek Tragedies*. Ed. David Grene and Richmond Lattimore.

Nussbaum, Martha C. *The Fragility of Goodness: Luck and Ethics in Greek Tragedy and Philosophy*. Cambridge: Cambridge UP, 1986.

Page, Norman. *Wilkie Collins: The Critical Heritage*. London: Routledge, 1974.

"Invite No Dangerous Publicity": Some Independent Women and Their Effect on Wilkie Collins's Life and Writing

Catherine Peters

My title comes from *The Woman in White*. Count Fosco writes to Marian Halcombe after she has rescued Laura from the asylum, warning her to go no further in trying to re-establish her sister's rights. "Dear and admirable woman! invite no dangerous publicity. Resignation is sublime—adopt it. The modest repose of home is eternally fresh—enjoy it. The Storms of life pass harmless over the valley of Seclusion—dwell, dear lady, in the valley." (412).

Marian takes no notice of Fosco's threats. But she cannot conclude Laura's rehabilitation without the help of a man. "[T]he Hand of God was pointing their way back to them," as Hartright puts it. And where Fosco fails, Hartright succeeds in suppressing Marian's independence. At the end of the novel she has dwindled into an aunt.

The dangers that face women who invite publicity is a central theme of Wilkie Collins's fiction. The real lives of many women were lived in secret, something he knew not only from the police reports and the gutter press—the accusation of his critics—but from the experiences of many of the women close to him. It is, therefore, worth examining some of those lives, and their relationship to the portrayal of women in his work.

The obvious way for a woman to achieve covert self-expression, inviting publicity while remaining hidden, was by becoming an actress: openly, on the stage, or secretly, adopting a false persona in ordinary life. Magdalen Vanstone uses her talent for impersonation legitimately, to entertain, and illegitimately, to deceive. Lydia Gwilt uses hers only for her own ends.

Wilkie Collins loved the theater, and had many actress friends. The aura of unrespectability still hung around the profession; a hint of scandal was almost expected. Other women hid the reality of their lives more carefully, aided, sometimes forced into secrecy by the men close to them.

In his own life, Collins seems to have been most comfortable with women who were intelligent, courageous, and capable of independent action, but ultimately needed the support of a man. This preference is sometimes reflected in his fiction, which often seems to betray contrary impulses. Strong, independent women are presented as capable of controlling their own lives, and influencing the lives of others, in ways that are sometimes reprehensible, sometimes wholly admirable; but this self-assertion is often followed by a retreat. Marian Halcombe is one example: Magdalen Vanstone in *No Name* is another. Ill and destitute, she is rescued at the last moment from the hospital or the workhouse by the aptly-named Captain Kirke, and becomes his wife. "The one dear object of all my life to come, is to live worthy of you!" she tells him after she has confessed her past and been forgiven (548). In *The Law and the Lady* Valeria Macallan, one of the earliest women detectives in English fiction, asserts herself magnificently, but only in order to rehabilitate her husband, so that she can again become a wife, though the reader is left doubting whether she will be a happy one. Examples could be multiplied from Wilkie Collins's works: the willing acceptance of renewed blindness by Lucilla, in *Poor Miss Finch*, is perhaps symbolic of such shifts. Are they an artistic loss of nerve, or a measured assessment of the true options available to women?

Collins knew many women who coped successfully with the world of work and lived unconventional and independent lives without retreating into dependence. His own family background provided an obvious example of a woman who made her way in a man's world. His aunt Margaret Carpenter became a successful portrait-painter without being either the daughter or sister of a male artist. Wilkie's friend Henrietta Ward was more typical in being the granddaughter, great-niece, daughter, and wife of painters. The advantages and disadvantages were finely balanced: she was always known as "Mrs. E. M. Ward" and dismissed as a talented follower of her husband. It is typical of the distortion of women's biography that some accounts of Margaret Carpenter insisted that she was the daughter of Andrew Geddes R.A., actually her cousin. While still very young, Margaret Geddes won three awards from the Society of Arts. Unusual for an unmarried woman of the period, she left home and lived on her own in London from the age of twenty-one, making her living as a painter. In 1817 she married; but her husband William Carpenter was hopeless at making a living for his wife and family. According to his obituarist in the *Gentleman's Magazine*, until he was made keeper of Prints and Drawings at the British Museum in 1845, his wife was the principal support of a rapidly increasing family; "she . . . would certainly have been a Royal Academician but for her sex; while many of the best names in the Academy were in favor of altering the law in her favor" (410). Between 1818 and 1866 she exhibited 147 paintings at the Royal Academy, 50 at the British Institution, and 19 at the Society of British Artists. There are portraits by her in the National Portrait Gallery in London, and six of her paintings are in the Sheepshanks collection of British artists in the Victoria and Albert museum. Her twin sons William and Percy and her daughter Henrietta also became painters. Margaret Carpenter was an outstanding portraitist and an exceptional woman; yet her biography has yet to be written. She rates only half a sentence in Wilkie's biography of his father, and her life does not provide a direct model for any of his female characters. Though he used the secret marriage of Henrietta and Ned Ward twice in his fiction, Wilkie did not grant Henrietta's successful artistic career to any of his characters.

Perhaps Wilkie found such women intimidating. He was more intrigued by the hidden struggles of his dearly loved mother, Margaret's elder sister Harriet. She too had known what it was to be dependent on her own resources, and without the advantage of her sister's talent. But her true history was suppressed by her husband and her son.

In the summer of 1855 Wilkie Collins spent over a month with Dickens and his family at Folkestone. He and Dickens were hard at work planning the Christmas number of *Household Words*, but Wilkie found time to look at a manuscript entrusted to him by an unpublished author, who wanted his advice on making her book publishable. Wilkie had learned from Dickens to be helpful and patient with inexperienced authors. This time there was an extra incentive: the author was his mother. On 2 September 1855 he wrote to her explaining how he was getting on:

I began to work again on your MS three weeks ago. After I had done fifty pages, leaving out many things, and transferring others, but keeping as close as I could to the simplicity of your narrative, I began to have my doubts whether it would not be necessary (with the public) to make a story to hang your characters and incidents on. I had told Dickens, in confidence, the history of the manuscript—and I now read to him what I had done. He thought it a good notion and well worth going on with, but felt as I did that without more story it would not do with the public. Strangers could not know that the thing was real—and novel readers seeing my name on the title page would expect a story.

So I am going to throw a little dramatic interest into what I have done—keeping the thing still simple, of course, and using all the best of your materials. As soon as I have made the alterations and have started again, I will let you know how I proceed.[1]

We may wonder whether it was her suggestion that the book should appear under his name, in the guise of fiction; another example of the suppression of a woman's identity that was taken for granted by women themselves. No more is ever heard of Harriet Collins's manuscript in Wilkie's correspondence. It was never published. It has always been assumed that the manuscript had disappeared. But it has not.

It consists of 158 pages, written on one side of the paper, in Harriet Collin's hand.[2] There are alterations in Wilkie Collins's writing, using pencil, or Dickens' blue ink, rather than the black ink he always preferred when he was at home. For the first sixty-eight pages these consist of cuts marked on the manuscript and brief suggestions for rearrangement of material and for chapter breaks, but there is no substantial rewriting. Thereafter there are suggestions for chapter breaks only. These editorial emendations are nothing like as numerous or as far-reaching as Wilkie's letter to his mother would suggest. Perhaps he made more extensive alterations on separate sheets. If so, they have not yet come to light.

Harriet Collins's manuscript is untitled and unsigned, but headed ''April 25th 1853,'' six years after the death of William Collins. It is a lively and amusing, if disorganized, account, which throws considerable light on the characters of her parents and siblings, and the personalities of Harriet herself and her future husband. It provides hundreds of fascinating details about the freedom of her country childhood, her experience of the provincial society of Salisbury, and her courtship by the rising young painter William Collins. But it also reveals that the respectable wife of the ultra-respectable R. A. intended, in her youth, to earn her living on the stage. Thwarted in this, she did in fact support herself and, in part, her improvident parents, by going out to work, first as a teacher in a London girls' school, and then as a governess. She was a working woman for eight years, from 1814 until her marriage in 1822. If her son knew these facts when he was writing the life of his father he did not think to mention them, and we can be sure, I think, that William Collins would not have wished him to. Harriet wrote that, when she first met him, ''I had gathered as I thought from his talk, that a degree of pride . . . was mixed with his opinions on the pursuits and callings of women. I fancied he did not think it fit they should work for their bread in any way'' (110). An artistic vocation such as that of her sister Margaret was a different matter. Harriet herself later took the conventional point of view on married women working when she scolded Henrietta Ward for not giving up art and devoting herself to her children. Whether Harriet would have felt the same if she had achieved her ambition to go on the stage, we cannot know. One thing seems certain, as an actress she would never have become the wife of William Collins, and the mother of Wilkie.

The statements in her manuscript that can be checked against known facts either tally, or the reasons for altering them are clear. Wilkie's comments that "strangers could not know that the thing was real" and that the account needed more story, strongly suggest that her manuscript may be relied upon, though names and some minor details are altered. The essential background facts that emerge are that the Geddes family, always on the brink of poverty, was, by about 1810, left with an income of only £50 a year. Harriet, the eldest daughter, was twenty, and there were five younger children, four girls and a boy. Her sister Margaret's precocious talents had for some years subsidized the family finances, and Harriet was already aware that she must either land a husband, or earn her living. Her flirtations with officers in Salisbury had failed to produce an eligible suitor, and her immediate response was that she would realize her longing to go on the stage, making her *debut* in *She Stoops to Conquer*. She was quite unfitted for the standard alternative, becoming a governess. "I had never learnt music, had no taste for drawing, knew little of history, Grammar, arithmetic or Geography . . . now I knew I could act, and I would go on the stage, if I had money to take me to Bath I would go there and beg the manager of the Theatre to give me a trial" (56).

At this point the story begins to sound familiar. Wilkie Collins obviously drew on his mother's manuscript when he came to write *No Name* in 1862. In that novel Magdalen Vanstone does as Harriet Geddes would have liked, taking the glamorous but wicked theatrical path. Her sister Norah becomes a well-behaved governess, Harriet's actual destiny. The character of Magdalen as a young girl is modelled on Harriet's description of herself. Moreover Andrew Vanstone's early life in Canada was suggested by the life of Alexander Geddes, Harriet's father. Alexander Geddes served as an Ensign and then Lieutenant in the Thirty-first Regiment of Foot, stationed in Quebec, for eleven years. The regiment returned home in 1789.[3] Lieutenant Geddes, possessing neither the fortune Wilkie Collins gives Andrew Vanstone, nor the sensational disadvantage which sets the plot of *No Name* going, of having contracted a secret marriage in Canada, was free to marry Harriet Easton of Salisbury, where his regiment was then quartered.[4] In 1791 Alexander Geddes left the army,[5] as Andrew Vanstone does. From his daughter's account of her parents' marriage, there must have been times when the Captain wished he had not been free to marry. The relationship of the retired soldier Major Milroy and his invalid wife in *Armadale*, in "the typical cottage of the drawing master's early lessons," relates, to some extent, to the marriage of Captain and Mrs. Geddes at Shute End House, Alderbury, as described by their daughter.

Harriet Geddes was encouraged by her fantasizing mother in her theatrical ambitions, and got as far as an invitation from the manager of the Theatre Royal, Bath, for her to appear in the following season. "Between my delight in reading novels and my extreme relish for the drama as displayed at the Theatre Royal D. [Salisbury] I was in a fair way to be made anything but an estimable member of society" (18). But her father, with more knowledge of the world, was horrified, as was an Evangelical clergyman who took her in hand, converted her, and put her through a course of instruction to fit her to become a governess. When she was considered fit to hold down a job, she was despatched to London to join her sister Margaret, whose training and expenses in the capital were being funded for a year by the generosity of Lord and Lady Radnor, her first patrons. Margaret was lodging in the house of a dressmaker in Mortimer Street, and Harriet went to be a teacher in a nearby school run by a Frenchwoman, wearing dowdy caps to make herself look older and plainer than she really was. From the mention of certain external events, her arrival can be dated to January 1814.

It was a hard initiation. She had to share a room with four of the pupils, and did not even have a bed to herself. Her salary was twenty pounds a year, of which she only received the first quarter. The school was cold, dirty, and disorganized. Harriet was in no position to complain: indeed she thought it fortunate that Madame, being a Frenchwoman, was not fully aware of her new teacher's shortcomings. Wilkie Collins's account of Sydney Westerfield's sufferings as a pupil-teacher in the school of her aunt Miss Wigger, in his late novel *The Evil Genius*, sensationalizes Harriet's account of this time. But it was at this low ebb in Harriet's fortunes, that she and her sister Margaret attended a ball given in London on 22 April 1814, by a group of young artists. They were escorted by two brothers, William and Francis Collins. The brothers are first named "Chester" in Harriet's manuscript, which is then altered to "Denham" throughout.

At her first meeting with her future husband, Harriet thought him melancholy, "apparently in a sort of reverie, his eyes cast down", (82), but she soon discovered how misleading an impression this was. Her account of him as a young man of twenty-five emphasizes his "happy flow of spirits," his "sallies of fun and wit" (87). He emerges from her story as a more lively young man than the respectful portrait of him in his son's *Life* often suggests. He was the prime mover in arranging a party in the hayfields at Hendon; he took her to see the fireworks in Hyde Park which celebrated the visit of the Emperor of Russia and the King of Prussia; he gave a hilarious supper-party at his mother's house where even the maid was so overcome with laughter that she threw her apron over her head. He was also a practical joker in the rather boisterous fashion of the times. Harriet was entranced by this witty, intelligent, and creative young man, and he seemed to single her out for attention. But neither had any money to marry on; marriage was not even mentioned at this time.

When Harriet had been a schoolteacher for about a year, her employer became bankrupt. Harriet had to find another job in a hurry. She became a governess in a merchant's family in a solidly-built house in Wandsworth. Here she was well-treated and better paid; but she was terrified by the intellectual demands of the highly-educated mother. The ten-year-old son was wilful and spoiled, and the six-year-old girl reluctant to learn anything at all. She gradually won them over; but her week's holiday at Easter 1816 came as a great relief. William Collins came to call on her sister, and stayed to sketch the back of Harriet's head and neck, to use in a painting he was engaged on: the first time she acted as his model. The following Sunday she dined at his house again, and he took her—this sounds more like the William Collins of later years—to hear a famous preacher. Harriet claims to have been "much edified by the sermon."

Harriet was not entirely surprised when she got the sack from her job at Midsummer 1816, ostensibly because she was unable to teach music. By then she had made a good relationship with the three children, and her account of the eldest daughter's distress, "my little Margaret when she heard I was going to leave went into quite an agony of grief," is drawn on and elaborated by Wilkie Collins in *The Evil Genius*, in his description of Kitty's distress at losing her governess Sydney.

> She looked at her father and mother. "Is she going away?" They were afraid to answer her. With all her little strength, she clasped her beloved friend and playfellow round the waist. "My own dear, you're not going to leave me!" The dumb misery in Sydney's face struck Linley with horror. He placed Kitty in her mother's arms. The child's piteous cry, "Oh don't let her go! don't let her go!" followed the governess as she suffered her martyrdom, and went out.
> (283–84)

Harriet was very reluctant to take her next situation, an engagement for two years as a "finishing governess" to a girl of fourteen in Scotland. The family was rich and aristocratic; the salary eighty pounds a year. But Edinburgh was six days' journey by coach from London, and to be so far away from her family, and, more importantly, from any opportunity of continuing her growing friendship with William Collins, was distressing. "What had I done? agreed to go to a new country, with perfect strangers, to teach I scarcely knew what, to a young lady who seemed to be anything but desirable as a pupil, and then as a winding up I should never again most likely see Mr. Denham before I returned he would very probably be married and why not? I could not answer that question satisfactorily" (103). She had no alternative.

Harriet goes into considerable detail about the family with whom she spent the next two years. The husband and wife were separated, the handsome, lively husband living in London, and his dour, Presbyterian wife, plain of feature, mean with the household comforts and food, and with a strong Scots accent, living partly in Edinburgh and partly in a country house in Lothian. Certain elements of this situation, and the Scottish setting, appear in *The Evil Genius*, where it is the governess who is the cause of the separation between her employers. Harriet, though she found the father charming when she met him in London, was more discreet. Her pupil was an awkward, plain child, bullied and half-starved by her mother. Harriet's task was to make this ugly duckling socially presentable and marriageable: schoolroom lessons were a very secondary consideration. Harriet held her own and defended her pupil courageously and spiritedly, gradually winning her confidence and coping with loneliness and the depressing climate of the Lowlands. There was some relief in visits to a large and jolly family, friends of her father's, in Edinburgh, whom she calls "Scott". These may be the Smiths, whom she and William Collins visited in 1822, and whom William took Wilkie to see when they were in Edinburgh twenty years later.

Harriet found herself, to her surprise, quite sorry to leave Scotland when her two-year contract was completed in July 1818. She had, like a true Victorian heroine, discovered strengths of character she did not know she possessed. She returned to Scotland only once, to marry William Collins in 1822.

Harriet first went to nurse her sister Margaret, now married to William Carpenter, through her first confinement. Harriet herself, at twenty-eight almost on the shelf by the standards of the time, seemed as far from marriage as ever, though she was delighted to discover that William Collins was still single when they met by accident in the street. But she had to take another job, her last, as it turned out. This had every advantage but one: the family's country house was near Salisbury, and Harriet was reluctant to appear as an employee in the society where she had grown up. Otherwise she thoroughly enjoyed herself. The salary was good; the family charming; she was treated more as an extra daughter than a governess, and she felt herself to be of real use in bringing some order and routine into a chaotic household. The description of Miss Garth's position in the Vanstone family matches Harriet's with the "Archers" as she calls them. "This was evidently not one of the forlorn, persecuted, pitiably dependent order of governesses. Here was a woman who lived on ascertained and honourable terms with her employers—a woman who looked capable of sending any parents in England to the right-about, if they failed to rate her at her proper value" (*No Name* 3).

Harriet visited home, very reluctantly, for the first time in four years. Her mother was querulous, her father depressed, the house bare of comforts. Her sister Kate had, she reports, "made a very rash marriage rather than go out as a Governess" (137). She gave her parents all the money she could spare, but the contrast between her life of comfort and their poverty was hard for both sides. It was a relief when her employers moved to London in 1821. William Collins at last declared his love, and in spite of his mother's opposition to his marrying a penniless young woman, he and Harriet finally became man and wife in Edinburgh in September 1822. Harriet's life as an independent wage-earner was over.

Wilkie Collins made very specific use of his mother's experiences in *No Name*, and there are other connections between Harriet's manuscript and that novel, not of relevance here. Perhaps it was the knowledge that his mother had made her way in the world as a young woman, alone and unprotected, that first aroused his interest in such situations. Harriet's courage in accepting work she had not chosen, and making something of it, shows that Wilkie had sound reasons for his admiration of his mother. Certainly Harriet's experiences reflect the position of governesses in Wilkie Collins's fiction. They are habitually well-treated and respected, by their employers, even when, as in *Armadale*, this confidence is abused.

Frances Dickinson, later Elliot, a friend of Wilkie Collins throughout most of his adult life, had very different experiences from Harriet Collins, though there are some correspondences in character and interests between the two. Frances Dickinson, four years older than Wilkie, was of a higher social class than the Collinses: an heiress from an old Somersetshire family with literary leanings. Her private life—as far as it can now be retrieved from oblivion—was as sensational as that of any Collins heroine, and must have intrigued the creator of Magdalen Vanstone, Lydia Gwilt, and Ann Sylvester. He dedicated *Poor Miss Finch* to her in 1872.

As a child Frances was allowed to run free on the family's Berkshire estate. Like Harriet Collins, she was a tomboy. "I had ridden wild horses, driven tandem with dogs, mounted ladders, bird's nested in lofty trees, waded in rivers, until I conceived myself as good as a boy," she writes of her first seventeen years.[6] But this freedom ended abruptly when she was taken to London for her first season, in 1838. If the pressures of being a correct and corseted young lady became unbearable, she would retreat to the attics of the London house to romp with her maid: "we fought and struggled with each other like schoolboys . . . spreading the feather-beds on the floor, we made believe it was a haycock, and rolled in them until . . . we were so exhausted . . . that neither of us could move, but lay there laughing at each other like a couple of happy fools. . . ."[7]

Frances Dickinson was no beauty, but she was intelligent and rich. She had numerous suitors, but she rushed into marriage with a Scotsman, John-Edward Geils, when she was only eighteen. They had four daughters, but the marriage was not happy. They parted in 1845, and Frances Dickinson returned to England and resumed her maiden name. According to her published accounts, her husband refused to allow her to keep or even to see her children. She started divorce proceedings in 1849, which was possible under Scottish law, though there was no divorce law in England until 1857. She alleged her husband's adultery with two of the household servants, and physical and verbal violence towards her. She was finally granted a divorce in 1855.[8]

Frances Dickinson spent a considerable amount of time in Italy, partly to escape from the unpleasant publicity and social stigma that attached to a woman, however innocent, first separated and then divorced from her husband. She writes bitterly of the defection of a close woman friend who insulted and finally forsook her.[9] Wilkie may have known her as early as 1849, when he was arranging amateur theatricals at his mother's house in Blandford Square, for she was a talented amateur actress. Both Frances Dickinson and Wilkie Collins had books published by Richard Bentley in 1851, and from 1852 to 1854 they were both contributors to *Bentley's Miscellany*, more than once appearing in the same monthly number. Frances Dickinson was in Florence in November 1853, when Wilkie Collins spent a few days in that city with Dickens and Augustus Egg, and Collins may have called on her there. She spent the winter and spring of 1853–54 in Italy.

She was a prolific writer, very popular in her day, though now forgotten. In addition to her contributions to *Bentley's Miscellany*, she wrote regularly for the *New Monthly Magazine*, under the pen-name "Florentia," from 1853 to 1857. Eight articles entitled "Diary of a First Winter in Rome" appeared in the *New Monthly Magazine* from May 1854 to October 1855. Seven more articles about Rome by "Florentia," all concerned with artists, appeared in the *Art Journal* in the same period, placed for her by Wilkie Collins. They have been claimed as being by Wilkie Collins himself, on the evidence of two letters he wrote about them,[10] but Frances Dickinson later reprinted two of them—with the pieces from the *New Monthly Magazine*—in a book she published in 1871,[11] and used substantial amounts of the material from the others in another book published in 1894.[12] Dickens published at least one article by her in *All the Year Round*, hitherto unattributed.[13] She also published four novels, some collections of historical sketches, and a number of travel books, all very successful on both sides of the Atlantic. When she republished "The Artists' Festa," one of the *Art Journal* pieces, it was singled out by a reviewer for praise as being "glorious for picturesque fun and frolic."[14]

Her journalism is gossipy, personal, and ephemeral. One article from a series entitled "The Baths of Lucca" (127) prompted a furious reply in the form of an anonymous pamphlet that identifies "Florentia" as an English lady who held up "even personal defects to public ridicule" and repaid the hospitality of her banker "by attempting to caricature almost every guest of his whom she names."[15] Most of her 1854 articles for *Bentley's*, the *New Monthly Magazine*, outline her unhappy married life in Scotland, her separation from her children, "by the malice of their father" and her secret meetings with them in Cornwall. Her descriptions of places in Cornwall and an account of going down a Cornish mine are strongly reminiscent of Wilkie Collins's *Rambles Beyond Railways*, though far less amusing and graphic. She also refers to "delightful converse" in London with "that friend whose support and protection alone enabled me to face the adversities that oppressed me—one whose fine literary taste and great acquirements had, by precept and example, taught me to draw consolation from . . . books; who encouraged and cheered me in the path of study, dissipating ennui and varying the course of weary hours by his kind visits and sound advice" ("Polperro" 56). It is tempting to speculate that this literary lover might have been Wilkie Collins. Frances Dickinson's subsequent career suggests that there would have been a wide field of admirers to choose from: she led, by what are generally though misleadingly considered Victorian standards, a sexually adventurous life, and seems to have gone out of her way to invite dangerous publicity.

In 1857, when Janet Wills, who originally played the part of the Scotch nurse in *The Frozen Deep*, was unable to continue because of lameness, Dickens wrote to Wilkie on 16 June, "You once said you knew a lady who could and would have done it. Is that lady producible?" (*Letters* II: 857).

The lady was Frances Dickinson, and she took over the part of "Esther" for all the performances at The Gallery of Illustration, being billed in the programme as "Mrs. Francis".[16] She was obviously an excellent actress, for when the public performances in the vast Manchester Free Trade Hall in August were in prospect, Dickens wrote to Wilkie that though his daughters' parts would have to be taken by professional actresses, "I have written to our friend Mrs. Dickinson to say that I don't fear her, if she likes to play with them" (*Letters* II: 866). Frances Dickinson evidently didn't choose to appear with professional actresses: the part of Esther was taken by Mrs. Ternan in the touring performances of *The Frozen Deep*.

Frances Dickinson seems to have had a gift for intimacy with men. Dickens' mode of addressing her, once they had got to know each other well, "My dear F. . . . Ever yours affectionately," was not one he habitually used to women outside his family. His frank letters to her provide a tantalizingly incomplete glimpse into her tangled private life, as well as increasing our knowledge of his. Frances Dickinson was one of the few people who dared to broach the subject of Dickens' relationship with Ellen Ternan to him—she was a friend of Ellen's sister Frances, who married Thomas Trollope. Dickens warned her against trusting Mrs. Trollope. Though she often exasperated him, Dickens always wrote with warmth and affection. He wrote to her about Wilkie's "flesh-coloured woman" (Caroline Graves), and commented on Frances's own unsatisfactory situation with an elderly lover:

> . . . . are you quite sure that what you are disposed to resent as indifference, is not the stealing apathy of advanced age? . . . I am inclined to think, on this ground alone, that you are better apart. . . . As to yourself I might be very moral in my admonitions and didactic remarks; but you are a woman and I am a man, and we should both know better, even if I were. There is no doubt that your position is a trying one. . . . But would it not be more trying still, if you were more pursued, sought out, and hovered about? (*Letters* III: 173)

On 9 August 1863 Dickens wrote to Wilkie warning him to be discreet about her past:

> She is extremely anxious you should know that profound confidence as to that adventure with the Doctor has become more than ever necessary, by reason of her having established the fact that the marriage (as no doubt he very well knew at the time) is no marriage and is utterly void. My own impression is that she contemplates a real marriage with somebody else, at no distant time.
> (*Letters* III: 359)

This "adventure with the Doctor" is clearly not her first marriage to Mr.

Geils, but some subsequent entanglement, probably made dubious by the conflict of Scots and English marriage law. Dickens' impression "that she contemplates a real marriage with somebody else" was correct. Three months later the irrepressible Frances Dickinson, now forty-three years old, married the Very Reverend Gilbert Elliot, Dean of Bristol, a widower of sixty-three. This respectable match turned out as disastrously as her earlier escapades, and Dickens was called in to mediate between the Dean and his lady, a task he eventually gave up in despair. The Dean was reluctant to relinquish his wife's fortune, and she resorted to blackmail, threatening to establish the validity of the earlier secret marriage, if he would not let her and her money go. Such a scandal would have ruined the Dean; eventually they reached some financial settlement and went their separate ways. Mrs. Elliot returned to live in Italy, where she died in 1898.

The Evil Genius, Wilkie Collins's picture of unhappy marriage and divorce, largely set in Scotland, reflects Frances Dickinson's experiences in her first marriage. The wife in that novel is threatened with separation from her child, and goes abroad with her. Until the divorce is granted, she—like Frances Dickinson—has no right of custody. She resumes her maiden name, as Frances Dickinson did. The divorce is granted in Scotland. Mother and child are shunned by polite society, as Frances Dickinson claims she was. Some of these experiences would have been common to the few women who successfully sued for divorce, but it seems plausible that Wilkie Collins's interest in their dilemmas was first aroused by the sufferings of his friend. Frances Dickinson's marriage tangles, and the conflict between Scottish and English law, are also reflected in *Man and Wife*, published in 1870, though the immediate impulse for that book was the 1868 report on the Royal Commission on the Marriage Laws. In more general terms, Frances Dickinson is an example, known to Wilkie from early in his adult life, of the kind of woman, independent, rash, sexually active and often leading a double life, who repeatedly figures in his novels. The bigamous shadow that first threatened to prevent her respectable marriage to the Dean, and then became a weapon against him, is reminiscent of the plots of Lydia Gwilt in *Armadale*, though Mrs. Elliot and the Dean avoided the sensational publicity of the Yelverton bigamy case, to which Wilkie Collins referred in *Man and Wife*.

Caroline Graves, Wilkie Collins's mistress and companion of many years, has always been seen as a helpless victim, largely because of the story connecting her with *The Woman in White*, which is quoted in every book on Wilkie Collins. In his life of his father, John Everett Millais's son recounted

how Wilkie and Charles Collins and their friend Millais encountered a distraught young woman in the middle of the night, and how Wilkie rushed after
her and rescued her from the clutches of a sadistic brute in a St. John's Wood
villa (278–79). This story—in a book that also inaccurately dates Wilkie
Collins's death to 1870—has always seemed doubtful. It was only published
after all the participants and witnesses, Wilkie and Charles Collins, Millais,
and Caroline herself, were dead. There is also an unexplained gap of four
years in the chronology. Millias moved from Gower Street in 1854; Wilkie
and Caroline did not live together until 1858. Yet, having rescued her he
could hardly abandon her again, without resources or a place to live. But
there is no mystery about his movements in the intervening years, nor about
his bank statements, as William Clarke has shown (228). If the story is untrue,
or, perhaps more likely, a sensationalizing of a more humdrum episode of
flight and rescue, where was Caroline Graves between the death of her husband in 1852 and her appearance in Wilkie Collins's life in 1858, and what
was she doing?

She was keeping a shop. When Caroline (or as she then was, Elizabeth)
Graves surfaces after the death of her husband, it is not as the helpless victim
of a poker-wielding villain, but at 5 Charlton Street, Fitzroy Square, which
happens to be on the direct route between Wilkie's home in Hanover Terrace
and Millais's in Gower Street. St. John's Wood is not. Mrs. Elizabeth Graves
is listed in the Post Office London Directory for 1853 as a "marine store
dealer" at that address. Entries in the Post Office Directories often refer to
the previous year: an entry in the 1853 Directory may indicate residence at
the given address in 1852.

A marine store had nothing to do with the sea: it was a junk-shop. According to Henry Mayhew:

> The *rag-and-bottle* and the *marine-store shops* are in many instances but differ-
> ent names for the same description of business. The chief distinction appears
> to be this: the marine-store shopkeepers (proper) do not meddle with what is a
> very principal object of traffic with the rag-and-bottle man, the purchase of
> dripping, as well as of every kind of refuse in the way of fat or grease. The
> marine-store man . . . will purchase any of the smaller articles of household
> furniture, old tea-caddies, knifeboxes, fire-irons, books, pictures, draughts and
> backgammon boards, bird-cages, Dutch clocks, cups and saucers, tools and
> brushes. . . . The *dolly* business [low-grade pawnbroking] is common to both,
> but most common to the marine-store dealer.   (II: 108)

Elizabeth Graves, the widow of a clerk, had sunk to scraping a living as best
she could in the grim world of the urban poor. If she was rescued by Wilkie

it was more probably in Fitzrovia than in the more romantic and sinister shadows of St. John's Wood, and the ''brute'' was more likely to have been an artisan or shopkeeper than a Sir Percival Glyde.

Two years later she was joined by her mother-in-law, Mrs. Mary Ann Graves, who kept a tobacconist's shop in Hertford Street, Fitzroy Square. Mary Ann Graves was described as a ''fund holder'' in the 1851 census, which suggests that she may have had small private means which enabled her to set up this business, and perhaps to help her daughter-in-law.[17] Then, near the time when we have positive knowledge that Caroline Graves became associated with Wilkie Collins, both women disappeared from the area. Elizabeth Graves's last appearance is in the 1857 Directory; Mary Ann's in the 1858 issue.[18]

Two more names in the Fitzroy Square area may be of significance for the relationship between Wilkie Collins and Caroline Graves. When she had failed to persuade Wilkie Collins to marry her, Caroline married Joseph Clow, the son of a distiller, in 1868. Clow is a fairly unusual name, but there was a Leonard Clow in business as an ale and stout merchant at 28 Grafton Street, Fitzroy Square.[19] It seems possible that young Joseph Clow, then a teenager, was apprenticed to a relative in the area where Elizabeth Graves was living and working, fell in love with the beautiful, unfortunate, older woman and finally rescued her from the betrayal of her first rescuer more than a decade later. When that marriage failed, Caroline went back to Wilkie Collins and stayed with him until his death.

If Caroline did require rescue in 1854, it was a temporary crisis: she remained in her shop for at least another two years. It is perhaps of relevance, however, that when Wilkie first took temporary lodgings on his own account in 1856, he chose them in Howland Street, adjacent to Fitzroy Square.

This little piece of the mysterious pattern of the lives of Wilkie Collins and Caroline Graves confirms that he was aware from the beginning of their relationship of her true origins and her widowed status. Her little girl and her mother-in-law, for whom he also took responsibility, would have been part of her everyday life. One might speculate that her occupation could have been one reason why he did not marry her. Harriet Collins, ex-governess and inveterate novel-reader, might have countenanced the victim of a gothic abduction as a daughter-in-law, but a marine store keeper was another matter. By the time Harriet died, Wilkie had entangled himself with Martha Rudd.

The second name in the Fitzroy Square region that struck a chord was one that Wilkie used in *The Woman in White*. A Henry Catherick was a ratepayer and shopkeeper in Charlotte Street in the 1850s. In spite of my scepticism over the St. John's Wood villa story, I do think that Wilkie's female skelelton, as Dickens once described her, was an inspiration for *The Woman in White*. The whole business of identity forcibly denied and remade, on which the plot of the novel turns, parallels in reverse the manufacture of Caroline's identity, with a new Christian name, a new father, a new class, a more romantic past, even a new date of birth. The reaction of Walter Hartright's mother and sister to his relationship with Laura Fairlie suggests the attitude of Harriet and possibly also Charles Collins to Wilkie's adventure: "My mother and my sister . . . believed me to be the dupe of an adventuress and the victim of a fraud" (380).

There is also a deleted passage in the manuscript of *The Woman in White* which points to Caroline. Walter Hartright, describing his love at first sight for Laura Fairlie, confesses, "Lower her to the rank of her own maid, raise her to the pinnacle of the peerage; disguise the maid as a lady, or the peeress as a servant; and the eyes would still have spoken the same language when they met, and the pen I wrote with must still have traced the same three words. I loved her" (ms79). Here the two women in white are merged, and the possibilities of disguise are raised at an early stage. The passage may have been omitted because the plot was being too obviously foreshadowed. Or perhaps the emergence of the butterfly Caroline Graves, the officer's widow, from the chrysalis of Elizabeth Graves, the carpenter's daughter, clerk's widow and marine-store keeper, needed to be more completely hidden.

This period of Caroline Graves's life is not transferred directly to Wilkie Collins's work: there are no women shopkeepers in his major fiction. But it is of interest that a woman who became an integral part of his life had, as part of her secret past, toiled to make a living for herself and her daughter, before retreating once more—no doubt thankfully—into dependence on a man.

Wilkie Collins's knowledge of the lives of poor working women, servants, and prostitutes in particular, aroused his indignation at their exploitation, and his fascination with the reality of their inner selves. In his own life, it was ultimately to such women that he turned when he came to make his most intimate relationships, first with Caroline and then with Martha. But the lives of unconventional and independent women from many different backgrounds had their effect on his novels. Victorian women often had experiences as varied as those of the men they supported, but they were not allowed to say so. The strains imposed on them by the male insistence that their true lives should be kept hidden from view became a major theme in the work of one of their greatest chroniclers.

NOTES

1. ALS to Harriet Collins, 2 September 1855, The Pierpont Morgan Library, New York. MA 3150, no. 45. I gratefully acknowledge permission to quote from manuscripts in the Library's possession. The interpretation of this letter by William M. Clarke, in *The Secret Life of Wilkie Collins* (London: Allison and Busby, 1988) 78–79, is incorrect. *Vide infra.*
2. Harriet Collins, MS, catalogued as by Wilkie Collins, Harry Ransom Humanities Research Center, University of Texas at Austin, Texas. I gratefully acknowledge the permission of the Center to quote from this manuscript.
3. Harriet Collins. 1: Army Lists, 1781–91.
4. *Gentleman's Magazine*, LIX (October 1789): 954
5. Army List, 1791.
6. Dickinson, Frances, 611.
7. Dickinson, "Adventures;" 51.
8. Scottish Record Office, Edinburgh (Ref. CS2.
9. Dickinson, "Adventures," 611.
10. See Jeremy Maas, *The Victorian Art World in Photographs* (London: Barrie & Jenkins, 1984) 168; William M. Clarke, "The Mystery of Collins's Articles on Italian Art." *Wilkie Collins Society Journal* IV (1984): 19–24; Clarke, 75–76.
11. See Frances Elliot, *Diary of an Idle Woman in Italy* 2 Vols. (London, 1871).
12. See Frances Elliot, *Roman Gossip* (London: J. Murray, 1894).
13. See "The Old Cardinal's Retreat," *All the Year Round*, NS III, 58 (January 8, 1870): 127–31.
14. See anonymous review in the *Bristol Times*, quoted in end pages of Frances Elliot, *Old Court Life in France* (London, 1873).
15. *Remarks upon the article termed "The Baths of Lucca" by "Florentia"* anon., privately printed, n.d.
16 Playbills for the Gallery of Illustration performances, also a photograph of the Dickens Dramatic Company in 1857 (not in costume) in which Frances Dickinson is sitting immediately behind Wilkie Collins, Dickens House Museum, Doughty Street, London.
17. 1851 Census Return for 11 Cumming Street, Pentonville, Public Record Office, London.
18. *Kelly's Post Office London Directory* (London, 1853, 1854, 1855, 1856, 1857, 1858).
19. Leonard Clow appears as the occupier of 28 Grafton Street in the *Post Office Directory* and the Rate Books throughout the 1850s.

WORKS CITED

Anonymous. *Remarks upon the article termed "The Baths of Lucca" by "Florentia."* privately printed.

Clarke, William M. "The Mystery of Collins' Articles on Italian Art." *Wilkie Collins Society Journal* IV (1984): 19–24.

———.*The Secret Life of Wilkie Collins*. London, Allism and Busby, 1988.

Collins, Harriet, ms. Catalogued as by Wilkie Collins, Harry Ransom. Humanities Research Center, University of Texas at Austin, Texas.

Collins, Wilkie. *The Evil Genius*. London: Chatto & Windus, 1866.

———. *No Name*. Oxford: World's Classics, 1986.

———. *The Woman in White*. Oxford: World's Classics, 1984.

———. *The Woman in White*. MS. Pierpont Morgan Library, New York.

Dickens, Charles. *The Letters of Charles Dickens*. Ed. Walter Dexter. London: Nonesuch, 1938.

Dickinson, Frances. "Adventures of a First Season." *Bentley's Miscellany*. 2 (December 1852); 34 (July 1853).

———. "The Baths of Lucca" *New Monthly Magazine*. 109 (February 1857): 127.

———. "The Old Cardinal's Retreat." *All the Year Round*. ns iii January 8, 1870: 127–31.

———. *Roman Gossip*. London: J. Murray, 1894.

———. "Polperro." *New Monthly Magazine*. 02 (September 1854): 56.

Elliot, Frances. *Diary of an Idle Woman in Italy*. 2 vols. London, 1871.

———. *Old Court Life in France*. London, 1873.

Gentleman's Magazine. ns ii October 1789, September 1866.

Kelly's Post Office London Directory. London: 1853–58.

Maas, Jeremy. *The Victorian Art World in Photographs*. London: Barrie & Jenkins, 1984.

Mayhew, Henry. *London Labor and the London Poor*. NY: Dover, 1967.

Millais, John G. *Life and Letters of Sir John Everett Millais*. London: Methuen, 1895.

Recent Dickens Studies: 1989

John Kucich

INTRODUCTION

The temporary suspension of the "Dickens Checklist" in mid-1989, upon the death of Alan Cohn, has made scholarly work on Dickens more difficult for us all. Traditionally dependent on the checklist, this review in particular has been severely hampered—especially since resumption of the checklist in the summer of 1990 occurred too late to be of much help. Besides the customary apologies for the brevity of my comments on each item, I wish to extend apologies to all those whose publications I have missed in my makeshift bibliographic search. I must also acknowledge that what success I have had in locating materials is entirely due to some expert help—inventive assistance with computer databases from John Price-Wilkin, and very empathetic research support from Robin Ikegami. I owe Robin and John great thanks for having made this review as extensive as it is.

I confess that my approach has been primarily descriptive, which may disappoint those who look to reviewers for histrionics. From an annual survey of this kind, however, most readers probably want to learn whose work might be useful to them, not what some reviewer's cleverly nuanced biases toward the entire field might be. My preferences, of course, are inscribed all over this review—in selection, arrangement, and emphasis. I have also not hesitated to make judgments, and have even, at times, indulged my deeply-ingrained snottiness against work that I think is misconceived. A reviewer always has a responsibility to appraise the quality and cachet of scholarship. But even in evaluating these projects, I have concentrated on conveying what I hope is a fair and neutral sense of their goals, and I may have paid the price, I am afraid, by being dull.

My own solution to the dilemma of reviewing essays published in *DSA* has been to make note of them in the appropriate contexts, but without extensive commentary.

PRIMARY SOURCES

In this perennially thin category, 1989 was an even more meager year than most. Aside from the usual reissues and paperback reprints, there have not been any significant publishing events—no new Clarendon novel, no new volume of the Pilgrim letters. The only notable re-publication of a novel was Oxford's *Hard Times*, in the World's Classics series, with a wide-ranging general introduction and notes by Paul Schlicke. Ewald Mengel has also published a useful collection of sketches about railways from *Household Words* and *All the Year Round*, though this is not an especially scholarly edition—it was prepared with perhaps more of an interest in railroads than in Dickens. Mengel has omitted many footnotes in the original articles because they are "not relevant in the context of this volume," and corrections made to the originals have not been noted. But Mengel's collection does make a few texts more easily available, since only one of the sketches included here had been previously reprinted.

BIBLIOGRAPHIC AND REFERENCE WORKS

Kathryn Chittick's bibliography of periodical reviews of Dickens' early writings was the single major reference tool published in 1989. The volume is handily organized under three cross-referenced systems: by chronology, by work reviewed, and by periodical. It is still a partial collection, but Chittick has exercised good judgment in her selection of 120 key periodicals out of the thousands available. The scope of the project would seem to cover everything of scholarly interest, and makes this an essential supplement to existing bibliographies of Dickens' critical reception. It is not clear exactly why Chittick has chosen to stop at 1841 (at least, the case she makes is weak), and Garland has no plans to extend the project forward in time, although the Garland bibliographies on individual novels do, of course, contain review citations. It is also not clear why Chittick includes a selective overview of general literary reviewing in periodicals from 1814 to 1841, which seems curiously half-hearted, especially since she does not explain the basis for her rather limited selections. The list she provides of secondary sources that helped shaped the periodical field for her is much more useful. The volume includes only British periodicals, which students of American or, indeed, of worldwide responses to Dickens will find annoying, but it must be admitted that wider horizons would have meant a dizzyingly more difficult project.

John Sutherland's substantial *Stanford Companion to Victorian Fiction* contains perhaps two dozen entries on Dickens, though these consist mostly of plot summaries of each of the novels as well as a few stories, along with a short biographical sketch. The *Companion* is probably most helpful on Victorian topics tangential to Dickens (e.g., the "Christmas Book" industry, various publishers, etc.), and for quick checks of dates or chronology. Besides the two 1989 installments of the "Dickens Checklist," also worth mention are Edward Cohen's "Victorian Bibliography for 1989" and Bruce White's "Victorian Periodicals 1988"—both useful resources for the period in general and Dickens in particular. There were no new bibliographies on novels from Garland, and no new volumes in the Dickens Companions series.

The biggest news in recent memory, in this particular category, comes in 1990 with Chadwyck-Healey's release of its monumental, microfilmed *Charles Dickens Research Collection*, but I must leave that to my successor.

BIOGRAPHICAL STUDIES

The most substantial contribution this year is Jules Kosky's *Mutual Friends: Charles Dickens and Great Ormond Street Children's Hospital.* Kosky has collected much published and unpublished material to provide an account of Dickens' absolutely critical support for Charles West's Children's Hospital—the first children's hospital in England and, perhaps, "the most favorite of [Dickens'] charities." Kosky, an Honorary Archivist to the Hospital, is ideally placed to unravel the record, and he does it with great care and discrimination, weaving biographical materials together with information taken from other Victorian sources, as well as from the records of the Hospital itself. The result is a useful glimpse of Dickens' attitudes toward children, and of his social activism. This account is all the more important because the Children's Hospital was the only institutionalized charitable organization that Dickens ever supported whole-heartedly. Kosky's work supplements the very brief narratives we already have of this episode in Dickens' life, even if it does not attempt to overturn them in any important respect. Though Kosky completely suppresses the dark side of Dickens' relationship to children, and though his occasional bursts of sentimentality about Dickens and childhood must be counterbalanced by what we know from Johnson, Kaplan, and others, the book is so responsibly documented that it can only serve to correct recent tendencies to look for psychological wolves in sheep's clothing. In addition, the book is a remarkably well-informed history of a Victorian charitable institution, of medical assumptions about childhood, and of general nineteenth-century attitudes toward children, especially poor children (some of which created strong resistance to the Hospital from the likes of Florence Nightingale and other reformers). It also chronicles Dickens' other activities in support of children's causes. In all these ways, Kosky's book is an important resource for Dickensians, even if his point of view is itself so Victorian that it often echoes the language and the ideology of patriarchal philanthropy. We could also do without Kosky's repetition of famous scenes involving children from the novels. One cause for more serious regret is that sources are not cited, nor is a bibliography provided, which means that the volume is a less reliable tool for scholars than it might otherwise have been.

The only other lengthy contribution to biographical study is John Frazee's *DSA* essay on Dickens and Unitarianism. But there were many shorter studies of note. Dick Hoefnagel has transcribed Dickens' annotations to Pepys's *Memoirs*. William Long has given us a straightforward but interesting account of Dickens' presence at the inauguration of the railway line to Deal in 1847, setting the event in the context of Dickens' brief flirtation with railway speculation—which is often overlooked in favor of his satires of speculative greed. Less usefully, J. Don Vann retells the history of Dickens' editorial conflicts with Elizabeth Gaskell, caused by his "tampering" with her work. David Roberts unveils the tumultuous events of Dickens' brief editorship of the *Daily News*, and describes what he sees as the scurrilous, inaccurate, incompetent, even inhumane editorial climate over which Dickens presided, warning understatedly that "to admirers of Dickens, these editorials will prove disappointing." In an even more disenchanting (but more to be expected) account of Dickens and the slavery question, Brahma Chaudhuri assembles Dickens' early abolitionist comments about slavery, including his denunciation of slavery in America, but points out how Dickens' attitude began to shift after 1842. His essay shows that, like many Englishmen, Dickens began to develop decided convictions about the inferiority of blacks, and by the 1850s was warning against emancipation. Chaudhuri recounts how Dickens' satire of Mrs. Jellyby's missionary zeal fueled anti-abolitionist sentiment among his readers, and how his concerns about economic profit affected his pro-slavery stance. Chaudhuri also corrects the perception that Dickens ever wavered in his support of the South during the Civil War. With a similarly jaundiced eye, Alan Watts catalogues Dickens' lapses in journalistic integrity through his longstanding concealment of poor conditions on emigrant ships in the 1850s and '60s. It seems that Dickens continued to support emigration enthusiastically as a panacea for social problems, despite his knowledge that conditions aboard emigration ships were, as Watts puts it, a national disgrace. Watts documents the extent of Dickens' personal knowledge of these conditions, and the instances in *Household Words* of his covering up those conditions by suppressing the dangers and deprivations of emigration. The last bit of bad news for Dickensophiles is provided by Nancy Fix Anderson's essay on Dickens and Eliza Lynn Linton, which demonstrates how Linton's antifeminism was catalyzed, in part, through her association with Dickens in the early 1850s.

In a more speculative mode, Jerome Meckier uses the letters and diaries of James and Annie Fields (recently made available in published form) to analyze a few testimonials to Dickens' emotional impact on his close friends, though Meckier's conclusions manage to sound overwrought, and highly questionable. An appropriate companion piece is Rita K. Gollin's ''Living in a World Without Dickens,'' which argues that the ''resignation'' Meckier attributes to Annie Fields at the news of Dickens' death was, in fact, profound anguish.

One of the more unique and valuable background essays on biographical topics is Angus Easson's brief account of the history of the Pilgrim edition of the letters. Easson explains the kinds of errors in the Nonesuch that the new edition corrects, and the nature of the information it supplies. He also includes a number of reflections on the various patterns he has found in the portion of Volume 7 for which he was responsible. Easson's essay shows, if anyone still doubts, the scrupulous and lavish care with which the Pilgrim editors have attempted to explicate what lies in and behind the letters.

GENERAL STUDIES

As the trend away from single-author critical studies continues, one ceases to look for major books on Dickens. Nothing published in 1989 appears destined to acquire landmark status. But without doubt the best of this year's lot is Edwin Eigner's *The Dickens Pantomime*, which modestly confines itself to exploring a single neglected topic in Dickens studies—the English Christmas pantomime tradition, and its influence on the novels. Eigner's book is useful in many ways: for its informative general discussion of pantomime; for its account of Dickens' deep engagement in pantomime; for its demonstration of the way various aspects of the novels are indebted to this tradition. In particular, Eigner concentrates on the impact pantomime had on Dickens' conception of character, on his grasp of comic vision, and on consistent features of the structure of the novels itself. Eigner's claims, it should be said, can sometimes seem too large. He over-generalizes pantomime's influence in such a way as to make it "the basis for [Dickens'] psychological insights and his social vision," as well as a key feature of his comic aesthetics. He also tends to reduce some novels entirely to their relationship to pantomime, claiming that "even the meaning of [Dickens'] vision can be . . . understood in terms of pantomime conventions." But while Eigner's claims for pantomime are sometimes extravagant, he does sketch out the many elements of the pantomime tradition that might be relevant to the novels.

In particular contexts, Eigner is very good on the way in which pantomime gave Dickens access to a medieval tradition of regenerative, iconoclastic energy, which he used to shape his general vision of a *theatrum mundi*. He has many interesting things to say about the relationship of various characters to pantomime types, and the transformations these types often undergo. He is good on the pattern of plotting that Dickens derives from the harliquinade, and on incidental conventions like that of the "pious fraud." He shows convincingly how the pantomime appeals to a world-view with which Dickens challenged what he took to be the dominant outlook of his age. The book is also surprising and instructive in the connection it draws between Dickens' "bad fathers" and the figure of Pantaloon, an insight that reorients this Dickensian preoccupation toward social concerns rather than psychological or biographical ones by foregrounding attitudes toward hierarchy and gentility in the pantomime tradition. But Eigner's emphasis on the Clown as the most important figure Dickens derives from pantomime is a focal point of the book that will generate the most interest and discussion. Eigner's argument that the Clown figure exploits ambiguities between the roles of hero and villain leads to striking and original readings of various enigmatic figures, notably Dick Swiveller, Mr. Dick, and Jenny Wren—but of Micawber most of all. Eigner makes the compelling case that Dickens' skeptical social vision in the "dark novels" coincides with his abandonment of this key pantomime figure.

The book is less convincing on the distinctions it makes between pantomime and melodrama (taking refuge in the fact that Dickens conflated the two forms), or, generally, on the integrity or autonomy of pantomime as a form. Eigner's argument about the transformative function of pantomime as a literary and social force is also open to serious question, drawing as it does on the essentializing side of "carnivalesque" theorists from Frye to Bakhtin. Less crucially, the book also fails to persuade in its defense of Dickens' pantomimic heroes, because it relies too much on commonsense psychologizing to try to make them appear useful models. Eigner makes the unlikely argument that Dickens' heroes are more sensitive to issues of social complicity than his readers, and thus threaten our complacency too much for us to identify with them comfortably. In general, the book is not as careful or as comprehensive in its general claims as it might be. But it draws attention to an important popular tradition underlying the novels, and it will be relied upon both for its insightful commentary, and as the basis for future explorations.

Richard Lettis's *The Dickens Aesthetic* takes on a bold and important project: to derive a coherent picture of Dickens' aesthetic judgment and taste, even a Dickens "theory of aesthetics," taken from his own statements about himself, from what we know of his reading and self-education, and from the comments of others about his abilities and opinions in the areas of sculpture, drama, architecture, painting, music, etc. Of course, conceiving the project in this way risks severe limitation, and not for the reason Lettis gives (i.e., that Dickens' education and aesthetic reflections are presumed to have been slim). Rather, the novels themselves are such self-consciously wrought reflections on art—as criticism of the last three decades has demonstrated—that it seems strange not to try to integrate them into the pursuit of a general Dickensian aesthetics. The result of this exclusion is more a biographical study than a critical one, and in this sense Lettis's project does have the advantage of assembling a vast range of neglected material—some of which is admittedly available elsewhere, but never in so concentrated a form. Lettis has done a particular service in providing the full record of Dickens' interactions with his illustrators (although his discussion of the feud with Cruikshank could have been fuller than it is), and there are many other instances in which he adds to the biographical record by so meticulously collecting material from such a broad range of sources. Perhaps it is because of the promise of the project, and its local successes, that the book as a whole disappoints as much as it does.

To be sure, this book will be an excellent resource for critics writing on any number of aesthetic issues in Dickens. But Lettis seems to lack synthetic skills. The material is presented in undigested form, and there is far too much incidental or familiar information that seems to have been included simply because it was there. Well-known biographical detail is retold at length (the story of Dickens' thwarted aspirations in the theater, and his later successes, is perhaps the most egregious in this regard, since the bare facts tell us little about Dickens' aesthetic leanings). The book often tends to string together quotations, blandly filling the gaps between them, even though Lettis does evaluate Dickens' abilities in particular cases quite well, and should have given his judgment freer scope. At times, we are given long lists of artists Dickens knew or the titles of books he owned, without any analysis of his acquaintance with either. The result is that we never get a "Dickens aesthetic"—the book is far too miscellaneous for that. When Lettis does risk generalizations, he often paints an unambitious portrait of Dickens as a champion of moralistic but non-didactic art, though even here Lettis does not make any consistent claims. One result is the unintended effect of drawing attention to just how much Dickens was confused about particular issues (about the nature and demands of "realism," for instance). There is also something so jingoistic about Lettis's defense of Dickens' intellect that the book becomes myopic: Lettis takes the effusions of Dickens and others about his abilities at face value, and uses them to argue tirelessly that Dickens was more perceptive than we had all thought. Despite all this, though, Lettis has made a significant contribution to our knowledge of Dickens' activities in various non-literary aesthetic spheres, and his book ought to be consulted by anyone doing work in these areas. A second volume, concentrating on Dickens' literary judgments, is due out in 1990. Lettis's work is very usefully supplemented, incidentally, by Robert Bledsoe's *DSA* essay on the significance of opera in Dickens' life and art.

Much less successful than both of these books is James A. Davies's *The Textual Life of Dickens's Characters*. Davies's book presents itself as a study of Dickens' characterization that is informed by semiotics and post-structuralist analysis, rather than being a simple retreat to mimetic criticism. Unfortunately, this theory is mostly window-dressing, and the book really is a retreat. Davies openly declares, at the end of his introduction, that he intends to go beyond what he calls the "anti-humanist approach," in order to take "the real world" into account. The result is a tortured, but interesting example of how critical vocabularies can be appropriated and eviscerated. Davies's primary claim is that the novels are interpretable entirely in the light of their protagonists' experience. Beneath the technical vocabulary and the somewhat forbiddingly clinical organization of topics, he gives us a pre-New Critical appreciation of the human experience and the personalities characterized in the novels, as well as Dickens' skill at provoking particular responses in his readers (reader-response theory also comes in for some domestication here). Though perceptive and careful, the book thus gives us little in the way of general knowledge. Its principal innovations are its willingness to discuss a few minor characters at some length—though this strategy often thins the book even further—and its thorough consideration of the narrators as characters. Davies urgently argues the claim that particular characters in Dickens advance particular themes, although this is not an issue that ought to provoke much debate. The themes Davies finds—alienation, social antagonism, difficulties of communication, and a countervailing sense of human potentials—will hardly surprise, either.

Mildred Newcomb's *The Imagined World of Charles Dickens* is strikingly passionate for a work whose methodology is also very dated—though it is more coherent and slightly more recent than Davies's. In an attempt to grasp ''Dickens' imagination,'' she pursues a set of thematic patterns made visible by recurrent clusters of images. She resolves these images into a unified but complexly textured and in any case ''totally felt'' experience. This experience is posited as both uniquely Dickens' and also that of a ''nineteenth-century Everyman.'' In her introduction, Newcomb makes a strong plea for a return to intrinsic studies of texts (though she seeks to avoid the excesses of New Critics by appealing to Kantian aesthetics), and she firmly refuses all ''preconceived'' models, which, for her, still means primarily Marxism and psychoanalysis. As a result of all this, the critical dialogue of the book—which is quite intense and exacting—is largely with work done before 1975, and often well before. The book is also marked by an inability to refrain from large pronouncements about Dickens and about the purpose of literature, as well as by a magnificently imperious tone. When she evaluates her peers, something she is not at all reluctant to do (the book includes an unusual appendix containing snapshot-like reviews of other works on Dickens), Newcomb takes wayward critics severely to task, and she nurses her favorites with great condescension in the direction of her own grand aesthetic syntheses. The caustic pomposity of the book makes reading it as astounding an experience as it might be to encounter Lewis Carroll's Queen of Hearts purging the stacks of the graduate library—''Off with their heads!''

Despite these difficulties, and if one can come to terms with her generalizations, Newcomb's book is quite good as a study of figurative language. Her analyses could be more compressed, but her tracing out of characteristic images from novel to novel is well done, and worth having. She is especially good at juxtaposing clusters of images that define particularly strong thematic axes, and at drawing connections between a central image (say, the marsh) and its complex progeny (''amphibious'' characters, reptilian behavior ticks, miasmic atmospheres, inert psychologies, etc.) The ultimate division of these patterns into life-images and death-images is not very helpful, but the local discussions are perceptive and energetic.

The only other single-author study this year was Keith Selby's *How to Study a Charles Dickens Novel*, in Macmillan's "How to Study Literature" series. The book is not of serious concern to scholars, though it is a treasure-trove in any number of ways for those interested in pedagogy.

Among critical anthologies, Colin Gibson's *Art and Society in the Victorian Novel* has a few essays on Dickens, which I have reviewed individually, and *Writers, Readers, and Occasions* reprints three of Richard Altick's Dickens essays. But the only collection completely devoted to Dickens is Carol Hanbery MacKay's *Dramatic Dickens*. MacKay's volume is a selection of thirteen essays (with the addition of her introduction and a "postscript" by Mary Margaret Magee) first presented at an interdisciplinary and multi-media conference, "The Dickens Theatre," held at the University of Texas at Austin. I have decided to review the essays together under this rubric because they are almost all on general topics, and because, taken as a whole, they give an extraordinarily broad view of contemporary approaches to theatrical topics in Dickens. Despite MacKay's attempt to focus the collection in her general introduction, the volume divides our attention in many different and incommensurable directions, and it is representative, most of all, for its diversity. MacKay herself has the opportunity to write at greater length about Dickens and drama in her *DSA* essay.

Two of the best essays in the collection focus on Dickens' relationship to modern, not Victorian theater. James Redmond's very strong essay charts an early Victorian debate about the competing claims of action and of psychologically complex language on the stage. In the 1820s and '30s, he argues, there was considerable resistance to the increasing place of "avant-garde" concerns with psychology, character, and lyrical language, at the expense of a more Aristotelean logic of action. Redmond provides a fascinating survey of the roots of modernist theater in these Victorian debates. He explores, in particular, one paradigmatic instance of the conflict—the rift between Browning and Macready over whether character ought to be conveyed through action or through language in Browning's own plays. Interestingly, Dickens appears in this instance as the reconciler, the figure most intent on synthesizing the demands of both action and language in a middling critical position. Redmond argues that the rarity of Dickens' synthetic position—and this is an argument that is at once more complex and more interesting than the sentimental affirmations of Dickensian theatricality that are a bit too prevalent in this volume as a whole—reveals the failure of Victorian theater to make room for "the lyrical sensibility at the heart of contemporary English poetry.'' Michael Goldberg also looks fruitfully at Dickens' relationship to twentieth-century drama, which he sees as more important than Dickens' influence on twentieth-century fiction. He points out that Shaw's well-known enthusiasm for Dickens was shared as well by Ibsen and Strindberg, who also openly acknowledged their debt. With great insight, Goldberg traces the borrowings of these dramatists, and also the ''shifting web of interactions among these three later writers themselves which produced a wide range of sometimes surprising permutations.'' Goldberg proposes a complicated but very concrete dynamic of reciprocal influences. Perhaps the most interesting part of his essay is his demonstration of how each of these figures used Dickens to focus what they saw as excessive in the others, and vice versa.

Another exciting contribution to the collection is Jean Ferguson Carr's essay, which looks at the metaphor of the theater in Dickens as a special form of self-revelation, and the way that this function contradicts the inherently performative dimensions of theater. In Carr's view, Dickens alternately uses theatrical performance as a vehicle of self-discovery, and of escapist fantasy—a contradiction expressed in Dickens' comments about his own acting abilities as well. Especially interesting is her discussion of *The Frozen Deep*, which Dickens saw as both an opportunity to test and explore some of his deepest, potentially scandalous impulses, but also a means to project an extreme of restless emotional savagery that would make his own domestic unrest appear more respectable by contrast. In this way, the theatrical self becomes a psychologically useful switching point, both identical to and different from convictions (or fears) about identity. Rather than being the means to some kind of metaphysical discovery about selfhood, the acting self is an instrument of psychic control, even if its mechanisms (as Foucault teaches) are themselves scripted. A less densely-argued essay on this same topic is James Kincaid's, which discusses the histrionic characters in Dickens—those for whom performance adds something to identity or social role. Kincaid uses these characters to explore what he sees as Dickens' notions about the divided or multiple self. Though Kincaid seems at times to confuse compulsive behavior with a belief in essentialism, and spontaneity or complexity with a fully liberated, de-centered self, his essay does pinpoint an important tension in the psychological energies of Dickens' characters.

Working in a more materialist vein, Michael Booth contributes a knowledgeable, well-researched essay about class lines in Victorian drama. Sifting through what evidence is available, Booth finds that over half the audience for theater in Victorian London was working class, and that its staple fare was melodrama—much more so than was the case for middle-class audiences of the West End. The content of melodrama, in which "class conflict . . . permeates the whole genre," no doubt has something to do with this popularity. From the 1830s on, in fact, East End melodrama usually featured conflict between the villainous rich and the moral poor, and also included a fresh realism about working-class life, including an emphasis on urban environments. In general, Booth argues that melodrama was the first form of drama that took the working class seriously—an important insight, which should qualify formalist or psychological theories of melodrama, and which also helps to explain some part of Dickens' popularity with the poor.

In a brief but very provocative essay, Nina Auerbach discusses how Dickens' occasional delight in theatrical cross-dressing is belied in his own boy-girl and child-adult figures, which are always stigmatized for their transgression of symbolic categories. Auerbach claims that Dickens was curiously resistant to one of the great features of the Victorian stage: its fascination with such mixtures of sex and age. She draws attention, too, to the strange displacement that allows Dickens as fictional/theatrical impersonator to play with subjective boundaries in ways that he denied to his characters. Also short but sweet is Mary Margaret Magee's essay, which engagingly discusses David Copperfield's "directorial role" in relation to his story, as well as to himself, showing how it highlights his inclinations to dissociation. In this sense, the metaphor of the tableau vivant, so pervasive in *David Copperfield*, is another means for David to explore the split between conscious and unconscious motivation.

Working on theatrical adaptations, Regina Barreca examines the 1838 adaptation of *Oliver Twist*, and finds, predictably enough, that much of the complexity of tone and psychological portraiture is lost in the translation. However, she argues that given the roots of Dickens' imagination in melodrama, it is surprising how much justice the play does to the fundamental concerns of the novel. John Glavin provides an interesting account of his own 1985 adaptation of *Little Dorrit*, according to the radically minimalist and interventionist principles of Jerzy Grotowski. His complete re-working of the novel sounds much more existentialist than Dickensian, but it is interesting nonetheless.

To round out the volume, Coral Lansbury—in a light-stepping and somewhat scattered essay—considers Dickens' "vulgarity," by which she means some inherently popular quality in his work that resists academic monopolization. She attributes this quality to his use of elements from popular theater, and goes on to explore at length the relationship between Pecksniff and the

Clown figure from pantomime. Carolyn Buckley LaRocque considers not theater, but ritual, and, specifically, the ritual stages of David Copperfield's development. She tries to broaden the argument by citing Dickens' borrowing of inherently ritualistic elements in the Victorian stage, but her essay is largely confined to tracing the three traditional phases of David's ritual passage in a set of isolated scenes from the novel. Mary Saunders points out that troubled women in Dickens often repeat a melodramatic gesture—they fall to the floor and expostulate. She claims that floor scenes transcend their melodramatic origins to express the characters' essential humanity and "to engage the reader in understanding that humanity." Robert Colby gives us a rambling but informative account of Dickens' and Thackeray's novels as reproduced on stage. Judith Fisher argues that Dion Boucicault's "sensation scene," first introduced in 1857, was influenced by similar scenes in Dickens' novels.

Turning now to articles in journals, one of the year's most important is S. J. Schad's "The I and You of Time: Rhetoric and History in Dickens." Schad contends that Dickens' conception of time, and also of the writing of history, is mediated by a rhetoric of direct address. The speech situation that generates any representation of temporality in Dickens implicitly challenges Victorian procedures of historiography, which, laying the groundwork for modern historians, attempt to efface subject and object, teller and receiver, from historical narrative. Ultimately, Schad argues, this eruption of rhetoric into the surfaces of time is antagonistic to any coherent ordering of history. It defeats notions of progress, or temporal purpose, as well as the possibility of any stable historical account. Schad effectively contrasts this tendency in Dickens with similar splicings of rhetoric and duration in Carlyle that work oppositely, toward sustaining the idea of progress within a history still rooted in speech situations. Schad develops his basic insight into what will seem a fairly standard conclusion: that, in Dickens, attempts to order the past suffer from the obstruction of rhetoric, and that historical "imperatives" are thereby revealed to be "convoluted and aberrant, indeterminate and quite subjective"—that is, that Dickens deconstructs Victorian historicism's implicit faith in the intelligible design and purpose of history. He insists as well, though, that this conclusion undermines the general attempts of post-structuralist criticism to caricature speech-act theory as theoretically conservative.

Juliet McMaster's essay on the act of reading in Dickens, originally drafted for an audience of language teachers, starts from the standard observation that, for Dickens, language is not a transparent medium, and that the act of reading becomes a subject of his novels. But McMaster goes on to show how we can recover what Iser has called the "contemporary reader" in Dickens' texts, a reader who is finally meant to transcend the signifier and to inhabit pure experience. The essay ranges widely—and very usefully—through the novels, exploring Dickens' manifold ideas about the tractabilities and intractabilities of language. It then concentrates on David Copperfield, an exemplary instance of a reader who, while aware of the surface of the medium, is also able to penetrate that surface to achieve "full imaginative involvement." Dickens generally seems to see language as an obstacle for the less skillful, but to believe that, for talented others, it "gives access to things." While the essay does not clearly distinguish between imagination and experience, it does offer a commonsensical corrective to those who would overlook Dickens' linguistic optimism and assimilate him to contemporary self-reflexive theories of language.

Brian Rosenberg's essay asks similarly large theoretical questions, this time about character in fiction. When are assumptions about character extratextual? When does explication of character become readerly projection? To what extent does literary character depend on non-literary discourses? After arguing that such questions are theoretically unanswerable, however, he goes on to discuss character in an entirely unproblematized way, assuming that it can be described as a stable element in a text, about which readers can arrive at consensus. This allows him—not a little reductively—to focus tensions between what a text "means" and what values characters within it express. He seeks to contrast "the lessons" of various Dickens' novels with the conflicting but still unitary values "embodied" in particular characters, concentrating on *The Old Curiosity Shop*, *Little Dorrit*, and *Dombey and Son*. Rosenberg's conclusion is that, by working against context, characters in Dickens regularly complicate our reading, and prevent us from deducing a "moral fable." He places heavy emphasis on characters whose behavior he determines to be excessive or inappropriate, arguing that such behavior inherently resists assimilation into the novels' structure—though this, of course, implies that narrative structure must be about unilinear, ordered, composed sorts of signification.

By far the most important work on intertextual topics is John Sloan's "The Literary Affinity of Gissing and Dostoevsky: Revising Dickens." Sloan's essay explores a dialogic relation between Gissing and Dostoevsky, as mediated by Dickens. Sloan finds a common revisionary program in the two later writers, which becomes the site of important similarities and differences between them. In particular, both writers adopt key Dickensian motifs—the oppressed heroine, the duality of idealistic hero and energetic villain—but transform them in different ways: Gissing through a characteristically English utopianism; Dostoevsky in the vein of psychological realism. Though using somewhat simple categories of opposition, Sloan shows how divergent ends can follow from similar revisionist impulses, particular from Gissing's and Dostoevsky's shared reaction against liberal humanist idealism. He also provides some cogent and useful examples of dialogic process within the literary tradition. His principle polemical argument is that Gissing's revision of Dickens remains more limited in its political implications because, unlike Dostoevsky, Gissing remains rooted in uncritical Victorian optimism. Much more modest in scope, Penelope LeFew's related essay studies a very early Gissing story, and reveals its complex Dickensian borrowings, pointing out how deeply Gissing's early work was shaped by his reading of Dickens, despite his later rejection of Dickens as a model. Frederick Nies and John Kemmey give us an interesting study of Dickens' often-overlooked influence on James, which finds pointed references to *David Copperfield* in *The Princess Casamassima* that signal James's conscious indebtedness. They trace a number of strong influences in characterization and plot, as well as the borrowing of scenes and wording. They conclude, specifically, that for James it was Dickens, more than either Balzac or Zola, who "taught him how to take possession of the metropolis," in addition to his more eclectic borrowings.

There were a number of formal studies of Dickens' language, though none were especially revisionary or compelling. Daniel Sheridan discusses the characteristic difficulties of reading Dickens, which seem, for him, to revolve around the radical unpredictability of the prose. Shrugging off the notion that this unpredictability represents a historical difference in the expectations of readers, Sheridan argues that Dickens' profuse and overly-detailed prose has the constant function of creating a sense of mastery by raising the level of unpredictability. He argues that Dickens gives us too much irrelevant detail in order to withhold important information, and that "the actual experience of confusion for the reader is valued above the intelligibility" of the prose. But Sheridan seems to reverse his point when he claims that we eventually learn to look for meaning in the "descriptive delays" themselves. Generalizing from his teaching experience, Sheridan concludes that the readability problem of a Dickens novel encourages various coping strategies, but that the "openness" of the prose in any case demands a struggle with the text. Rather simplistically, he argues that this struggle is ultimately what makes reading valuable. Knud Sorensen published two essays that extend his earlier study of linguistic innovation in Dickens. In "Dickens on the Use of English," Sorensen traces Dickens' fascination with linguistic behavior that deviates from the norm, and his dramatization of a range of peculiar idiolects.

Unfortunately, the categories of deviation Sorensen presents in this essay are too obvious: neologisms, slang, prolixity, etc. Strangely, too, in light of his other work, he concludes here that Dickens valued standard English very highly, and captured linguistic deviations mainly to criticize them. In "Narrative and Speech-Rendering in Dickens," Sorensen continues his documentation of "idiolectical variation" by looking at the speeches of various Dickens characters, while extending the analysis to include the interaction of narrative and speech. He confines himself to noting, however, that speech and narrative interrupt and qualify each other in various ways. Sorensen's comments are quite commonsensical, and he is a good reader, but his general conclusion is only that Dickensian speech-rendering involves "great variation," and, as in his other essay, the categories of his analysis are not especially novel or rigorous. In both essays, he seems to be furnishing further evidence for claims about Dickens' linguistic experimentalism and daring that have stood for generations. Also of note is Frank Patterson's essay, which shows that Dickens' frequent use of anaphora is complicated by his use of the tricolon, defined as a verbal unit having three parts, to convey urgency—which may, for all I know, be a meaningful discovery. Bernard Richards comments briefly on Dickens' use of simile, and Jill Matus on his use of metonymy.

Among brief studies of thematic topics, Benjamin Fisher notes that Dickens frequently used vampire motifs to express fascination with the divided self. Some of his examples are forced (Quilp a vampire because of his long fingernails? Krook because he profits from Nemo's death?), but he does show how Dickens draws on a staple of Gothic fiction. George Wing uncovers a little-noticed object of Dickens' ridicule—the unmarried—and shows one of the more uncharitable sides of Dickensian humor. Unfortunately, he accompanies this account with amateur psychologizing of Dickens' general needs for vengeance. Terrence Whaley castigates Dickens for his negative portrayal of schoolteachers. He sketches the main lines of the stereotype in Dickens, and its dependence on prevailing Victorian attitudes toward education, in a useful but pedestrian comparison of various figures. He seems to stack the evidence somewhat, leaving out idealized professional teachers, like the schoolmaster in *The Old Curiosity Shop*, and ruling out the relevance of figures like Dr. Strong, while over-emphasizing the typicality of Squeers. Mary Burgan's interesting essay on Victorian heroines and music (an essay reprinted from *Victorian Studies*) considers Dickens briefly, and shows musical talent in Dickens' women to be an ambivalent sign—either of a woman's frivolousness or her soulful character—that depends on the general codes of Victorian attitudes toward music. As studies of a single thematic topic in Dickens, all four of these essays are exceeded in thoroughness and discrimination by William Palmer's *DSA* essay on Victorian shipwrecks and their various functions in the novels—both practical and metaphorical. With a little stretching, this category might also include C. C. Barfoot's essay on romantic and anti-romantic tendencies in Dickens—a stale topic to which Barfoot adds only a series of facile generalizations.

Architectural topics have elicited interesting work from Phillippa Tristram and George Baird. Tristram's *Living Space in Fact and Fiction*, a study of the literary uses of domestic architecture, would appear to have a single chapter on Dickens, "Aspects of Chesney Wold: The Houses of the Great." The chapter does begin and end with images from *Bleak House*, and it refers throughout to that novel's disdain for the anachronisms of the aristocracy through nuanced descriptions of domestic space. But references to various eighteenth- through twentieth-century novels, including many others of Dickens, are spliced liberally throughout the chapter, and indeed throughout the work. In Dickens' case, the comments Tristram makes about the varieties of working-class abodes in Dickens, or about the middle-class embrace of domestic vulgarity that Dickens defiantly champions, are, in fact, much more enlightening than the claims she makes about Sir Leicester Dedlock's country house, which could easily be derived from, say, Mark Girouard's more impressive study of country house architecture. In general, Tristram's book is lavish in illustration and superficial in text. But it does have some intelligent things to say about domestic space in Dickens and elsewhere—ranging from decorating fads to house plants to servants quarters—and a quick tour through the book with the aid of the (badly prepared) index can be of use to Dickensians. Baird's essay very briefly discusses Dickens' conservative attitudes toward architectural innovation in a stimulating essay on the Victorian roots of cultural anti-modernism.

Two fascinating but antithetical works on Dickens and film are essays by Rick Altman and Neil Sinyard. In "Dickens, Griffith, and Film Theory Today," Altman reflects on Sergei Eisenstein's classic treatise (to which his title is an allusion) about the influence of the nineteenth-century novel—especially Dickens—on film, and he takes issue with this traditional piety. Altman argues that it was theatrical adaptation, not the novels themselves, that furnished filmmakers with their conventional techniques. He argues that the suppression of film's debt to theater, and especially popular theater, arises from the early cinema's appeals to literature as cultural authority. Altman's essay is not in its entirety useful to Dickensians, having more relevance to contemporary film theory, but he does offer a few important caveats for those interested in Dickens and film. Sinyard, on the other hand, discusses very intelligently Dickens' influences on and metamorphoses within contemporary, rather than classic film. He manages to define the kinds of uniquely Dickensian thematic elements that can be carried over from narrative to film. Sinyard discusses at length two films in particular, Christine Edzard's *Little Dorrit*, and Hanif Kureishi's *My Beautiful Laundrette*. His essay is well-supplemented by Michael Slater's discussion of Portuguese director Joaô Botlho's *Hard Times*.

STUDIES OF INDIVIDUAL NOVELS

If I order my treatment of the novels according to the amount of critical attention they have received, I must begin with *Bleak House*, which attracted the lion's share—especially, for whatever reason, from feminists. Of the many essays on *Bleak House*, Helena Michie's is perhaps the most ambitious. Michie's general argument is that the Victorian novel provides one legitimate space for representations of the female body: the discourse of sickness and pain. This means, in part, that Victorian women could exploit illness as a means of control—that is, as a means of suspending the body from domestic roles and articulating it differently, through a filter of fragmented or destabilized identity. Pain, therefore, is a process of both making and unmaking female identity, and, as such, a way for a novelist like Dickens to explore female agency. It is also a way for him to disrupt the passive roles conventionally assigned to women in realist fiction. Michie shows how both *Bleak House* and *Our Mutual Friend* permit female characters to construct a self through pain and fragmentation, in a kind of self-writing that runs counter to the romantic teleology of the conventional Victorian plot. Specifically, she sees Esther Summerson's illness as a movement away from the feared rigidities of the domestic angel—not a development of identity but a new textualization of it through a language felt to be more her own. Scarring, in particular, allows Esther to assert her fundamental difference from her mother, and from her positioning as an object of the admiring gaze of others. As such, it becomes a means of privatizing the self, and it prevents Esther from being simply absorbed in a conventional marriage plot. For Esther, illness, pain, and scarring signal a general choice for difference over sameness, self-construction over identity. In *Our Mutual Friend*, self-fashioning is correlated to physical pain and deformation through Jenny Wren. Michie shows persuasively how Jenny not only exploits her own shifting identity but is able to fashion a self for Lizzie. Michie does shy away from examining the more obviously oppressive aspects of this discourse, especially the intervention of medical expertise in the construction of femininity so well documented recently by Mary Poovey. One also keeps expecting from her essay a grand synthesis that never comes. But Michie's reading of the liberatory potential of illness, derived ultimately from her innovative synthesis of deconstructive and Lacanian analysis, is clever and extremely astute.

Monica Feinberg also channels feminist analysis into a sympathetic reading of *Bleak House*. Feinberg acknowledges Esther's familiar domestic ideology, but argues that Dickens exposes it as untenable and undesirable. While Esther's celebratory mythology of domestic relations may very well allow Dickens to explore his own potentially edenic fantasies, it also becomes a target of the novel's criticism, especially in its exploitation of thematic juxtapositions and contradictions. Feinberg claims that this criticism revolves primarily (and this will no doubt sound old hat) around Dickens' claustrophobic revulsion from domestic insularity. Besides being persuasive about the novel, though, Feinberg also takes the opportunity to theorize the subtle relations between de-mythologizing and re-mythologizing ideological practices, an understanding of which allows her to escape any reduction of Dickens to the reified roles of spokesman for, or rebel against, the Victorian hearth. In fact, she shows how Dickens explores the processes of ideological reduction, or what she calls "the dynamics of the adage," in which complex ideological stances are reduced to formulas that can easily be consumed and reproduced. In the course of this discussion, she instructively situates Dickens' attitudes toward domesticity in relation to other Victorian writers. There are a few too many tired passages in her essay about nineteenth-century uses of the family as a means of social control, however, and her reading itself is much more detailed than it needs to be.

A third feminist reading of *Bleak House* (though she would call it a discursive analysis rather than a "reading") is featured in Robyn Warhol's book on "feminist narratology," which includes a chapter on *Bleak House* and *Can You Forgive Her?*. Warhol's *Gendered Interventions* is a much-anticipated attempt to unite two oddly separated movements in contemporary theory. It concentrates on instances of direct address in Victorian fiction, and argues (somewhat long-windedly) that these textual strategies are gendered in the mid-nineteenth century so as to privatize the narratorial appeals of female narrators. She claims that writers' gradual aversion to direct address stems from this feminization. What is crucial methodologically is her attention to discursive modes, not to content, which she promotes as an important advance in feminist criticism's attempt to pinpoint the gendering of writing. At the same time, she seeks to historicize narratology by opening it to various ideological contexts. The key to her narratological model is a distinction between techniques of engagement, employed by women, and of distancing, employed by men. These have less to do with affective dispositions than with rhetorical strategies that create a narratee, and situate the narratee in relation to "actual readers." The objectivity of Warhol's approach, however, would seem to be seriously compromised by including tropological elements like irony, or a narrative's explicit or implicit "stance" toward both characters and its own status as story. One might also object that her distinction between male and female narrators is too rigid and elementary. Warhol's chapter on *Bleak House* argues, in part, that Dickens "borrows" the female strategy of engaging direct address. She provides no analysis of Dickens' motives or of the ideological implications of this move (she does insist, somewhat simplistically, that Dickens' access to public forums allowed him the luxury of dabbling in feminine modes of address in his novels), but merely notes how in *Bleak House* Dickens uses a number of different narratorial modes, which combine both distancing and engaging structures. Warhol reads several passages from the novel closely, and shows how rapid and subtle shifts in narrative posture can be. She argues that certain techniques of Dickens' narration seem to have been borrowed from Harriet Beecher Stowe and Elizabeth Gaskell.

In yet another of her important contributions to Dickens scholarship, Kathleen Tillotson shows how critics have been misled by Forster's remarks into thinking that Jo was central to Dickens' original conception of the novel. She demonstrates, in fact, that Jo played no role at all in Dickens' early designs. Besides Jo's absence from Dickens' memoranda, he is conspicuously absent from the pictorial cover, which Dickens discussed thoroughly with Hablot Browne. In addition, a strong source for Jo (besides the notorious case of George Ruby, several years before the composition of the novel) was an orphan Dickens met while visiting at the Ragged School in Farringdon Street during late February of 1852. Dickens' remarks about Jo during the composition of *Bleak House* include topical references to "ragged schools" that make this connection seem highly likely. Tillotson goes on to build a solid case for the way Jo's role evolved in response to pressures both within the novel as it developed and within the events of Dickens' life of 1852–53.

Ralph Rader's essay on *Bleak House, Vanity Fair*, and *Middlemarch* is presented as the "precursor" of a larger project on the formal development of the novel. Generally speaking, Rader seeks to analyze "leading master-piece novels of successive periods as creative adaptations of the intrinsic possibilities of a historically invented and inherited form in response to the extrinsic norms characteristic of the periods on the one hand and the authors' pre-given psychological set on the other." In this sententious style, Rader explores rather uneventfully the apparent conflict between the social "message" in Victorian fiction and possibilities for "organic form," a conflict that Rader attempts to understand in a new way. His resolution: that each novel has a "peculiar plot intention" meant to distinguish itself from other novels. This idiosyncratic intention results not only in Jamesian "bagginess," but in the distinct and different bagginess of each novel. Thus, Rader wants to show how social signification in the Victorian novel must be seen not just as a theme, but as in principle antithetical to "the aesthetic purity of fully integrated organic form." In the case of *Bleak House*, Dickens attempts to posit the social connectedness of what seem to be unconnected social traumas, in pursuit of an atmosphere of "diffuse, inspecific guilt." This well-known theme, for Rader, explains specific fragmentations in the novel—the double narration, protracted thematic patterns—as well as an opposing drive toward synthesis.

Ann Smalley's essay also focuses on *Bleak House*'s famous desire to bring together individuals of disparate social contexts, in her case by examining the way gulfs of class and power are bridged. She largely repeats the conventional wisdom about the novel, even as she tries to differentiate her essay by claiming that these cross-class connections are dynamic, not static. Though she recognizes that such bridgings are the occasion for the growth or development of one of the characters involved, it will come as no surprise that this process revolves around sudden recognitions of kindred human status. Smalley does point out, however, that Dickens seemed to believe that complex aspects of human nature might be reconciled in socially "mixed" relationships—in other words, that contact between various classes might "enrich" individual characters. Smalley herself endorses this perception, and speaks rather riskily of the "higher" and "lower" aspects of human nature that are complementarily embodied in figures from different social ranks.

A brave attempt to totalize the novel is James Roy King's "*Bleak House* as Metaphor." King explains the basic structure of the novel in terms of the metaphorical sentence, which he defines as a grammatical sequence that moves a particular element from one context to another. Very reductively, he explains everything in the novel—form, structure, character, theme, motifs—in terms of such metaphorical movement. While claiming that metaphor dominates the novel, he defines metaphor so broadly that his more erudite attempts at structural analysis simply become amorphous. Kenneth Muir gives us a more pedestrian and mostly recycled proof of totalization of a different kind—namely, that "Dickens organized his material with great care, and he knew exactly what he was doing."

The most interesting minor piece on *Bleak House* is Jenny Graham's essay on character sources. Graham studies two characters based on historical figures of the late eighteenth century, which Dickens seems to have modeled out of Samuel Rogers' *Table Talk*. Horne Tooke, who was mysteriously involved in seditious activities of the 1790s, but was able to outwit the prosecution at his trial, served as a source for Tulkinghorn (as the inversion of his name would suggest); and Dr. Samuel Parr, a scholarly parson, was a model for Jarndyce. Besides cleverly tracing these sources, Graham shows how Dickens used his information selectively, and transformed much of it in creating each character. Other minor essays on *Bleak House* include James Hill's useful summary of mid-nineteenth-century knowledge about smallpox, which explains apparent inconsistencies in Woodcourt's treatment of Jo; and Carolyn and James Misenheimer's rather bland study of four sets of "paired" chapters, meaning to augment our appreciation of Dickens' artistry by showing formal and thematic continuities. Camilla Humphreys also gives us a desultory study of the various functions of letters and letter-writing in the novel, showing how letters often signal important clues to character and plot. And Richard Currie has written an interesting if somewhat strained analysis of Esther's coping mechanisms, as an example of D. W. Winnicott's phenomena of "transitional relatedness"—that is, Esther survives trauma through transitional objects that supply the emotional comfort she cannot obtain from her mother. In the category of teapot tempests is an exchange between John P. Frazee and Michael Steig about a figure in Hablot Browne's cover for the monthly parts of *Bleak House*. Frazee is convinced this figure is a dog, but Steig argues eloquently that it is a fox. Both develop highly involved symbolic interpretations of little consequence, which depend on resolving the species of this beast, and deciding, furthermore, whether its posture seems protective or threatening.

Finally, Elliot Gilbert's collection of reprinted essays on *Bleak House* lives up to the high standards of G. K. Hall's Critical Essays on British Literature series. It contains no new essays, except for Gilbert's gracious and intelligent introduction, and some might regret that the volume features neither indisputably "major" essays (Gilbert has left out anything reprinted elsewhere) nor new work. But a volume like this does good service in making available some widely-known essays that deserve to be known even more widely, without pretending to be a comprehensive collection. A more serious objection might be that the volume leans rather lopsidedly toward traditional approaches.

Great Expectations, for some reason, tended to be used to illustrate general theoretical arguments. One of the most important and controversial studies of any single Dickens novel this year is Daniel Cottom's chapter on *Great Expectations* in his *Text and Culture: The Politics of Interpretation*, a volume in the (now bloated) Theory and History of Literature series from Minnesota. Cottom's position on the politics of interpretation is difficult to summarize, because his ideas depend on elaborately textured arguments. But in general terms, Cottom argues—in ways that will strike some too quickly, perhaps, as new historicist—that interpretation is always politically situated and can never be endowed with neutrality. This means, among other things, that no interpretation can be justified that excludes the possibility of differing and contradictory readings. Cottom develops his non-reductive position in a lively chapter on the reversibility of jokes in differing political contexts. He goes further than most new historicists, however, in his emphasis on the motility of context, which can never be subjected to totalizing explanations (one characteristic consequence, however, is that Cottom rejects any "ideal political authority" as essentialist). For he insists that "no way of reading is wrong except as it may become so under specific political conditions." This position, open to the infinite re-describability of all discourse, and willing to defer endlessly the naming of political stakes, leaves Cottom free to speak in general terms of the conditions of political discourse without any need to define or stabilize its Victorian implications in unitary terms. From one point of view, the result is a nightmarish game of political one-upsmanship; from another, a liberation from political naîvete of all kinds. Cottom further extends his position to the category of culture, rejecting any attempt at a totalizing conception of culture, and arguing for the perception of culture as heterogeneity—though he commits the by now familiar mistake of not acknowledging the totalizing gestures in his own method (e.g., in using "oppression" as a pseudo-ethical category or "heterogeneity" as an ideal). He claims, further, that cultural power lies not so much in its ideological context as in the "enchantment" of the discourse of law and rebellion that organizes such heterogeneity into deceptively straightforward social structures. At the bottom of all this is Cottom's (equally totalizing) argument that culture always depends on the repression of differences and conflict.

In the case of *Great Expectations*, Cottom argues that unitary readings of the novel have systematically disguised its politics of rhetoric. Cottom concentrates on what he calls the "rule of irony" in the novel, according to which unrestrained individualism, the hallmark of middle-class ideology, is subjected to subtle but regular qualifications. This "rule" of irony, he suggests, prevents irony from contaminating individualism in some general way, and also displaces the ideologically archaic question of origins with which the novel initially seems preoccupied. The rule of irony, though ideologically simple, has great consequences: for various reasons, it can easily be represented as character, as feeling, as truth, as nature, as history, and, finally, as universal subjectivity. Cottom emphasizes that this mode is rhetorical—not the reflection of "real" historical events—but that it must be evaluated as a historical and political practice, not simply as a formal mode. He is then able to show how various unitary readings depend upon taking these central themes as givens—in particular, the logic (or illogic) of desire. Ultimately, his goal is to demonstrate that the novel itself reveals both the repression of differences within culture, and the inescapability of such repression, though Cottom suggests finally, in a moment of Foucauldian "liberatory pessimism" (Terry Eagleton's term) that awareness of the conditions of culture is the precondition for change. His essay is a stimulating, sophisticated, often brilliant meditation on *Great Expectations*, with which all critics of the novel will have to come to terms, as well as an important contribution to contemporary theoretical debate.

Of similar theoretical weight, though her treatment of the novel itself is much slighter, is Laurie Langbauer's essay. Langbauer discusses *Great Expectations*, together with novels by Collins and Mrs. Henry Wood, in a general study of patriarchal associations of the madwoman with the mother. Her ultimate aim is to expose male appropriations of feminism that depend on the collapse of gender distinctions, and her essay tends to claim that all versions of feminism employed by men are fundamentally contaminated by such strategies of co-optation. The principle conclusion she draws from *Great Expectations*, which supports only one phase of her general theoretical argument, has to do with displacements of authority that take place between the figure of the mother and that of the madwoman. In both *Great Expectations* and *The Woman in White*, the mysteries embodied by two hysterics—Miss Havisham and Anne Catherick—are ultimately resolved by appealing to textually marginalized mothers—to Mrs. Catherick, and to Estella's real mother, Molly. This pattern conforms to recent feminist object-relations psychology, which argues that mothers are reviled and occluded precisely because of their power over creation. In both cases, the mother is linked to fantasies of totalizing power, and the utility of the madwoman as a vehicle for male fantasies depends on her complex distance from and incorporation within that power.

James Phelan's essay, "Reading for the Character and Reading for the Progression: John Wemmick and *Great Expectations*," is an adapted version of sections from his *Reading People, Reading Plots: Character, Progression, and the Interpretation of Narrative*. The condensed, essay version—with its focus on the novel, and its tighter exposition of conceptual background—may ultimately be more helpful for Dickensians. Phelan uses *Great Expectations* to illustrate a general theoretical discussion of character. Specifically, Phelan proposes a series of categories and structuring tensions within novelistic character as a way to theorize the relation between character and plot (or "progression," as he terms it, in order to include the activity of the reader). This strategy is largely conceived as a corrective to Peter Brooks's *Reading for the Plot*, which Phelan sees as subordinating the dynamics of character to temporal structures. Phelan's various idiosyncratic categories are generally meant to avoid an analysis of "deep structures" through a focus on "surface structures," in an attempt to forestall premature leaps to meta-narrative explanatory paradigms, which he finds constraining. Instead, Phelan hopes to capture the "experiential dynamics" of the narrative. One might object that Phelan's theoretical machinery is itself monological, that it is trapped in the idealization of a unitary reading (Phelan must assume certain responses from the reader that are nevertheless "built into" the novel), and that it presupposes various "deep structures" itself in the hard and fast distinctions it makes between character, plot, theme, "mimetic function," and an array of other methodological instruments. But for Dickensians, there remain original and illuminating readings of the intersections of various plots in *Great Expectations* and the effect of these intersections on the development of Pip as a character. In particular, Phelan reveals how Wemmick functions to shape the narrative's view of Pip not simply in a thematic way, but more temporally as well.

In yet another theoretical study that uses *Great Expectations* as exemplum, Douglas Brooks-Davies studies four texts that have an unusually strong commitment to *Hamlet*, arguing that the Oedipal material in the play has assumed a strong role in literary myths about "the creative male psyche" and about gender difference. Firmly grounded in Freudian, Lacanian, and (French) feminist psychoanalysis, Brooks-Davies begins with a model of the Oedipal crisis that revolves around a primal experience of loss and the fear of death, which is then projected across the field of the symbolic order in gendered terms. It is not clear exactly how Shakespeare's play functions in this model, but

Brooks-Davies tends to see it generally as a "parent text" that these particular works absorb, revisit, and revise, in yet another relationship of Oedipal anxiety. The book is structured as a developing argument that critiques the Oedipal model, especially in light of Iris Murdoch's revelation of its inherent misogyny. The chapter on *Great Expectations* is a strong analysis of the dynamic of maternal and paternal absence in the novel, as well as its "thanatological" relationship to *Hamlet*. Brooks-Davies shows how *Great Expectations*, like all Oedipal narratives, represents the mother as fully mediated by the figure of the father. Apart from a few over-readings of symbols and relationships, and an overly-close, conceptually static reading of textual details, Brooks-Davies presents a strong case for the existence of a Shakespearian Oedipal pattern in the novel. In this pattern, the quest for the mother is completely managed within the terms of the father-son bond, which insists that the mother be a strange blend of Gertrude and Ophelia. Perhaps the most interesting part of the reading is its tracing of the feminization of Magwitch, which helps subsume the mother within a masculine order.

Brooks-Davies has repeated and extended his psychoanalytic reading of *Great Expectations* in a Penguin Critical Studies volume. Like other works in this series, however, Brooks-Davies's book runs into problems of audience—it never does decide whether it is a companion to the novel meant for undergraduates or whether it is aimed at scholars. It tends to veer crazily from one mode of address to the other. On the one hand, we are told all about the blacking warehouse episode, along with other well-known biographical chestnuts, and, far worse, we are treated to saccharine expostulations about Dickens' "creative exuberance" (the concluding sentence of the book, for example, is: "I am dazzled by [the novel's] brilliance and wish to say, simply, that I love it and enjoy it in all its moving vitality"). On the other hand, Brooks-Davies often switches critical focus glibly, with only a few cues for the knowledgeable insider, and he often unwinds elaborate conceptual schema appropriate to a full-fledged (and sometimes obsessive) Oedipal reading. The book is full of clever explanations of Dickens' word-play, and it does make a number of valuable suggestions. But it is ultimately too fragmentary, too meandering, and too simplistically Freudian.

Several less emphatically theoretical studies of *Great Expectations* actually managed to sneak into print. Thomas Loe, in "Gothic Plot in *Great Expectations*," demonstrates the multiplicity of the novel's plot lines, even though *Great Expectations* is usually seen as the most unified of Dickens' novels. In particular, he argues convincingly that the bildungsroman plot, usually taken in isolation, is given shape and focus by the gothic plot, which provides a sharper sense of progression. The layering of mystery upon mystery, which Dickens takes from gothic form, advances the bildung plot by steady degrees, and also ties together the various strands of action. Loe highlights Dickens' borrowings instructively, and shows their unexpected structural function.

Linda Raphael takes up the issue of differences between readings by a novel's contemporaries and subsequent readings, and she attempts to balance the claims of each in analyzing the novel. In the particular case of Miss Havisham, she stresses the social facts of spinsterhood, family structure, and class conflict in the period, so as to define the Victorian-ness of Miss Havisham's dilemma. But she also sees room for contemporary psychoanalytic diagnoses, and tries to synthesize both perspectives, finally, in a reading of the vicious circularity of Miss Havisham's behavior.

In an interesting but minor note, Stanley Friedman shows how Pip distorts the details of an oriental story taken from Ridley when he retells it, in such a way as to suggest a doubling in his own attitude toward his inheritance. Through his distortion, Pip seems to suggest that he is both guilty and the victim of others, that he is both reprehensible and a heroic figure. This new discovery sheds fresh light on an old topic: Pip's self-consciousness about the moral ambiguities of his situation. Less interestingly, and with little subtlety, Michael L. Richmond argues that the portrait of Jaggers is Dickens' argument for the need of literary values among attorneys.

As usual, the issue of Dickens' politics—and the difficulties it presents for twentieth-century readers—frames discussions of *Hard Times*, though a number of critics have tried very hard to escape it. Gorman Beauchamp argues that the critical focus on Dickens' (admittedly simplistic) class analysis in *Hard Times* has diverted attention from other aspects of his thinking about industrialization. What interests Beauchamp is an issue he calls ''mechanomorphism''—the notion that human beings should pattern their behavior on the model of the machine. Beauchamp notes the remarkable dearth of nineteenth-century fiction addressing this intellectual phenomenon, considering that both proponents and opponents during the period saw mechanical approaches to human behavior as one of the most fundamental currents in their rapidly changing society. This novelistic aphasia gives Beauchamp reason to champion Dickens' rare reflections on mechanomorphism in *Hard Times*. Urging that we put aside the focus on class and labor relations that has been the legacy of left-leaning (and especially Marxist) criticism of the novel, he traces instead Dickens' perception of what he believed to be more fundamental social changes—though one might object that Marxism has always tried to incorporate this particular insight about industrialism. Beauchamp contends that the caricaturing of Gradgrind, in particular, does not identify him with a single philosophy or figure, but as "the satirical archetype of a generic intellectual figure, the modern social scientist." Rather than equate Gradgrind solely with Bentham or utilitarianism, Beauchamp draws connections between Gradgrind's philosophy and such figures as Bacon, Hartley, Smith, Malthus, and, most important of all, Newton. Beauchamp thus seeks to defend the subtlety and sophistication of *Hard Times* by understanding it as an attack on a certain general mentality, rather than on a specific form of social organization.

A different kind of aversion to traditional political discussion is John Holloway's chatty, impressionistic, but insightful essay. Holloway calls attention to the positive aspects of Bounderby, especially his resilience and strength of will, which Holloway argues gives him a dignity rare among characters in this novel. Holloway claims that the positive side of Bounderby is evidence that the character escaped Dickens' control, but also that Bounderby is endowed with some of the fabular qualities Dickens always associated with his villains. His most controversial point (at least, it might be controversial if the essay were clearer) is that these fabular qualities of the novel have been systematically overlooked because critics insist on tying the novel too closely to contemporary events and social issues, as a commentary or a reaction. Arguing the partial autonomy of the novel from such a framework, Holloway points out that the treatment of Benthamism, for which Dickens is often praised, is hardly more fair than the treatment of trade unionism, for which he is faulted. Holloway ties this general claim to intriguing comments about the ways in which the form of the novel underscores the lack of genuine social community and vitality in Coketown. These considerations lead him to conclude that the novel ultimately valorizes individualistic energy, as a counter to such inertia, and—through what seems like a twist in logic—that Bounderby embodies in a fabular way the social forces that work to squelch such individualism. A similar formalist tack is taken by Grahame Smith's *DSA* essay, which also dissociates the aesthetic structure of the novel from direct political assertions, locating it instead within what he calls principles of "comic subversion."

Both of these essays about formalist modes of discourse in *Hard Times* are usefully countered and complemented by Jean Ferguson Carr's excellent *DSA* essay on Dickens' incorporation of feminized modes of discourse into the novel, as a way to exploit the social position of the marginalized outsider for his own interests. Another useful approach to the novel's politics is taken by Cynthia Northcutt Malone, who argues that although *Hard Times* denounces utilitarian approaches to social reform, it attempts to substitute for them a more sophisticated system of social control, based on the ideology of middle-class reform. She argues that despite the novel's emphasis on tolerance and imagination, it aims at the disciplining of individuals in conformity with middle-class values. Ironically, the novel borrows from the utilitarians the tactic of surveillance to achieve its disciplinary norms. Malone demonstrates how beneath the novel's various oppositions—fancy/fact, circus/society, heart/head—is an essentially homogeneous system of surveillance. She shows, for example, how the opposition between society and the circus is undermined by the way the circus uses spectacle to normalize physical performance, thereby mirroring wider patterns of social control. She sees in Sleary a figure of all-reaching sight, who punishes whenever he detects deviation. She compares the strategies of various "good characters" as well as the narrative as a whole to the disciplinary devices of Gradgrind. Ultimately, Malone argues that the novel's policing is focused on the sexual discipline carried out against Louisa. Though somewhat sketchy, and immune to the considerable ambivalence of the novel toward both class and moral boundaries, Malone's essay is full of intriguing insights about such things as the regulative power of Sissy Jupe's presence and observation, the education of Stephen Blackpool into self-discipline, and, most of all, the "naturalization" of middle-class norms of moral reform that Dickens imposes by embodying such norms in a working-class girl.

In an intricate attempt to defend Dickens' politics, Patricia Johnson argues for the ideological coherence of Dickens' representation of industrialism, a coherence achieved through his use of the factory as a metaphor both for destructive social conditions and for the aesthetic unity of the novel itself. Her analysis thus runs counter to recent work by Catherine Gallagher or Stephen Spender, who have argued that the metaphorics of the novel are not unified. The "closed economy" of the factory system, in Johnson's view, offered Dickens a way to link the metaphoric and metonymic structures of the novel in ideologically expressive ways. Johnson's claims are based on somewhat strained analogies between novelistic structure and theme: for example, that the lives of Stephen and Louisa are presented as the novel's "coke"—the fuel and also the eventual waste products of factory production, and of the patriarchal family. While proposing a unified reading, she also focuses only on these two characters, and she provides a purely formalist explanation of how capitalist production and sexual reproduction intersect. In many respects, however, this is a clever reading of the novel, and Johnson does succeed in re-directing the usual controversies over Dickens' political intentions by conceiving the novel as a self-consuming, mirroring instrument.

That is, she situates the novel as an ideological drama, in which the dynamics of the factory system demonstrate the costs of their own maintenance, without allowing the narrative to speak from any outside, critical perspective.

The most substantial reading of any single novel is Charlotte Rotkin's *Deception in Little Dorrit*, a monograph in Peter Lang's English Language and Literature series. Rotkin pursues deception both as a theme and as the basis of Dickens' own narrative strategies: *Little Dorrit* is "a deceptive presentation of deception." The difficult task she sets herself is to show how psychological portraiture is ambiguously drawn so as to misguide interpretation. Furthermore, Dickens has covered his tracks by delineating most of his characters candidly, and reserving key deceptions for just a few of the protagonists. For Rotkin, Dickens' deceptions do not come to depend on some central repression, but stem instead from what seems to be a polymorphous mendacity that has its roots in a deeply pessimistic, even cynical vision. As she puts it, Dickens means to show "that improbity is ubiquitous, is part of the ritual of social life. . . . It is an international social evil, integral to social conventions." Even more darkly, "the manifestation of ill will, which Dickens sees as a pervasive human force, is intrinsic to *Little Dorrit*." Rotkin is very good at documenting the loose lines of truth in various quarters of the novel, but her study often walks the thin line between penetration and paranoia. To make her claims, Rotkin's argument must hinge on inflexible assertions about what Dickens really intended, and about how readers are systematically manipulated into specific psychological misreadings that fall short of his intentions (e.g., that all readers are maneuvered into overlooking what Dickens sees as Amy's egotism and aggression—which is simply not true, as the critical record shows quite plainly). Other readers, less univocal in their interpretations, might also define the techniques of ambiguity that she identifies as narrative subtlety. The reading she develops can seem very tenuous, and, almost inevitably, she must protest a bit too much about her own originality, and about other critics' obtuseness.

In the context of *Little Dorrit*, Joseph Childers takes one aspect of new historicist criticism—its refusal of totality to either author, work, or period—and considers the resultant pitfalls: inabilities to contest competing interpretations or events and failure to ground an oppositional politics. Arguing that these problems can be overcome by keeping the issue of totality in the foreground, without yielding to the sin of totalization, he discusses the "dynamic totalization" of *Little Dorrit*, by which he appears to mean its play with processes of totalization, though in practice this appears to return him

to the cultural idealism that grants novelists the ability to perceive and decons-
truct the unified discourses of others. Arguing that *Little Dorrit* is a set of
ambivalent, sometimes contradictory reflections on the Victorian discourse of
progress, Childers manages to locate discursive fluidity within the novel,
making it, in effect, the deconstructor of this "dominant ideology." Childers
feels the need to advance evidence to shore up the idea that myths of progress
were, in fact, widely-shared in Victorian culture, and it will come as no
suprise to Dickensians to hear that *Little Dorrit* is skeptical about social
progress, and exposes the ways in which institutions use the discourse of
progress to contain it. The theoretical generalizations Childers draws from
this account are cheerfully dialectical at times (that dominant ideologies are
always riven by contradictions, and that these contradictions, besides constituting the dominant ideology, are also the mechanisms for changing it); but
materialist at others (that our linguistic descriptions of change must always
respect the pressure of the referent); and occasionally idealist (that descriptions of the world ultimately manage change, and therefore should be drafted
with the consequences of change in mind). Ultimately, Childers argues con-
fusedly that skepticism about totalizing concepts has an inherent affinity with
political resistance, and his position finally looks something like a simple
liberal pluralism that recognizes the importance of choice. Despite the ram-
shackle nature of the argument, this remains, nevertheless, an interesting set
of reflections on very complex and urgent issues.

   Little Dorrit also attracted two important feminist readings in *DSA*: Nancy
Aycock Metz's essay on Dickens' use of narratives that subvert expectations
of linearity, which she connects with Cixous's model of feminine writing;
and Sarah Winter's more traditional critique of Dickens' validation of female
deference.

   There were a number of interesting pieces published in 1989 on Christine
Edzard's film version of *Little Dorrit* (released in 1988). I have neglected
those that concentrate only on the film, but there were at least two worth
noting because they throw useful light on the novel as well. Raphael Samuel's
essay is one of the more sensitive hostile reviews of the film, detailing even-
handedly a number of widespread complaints: that realistic attention is conflated with rendering a "period piece," that Victorian social critique is turned
into pure spectacle, and that melodramatic effects are erased in the name of
representational accuracy. Samuel contrasts the film's limitations to what he
sees as the greater success of the RSC's *Nicholas Nickleby*, David Lean's
version of *Great Expectations*, and numerous other dramatized versions of
the novels, which have all taken creative liberties with Dickens' texts to their

own great advantage. But he also remains critical of the way Dickens is
appropriated for conservative ideological ends by all of these adaptations. A
much less fair analysis is Garry Wills's "Dorrit Without Politics," which
dismisses the film as "a soupy love story peopled at the edges with decorative
oddities," and which argues that the film's entire purpose is to revitalize the
love story at the expense of other elements in the novel, particularly its social
critique and its anger.

Steven Connor tries to explore the self-conscious textuality of *Oliver Twist*,
without reducing the novel to "an undifferentiated ocean of textuality." He
does so by exploring the relationship between self-reflexive narrativity and
social power. Somewhat problematically, however, he returns to a few much-
contested distinctions when he labels the specificity of Dickens' narrative
strategies. That is, he differentiates between "public" and "private" narratives, finding the public to be characterized by impersonality and a tendency
to encroach on personal agency, whereas the private is characterized by
"vigorous adaptability." In his reading of *Oliver Twist*, Connor also seems
to discover a fairly traditional progression: Oliver is at first "dispossessed" of
narrative power, which allows others to write his story in official, institutional
terms, but the novel eventually allows for Oliver's private and "true story"
to be told. Connor does show, however, how Oliver's final narrative never
really recovers an extra-textual explanatory origin. The "true" revelations at
the end of the novel are, in fact, the result of competing narratives. Thus,
even if the novel dissolves "false narratives" it cannot disperse a general
economy of narration that prevents anything like full presence. Connor seems
to want to distinguish this kind of reading from typical post-structuralist
accounts by claiming that Dickens' textual strategy is affiliated with "resistance" to social power. But he makes this claim only by showing how the
narrative has resisted its own inclinations toward closure, thus resisting middle-class claims to ideological legitimacy that an originary narrative would
supposedly have supplied. That readings of *Oliver Twist* have, indeed, always
affirmed those kinds of ideological legitimacy is a problem that Connor does
not explain. Another interesting, if quite different, semiotic approach is taken
by John Jordan's *DSA* essay, which explores the social and symbolic significance of the novel's use of handkerchiefs.

Focusing on a more specific aspect of *Oliver Twist*, Nancy West claims
that Dickens anticipates the surrealist movement in much more concrete ways
than scholars have realized, in the sense that the hallucinatory or dream-like
qualities of his work are a significant attempt to explore the unconscious—though it is doubtful that she would get much resistance on this point.

But in *Oliver Twist*, she does take elements usually thought to reflect immature technique—a disproportionate blend of detail within fantasy, the passivity of Oliver, visual condensation of images, a suggestive use of "stillness," etc.—and argues that they are strategies of psychological investigation.

John Watson's reading of *Oliver Twist* seeks to explore how Dickens uses comedy and "imagination" to confront "the cruelty of life," and to show how point of view is crucial to this project. Watson's terms are very ill-defined, and it is difficult to know exactly what he is proposing. The essay is more a miscellaneous collection of observations about humor and nightmare in *Oliver Twist* than a sustained argument. Watson is insightful about the underworld characters, and about the inappropriate attempts at comedy in the ending, but the essay as a whole makes too many unfounded generalizations about when we laugh and why, or about the sequence of reflections embedded within "our" laughter in reading a particular scene. Another unsatis-fying—but much more interesting—look at the novel is Garry Wills's "Love in the Lower Depths." Wills insightfully locates *Oliver Twist* at the head of a boy's book tradition, including works by Twain, Stevenson, and others, which revolves around the good boy's socially enlightening encounter with social outcasts. But Wills commits quite a few sins of interpretive excess. He over-idealizes Fagin's gang as a social site of equality and humanity. Worse, he assumes matter-of-factly that Fagin is a pederast, that his homosexuality was perfectly obvious to Victorian readers, and that the force of the mob's revulsion at the conclusion of the novel lies in its homophobia. This enables Wills to over-state Dickens' radicalism, by claiming that *Oliver Twist* declares even pederasty to be better than corrupt social institutions like the workhouse. Wills also perversely finds Nancy to be the most fully-realized and deeply-felt of all Dickens' female characters, and he chides readers who do not appreciate her with class prejudice. The essay concludes with a vivid, if familiar, evocation of Dickens' desire to explore the criminal mind.

Turning now to *David Copperfield*, Natalie and Ronald Schroeder provide a modest but useful reading of one minor textual pattern, the polarized roles of David's two aunts (static vs. dynamic, evil vs. good). They point out the uncanny symbolic and psychological similarities between these two figures: the resonance of their names; their masculinization; their antipathy to men; their tendency to criminalize David; their mutual mistreatment of Clara; etc. The Schroders argue convincingly that these parallels lend significance to the dramatic confrontation between the two women, which precipitates a sudden change in Betsey's character. Betsey's repudiation of the Murdstones is thus part of an internal struggle, a purging of parts of her personality that had the potential to distort her strong traits into loveless ones.

Torsten Pettersson tries to divide critics of *David Copperfield* into two basic camps: those who claim David represents a coherent, unified self, and those who identify damaging conflicts or contradictions within his personality. He argues that this polarization warrants a third view: he argues for the coexistence of tensional elements in David's personality, as well as David's self-conscious integration of these elements into a mature balance. Pettersson thus argues that conflicts within David's personality are "psychologically understandable and need not undermine our confidence in David's narratorial judgments." It is difficult, however, to see how this is not a retreat to the first camp Pettersson describes, especially in that Pettersson attributes the conflicts he identifies entirely to the gap between David's "spontaneous emotions" and his growing sense of morality. This approach greatly reduces the range of subjective slippage identified by other readings of David's motivations and his self-knowledge, and it leads Pettersson toward traditional speculations about Dickens' use of David as a positive (but perhaps impossible) model for resolving his own personal dilemmas.

Heather Henderson's book on autobiography and Biblical narrative contains a short but substantial section within the epilogue (about fourteen pages) on *David Copperfield*. *The Victorian Self* is an important contribution to work on Biblical typology in Victorian writing, with excellent chapters on Newman, Ruskin, and Gosse. Henderson's main thesis is that Victorian writers often deliberately "misuse" typological patterns to subvert their traditional meanings. But rather than seeing this subversion as merely a strategy of apostasy, Henderson shows how it opens up many possibilities for new narratives of doubt, "unconversion," progressive enlightenment, parody, or even transcendence, and especially new narratives of subjectivity—all informed by self-conscious fictionalizing. The section on *David Copperfield*—which is weaker than the book as a whole, unfortunately—argues that the novel uses the Biblical story of David to define a quest for self-knowledge that is ultimately secularized, and diverted from the typological pattern. While conversion thus remains a key element in the narrative of the self, its meaning is radically changed. Perhaps the most interesting—but most arguable—part of this discussion is Henderson's contention that Dickens avoids the darker implications of the Biblical story, suggesting that his departures from the model are signs of fear, not deliberate revision (in what sense, one might ask, does Dickens really "repress" David's attraction to Steerforth, or his parallels with Uriah?). This section is followed by a companion piece on *Jane*

Eyre that demonstrates how the same narrative pattern could be adapted to a woman's history. Henderson's claim that nineteenth-century novels try to plant authority in the self, and do so by sublimating external authority, will not surprise many people. But the way this pattern informs novelists' use of typology will nicely supplement and correct recent work in this area.

Perhaps the most important essay likely to be overlooked because of its focus on a minor novel is Kim Ian Michasiw's "*Barnaby Rudge*: The Sins of the Fathers." Michasiw addresses the persistent problem of a gap between historical and psychobiographical accounts of the novel, as well as critical struggles with larger issues embedded in this disjunction: the relation between writer and precursor, between generational conflict and social forms, or between individual and society. He uses a Bloomian model of the text—in which the text is a terrain of conflict with the father—to illuminate these various issues. Michasiw negotiates these issues persuasively, though he runs the risk (as he admits) of reifying both particulars and systematic structures, which is the tendency of Bloomian analysis. With some justification, he sees this risk as necessary to articulate a level of agonism in and behind the text, an agonism that makes discussions of agency possible within the context of contemporary theories of history, and their emphasis on embeddedness. In general, Michasiw argues that the constructed opposition between writer and precursor can open up a space of agency, and, therefore, of the historical viability of agonistic strategies—a model somewhat more complicated than Bloom's, and more willing to admit social pressures and constraints that shape any particular construction of the past. In Dickens' case, his relationship to Scott opens up an oppositional stance toward a number of contemporary discourses, for Dickens focuses his social perspectives through objections to Scott's rather static model of history, and his lack of faith in exceptional individuals or actions. Michasiw's reading of the novel, in which he sees Dickens interpreting social relations entirely through generational conflict in order to articulate his ambivalence about both authority and rebellion, is less original and less instructive than his theoretical suggestions, and it remains somewhat sketchy. Nevertheless, he does have illuminating insights about the motives of Barnaby in several instances, and about Dickens' own affinities with Hugh, specifically through his association of Hugh with Carlyle. He also shows how Dickens bases prophetic ability on the recognition and incorporation of "ancestral voices," both literary and social, which means, in effect, that writers must "name the father" to be empowered.

Another essay that Dickensians should not overlook, though it is only partially on *Tale of Two Cities*, is Garrett Stewart's "Leaving History: Dickens, Gance, Blanchot." Taken broadly, this is a study of film and literature as "unique but related textual systems." Stewart examines *The Tale of Two Cities*, an essay by Blanchot on textuality and revolution, and Gance's film *Napoleon* to explore the relationship between insurrection and signification. In all three of these works, Stewart finds a similar set of tensions, in which the textual medium is seen as the limit of all subversion, but also the ground from which all subversion must be authorized. Each work is divided from within, then, by its ambivalent representation of textuality itself. In each work, however, Stewart finds posited "a different escape route from the confines of its own textuality." Through this set of concerns, Stewart seeks to theorize within textuality—or to coax such theory out of his three texts, and especially out of the Blanchot—some space for revolutionary overturning. Not itself a historicist reading, the essay examines a set of illusions about the flight from history that are inevitably generated by narratological practices. Dickensians will be particularly interested in Stewart's careful and perceptive analysis of textuality as a theme in *Tale of Two Cities*, which demonstrates how writing for Carton becomes an instrument of emptying and effacing, and also how, ironically enough, "vision" comes to replace script as the sign of the insurrectionary text. In particular, by appealing to the language of vision, Dickens anticipates the cinematic means of erasing history as fixed sequence, figuring it instead as a palimpsest of simultaneous events and ideas.

While I am on the subject of buried gems, one of the more intriguing and important contributions to literary theory to come out of a minor Dickens novel is Michael Hollington's translation of Adorno's short 1931 essay (revised in 1967), "Rede über den *Raritatenladen* von Charles Dickens." Adorno's essay sheds less light on *The Old Curiosity Shop* (despite Hollington's claims) than it does on his own intellectual development, but for that reason alone its translation is a significant event. The essay is largely a vindication of Dickens' allegorical method (and of allegorical method in general), which Adorno roots in tensions within bourgeois culture that ultimately serve to unmask that culture. In this sense, Quilp and Nell are seen neither as psychological studies nor as expressions of metaphysical opposites, but as figures determined by the dialectic of bourgeois history. Nell, in particular, is destroyed by the new bourgeois order, even as Dickens glimpses the dialectical potential for redemption in the new world of things in which she is embedded. In an excellent prefatory essay, Hollington explores the importance of Benjamin's influence at this early stage of Adorno's career, especially Benjamin's theory of allegory.

Writing in an entirely different vein about *The Old Curiosity Shop*, Adriane LaPointe's *DSA* essay offers a brave defense of Little Nell that sees her as an expression of Dickens' complex feelings about theological authority. Marcia Eaton uses *The Old Curiosity Shop* to revise what she sees as commonplace separations made between the ethical and the aesthetic. Instead of relying on the long tradition of post-Kantian thought that theorizes their relation, however (Eaton is a philosopher), she argues quite simplistically that such interrelation is necessary "for a meaningful life." There is a good deal of reinventing the wheel here, for both philosophic and literary critical travel, and the analysis of sentimentality is completely ahistorical. Eaton assumes that sentimentality is bad in some absolute way, but she does make the valuable point that condemnations of sentimental art are almost always grounded in moral objections.

Lewis Horne's point of departure, in a relatively uncomplicated essay on *Nicholas Nickleby*, is the critical consensus that the novel lacks aesthetic structure and coherence. Horne argues that attention to its form leads instead to a general recognition about the unity of the novel: *Nicholas Nickleby* is about a world that functions according to structures of power that link family, society, and individual psychology. Horne sees the novel mainly as a story of how "strength of spirit" overcomes restrictive relationships of various kinds, and he charts how Nicholas is able, eventually, to discriminate between harmful and benevolent kinds of power. He focuses on Newman Noggs as a figure of guidance and support, the principle character who leads Nicholas toward recognition of his "covenant with the human community."

David Parker's unassuming but fascinating essay explores the origins of *Pickwick Papers* in Seymour's illustrative project, attributing a greater influence to Seymour than Dickens and most Dickensians would like to credit. His contention is that Seymour's sporting emphasis was modified by Dickens, not dropped, and that the Cockney sporting mishap tradition allowed Dickens great opportunities to explore various kinds of contemporary social change. Parker is very good on the class coding of elements of the sporting tradition, especially the importance of a knowledge of horses. Dickens' own anxiety about "horsey" knowledge, shared with Mr. Pickwick, is a response to a peculiar nineteenth-century alliance of stablish *savoir faire* between upper and lower class figures that excludes members of the lower middle class. Sporting scenes involving horses thus serve to focus the class advantages that certain kinds of equine knowledge afforded middle-class protagonists, and Parker demonstrates how Pickwick's moral education parallels his initiation into the mysteries of stable life.

In addition to Michie's important essay on *Our Mutual Friend*, there were three fairly minor essays on the novel. A short essay by Michael Miller describes the basic contrasts between the Fellowship-Porters and the Veneerings', which direct the reader toward a set of judgments that help unify the novel. His essay is a good close reading, though it only underlines the usual contrasts between hypocrisy and authenticity, and affirms Dickens' commitment to ideals of "justice." S. J. Newman returns us to long-standing complaints (he tangles with Henry James and F. R. Leavis) that *Our Mutual Friend* lacks both exuberance and coherence. Daring to challenge such eminent authority, he endorses the novel's various "breakdowns" with great fanfare, seeing them as socially diagnostic and imaginatively fertile—as if no one had ventured such opinions before. Peter Smith argues that *Our Mutual Friend* is not primarily about social issues, but that its theme is "beauty," and that it looks forward to Pater rather than backward to Carlyle. Smith's contention, not very rigorously situated in terms of nineteenth-century aesthetic theory, is simply that the novel is about the power of art to transform self and society through the filter of aesthetic consciousness. He does make the interesting point that the novel propounds a bourgeois version of aestheticism, and that it resists the aesthetic elitism that it might otherwise seem to endorse.

Based loosely on *Martin Chuzzlewit*'s Sarah Gamp, Anne Summers's essay—an important contribution to feminist studies—shows how Dickens' literary stereotype of the domestic nurse reflects widespread prejudice against nursing, which arises, she claims, from fears about the professionalization of female work. Misinformation about the state of early Victorian nursing, Summers claims, has actually contributed to an exaggeration of the reforms carried out by Florence Nightingale and others. Her article is concerned mostly with correcting our view of the early Victorian female nurse, who was both more competent and more respectable in background and education than the Gamp syndrome acknowledges.

Gerhard Joseph and Jay Fellows's essay on *Martin Chuzzlewit*—an essay that would have been considered "trendy" several years ago—repeats in formal terms its deconstructive paradigms. Claiming that the "diffusionary impulses" of the novel make it impossible to achieve a comprehensive critical perspective, they fracture the surface of their own essay, paralleling Joseph's lucid "host text" with Fellows's marginalized "guest text," which turns out to be a rhapsodic, delirious, obstreperous, hysterical intertextual expression of the jouissance/anxiety that textual fragmentation provokes. As the essay proceeds, of course, the guest text progressively encroaches on the host text, both graphically and conceptually. Further, Joseph and Fellows in different ways blur the boundaries between center and margin, reason and unreason.

Etc., etc. The net effect is not so much unreformed de Manian critique or Barthesian bliss as it is simply precious. Still, Joseph and Fellows are extremely skillful readers and writers, and the analogies they draw in the midst of all this rhetorical pirouetting are often provocative—especially Joseph's remarks on architectural metaphors in Dickens, and the way in which such metaphors help to express certain moral and aesthetic dilemmas.

The unfinished ending of *Edwin Drood* continues to attract banal but strident speculation. Benny Reece's study, though more tongue-in-cheek than most, shares the usual overweening pride in having discovered the single possible (and, in this case, absolutely bizarre) solution. Reece is also very proud about having a great number of other eccentric opinions. By not revealing his discovery, I trust I leave my readers breathless with suspense. W. W. Robson has also contributed a long, rambling essay on the subject that has little focus or originality. It restates the case against Jasper, rehearses old speculations on how the events of the murder actually fell out, and retells some of the hunches of Forster and others close to Dickens, as well as some of the more elaborate theories of later critics. The essay adds little of note to the old debate, but does risk an innovative (if loosely argued and tenuously-held) suggestion: that Datchery is Charles Dickens himself, and that Dickens intended to play with the gap between the author and the world of his characters.

The only two essays published on *Dombey and Son* were two works in *DSA*: Gerhard Joseph's study of the novel's preoccupation with change of various kinds, and Robert Newsom's essay about its structures of variety and coherence.

Among studies of more peripheral works, Caracciolo and Hampson's piece is easily the most entertaining. It cleverly explains a puzzling reference found in both *The Lazy Tour of Two Idle Apprentices* and in *The Secret Agent* to an *Arabian Nights* tale that has mysteriously eluded scholarly research. Caracciolo and Hampson show how the references are the result of a Victorian mistranslation of a somewhat misleading French translation of the *Arabian Nights*. Joel Brattin writes on the composition of *The Lamplighter*, and its transformation into a short story, detailing the circumstances of composition. He also considers various changes, as well as continuities, and reflects randomly on their significance. Peter Merchant discusses ''The Battle of Life'' in an interesting essay on children's literature in the 1840s and '50s, which Merchant sees as deliberately revising classical narratives of heroism to promote self-abnegation over valor. Finally, David Greenman argues that the last two ghost stories Dickens wrote represent his highest success in this genre, and that they are equal in sophistication to the best stories of the gothic genre. He tries to substantiate these claims with much praise for the stories' structure, dialogue, psychology, and irony.

CONCLUSION

Besides being exhausted and overwhelmed—and, certainly, resentful of a publishing treadmill that generates far too much repetitious or unnecessary scholarship—I am also struck by how little conflict there is in Dickens studies. While the entire range of methodological and professional interests would seem to be represented in this body of work, one can easily read through it all with a minimal sense of argument, disagreement, or debate. The Dickens heterocosm seems to be a strangely frictionless one—if it is really a hetero-cosm at all, since a great many of these projects seem to feature the stitching together of various approaches, rather than their differentiation, much less the championing of one over another. Not that there is no conflict at all in this work—indeed, I hope I have highlighted some of it. But such conflict does seem ominously subdued, and strangely overshadowed by the choral, often shrill agreement we have come to expect on a few contemporary pieties. All this, if I may be allowed to revel in my gall, is only symptomatic of the state of the profession as a whole in the late 1980s.

My other principle reflection is a certain regret about the narrow way I went about organizing this review. Given the increased blurring of critical categories and boundaries in the profession, there is an increase in the kind of scholarship that takes up Dickens only briefly in the context of some wider cultural or historical topic. This kind of work is becoming much more central to our collective sense of what we, as literary or cultural intellectuals, do. It may have been easier to see it as peripheral to "Dickens Studies" only a few years ago than it is now. In reading for this review, it has occurred to me that the Dickens industry is somewhat less amenable to this change than is criticism of, say, women writers, or romantic poetry, or detective fiction (as all single-author criticism must inevitably be, I suppose), but it has certainly not been immune. Some of this kind of work has been included in my review (MacKay's volume contains many examples; I think also of essays by Stewart, Langbauer, Parker, and a few others), but much of it, I fear, has necessarily been displaced by more narrowly-focused Dickensiana. And while it would complicate the task of this reviewer enormously—perhaps impossibly—I wish

I had found some way to frame the review more widely, in order to capture this distinct change in what Dickens studies has become, or is becoming.

WORKS CITED

Adorno, Theodor. "An Address on Charles Dickens's *The Old Curiosity Shop*." Trans. of "Rede über den *Raritatenladen* von Charles Dickens." *Dickens Quarterly* 6 (1989): 96–101.

Altick, Richard D. *Writers, Readers, and Occasions: Selected Essays on Victorian Literature and Life*. Columbus: Ohio State UP, 1989.

Altman, Rick. "Dickens, Griffith, and Film Theory Today." *South Atlantic Quarterly* 88 (1989): 321–59.

Anderson, Nancy Fix. "Eliza Lynn Linton, Dickens, and the Woman Question." *Victorian Periodicals Review* 22 (1989): 134–41.

Auerbach, Nina. "Dickens and Acting Women." MacKay. *Dramatic Dickens*. 81–86.

Baird, George. "The Labor of our Body and the Work of our Hands." *Harvard Architecture Review* 7 (1989): 82–99.

Barfoot, C. C. "Swivelling Dick: Dickens as Romantic and Anti-Romantic." *Dutch Quarterly Review of Anglo-American Letters* 19 (1989): 281–93.

Barreca, Regina. " 'The Mimic Life of the Theatre': The 1838 Adaptation of *Oliver Twist*." MacKay. *Dramatic Dickens*. 87–95.

Beauchamp, Gorman. "Mechanomorphism in *Hard Times*." *Studies in the Literary Imagination* 22 (1989): 61–77.

Bledsoe, Robert. "Dickens and Opera." *Dickens Studies Annual: Essays on Victorian Fiction* 18 (1989): 93–118.

Booth, Michael R. "Melodrama and the Working Class." MacKay. *Dramatic Dickens*. 96–109.

Brattin, Joel J. "From Drama Into Fiction: *The Lamplighter* and 'The Lamplighter's Story.' " *Dickensian* 85 (1989): 130–39.

Brooks-Davies, Douglas. "Dickens: *Great Expectations* and the Ghost of the Father" in *Fielding, Dickens, Gosse, Iris Murdoch and Oedipal* Hamlet. London: Macmillan, 1989. 60–114.

———. *Great Expectations*. Penguin Critical Studies. London: Penguin, 1989.

Burgan, Mary. "Heroines at the Piano: Women and Music in Nineteenth-Century Fiction." *The Lost Chord: Essays on Victorian Music*. Ed. Nicholas Temperley. Bloomington: Indiana UP, 1989. 42–67.

Caracciolo, P. L. and R. G. Hampson. " 'Money Turned to Leaves': Conrad, Collins, Dickens, and the Barber's Fourth Brother." *Notes and Queries* new series 36 (1989): 193–96.

Carr, Jean Ferguson. "Dickens's Theatre of Self-Knowledge." MacKay. *Dramatic Dickens*. 27–44.

———. "Writing as a Woman: Dickens, *Hard Times*, and Feminine Discourses." *Dickens Studies Annual: Essays on Victorian Fiction* 18 (1989): 161–78.

Chadwyck-Healey. *The Charles Dickens Research Collection*. Cambridge, England: Chadwyck-Healey, 1990.

Chaudhuri, Brahma. "Dickens and the Question of Slavery." *Dickens Quarterly* 6 (1989): 3–10.

Childers, Joseph W. "History, Totality, Opposition: The New Historicism and *Little Dorrit*." *Dickens Quarterly* 6 (1989): 150–57.

Chittick, Kathryn. *The Critical Reception of Charles Dickens, 1833–1841*. New York: Garland, 1989.

Cohen, Edward H. "Victorian Bibliography for 1988." *Victorian Studies* 32 (1989): 611–734.

Cohn, Alan M. "The Dickens Checklist." *Dickens Quarterly* 6 (1989): 31–35; 6 (1989): 79–82.

Colby, Robert A. "Thackeray and Dickens on the Boards." MacKay. *Dramatic Dickens*. 139–51.

Connor, Steven. " 'They're All in One Story': Public and Private Narratives in *Oliver Twist*." *Dickensian* 85 (1989): 2–16.

Cottom, Daniel. "Paranomasia, Culture, and the Power of Meaning" in *Text and Culture: The Politics of Interpretation*. Theory and History of Literature series, vol. 62. Minneapolis: U of Minnesota P, 1989. 103–153.

Currie, Richard A. "Surviving Maternal Loss: Transitional Relatedness in Dickens's Esther Summerson." *Dickens Quarterly* 6 (1989): 60–66.

Davies, James A. *The Textual Life of Dickens's Characters*. London: Macmillan, 1989.

Dickens, Charles. *Hard Times*. Ed. Paul Schlicke. The World's Classics. Oxford: Oxford UP, 1989.

Easson, Angus. "Towards the Celestial City: The Pilgrim Edition of Dickens's Letters." *Dickensian* 85 (1989): 18–28.

Eaton, Marcia Muelder. "Laughing at the Death of Little Nell: Sentimental Art and Sentimental People." *American Philosophical Quarterly* 26 (1989): 269–82.

Eigner, Edwin M. *The Dickens Pantomime*. Berkeley: U of California P, 1989.

Feinberg, Monica. "Family Plot: The Bleak House of Victorian Romance." *Victorian Newsletter*, (1989): 5–17.

Fellows, Jay, and Gerhard Joseph. "Mixed Messages in Mr. Pecksniff's Grammar School: A Defense of that Celebrated though Much-Maligned Parasite's Architectural Principles, as Necessitated by a Universal Misunderstanding of Them, of Him, and of Chapter 35 of *Martin Chuzzlewit*, by Charles Dickens, the Drunken Architect of the House of Chuzzlewit or The Rift in Pater's Lute." *Perspectives on Perception: Philosophy, Art, and Literature*. Reading Plus, vol. 3. Ed. Mary Ann Caws. New York: Peter Lang, 1989. 225–59.

Fisher, Benjamin Franklin, IV. "Dickens and Vampirism." *Dickens Quarterly* 6 (1989): 162–66.

Fisher, Judith L. "The 'Sensation Scene' in Charles Dickens and Dion Boucicault." MacKay. *Dramatic Dickens*. 152–67.

Frazee, John P. "Dickens and Unitarianism." *Dickens Studies Annual: Essays on Victorian Fiction* 18 (1989): 119–44.

———. "Of Foxes, Dogs, and the Monthly Cover of *Bleak House*." *Dickens Quarterly* 6 (1989): 112–16.

Friedman, Stanley. "Ridley's *Tales of the Genii* and Dickens's *Great Expectations*." *Nineteenth-Century Literature* 44 (1989): 215–218.

Gibson, Colin, ed. *Art and Society in the Victorian Novel: Essays on Dickens and his Contemporaries*. New York: St. Martin's, 1989.

Gilbert, Elliot L. *Critical Essays on Charles Dickens's* Bleak House. Critical Essays on British Literature series. Boston: G. K. Hall, 1989.

Glavin, John J. "*Little Dorrit* as 'Poor Theatre': Dickens through Grotowski." Mackay. *Dramatic Dickens*. 110–24.

Goldberg, Michael. "Dickens and the Early Modern Theatre." MacKay. *Dramatic Dickens*. 168–83.

Gollin, Rita K. "Living in a World Without Dickens." *The Huntington Library Quarterly* 52 (1989): 415–19.

Graham, Jenny. "Two Characters in *Bleak House*." *Dickens Quarterly* 6 (1989): 43–52.

Greenman, David J. "Dickens's Ultimate Achievements in the Ghost Story: 'To Be Taken with a Grain of Salt' and 'The Signalman.' " *Dickensian* 85 (1989): 40–48.

Henderson, Heather. "Typology and Autobiographical Fiction: The Story of David" in *The Victorian Self: Autobiography and Biblical Narrative*. Ithaca: Cornell UP, 1989. 159–90.

Hill, James. "Dickens's *Bleak House*." *The Explicator* 47.3 (1989): 21–22.

Hoefnagel, Dick. "Charles Dickens's annotated copy of Pepys's *Memoirs.*" *Dickensian* 85 (1989): 162–66.

Hollington, Michael. "Adorno, Benjamin, and *The Old Curiosity Shop.*" *Dickens Quarterly* 6 (1989): 87–95.

Holloway, John. "Form and Fable in *Hard Times.*" Gibson. 29–42.

Horne, Lewis. "Covenant and Power in *Nicholas Nickleby*; or, The Guidance of Newman Noggs." *Papers on Language and Literature* 25 (1989): 165–77.

Humphreys, Camilla. "Dickens's Use of Letters in *Bleak House.*" *Dickens Quarterly* 6 (1989): 53–60.

Johnson, Patricia E. "*Hard Times* and the Structure of Industrialism: The Novel as Factory." *Studies in the Novel* 21 (1989): 128–37.

Jordan, John O. "The Purloined Handkerchief." *Dickens Studies Annual: Essays on Victorian Fiction* 18 (1989): 1–18.

Joseph, Gerhard. "*Dombey*, Change, and the Changeling." *Dickens Studies Annual: Essays on Victorian Fiction* 18 (1989): 179–96.

Kincaid, James R. "Performance, Roles, and the Nature of the Self in Dickens." MacKay. *Dramatic Dickens.* 11–26.

King, James Roy. "*Bleak House* as Metaphor." *Metaphor and Symbolic Activity* 4 (1989): 39–54.

Kosky, Jules. *Mutual Friends: Charles Dickens and Great Ormond Street Children's Hospital.* New York: St. Martin's, 1989.

Langbauer, Laurie. "Women in White, Men in Feminism." *The Yale Journal of Criticism* 2.2 (1989): 219–43.

Lansbury, Coral. "Pecksniff and Pratfalls." MacKay. *Dramatic Dickens.* 45–51.

LaPointe, Adriane. "Little Nell Once More: Absent Fathers in *The Old Curiosity Shop.*" *Dickens Studies Annual: Essays on Victorian Fiction* 18 (1989): 19–38.

LaRocque, Carolyn Buckley. "The Initiation of David Copperfield the Younger: A Ritual Passage in Three Acts." MacKay. *Dramatic Dickens.* 52–67.

LeFew, Penelope A. "Evidence of a Dickensian Gissing in 'Joseph Yates' Temptation.' " *English Language Notes* 26.3 (1989): 82–87.

Lettis, Richard. *The Dickens Aesthetic.* New York: AMS, 1989.

Loe, Thomas. "Gothic Plot in *Great Expectations.*" *Dickens Quarterly* 6 (1989): 102–110.

Long, William F. "Dickens and the Coming of Rail to Deal: An Uncollected Speech and its Context." *Dickensian* 85 (1989): 66–80.

MacKay, Carol Hanbery. " 'Before the Curtain': Entrances to the Dickens Theatre." MacKay. *Dramatic Dickens.* 1–10.

———, ed. *Dramatic Dickens.* New York: St. Martin's, 1989.

———. "The Encapsulated Romantic: John Harmon and the Boundaries of Victorian Soliloquy." *Dickens Studies Annual: Essays on Victorian Fiction* 18 (1989): 255–76.

Magee, Mary Margaret. "Postscript: Theatricality and Dickens's End Strategies." MacKay. *Dramatic Dickens.* 184–93.

Malone, Cynthia Northcutt. "The Fixed Eye and the Rolling Eye: Surveillance and Discipline in *Hard Times.*" *Studies in the Novel* 21 (1989): 14–26.

Matus, Jill. "Proxy and Proximity: Metonymic Signing." *University of Toronto Quarterly* 58 (1989): 305–326.

McMaster, Juliet. "Dickens and David Copperfield on the Act of Reading." *English Studies in Canada* 15 (1989): 288–304.

Meckier, Jerome. " 'A World Without Dickens!': James T. to Annie Fields, 10 June 1870." *The Huntington Library Quarterly* 52 (1989): 409–414.

Mengel, Ewald, ed. *The Railway Through Dickens's World: Texts from* Household Words *and* All the Year Round. Britannia Texts in English, vol. 1. New York: Peter Lang, 1989.

Merchant, Peter. " 'Fresh Instruction o'er the Mind': Exploit and Example in Victorian Fiction." *Children's Literature in Education* 20 (1989): 9–24.

Metz, Nancy Aycock. "The Blighted Tree and the Book of Fate: Female Models of Storytelling in *Little Dorrit.*" *Dickens Studies Annual: Essays on Victorian Fiction* 18 (1989): 221–42.

Michasiw, Kim Ian. "*Barnaby Rudge*: The Since of the Fathers." *ELH* 56 (1989): 571–92.

Michie, Helena. " 'Who is this in Pain?': Scarring, Disfigurement, and Female Identity in *Bleak House* and *Our Mutual Friend.*" *Novel* 22 (1989): 199–212.

Miller, Michael G. "The Fellowship-Porters and the Veneerings': Setting, Structure and Justice in *Our Mutual Friend.*" *Dickensian* 85 (1989): 30–38.

Misenheimer, Carolyn, and James B. Misenheimer. "Structural Unities: Paired Parallel Chapters in Dickens's *Bleak House.*" *Dickensian* 85 (1989): 140–49.

Muir, Kenneth. "Bleak House Revisited." *The Aligarh Critical Miscellany* 2 (1989): 85–100.

Newcomb, Mildred. *The Imagined World of Charles Dickens.* Columbus: Ohio State UP, 1989.

Newman, S. J. "Decline and Fall Off? Towards an appreciation of *Our Mutual Friend.*" *Dickensian* 85 (1989): 99–104.

Newsom, Robert. "Embodying *Dombey*: Whole and in Part." *Dickens Studies Annual: Essays on Victorian Fiction* 18 (1989): 197–220.

Nies, Frederick and John Kimmey. "*David Copperfield* and *The Princess Casamassima.*" *The Henry James Review* 10 (1989): 179–84.

Palmer, William. "Dickens and Shipwreck." *Dickens Studies Annual: Essays on Victorian Fiction* 18 (1989): 39–92.

Parker, David. "Mr. Pickwick and the Horses." *Dickensian* 85 (1989): 81–98.

Patterson, Frank M. "Dickens's *A Tale of Two Cities.*" *The Explicator* 47.4 (1989): 30–31.

Pettersson, Torsten. "The Maturity of David Copperfield." *English Studies* Feb. 1989: 63–73.

Phelan, James. "Progression and the Synthetic Secondary Character: The Case of John Wemmick" in *Reading People, Reading Plots: Character, Progression, and the Interpretation of Narrative*. Chicago: U of Chicago P, 1989. 107–132.

———. "Reading for the Character and Reading for the Progression: John Wemmick and *Great Expectations.*" *Journal of Narrative Technique* 19 (1989): 70–84.

Rader, Ralph W. "The Comparative Anatomy of Three Baggy Monsters: *Bleak House, Vanity Fair, Middlemarch.*" *Journal of Narrative Technique* 19 (1989): 49–69.

Raphael, Linda. "A Re-Vision of Miss Havisham: Her Expectations and Our Responses." *Studies in the Novel* 21 (1989): 400–412.

Redmond, James. "Action, Character, and Language: Dickens, His Contemporaries, and the Lure of the Stage." MacKay. *Dramatic Dickens*. 125–38.

Reece, Benny R. *The Mystery of Edwin Drood Solved*. New York: Vantage Press, 1989.

Richards, Bernard. "Emblems and the TV Image-Merchants: Electronic Woodcuts." *Encounter* March 1989: 65–68.

Richmond, Michael L. "In Defense of Poesie." *Fordham Law Review* 57 (1989): 901–929.

Roberts, David. "Charles Dickens and the *Daily News*: Editorials and Editorial Writers." *Victorian Periodicals Review* 22 (1989): 51–63.

Robson, W. W. "The Choir-master and the Single Buffer: an Essay on *The Mystery of Edwin Drood.*" Gibson. 43–62.

Rosenberg, Brian C. "Character and the Demands of Structure: The Example of Dickens." *The CEA Critic* 51.2-3 (1989): 42–54.

Rotkin, Charlotte. *Deception in Dickens' Little Dorrit*. English Language and Literature series, vol. 80. New York: Peter Lang, 1989.

Samuel, Raphael. "Dickens on Stage and Screen." *History Today* Dec. 1989: 44–51.

Saunders, Mary. "Lady Dedlock Prostrate: Drama, Melodrama, and Expressionism in Dickens's Floor Scenes." MacKay. *Dramatic Dickens*. 68–80.

Schad, S. J. "The I and You of Time: Rhetoric and History in Dickens." *ELH* 56 (1989): 423–38.

Schroeder, Natalie E. and Ronald A. Schroeder. "Betsey Trotwood and Jane Murdstone: Dickensian Doubles." *Studies in the Novel* 21 (1989): 268–78.

Selby, Keith. *How to Study a Charles Dickens Novel*. How to Study Literature series. London: Methuen, 1989.

Sheridan, Daniel. "The Unreadable *Dombey*." *Dickens Quarterly* 6 (1989): 142–49.

Sinyard, Neil. "Dickensian Visions in Modern British Film." *Dickensian* 85 (1989): 108–117.

Slater, Michael. "*Hard Times* Through Portuguese Eyes." *Dickensian* 85 (1989): 176–77.

Sloan, John. "The Literary Affinity of Gissing and Dostoevsky: Revising Dickens." *English Literature in Transition, 1880–1920* 32 (1989): 441–53.

Smalley, R. Ann. "Crossing the Gulfs: The Importance of the Master-Servant Relationship in Dickens's *Bleak House*." *Dickensian* 85 (1989): 150–60.

Smith, Grahame. "Comic Subversion and *Hard Times*." *Dickens Studies Annual: Essays on Victorian Fiction* 18 (1989): 145–60.

Smith, Peter. "The Aestheticist Argument of *Our Mutual Friend*." *Cambridge Quarterly* 18 (1989): 363–82.

Sorensen, Knud. "Dickens on the Use of English." *English Studies* 70 (1989): 551–59.

———. "Narrative and Speech-Rendering in Dickens." *Dickens Quarterly* 6 (1989): 131–41.

Steig, Michael. "*Canis* or *Vulpes*? The Esther Vignette in the *Bleak House* Cover-Design." *Dickens Quarterly* 6 (1989): 158–61.

Stewart, Garrett. "Leaving History: Dickens, Gance, Blanchot." *The Yale Journal of Criticism* 2.2 (1989): 145–90.

Summers, Anne. "The Mysterious Demise of Sarah Gamp: The Domiciliary Nurse and her Detractors, c. 1830–1860." *Victorian Studies* 32 (1989): 365–86.

Sutherland, John. *The Stanford Companion to Victorian Fiction*. Stanford: Stanford UP, 1989.

Tillotson, Kathleen. "*Bleak House*: Another Look at Jo." Gibson. 16–28.

Tristram, Philippa. "Aspects of Chesney Wold: The Houses of the Great." *Living Space in Fact and Fiction*. New York: Routledge, 1989. 30–65.

Vann, J. Don. "Dickens, Charles Lever, and Mrs. Gaskell." *Victorian Periodicals Review* 22 (1989): 64–71.

Warhol, Robyn R. "Men's Narrators Who Cross Gender: *Can You Forgive Her?* and *Bleak House*" in *Gendered Interventions: Narrative Discourse in the Victorian Novel*. New Brunswick: Rutgers UP, 1989. 134–56.

Watson, John. "Laughter, Imagination, and the Cruelty of Life: a View of *Oliver Twist*." Gibson. 1–15.

Watts, Alan S. "Dickens and Emigrant Ships: A Matter of Whitewashing?" *Dickensian* 85 (1989): 167–75.

West, Nancy M. "Order in Disorder: Surrealism and *Oliver Twist*." *South Atlantic Review* 54.2 (1989): 41–58.

Whaley, Terrence. "The Dickensian Image of the School Teacher." *From Socrates to Software: The Teacher as Text and the Text as Teacher*. 89th Yearbook of the National Society for the Study of Education. Ed. Philip W. Jackson and Sophie Haroutunian-Gordon. Chicago: U of Chicago P, 1989. 36–59.

White, Bruce. "Victorian Periodicals 1988: An Annotated Bibliography." *Victorian Periodicals Review* 22 (1989): 167–81.

Wills, Garry. "Dorrit Without Politics." *New York Review of Books* 2 Feb. 1989: 16–18.

———. "Love in the Lower Depths." *New York Review of Books* 26 Oct. 1989: 60–67.

Wing, George. "The First of the Singles: Watkins Tottle." *Dickens Quarterly* 6 (1989): 10–16.

Winter, Sarah. "Domestic Fictions: Feminine Deference and Maternal Shadow Labor in Dickens's *Little Dorrit*." *Dickens Studies Annual: Essays on Victorian Fiction* 18 (1989): 243–54.

Index

361

Contents of Previous Volumes

Volume 2 (1972)

Volume 8 (1980)

Volume 9 (1981)

Volume 10 (1982)

Volume 11 (1983)

Volume 12 (1983)

Volume 13 (1984)

Volume 14 (1985)

Volume 15 (1986)

Volume 16 (1987)

Volume 17 (1988)

Volume 17 (cont'd)

Volume 18 (1989)

Dombey, Change, and the Changeling
GERHARD JOSEPH
Embodying Dombey: Whole and in Part
ROBERT NEWSOM
The Blighted Tree and the Book of Fate: Female Models of Storytelling in
Little Dorrit
NANCY AYCOCK METZ
Domestic Fictions: Feminine Deference and Maternal Shadow Labor in
Dickens's Little Dorrit
SARAH WINTER
The Encapsulated Romantic: John Harmon and the Boundaries of Victorian
Soliloquy
CAROL HANBERY MACKAY
Faith's Incubus: The Influence of Sir Walter Scott's Folklore on "Young
Goodman Brown"
BARBARA FASS LEAVY
Novels by Eminent Hands: Sincerest Flattery from the Author of Vanity Fair
JULIET McMASTER
William Thackeray's Fiction and Caroline Norton's Biography: Narrative
Matrix of Feminist Legal Reform
MICAEL M. CLARKE
The Professor:Charlotte Brontë's Hysterical Text, or Realistic Narrative and
the Ideology of the Subject from a Feminist Perspective
RUTH D. JOHNSTON
Review of Brontë Studies: 1981–1987
KATHLEEN BLAKE
Recent Dickens Studies: 1987
GEORGE J. WORTH

Volume 19 (1990)

Male vs. Female Self-Denial: The Subversive Potential of the Feminine Ideal
in Dickens
CAMILLE COLATOSTI
Debtors and Creditors in Dickens' Fiction
C. R. B. DUNLOP
Anorexia Nervosa vs. the Fleshpots of London: Rose and Nancy in Oliver
Twist
SIMON EDWARDS